AMERICAN POETS IN THE 21ST CENTURY

Also by Wesleyan University Press

American Women Poets in the 21st Century: Where Lyric Meets Language
Edited by Claudia Rankine and Juliana Spahr

AMERICAN POETS
IN THE
21ST CENTURY

THE NEW POETICS

EDITED BY

Claudia Rankine

AND

Lisa Sewell

Wesleyan University Press

MIDDLETOWN, CONNECTICUT

Published by Wesleyan University Press,
Middletown, CT 06459
www.wesleyan.edu/wespress

Printed in the United States of America
5 4 3 2 1

Library of Congress Cataloging-in-Publication Data

American poets in the 21st century : the new poetics /
edited by Claudia Rankine and Lisa Sewell.
   p.   cm.
ISBN-13: 978-0-8195-6727-7 (alk. paper)
ISBN-10: 0-8195-6727-2 (alk. paper)
ISBN-13: 978-0-8195-6728-4 (pbk. : alk. paper)
ISBN-10: 0-8195-6728-0 (pbk. : alk. paper)
1. American poetry—21st century. I. Rankine, Claudia, 1963–
II. Sewell, Lisa, 1960–
PS617.A55 2007
811'.608—dc22   2006102844

CONTENTS

ACKNOWLEDGMENTS

THE EDITORS would like to thank Suzanna Tamminen for her support of this project. Many thanks as well to Rachel Luckenbill, Jana Diemer, Fay Ellwood and especially Alanna Reeser for invaluable administrative support and assistance. Permission to reprint copyrighted material has been obtained whenever possible. The editors gratefully acknowledge permission to reprint from the following sources:

Joshua Clover's poems from *The Totality for Kids* (University of California Press, 2006) are reprinted by permission of the author and the Regents of the University of California, University of California Press. Excerpts from *The Totality for Kids* by Joshua Clover © 2006 in Charles Altieri's "The Pleasures of Not Merely Circulating: Joshua Clover's Political Imagination" are reprinted by permission of the author and the Regents of the University of California, University of California Press.

Stacy Doris's "A Month of Valentines," originally appeared in *Paramour* (Krupskaya, 2001) and is reprinted by permission of the author and Krupskaya. Selections from *Conference* (Potes and Poets Press, 2001) are reprinted by permission of the author. Selections from *Knot* (University of Georgia Press, 2006) are reprinted by permission of the University of Georgia Press. Excerpts from *Paramour* by Stacy Doris © 2001 in Caroline Crumpacker's "The Poetics of Radical Constraint and Unhooked Bedazzlement in the Writing of Stacy Doris" are reprinted by permission of Krupskaya. Excerpts from *Conference* by Stacy Doris © 2001 are reprinted by permission of the author. Excerpts from *Knot* by Stacy Doris © 2006 are reprinted by permission University of Georgia Press.

Excerpts from *Fidget* by Kenneth Goldsmith © 2000 in Raymond McDaniel's "Affect and Autism: Kenneth Goldsmith's Reconstitution of Signal and Noise" are reprinted by permission of Coach House Books. Excerpts from *Soliloquy* by Kenneth Goldsmith © 2001 are reprinted by permission of Granary Books. Excerpts from *The Weather* by Kenneth Goldsmith © 2005 are reprinted by permission of Make Now Press.

Peter Gizzi's poems from *Some Values of Landscape and Weather* (Wesleyan University Press, 2003) and *The Outernationale* (Wesleyan University Press, 2007) are published by the permission of Wesleyan University Press.

Myung Mi Kim's poems from *Commons* (University of California Press, 2002) are reprinted by permission of the author and the Regents of the University of California, University of California Press. Excerpts from *Commons* by Myung Mi Kim © 2002 in Warren Liu's "Making Common the Commons: Myung Mi Kim's Ideal Subject" appear by permission of the author and the Regents of the University of California, University of California Press. Excerpts from *Under Flag* by Myung Mi Kim © 1991 are reprinted by permission of Kelsey Street Press. Excerpts from *Dura* by Myung Mi Kim © 1998 are reprinted by permission of the author and Sun & Moon Press.

Mark Levine's poems from *Debt* (William Morrow, 1993) are reprinted by permission of the author. Poems from *Enola Gay* (University of California Press, 2000) and *The Wilds* (University of California Press, 2006) are reprinted by permission of the author and the Regents of the University of California, University of California Press.

Excerpts from *Debt* by Mark Levine © 1993 in Sabrina Orah Mark's "Mark Levine: The Poetics of Evidence" are reprinted by permission of the author. Excerpts from *Enola Gay* and *The Wilds* by Mark Levine © 1998 and 2006 are reprinted by permission of the author and the Regents of the University of California, University of California Press. Excerpts from Walter Benjamin's *Reflections Essays, Aphorisms, Autobiographical Writings*, and *Illuminations* in Sabrina Orah Mark's essay "Mark Levine: The Poetics of Evidence" are reprinted by permission of the publishers of *Walter Benjamin: Selected Writings, Vol 1, 1913–1926*, edited by Marcus Bullock and Michael W. Jennings (Harvard University Press © 1996 by the President and Fellows of Harvard College).

Mark Nowak's poems from *Shut Up Shut Down* (Coffee House Press, 2004) are reprinted by permission of the author and Coffee House Press.

Excerpts from *Shut Up Shut Down* by Mark Nowak © 2004 in David Ray Vance's essay "Mark Nowak: Radical Documentary Praxic [Redux]" are reprinted by permission of the author and Coffee House Press. Excerpt from "Why I Refused the National Medal for the Arts," by Adrienne Rich was originally printed in Adrienne Rich, *Arts of the Possible: Essays and Conversations* (W.W. Norton & Company, 2001). Used by permission of the author W. W. Norton & Company, Inc. Excerpt from Michael Davidson's essay "On the Outskirts of Form: Cosmopoetics in the Shadow of

NAFTA" is from an unpublished book chapter and appears by permission of the author.

D. A. Powell's poems from *Tea* (Wesleyan University Press, 1998) and *Lunch* (Wesleyan University Press, 2000) are published by the permission of Wesleyan University Press.

Karen Volkman's poems from *Spar* (University of Iowa Press, 2002) are reprinted by permission of the author and University of Iowa Press. Excerpts from "Shipwreck Poem," "Infernal," "Infidel," "Looking Back," "Equations," "Casanova In Love," "Chronicle," and "Persephone at Home" appear in Paul Otremba's "A Space for Desire and the Mutable Self: Karen Volkman's Experimentations with the Lyric." All are from *Crash's Law* by Karen Volkman © 1996. Used by permission of W.W. Norton & Company, Inc. Excerpts from *Spar* by Karen Volkman © 2002 are reprinted by permission of University of Iowa Press.

Juliana Spahr's "Gentle Now, Don't Add to Heartache" originally appeared in *Tarpaulin Sky* (http://www.tarpaulinsky.com), Volume 3, Issue 2, Summer 2005 and is reprinted by permission of the author and *Tarpaulin Sky*. Excerpts from *Fuck You-Aloha-I Love You* by Juliana Spahr © 2001 in Kimberly Lamm's "All Together/Now: Writing the Space of Collectivities in the Poetry of Juliana Spahr" are reprinted by permission Wesleyan University Press. Excerpts from *This Connection of Everything with Lungs* by Julianna Spahr © 2005 are reprinted by permission of the author and the Regents of the University of California, University of California Press. Excerpts from *Response* by Juliana Spahr © 1996 and "Changing Rooms" are reprinted by permission of the author.

Susan Wheeler's "The Debtor in the Convex Mirror" originally appeared in *Ledger* (University of Iowa Press, 2005) and is reprinted by permission of University of Iowa Press. Excerpts from *Smokes* by Susan Wheeler © 1998 in Lynn Keller's "Susan Wheeler's Open Source Poetics" are reprinted by permission of the author and Four Way Books. All rights reserved.

INTRODUCTION

Lisa Sewell

I

To claim the new, as the subtitle to this volume does, is always a risky proposition. It smacks of marketing strategy and insists on a lockstep trajectory of progress, as the inevitable "and improved" lurks in the background; it is permeated with forgetting and the obliteration of memory and history, seemingly cutting ties with all that has come before. But *new* can also indicate lateness, as in lately, as in having but lately come or been brought into being, as well as the excitement and upsurge in energy that generally accompanies a birth.[1] In this instance, the new designates the advent of a poetry that is vital and energized, but also notably various, exploring a range of modes and directions, countering the lament that the field is in crisis, or that poetry as a genre no longer matters.[2] The new of this anthology also glances backward, encompassing a sense of relation and origin, insisting on indebtedness to the poetry movements and schools of the late twentieth century, from the Confessional poets to the Black Arts movement, from the Beats to Language poetry.[3] While no particular rubric has emerged to designate and name the poetries of this new century, a generation worth recognizing is currently coming into its own, revisiting and developing established and emerging modes of poetic inquiry.

This collection is among those beginning to chart and situate the progress of this current generation, focusing on thirteen poets whose work provides an introduction to the breadth and vitality of the field: Joshua Clover, Stacy Doris, Peter Gizzi, Kenneth Goldsmith, Myung Mi Kim, Mark Levine, Tracie Morris, Mark Nowak, D. A. Powell, Juliana Spahr, Karen Volkman, Susan Wheeler, and Kevin Young. Because of space limitations, it isn't possible to present a thorough sampling from this "radically democratized" field, but each of the writers collected here is evolving a distinct poetic that in some way revises, extends and/or counters the traditions of the previous century.[4] Following the format of *American Women Poets in the 21st Century* (University Press of New England/Wesleyan University Press, 2001), each chapter includes a selection of poems, a brief statement, and a critical essay that provides a historical context as well as an analysis of the ways the specific work alters and extends the understanding of what the new American poetries can look, feel, and sound like. Thanks to the wonders of technology, a recording of each poet reading some of his or her work has also been included.

The task of delineating, naming, and defining either the important movements in twenty-first-century American poetry or its central figures is nearly impossible; as Hank Lazar has suggested, the field is so "atomized, decentralized, and multifaceted" that "no one can pretend to know what is out there, or what is next."[5] At the same time, several broad trends did emerge from the transformation in poetry that took place during the 1960s and early 1970s: the postconfessional, mainstream voice–centered lyric of introspection and revelation, which continues to be widely published in literary journals and by academic presses; the identity-based feminist and multicultural poetries that are also voice-centered but rely on the representational qualities of language to convey difference, claiming subjectivity as well as social and political authority for the marginalized and ignored; and the experimental work of Language-oriented writing, which is theoretically informed, Language-focused, and formally innovative with an eye toward critiquing and resisting social convention and ideology at the level of language—in many ways revisiting the radical materialist experimentation of early Modernism.[6] These designations do not account for significant overlap or variation within each trend (for example, socially grounded speech and performance-based slam poetry) but they do paint a picture of the aesthetic and ideological concerns each writer included in this anthology must respond to in some way, whether through rejection or some form of engagement.[7]

A number of critics have documented the ways these trends led to a sense of division and conflict in contemporary American poetry during the 1990s, and to the so-called turf wars between conventional voice-centered verse and the language-focused avant-garde.[8] Charles Bernstein's description of mainstream poetry as "official verse culture"[9] suggests the political stakes of the division, while Charles Altieri's phrase the "scenic mode" lays out the aesthetic faults of this mode:

> the work appears spoken in a natural voice; there must be a sense of urgency and immediacy to this "affected naturalness" so as to make it appear that one is reexperiencing the original event; there must be a "studied artlessness" that gives a sense of spontaneous personal sincerity; and there must be a strong movement toward emphatic closure.[10]

Language-oriented writing also had its detractors. With its emphasis on the nonrepresentational, material aspects of language itself, its techniques of rupture and disjunction, and its interrogation of the subject as a construct in and of language, it was perceived as either too conceptual or too chaotic, far too opaque either to galvanize readers or to effect social change. A sense of division and antagonism between those who align themselves with Language writing and those who do not persists, but the line between innovation and tradition, between experiment and expression, is no longer clear or easy to draw. As Jed Rasula notes in *Syncopations: The Stress of Innovation in Contemporary American Poetry*, "Language poetry . . . seems to have nourished poetic practice in markedly nondenominational ways."[11]

Innovative, materialist poetic practices have been absorbed by both the lyric mainstream and the multicultural poetries of identity politics: writers on either side of the ostensible divide employ interruption, parataxis, narrative discontinuity, and alinearity to produce fragmentation and disjunction. And, to one degree or another, the writers collected here embrace what Mark Wallace has identified as a "free multiplicity of form" that cannot be easily relegated into movements or schools.[12] They bring into play whatever seems to be useful, deliberately and self-consciously engaging with the lyric tradition but also questioning that tradition through techniques of disruption, diversion, and resistance, producing a "humming sphere with many different parallel poetries, relatively equal, blurring and fusing across their boundaries."[13] In his poetics statement, Peter Gizzi is explicit about the contradictions that are central to his work, admitting to a general acquisitiveness that leads him to draw on "gestures of narrative disturbance, . . . quoting out of context, . . . bending and borrowing and blending . . . tradition . . . to create depth, emotive effect, even sincerity."

At the same time, it's worth noting the tendencies that do emerge. While many of these poets claim a space for lyric interiority and "emotive effect," almost all treat the speaking subject as provisional, expressing doubts about a lyric poetry that dramatizes the self's fixed relationship to the world. The work of writers as apparently at odds as the lyric-influenced Mark Levine and the language-oriented Juliana Spahr confirms Rasula's sense that one of the most notable effects of Language poetry is "its erosion of the complacent security on which the lyrical ego hoists its banner." But, he immediately adds, "The lyrical ego is by no means deposed as such."[14] In other words, while a poetics of utter sincerity and authenticity is less and less the standard, the lyric is by no means exhausted. Poets like Karen Volkman and D. A. Powell provide new instances of the "slipperiness between reality and imagination" that has always informed lyric utterance.[15] Several poets in this collection situate their work in the long-standing formal traditions of the lyric, whether by reimagining the sonnet sequence (as Kevin Young does), or by overturning and interrupting traditional forms like the ballad and the rondelle (as Stacy Doris does).

Another trend this collection helps bring to light is the ongoing project of extending the poem into external social and political worlds, moving toward what Juliana Spahr has called a "connective poetics," which can be found in works that "present and engage with large, public worlds that are in turn shared with readers."[16] Poets as diverse as Susan Wheeler, Joshua Clover, and Mark Nowak are engaging with a range of "public worlds," constructing a lyric mode that is historically aware, socially generative, and overtly interested in moving toward an expansive and connective consciousness. This sense of inclusiveness, coupled to an acute awareness of history, informs the work of many the writers collected here. As Myung Mi Kim writes in her poetics statement, "historical consciousness [is] charismatic—mobile." By sharing this sense of the poem as a document that extends into and participates in history, in quite different manifestations, many of the poets in this collection insist on a poetics of community.

As I have already suggested, this collection presents particular but representative shadings along the continuum of contemporary poetry; the ordering of the chapters attempts to map the arc of that continuum, emphasizing formal and ideological differences at either end, but also foregrounding the ways shared concerns can be explored through the use of divergent modes and forms. One question that persists throughout is the use to which experimental modernist strategies are put, whether disorienting and disjunctive techniques are used merely for aesthetic purposes or for their oppositional function. Taking a closer look at the specific focus of each section can illuminate the ways these writers blur and interrogate such distinctions through sound, form, and content.

II

In his poetics statement, Mark Levine makes his faith in expressive language clear, suggesting that poetic language specifically can produce presence: "I ask poetry for an instrument with which to listen and listen closely, to the most inward, and desire-riddled, and perhaps embarrassing, voices of feeling—." But his work is marked by an explicit self-consciousness about that engagement, "a sharp skepticism about the . . . sharp need to represent a self-conscious individual, one equipped with emotions and moral demands."[17] In "Belongings," this conjunction of skepticism and need is clear as Levine asks:

> Who was the speaker
> (hand in a bowl of dates)
> believing the leaves to be
> a diagram worn by the land
> sweeping over his home?
>
> Which piece of him dug at the
> orchard with his unshod
> heel . . .

Here Levine traces the dislocations inherent in subjectivity, attempting to map the space between activity and awareness of that action, and resisting the "scenic mode" that Altieri disparages through his investigation of the lyric speaker. As Sabrina Orah Mark argues in her essay "Mark Levine: The Poetics of Evidence," Levine's poetry traces the world as it is experienced by a discontinuous, provisional subject, but also "folds self-investigation into historical interrogation." Situating Levine as the inheritor of the modernist sensibility found in writers like Beckett and Stevens, and philosophers like Benjamin and Levinas, Mark argues that through his investigation of the shattered subject, Levine "interrogates the lyric and its conversation with history."

Like Levine, Karen Volkman does not shy away from the inwardness and introspection associated with lyric poetry. Her subject matter appears to be standard post-Romantic lyric fare: seduction, heartbreak, and revenge. But no locatable personality or stable subject emerges as she adapts a fluid and destabilized speaker, and completely discards narrative continuity. Sentences develop based on associations of idiom, sound, meter, and rhyme to create rhythms that seem familiarly meaningful but ultimately foreground language:

> How does a namelessness name?
> Suppose it were better off dead.
> Or its tongue were a species of beam
>
> jouissance of the burning to seem
> occult, aureate, aspect, thread,
> not number that nevers the scheme.

The dactyls and iambs, even rhyme itself seem to dictate the emergence of utterance, resulting in a decidedly twenty-first-century remaking of form. In her poetics statement Volkman explains: "I'm intrigued by deformations of convention, ways in which traditional lyric gestures, embodying cultural codes, can be made malleable and strange." In "A Space for Desire and the Mutable Self: Karen Volkman's Experimentation with the Lyric," Paul Otremba argues that Volkman's poems create experience from "the material of language and its endless capabilities for making meaning." Otremba shows that in Volkman's most recent work in *Spar* and the unpublished *Nomina* the formal elements of lyric poetry—meter, rhyme, assonance—form the real content of her work as she "introduces a poetics of elemental lyric gestures."

D. A. Powell takes the exploration of form and lyric interiority in a distinctly different direction from Volkman. His investment in the expressive possibilities of the lyric tradition is clear in his intensely personal, even intimate poems. In "The Flesh Failures," he explains that for him poetry provides the writer with "a place to explore . . . passions" and to be opened up to the ecstatic. But he depends on "Full stops. Broken phrases. Rising and falling rhythms welded within the same line" to shape and make his poems as he forges a new poetry of gay identity and HIV/AIDS. While poets of the previous generation—Thom Gunn, Mark Doty, and Paul Monette—have explored this territory through elegy, Powell gives his response to the devastation of AIDS a broken but continuing formal body. The expressive queer politics of the work is tempered by formal disruption: his lines stretch into the margins of the page, incorporating breaks and hesitations, as well as midline syntactical dislocations. Focusing on his most recent book *Cocktails*, in "'Here is the Door Marked *Heaven*': D. A. Powell" Stephen Burt demonstrates that Powell's extended metaphors allow him to project communal, ritual experiences whose performative language exalts a vulnerable (gay) male body. Burt argues that Powell's work challenges models (such as Leo Bersani's or Jonathan Dollimore's) that consider gay or queer experience inherently inimical to liberal individualist ideas of the subject. Powell's style imagines the gay subject's delight and survival, in part by troping that subject's connection to a community perhaps endangered, or mourning, but very much alive. In this way, Powell highlights the connective possibilities of a queered lyric poetics.

As coeditor and cofounder of the journal *o·blēk* and editor of the lectures of Jack Spicer, Peter Gizzi is more strongly associated with the New York School and Language poetry than with the meditative lyric tradition. But his interest in the lyric (made explicit in the poem "History of the Lyric"), his ease with personal self-revelation in poems that meditate on classical Romantic subjects such as nature and loss, allow for a more expansive, politicized understanding of that tradition. Like Levine, he sees himself as the instrument or vehicle through which the poem can coalesce and, like Powell, he establishes some of the expansive possibilities of the lyric. As he explains in "Extract from a Letter to Steve Farmer," in his work, he is "after" "both a construction of self and an emptying of self—not autobiographical but autographical." The distinction between pure self-expression and self-expression that is mediated via the material world is crucial, and it is this balancing act between Romantic introspection and modern/postmodernist self-consciousness that Cole Swensen explores in "Peter Gizzi's City." Swensen argues that Gizzi's emphasis on dailiness and the quotidian "sites" his poetry in the body politic; full of everyday objects and common speech, Gizzi's poems encompass both the heterogeneity and community that inheres in city life. Whereas the ways Levine, Volkman, and Powell reinvigorate and investigate the lyric is more enclosed in aesthetic effects, Gizzi's lyricism swerves deliberately toward the world, linking the lyrical quotidian to an exploration of mass culture.

Like Gizzi, Juliana Spahr has clear ties to Language poetry and the contemporary avant-garde, having coedited *o·blēk* with Gizzi, and the innovative journal *Chain*, with Jena Osman, but her work also draws on and extends the possibilities of the lyric tradition. Though clearly interested in the unreliability of language as it is used to convey information, observations, political and personal realities, many of Spahr's poems display a musical if hypnotic lyricism that accumulates sound and rhythm as it revisits details and phrases. But Spahr's version of the lyric is not timeless; she formulates a documentary poetics that depends on technology, cataloguing and recording our specifically located and time-bound moment. By emphasizing the ways the "open" text can forge connections between authors and readers, and create connection and community through reading, Spahr's work also rejects the individualism of the lyric. Instead she investigates lyric's "intimate pluralisms" and "shared, connective spaces," as well as the difficulties of forging links in a culture where language is debased and deracinated by mass media.

In "Gentle Now, Don't Add to Heartache," the pronouns "we" and "our" predominate even as Spahr describes specific and particular observations of the natural world that become formative and shared through this insistence:

> We loved the stream.
> And we were of the stream.
> And we couldn't help this love because we arrived at the band of the stream
> and began breathing and the stream was various and full of information
> and it changed our bodies with its rotten with its cold with its clean with
> its mucky with fallen leaves with its things that bite the edges of the skin
> with its leaves with its sand and dirt with its pungent at moments with its
> dry and prickly with its warmth with its mush and moist with its hard flat
> stones on the bottom with its horizon lines of gently rolling hills with its
> darkness with its dappled light with its cicada buzz with its trills of birds.

The poem goes on to detail the ways "we" also participate in the desecration of nature by letting in "soda cans . . . cigarette butts . . . pink tampon applicators and . . . various other pieces of plastic that would travel through the stream." As Kimberly Lamm points out in "All Together/Now: Writing the Spaces of Collectivities in the Poetry of Juliana Spahr," questions about the possibility of community and collective action are central to all of Spahr's work: poetry, essays, and literary criticism.[18] Focusing on *Fuck You-Aloha-I Love You* and *This Connection of Everyone with Lungs*, Lamm elaborates the various means Spahr uses to inspire and engender "collectivities that are resistant and responsible, open to the alterity of the planet and the ethical impossibilities it requires."

"Obsessed with the modern/and its endnotes" in his poems, Joshua Clover makes formal experimentation, fragmentation, and pastiche his primary modes of poetic exploration. Like Gizzi and Spahr, he also engages the conventions of lyric poetry, but does so through critique, seeking a locus for subjectivity that is based on resistance to both lyrical and social conventions.

His irreverent and yet deadly serious poetics statement submits "Superinformation" as an aesthetic that can successfully balance the incorporation of the real and the imaginary: "Superinformation is the set of relations through which, within the excess of signification, the immanence of actual life and its frantic dissimulation, we live more, not less." In conversation with Andreas Gursky, Frank O'Hara, and Jacques de la Villeglé, Clover's statement asserts a definitive politics, a concern for the social world, and a desire to achieve the beauty and pure pleasure poetry can offer.

In "The Pleasures of Not Merely Circulating: Joshua Clover's Political Imagination," Charles Altieri explores the specific ways Clover's work resists the pleasurable seductions of beauty and subjective identification prevalent in traditional lyric poetry. As Altieri shows, rather than projecting the inwardness of the subject, Clover makes poetry a site where the subject has to experience the strange impersonal or transpersonal dependencies that bind us to our cultural moment. Altieri suggests that through the use of excessive formal constraints Clover calls the reader's attention to the work that pleasure has to do thematically and emotionally on the discursive level. He also situates Clover's work within a Situationist aesthetic that insists that the spirit of play is precisely what art can contribute to our resources for engaging the real. But this intention does not devolve into the reiteration and rehearsal of critical theory; Clover is deeply committed to *making*. For him, poetry must begin by asking how one might get any hold at all on what reification and alienation make of our psychic lives. As Altieri demonstrates, his poetry begins with the desire to make, not to know; he then pursues the shaping of immaterial thoughts and feelings to see how they might attach to the insistences of the world.

The merging of form and content to develop and explore the politics and social meanings of a particular subject position also informs the work of Kevin Young, who like Powell, Levine, and Volkman is associated with the mainstream of contemporary poetry. But Young is also the inheritor of the legacy of the Black Arts movement, and in his work he reformulates and reenvisions their priorities—the celebration of African American artists and traditional African American forms, the incorporation of black vernacular English— taking them in new directions and ultimately formulating a poetics that has been influenced by both the Western tradition and the Black Arts tradition. In "Mixed-up Medium: Kevin Young's Turn-of-the-Century American Triptych," Rick Benjamin focuses on three linked volumes—*To Repel Ghosts*, *Jelly Roll*, and *Black Maria*—in which Young chronicles and preserves black history. Innovatively structured to evince mass cultural forms, with each section of the book designated as a "side" of a record, *To Repel Ghosts* investigates the effects of fame on some of the greatest black artists of the twentieth century, including poems about Billie Holiday, Charlie Parker, and Jimi Hendrix, but focusing in particular on the artist Jean-Michel Basquiat. In *Jelly Roll*, he self-consciously structures his poems via jazz and the blues, simultaneously reimagining the sonnet sequence while also reinventing the blues. Benjamin shows that Young's project is epic and very much American, as he takes on pop culture and mass media, traditional blues, hip-hop and terza rima, film noir, and couplets in order to conduct a sustained cultural critique and examination of the place of the black artist in American society.

The sound poetry of Tracie Morris also extends the efforts and ideals of the Black Arts movement but along a very different trajectory from Young. Morris pushes the Black Arts investment in the African American oral tradition to its limits, experimenting with the materiality of language as sound. Christine Hume's essay "Improvisational Insurrection: The Sound Poetry of Tracie Morris" charts the evolution of Morris's sound-based poetry, from her participation in the popular and populist slam/performance poetry, to her more recent experimental, nonlinear, non-narrative work. Hume demonstrates that Morris's new work bypasses the more programmatic features of these two poetic praxes—slam and contemporary avant-guard—by standing against reified notions of authenticity and sincerity as well as ready-made loopholes of indeterminacy and alienation. Morris's "tone poems" retain the immediacy and accessibility of performance but take spoken word and black oral traditions in entirely new directions, calling attention to both the referential and nonreferential possibilities of language at the intersection between standard and black vernacular English.

While their work appears to be diametrically opposed, the poetry of Myung Mi Kim shares surprising affinities with Morris's sound poems. Kim's use of disconnected statements, interruptions, and fragments—as well as the meaningful use of the white space of the page—clearly signals her interest in the nonreferential material aspects of language. But as with the work of Morris and Volkman, the lyrical aspects of her poems are based in elements of sound and song. Her varied use of double and triple line spacings could even be read as a kind of musical score: many lines from her poems must be read out loud in order to be understood, as with these lines from section 315 of "Lamenta":

> how to false bottom log
> whom I saw beautiful as a boy
>
> *nuph- juk- pahn*
> *nubh-jjuk-paan*
>
> shun . nestle
>
> ravenous . seal
>
> ash . gust

Alliteration, internal rhyme, metrical patterning—even typography—are all essential elements of the poems.

However central these traditional lyric elements are, Kim also uses techniques of disruption—collage, parataxis, the juxtaposition of the theoretical and the poetical within the same piece of writing—to examine questions of globalization and identity politics, in particular the cultural and linguistic displacement of immigration and the necessity and impossibility of assimilation. But as Warren Liu demonstrates in "Making Common the Commons: Myung Mi Kim's Ideal Subject," Kim's examination of identity politics is truly an investigation of language itself and the ways that language mitigates and disrupts but also allows for any sense of identity. "For Kim, the exploration of how language functions to mask or suppress the fundamental power relations amongst generalized forms of knowledge production . . . is intimately linked to the recognition that we must also use that same language to define, understand and uncover specific iterations of power (or powerlessness)." In her poems, language is used to portray the irreducibility of difference—ethnic, national, gender—as she demonstrates that identity cannot be assimilated to one particular locus. Following quite different trajectories, Kim, Morris, and Young demonstrate that issues of race and identity can be addressed and illuminated through innovation, and that the lyric can be the site of a language-based investigation and critique of racial politics.

Like Kim, Stacy Doris is a poet whose work is particularly and specifically grounded in the aesthetics and politics of Language writing; she has said that "it was initially through an acquaintance with Language Writing that the notion of poetry as revolutionary came to valorize and energize [her] own pursuit of writing."[19] Full of palindromes, puns, anagrams, and other word games, Doris's poetry conveys a clear delight in the materiality of language. She also takes the destabilization of a central consciousness to extremes with speakers who change genders and positions, morphing into one another. Her book-length poem *Conference* (excerpted here) combines procedural verse and a thirteenth-century poem about the Sufi path to divinity, speaking through characters who are multiple and endlessly mutable. Form is also central to Doris's project. In "I Have to Check My e-mail," she claims that her interest in poetry began with a problem with form. In particular, poetry allowed her to address her dissatisfaction with the apparently fixed assignment of form that the body imposes: "I have never agreed with form in the sense that it was assigned to me at birth with my body. Why this form and why stay in it for more than an instant? There is no stability of form; all science extols that. . . . The reason to create form might be as a way of charting its fleet malleability." This disagreement with form is made manifest in her work as she engages with strict forms and patterns but interrupts them with an equally strict regularity, thus emphasizing radical openness in a way that is distinct from Spahr's "documentary poetics." "A Month of Valentines," which is the "centerfold" of her book *Paramour*, a meditation on love and sex, coupling and copulation, creates a sense of this openness, providing no real guide as to how to read the cryptic, playful poems laid out in boxes like an advent calendar.

As Caroline Crumpacker suggests, Doris's poetry "questions the role of formal (and romantic) convention—celebrating and transgressing its manifestations—vis-à-vis literary (and social) innovation." In "The Poetics of Radical Constraint and Unhooked Bedazzlement in the Writing of Stacy Doris," Crumpacker charts the ways Doris's exploration of convention and form links cyberspeak to literary innovation. Doris not only engages with ancient traditions; she demonstrates that these traditions inhere in the modes of interaction that inform twenty-first century discourse, drawing on the Internet as a source and resource for her textual deformations.

Like many of the other poets in this collection (Clover, Spahr, Gizzi, Young), Susan Wheeler's poetry displays an obsessive engagement with American life and Western culture—from pop songs and crass consumerism to Renaissance painting—taking pleasure in both the high and the low, celebrating and critiquing each in equal measure. She "cobbles" together a unique poetics through polysemy and linguistic aggregation, juxtaposing contrasting dictions, from hip-hop vernacular to Middle English; through this gleeful borrowing, she lifts and reworks a wide range of sources. Taken together, her four books of poems make an extended argument for the legitimacy of accrual and acquisition as a literary aesthetic. And Wheeler has been forthright about the joys and necessities of making use of whatever poetic sources present themselves; as Lynn Keller notes in her essay, "Susan Wheeler's Open Source Poetics," Wheeler rejects the notion that adapting innovative techniques from Language writing results in "mere aestheticism." Announcing her indebtedness to John Ashbery with her title, Wheeler's long poem, "The Debtor in the Convex Mirror" suggests that the accumulation of various debts (and uneasy guilt) are as much a part of the twenty-first-century poet's trade as they were for moneylenders and their clients in Renaissance Antwerp. In her essay, Keller suggests that in her third book, *Source Codes*, Wheeler makes the relationship between poems and their sources her subject of investigation. Keller demonstrates that by assimilating multiple sources, Wheeler's "cobbled solutions" and crossover poetic succeed in "invigorat[ing] poetry's radical cultural force . . . [by] foregrounding both formally and in her poems' content, the contemporary 'problems' of 'steam roller' consumerism/commodification and of artistic assimilation so as ultimately to recast them as opportunities and resources."

The work of labor activist, publisher, and poet Mark Nowak also argues for the legitimacy and power of a poetics of acquisition and collage but to entirely different effect and for quite different purposes. Exploring and exposing the legacy bequeathed to the working class by corporate culture and global capitalism, Nowak's documentary poetry creatively bridges the gap between poetic innovation and political critique. In the tradition of Charles Reznikoff and Muriel Rukeyser, Nowak's work documents and protests the conditions suffered by the economically and socially disenfranchised. Mixing brief lyrics, prose, and photographs, he records the effects of plant closings and unemployment for workers living in the Rust Belt of America. Like Spahr, his work is firmly situated in history, in a specific time and place, but the poems are entirely composed out of "found" and "collected" sources ranging from a grammar guide and the published testimonies of workers, to photographs of "shut down" businesses and localized unemployment statistics.

In "Notes toward an Anti-capitalist Poetics II," Nowak makes explicit his goal of creating a poetry that can explore and expose "the relationship between a U.S.-controlled agenda for globalization (with Bush crony Paul Wolfowitz as president of the World Bank) and the future of language and the imagination amidst ubiquitous privatization." David Ray Vance's essay "Mark Nowak: Radical Documentary Praxis [Redux]," strongly suggests that Nowak has indeed responded to his own call. Situating Nowak's praxis within both a documentary tradition and the sampling techniques of hip-hop and rap, Vance emphasizes the ways that Nowak's work goes much further in its critique than much political "poetry of witness," addressing and examining overarching ideologies, structures, and economic practices. Vance delineates the ways Nowak's "multivalent dialectic" "doesn't assert claims so much as invite inquiry," calling attention to the effects of capitalism on individual lives, while exposing the interrelationship between economic and language systems.

The final chapter of the collection presents the work of Kenneth Goldsmith, who perhaps takes the procedural and material emphases of experimental writing to its logical extreme, dealing not merely with found texts but with language itself as found object. In "Being Boring," he explains that over the past ten years his writing practice "has boiled down to simply retyping existing texts." For example, for No. 111, he spent two years "collecting" phrases that ended in "r" and then arranged them by syllable count. For his book *Day* he retyped the entire *New York Times* for Friday, September 1, 2000. Instead of adding to the "texts in the world," Goldsmith engages with those texts that already exist, working as a collector, compiler, and arranger of everyday speech and the discourse of common culture, measuring the relative weight or lack thereof that words possess, and how they are woven throughout the fabric of lived life.

As Raymond McDaniel suggests in "Affect and Autism: Kenneth Goldsmith's Reconstitution of Signal and Noise," Goldsmith's "uncreative practice" extends that of various avant-garde movements that preceded him—Dada, the concrete poets, Fluxus, Oulipo—but succeeds where his predecessors failed by completely evacuating the locus of the creative author/ maker. Finding ties between the *DSM* (*Diagnostic and Statistical Manual of Mental Disorders*) characterization of Asperger's syndrome and Goldsmith's poetic practice and output, McDaniel shows that Goldsmith's work makes literal-mindedness as literal as it can get; it is emphatically *not* haunted by the specter of the "creative impulse." As McDaniel convincingly shows, this erasure of the creative impulse successfully "dissolve[s] the normally invisible boundaries upon which meaning rests, . . . finally allow[ing] language to wreak its own derangements."

It is not easy to locate traces of a lyric impulse in Kenneth Goldsmith's work, although there are passages of great beauty in "Page One" from *The Day*, a transcription of the front page of the *New York Times* on September 11, 2001. Certainly, despite Goldsmith's "uncreative" techniques, his reader is aware of the author's *presence*, in particular, his physical efforts to complete his tasks. In this way subjectivity, if not originality, becomes an issue and question in his work.

The question of subjectivity is explored by all the poets collected here, whether by distributing the speaking subject among multiple pronouns or inventing characters that morph and shift into one another. Form is also of central concern: variously treating it as an untapped resource and a limiting constraint, the writers here grapple with form and its legacy. The poems and essays collected here present a sampling of the exciting work being done by a new generation of poets, poetries that cannot be neatly aligned with one camp or another or confined to a particular rubric. The publication of this collection marks one starting point for the serious consideration of these writers and their peers and an exploration of the various but connected poetics being invented at the start of this new century.

NOTES

1. *Websters's New Universal Unabridged Dictionary* (New York: Barnes & Noble, 2003), 1293.

2. This sense of crisis or dissipation has been widely discussed and bemoaned. See, for example, Vernon Shetley, *After the Death of Poetry: Poet and Audience in Contemporary America* (Durham: Duke Universty Press, 1993), as well as Dana Goia, *Can Poetry Matter? Essays on Poetry and American Culture* (St. Paul, Minn.: Graywolf, 1992).

3. There are numerous accounts of this period in American literary history. See, for example, James Longenbach, *Modern Poetry after Modernism* (New York: Oxford University Press, 1997); Marjorie Perloff, *The Poetics of Indeterminacy: Rimbaud to Cage* (Princeton: Princeton University Press, 1981) James E. B. Breslin, *From Modern to Contemporary: American Poetry, 1945–1965* (Chicago: University of Chicago Press, 1984); Jerome Mazzaro, *Postmodern American Poetry* (Urbana: University of Illinois

Press, 1980); Paul Breslin, *The Psycho-Political Muse: American Poetry Since the Fifties* (Chicago: University of Chicago Press, 1987); and Mutlu Konuk Blasing, *Politics and Form in Postmodern Poetry* (New York: Cambridge University Press, 1995).

4. Hank Lazer, "The People's Poetry," *Boston Review* 29, no. 2 (April–May, 2004): 1.

5. Ibid.

6. In *Twenty-First-Century Modernism: The "New" Poetics* (London: Blackwell, 2001), Marjorie Perloff convincingly argues that contemporary innovative and experimental poetry is indebted to early Modernist writings at the beginning of the twentieth century; thus it is perhaps less innovative than has been claimed.

7. Clearly there are other ways to map the trends in contemporary poetry since the 1970s and 1980s. I am indebted to Timothy Yu's formulation in "Form and Identity in Language Poetry and Asian American Poetry," in *Contemporary Literature* 61, no. 3 (Spring 2000): 422–61. Yu maps out these distinctions in order to explore the impact the radical critique of Language poetry has or has not had on contemporary Asian American poetry. In "Toward a Multiplicity of Form," in *Telling It Slant: Avant-Garde Poetics of the 1990s*, ed. Mark Wallace and Steven Marks (Tuscaloosa: University of Alabama Press, 2003), Mark Wallace usefully creates five distinctions that roughly mirror the three I have laid out, but also include New Formalism and "the New American poetry speech-based poetics, often associated with spoken-word, ethnopoetics or New York School Writing" (193).

8. Hank Lazar's *Opposing Poetries: Part One: Issues and Institutions* (Evanston, Ill.: Northwestern University Press, 1996) provides a thorough if biased account of these poetry wars, and Jed Rasula's *The American Poetry Wax Museum: Reality Effects, 1940–1990* (Urbana, Ill.: National Council of Teachers of English, 1996) explores the divergences in the field by examining the processes and effects of the anthologization of poetry. Christopher Beach's essay "Poetic Positionings: Stephen Dobyns and Lyn Hejinian," in *Contemporary Literature* 38, no. 1 (Spring 1997): 44–77, usefully summarizes the differences between conventional mainstream poetry and Language-oriented work.

9. Charles Bernstein, *Content's Dream: Essays, 1975–1984* (Evanston, Ill.: Northwestern University Press, 2001), 246. See Lazar, *Opposing Poetries*, and Rasula, *American Poetry Wax Museum*.

10. Charles Altieri, *Self and Sensibility in Contemporary American Poetry* (New York: Cambridge University Press, 1984), 10. See also Marjorie Perloff, *Twenty-First-Century Modernism* and *Poetics of Indeterminacy*; Charles Bernstein, *Content's Dream*; and Ron Silliman, *In the American Tree* (Orono, Me.: National Poetry Foundation, University of Maine at Orono, 1986) for descriptions of the ways so-called mainstream poetry upholds the status quo.

11. Jed Rasula, *Syncopations: The Stress of Innovation in Contemporary American Poetry* (Tuscaloosa: University of Alabama Press, 2004), 24.

12. Mark Wallace, "Toward a Fee Multiplicity of Form," in *Telling It Slant*, ed. Wallace and Marks, 196.

13. Richard Silberg, *Reading the Sphere: A Geography of Contemporary American Poetry* (Berkeley, Calif.: Berkeley Hills Books, 2001), 40.

14. Jed Rasula, "Ten Different Fruits on One Different Tree: Experiment as a Claim of the Book," *Chicago Review* 43, no. 3 (Fall 1997): 28.

15. Elizabeth Willis, "Thoughts on the Late Lyric," in *Telling It Slant*, ed. Wallace and Marks, 229.

16. Juliana Spahr, *Everybody's Autonomy: Connective Reading and Collective Identity* (Tuscaloosa: University of Alabama Press, 2001), 4.

17. Stephen Burt, review of *Enola Gay*, in *Boston Review* (Summer 2002), http://bostonreview.net/BR25.3/burt.html.

18. See Spahr, *Everybody's Autonomy*. In her poetics statement (in this book), Spahr mentions that Lyn Hejinian's essays on poetry as a language of inquiry are central to her own thinking about poetry.

19. Stacy Doris, "After Language Poetry," in *After Language Poetry: 10 Statements*, ed. Anders Lundgerg, Jonas Magnusson, and Jesper Olsson (Sweden: OEI, 2001). Also available on UBU Web at http://www.ubu.com/papers/oei/doris.html.

MARK LEVINE

WORK SONG

My name is Henri. Listen. It's morning.
I pull my head from my scissors, I pull
the light bulb from my mouth—Boss comes at me
while I'm still blinking.
Pastes the pink slip on my collarbone.
It's OK, I say, I was a lazy worker, and I stole.
I wipe my feet on his skullcap on the way out.

I am Henri, mouth full of soda crackers.
I live in Toulouse, which is a piece of cardboard.
Summers the Mayor paints it blue, we fish in it.
Winters we skate on it. Children are always
drowning or falling through cracks. Parents are distraught
but get over it. It's easy to replace a child.
Like my parents' child, Henri.

I stuff my hands in my shoes
and crawl through the snow on all fours.
Animals fear me. I smell so good.
I have two sets of footprints. I confuse the police.
When I reach the highway I unzip.

I am a zipper. A paper cut.
I fed myself so many times
through the shredder I am confetti,
I am a ticker-tape parade, I am an astronaut
waving from my convertible at Henri.

Henri from Toulouse, is that you?
Why the unhappy face? I should shoot you
for spoiling my parade. Come on, man,
put yourself together. You want so much to die
that you don't want to die.

My name is Henri. I am Toulouse. I am scraps
of bleached parchment, I am the standing militia,
a quill, the Red Cross, I am the feather
in my cap, the Hebrew Testament, I am the World Court.
An electric fan blows
beneath my black robe. I am dignity itself.

I am an ice machine.
I am an alp.
I stuff myself in the refrigerator
wrapped in newsprint. With salt in my heart
I stay good for days.

SCULPTURE GARDEN

I

I won't speak for everyone. But my father, not
sleeping for six weeks, turns
into the crumbling Czar-on-horseback
statue in the central square of his birthplace.
He just stands there, life-like.
Didn't he listen? He wasn't supposed to look

back while escaping. Everyone died.
The bodies spread around the statue like linked cobblestones.
They died. He didn't. *It wasn't his fault.*
Why am I looking at him like this?

2

This is the house my father tried to build.
That patch of dirt raked
in geometric planes is a Japanese garden.
Those gaps the pigeons roost in are French windows.
A step-ladder—a spiral staircase—a helix. My father hasn't

slept in six weeks. There is a crack in the living
room wall. There is an icy roof.
He is watching the plaster.
Certain the house will collapse.
Should I talk to him when he doesn't talk back?
His tongue coated white.
Should I touch him? He is dirty.

3

I can't help it.
When I think of that house I think of
the wreckers taking it down in ten minutes.
Neighbors carrying off faucets and two-by-fours.
My mother in drugged sleep with a ten-syllable disease.
A *galloping* disease.
My father next to her, his cracked lips the only moving thing
in sight.

4

What did they find with their shovels,
the Americans?
Was the thing stacked very high? Was the thing
visible from a single angle?
Did they have to walk around it,
the thing?

5

Hold still, my father says. The shutter clicks.
And again. My mother and I blink.
Pose after pose around the sickbed. White spots.

Once in a dream I made love to my mother.
It did no good.

6

I sit in my room hands blackened with newsprint.
Why not believe the papers.
Things turning wrong.
Gets in the dirt gets in the water.

7

Gets in the dirt gets in the water.

JOHN KEATS

Here we were. Here here we were.
Graphite and plaster and cardboard and canvas.
A dozen human fingers of yellow rays.
Here fully exposed here fully protected.
Reclining like fresh-blasted stone, poised
here beneath the cracked canopy, clutching at flat planets,
adjusting the grains of light here
on our hair and throats.
The newly-dead were not lazier than we.
Our rings were melted for resembling rings.

Sleep had not touched us in however long.
The ill wind collapsed against the bole of the aspen
and could not reach us; and the hungry doves

thrashing above us were our shield
against the unverifiable rain.
                    Our ideal vase
was still with us; and as we passed it among us
the canopy changed in its mirrors—
changed to an arbor swelled with purple vines; changed to
a corridor of polished stone; to a silver pond
and silver moss; to a grove of coal-trees; to a chemical
grove. We plucked from the ground thick strands
of an ashy growth; and we saw in the veins
of the ideal vase blue boulders striking the walls
of the great city and pocking the avenues
of the great city. And we saw thunder
float above us in a spool of cloud.
                    Our machine
was wired with forgetfulness and failed to ease
the pressure in our mouths, the pressure of the
ground in prayer. Our machine coaxed us
with half-messages from the dying system;
and we saw the machine was weak,
in need of rites; so we touched it with
leaves and with thistles and with dirt
and with a white flame and with uranium.
We touched it with sleep and we saw it
in a cloud uplifted on the wings
of nervous hawks. When would the great city
open itself to us? The ideal vase
recited to us treatment methods
we were eager to share.
                    Our pilgrimage
is long and narrow and pitted with traps
scattered by man and by beast: mud; vipers; opiates;
virus; fallout. And the great city
is guarded by personal machines familiar
with suffering; machines with copper voices
high-pitched and trilling in the blank cold night.
Yes we have an offering to make to the earth.

Come here, and closer, and here, and here.
Our blue misleading box of soil
has grown crowded; crowded with ornaments
and with the anonymous powder of skeletons
and with laments.
We were sorry to hear of the earth's loss.
We send our regrets, burdens and regrets.

LIGHT YEARS

The failure to transport himself to the green green
woods—through the sun-raked hollows of the marsh,
through convolutions of bramble and desiring thorns—
was a chronic failure. And yet he loved the earth.

The birds of poetry, like paper birds installed
against a geometric fog, addressed
themselves to him in guilty hush, wanting
him, his sleep, his torpor, his signal, crest,

scenarios of daylight and of noise.
The little triangle that was his home withdrew,
blanched and withdrew in wind. Whose harshest fingers,
lit by glossy rings, strummed at his window now?

He was not alone. The fish of poetry,
teased from the cool white mud, eyed him always on their slow
ascent to the dawnlit surface; and the moon
crossing the water, anonymous hero,

was sent to incite him and remove him to
the woods where he would be almost alone.
He could smell the crumbling bloom of the acacia.
The night stammered through mist and moss and stone.

Once more he turned to the chronic water
looking for an end, and once more saw the watery
bent image of a plane dangling from clouds.

ONTARIO

Beauty in its winter slippers
approached us by degrees
on the gravel path. We were
hitching a ride out; had been hitching.
Our suitcase freighted with a few
gardening tools lifted from the shed
while the old man, old enough,
looked away. He who
went fishing at night (so he said)
carrying in his pail
a nest of tiny flame.

We were headed, headed out, we
were going in a direction.
No tricks
or intrigue, just a noisy
ineptness.

If that's a word. Beauty, dipped
in resin beneath its shag,
was always ready with the right
curse to recite to
our nature. It is
in us, it is,
in the smokehouse in the woods and the old man
looked away. Song of
experience.

There were treads in the snow.
We waited for our hitch.
There were train tracks which
stung with clods of this region's
rare clay.

We were boys, boyish, almost girls.
Left alone on the roof, we would have dwindled.
Incrimination called to us
from the city and its fog-blacked lake,

called to us from the salvaged farms beyond the lake,
from the wilds beyond that.
Guilty was good.

DOCUMENT

They (the same ones) are to be
got at by tilling a ground
fretted with frost in which
the speaker would place them.
They are in it in winter wheat
in inappropriate shoes scorned by farmers
and arrayed in magnetic single file
uphill.

Birdless wind alongside them
along implements and papers
from the forge
alighting.

They (being got at) are cresting,
puppetry, decampment,
one leg crooked
one leg brought down on the unpacking slope
dulled by weather and hacked
tree stumps and the picked-over
remains of the pile
and trod.

Tunnels in the hill
altering the hill without altering its
shape. Hill drops away.
Can you see the hill, you?
It is here in the foreground
a hunting hill.

THEN

Thrift built us a shed
out back in which to stow
our set. I see a sky.
A cloud with a carpenter's hand in it.

I see a shed
an all-day affair with particle
board and steel hinges.
All of us standing at attention, feeling
—my family and I—
(and I was youngest, and we were all still there)
like homeowners. Owning
a yard.

I see a fountain its
waters reeling elsewhere.

Then there were stairs to hide beneath
with the wood-destroying insects.
Look: I wasn't that young. Had
already done some of the worst moral
things, and others. Yet we stood at attention
in the shed at the end of that day among
shelves and safety hooks and nearly
marveled. There is, there is a
moment before infiltration,
is.

I see a tool
left out in grass like a new thought
painted by night with
efflorescence.

I didn't have to leave that place. I did.
We all left. One at a time
by different means (extractive/bitter/ceasing/yielded)
and the owned yard softened at night.
My father's assignment was:
last to go. What was that like
when they peeled him from it.
And pulled up the lawn by its handmade nails.
And found a circuit of passageways
laden with scrap. Which then was sold
rather auctioned.
As he watched, knowing.
And how did he bear.

WILLOW

Okay, willow, breathe on me
from the sunless opening in you—
crescent of gouges and breezes—slope
on which beetles stumble and are
flushed out—

Traffic, human traffic with its rinse
of promises and pauses is coming
for keeps.
And look there goes a swallow transplanting soil.
Me (let me think it)
I can sit on this bench longer than nature
and not know or crave a thing
about this bench, bottle cap dented into its plank

and initials scratched beside it, beside
the point: two raw letters forward to back just
as rare as any combination.
And now the date, plume of digits, daily
statistic.

This is behavior, willow, this
drone, it accompanied you once
in your grove of which
you have a memory—a lush one—don't you?
Was there no breath of you there?

I crossed the arc of your silhouette and lapped
your leaves's signature.
Things grew from you
beneath you in the patched grass
and not far away sat a man on
a bench.

You take it in or you don't.
You hide the sky or else.
Things lived in you.
You, stranger.

POETICS STATEMENT

ABOUT TWENTY years ago, when I began writing poetry with some serious
exuberance, and at an age when it seemed that everything had to be engulfed
in political and erotic flames in order to be meaningful, it was important to
me to make statements along the lines of "Poetry must change the world."
I would never want to think that I have lost that ideal, but I have lost the
desire to make such a statement. I prefer to search for guidance about poetry
from poems themselves. "There are countless hiding places but only one sal-
vation," Kafka wrote in his diaries. "But then again, there are as many paths
to salvation as there are hiding places." One seeks the strength to proceed as
oneself, with all the attendant missteps and uncertainties. For me, the most
trustworthy statement of poetics is the statement that a poem makes in being
itself and not another.

"Leap of faith" seems to me a suitable description of the enterprise of
valuing poetry as a way of life. Let the faith be wide-eyed, and not blind,
not a faith that clings too feverishly to the notion that its rewards are attain-
able; but a faith nonetheless. Among its tenets: that states of mind and feel-
ing can be made most apprehensible, and increasingly so, through language;
that the natural world can be known more accurately—more faithfully—
in language than outside of it, and the human domain known more accu-
rately through the natural; that our bodies and minds, working in concert,
can recognize authenticity—honesty, that is—in a poetic utterance, and can
recognize lapses from authenticity, and can resolve, through poetic craft, to
become more authentic; that "truth," while never absolute, is never nothing,
either, and that it makes a difference to strive for truth, rather than to dis-
count its possibility.

When I write poems, I try to focus on the nuts-and-bolts of composition.
I enjoy attending to technical minutiae. I greatly admire craft in poets, as one
tends to admire qualities in others that one finds deficient in oneself. I am
always trying to extend and improve my technique. I want to learn to express
myself more fully. So, for example, in writing my first book, *Debt*, I experi-
enced as a liberating gesture the assumption of persona. Since then I have
found it liberating, though more difficult, to shed the pretense of persona.

In that first book I insisted on placing my speaker in what felt like a specific place and a specific moment, and I tended to activate some kind of narrative to guide my way through the poem. Since then I have tended to aim at action without narrative. The use of the first-person pronoun no longer seems to me to have a privileged claim to immediacy; nor do I find "I" to be any more troubling than other pronouns. Early on, I wanted pared-down, blunt diction and staccato syntax; that is no longer the case, or at least not all the time. I dislike my ironic bent. I don't want to use tonal gestures—a wink and a nod—to offer commentary on my poem-in-progress. Nothing matters more to me than attempting to produce acute sensory experience through imagery, to produce in a jolt the mystery and clarity of uninterpreted physical knowledge. "O for a Life of Sensations rather than of Thoughts," as Keats, a hero, put it.

I don't imagine a "reader" of my poems—which, as the joke might go, is only realistic. But I do have a listener, a single listener, to whom I attend. At times it seems that our knowledge of each other and of ourselves—the two of us—is transacted by poems. This listening to each other in poems is an ongoing education. It is my experience of Stevens's "intensest rendezvous." I don't presume or expect or even really want anything so grandiose as an "audience" for my private work of poetry—just as one wouldn't ask for an audience larger than a single member for one's prayer. It wouldn't be prayer if it were spoken to many. It is difficult to proceed without that single listener, though one does proceed, one posits that listener in uncertainty. To have a listener, to whom one is present, whose presence compels one's own, in language—the gift is measureless, beyond gratitude.

RECORDING DEVICES

Mark Levine's Poetics of Evidence

Sabrina Orah Mark

> But never did Henry as he thought he did,
> end anyone and hacks her body up
> and hides the pieces, where they may be found.
> He knows: he went over everyone, & nobody's missing.
> Often he reckons, in the dawn, them up.
> Nobody is ever missing.
>
> —John Berryman, from *The Dream Songs*

> Quiet. The Jew Levine is coming to collect
> with his chisels and his sack of flesh.
>
> —Mark Levine, from *Debt*

READING ACROSS Mark Levine's three books of poetry, *Debt* (1992), *Enola Gay* (2000), and *The Wilds* (2006), Samuel Beckett's invention of a man named Krapp, surrounded by reels of recorded tapes, emerges, unspectacled, in strong white light. It is not so much Krapp, the actual man, we remember, although his rusty clothes, surprising boots, capacious pockets, cracked voice, nearsightedness, and laborious walk can easily, like leftover souvenirs, be reminiscent of what is found among the body of Levine's magnificent voices.[1] What more eloquently binds them, though, is their project. Their copious rewinding and fast forwarding. Each bends over the recording device not only to create for the world a testimony, but also to listen to testimonies barely remembered as their own. Ledgers are consulted. Fingers carefully run over entries, as if without these entries existential coordinates would be lost. For each, evidence is crucial. But what ultimately edges Levine's voice off the stage, and beyond the dusty reels of tape, is how seamlessly Levine folds self-investigation into historical interrogation. The debt, always part personal, part historical, becomes like a spool spinning endlessly as it collects the consequences of a world struggling wildly beneath it. And then the spool rewinds. And then it plays again. Stop. Rewind. Fast forward. Play.

"Nothing," writes Emmanuel Levinas, "was official anymore."[2] If through the activity of spinning the tape forward and back a deletion occurs, it is because this deletion was already present. Levine's poems crave for what is officially no longer a dwelling place. He goes back into the past and retrieves, not only like a collector engaged in platonic anamnesis, but also like a collector who, through recollection, disrupts a metanarrative that once marked

Enlightenment and later informed Modernity's desire to fragment. Levine writes to interrupt and intervene, and what becomes felt in this process is the energy of absence: that mother; that lyric; that war; that innocence; that list; that vision; that history that always is and is no longer. Consider the first two lines of "Landscape," the first poem in Levine's first collection, *Debt*: "I am caught at the end of a wooded cul-de-sac / in the glare of a light circling me."[3] Levine begins caught at the end, circled by a new architecture made entirely out of harsh light. It is a poetic enactment of what the architect Daniel Libeskind, in "Traces of the Unborn," is looking to physically construct when he calls for "a need to respond to history, the need to open up the future: that is, to delineate the invisible on the basis of the visible."[4] Levine begins in a "glare." He begins in an image of amnesia that remembers an unspeakable event. Glare, through its disorienting characteristics, suggests how something alive and untranslatable can dwell in permanent exile. And from this too illuminated, bombed-out place, Levine lifts off. There is always the sense, reading Levine, that he is transcribing off of a glare, as he imagines what is forever obscured by too much accounting for, and too much knowledge. *"Where does he live?"* the poem continues. "Across the steel fence, across the canal that slices / the landscape in two?" (*D* 13). Habitation, for Levine, is contingent on displacement, on question. "It is as if in going toward the other," writes Levinas, "I met myself and implanted myself in a land henceforth native, and I were stripped of all the weight of my identity."[5] Levine's obsessive encounter with the uprooted Other is imagined alternately as collapse and eclipse. What becomes of this is a search toward coordinates that slip from the hand only to rise up again as a constellation of loss. In Levine's essay "W. G. Sebald: Other Places," he quotes from Sebald's *Vertigo*: "Despite a great effort to account for the last few days and how I had come to be in this place, I was unable even to determine whether I was in the land of the living or already in another place."[6] The same dialectic of proximity and distance in Sebald is what often propels Levine's voice forward, as is the dialectic of erasure and account. The question as to where the *I* lives, if not here, if already in another place, becomes the jagged sheen that casts itself over Levine's poetics, as he interrogates the lyric and its conversation with history.

Let's fast forward, for a moment, to the end, where "Willow," the last poem in Levine's latest collection, *The Wilds*, imagines an I who can sit on a "bench longer than nature / and not know or crave a thing / about this bench, bottle cap dented into its plank // and initials scratched beside it, beside / the point: two raw letters forward to back just / as rare as any combination" (*TW* 64). The initials, like the nature of Levine's interrogative lyric, are half anamnestic and half amnesiac. Like a record the initials are scratched. And like Sebald, who can no longer make a final account for the sake, perhaps, of authenticity, the I, for Levine, after three entire collections that desperately make a plea for the I, knows nothing, nor craves to know anything about his final dwelling, his sparse bench. He is empty of the knowledge experience is expected to make accessible. The carved initials are "raw" and "beside / the point" (*TW* 64). They are the superfluous evidence of life, (superfluous because evidence obscures the actual life), and yet they are "forward to back just / as rare as any combination" (*TW* 64). This composition of "forward to back" choreographs a figure reminiscent of Walter Benjamin's Angel of History:

> A Klee painting named "Angelus Novus" shows an angel looking as though he is about to move away from something he is fixedly contemplating. His eyes are staring, his mouth is open, his wings are spread. This is how one pictures the angel of history. His face is turned toward the past. Where we perceive a chain of events, he sees one single catastrophe which keeps piling wreckage upon wreckage and hurls it in front of his feet. The angel would like to stay, awaken the dead, and make whole what has been smashed. But a storm is blowing from Paradise; it has got caught in his wings with such violence that the angel can no longer close them. This storm irresistibly propels him into the future to which his back is turned, while the pile of debris before him grows skyward. This storm is what we call progress.[7]

At the end, Levine addresses a willow, an image that bends, like the blown Angel, according to the events in the air: "Okay, willow, breathe on me / from the sunless opening in you" (*TW* 64). Here is Levine irresistibly quiet, almost kneeling again (as he kneels in his earlier collections), but this time he is humbled by what grows wild. He asks of it to breathe on him, as if to swallow out all the experience that has left him like a man on a bench without memory beside initials that may or may not be his. Progress, both for Levine and Benjamin, means a movement that always has its face turned toward an inconceivable past. "I crossed," writes Levine, "the arc of your silhouette and lapped / your leaves's signature . . . and not far away sat a man on / a bench" (*TW* 65). The lyric for Levine, like progress, becomes a propagation that relies on retreat. An emanation that relies on limitation. The lyric is the altered-ego, flickering, but never flickering out. It is the altered-ego watching itself not watch itself. The lyric is the hero always on the verge of forgetting his own name. In *Debt*, Levine introduces Henri in the poem "Work Song." Henri embodies the lyrical draught of lyric; namely, the inadequacy of language to adequately remember. "My name is Henri," writes Levine. And then later on he writes, "I am Henri, mouth full of soda crackers." And then later on: "I am an astronaut / waving from my convertible at Henri" (*D* 17). Like the man on the bench, in "Willow," who sits beside the scratched initials, and then later crosses an "arc" to distance himself from himself, Henri's pose marks the same movement: from inscribe, to muffle, to scratch, to split—leaving us to wonder if that man on the bench *is* Henri, reincarnated perhaps as the record of Levine's lyrical patterns. "I am scraps / of bleached parchment, writes Levine. "I am the feather / in my cap, the Hebrew Testament . . . I stuff myself in the refrigerator / wrapped in newsprint. With salt in my heart / I stay good for days" (*D* 18).

Unlike the voices in Levine's earlier collections, the voices throughout *The Wilds* are stark and contemplative. The landscape is often overgrown, undone. And still there is that eerie sense that someone has been here before, as much as there is a sense that the ones who are beginning here have ended, already, elsewhere. This world is as preapocalyptic as it is postapocalyptic. "We will not stare in that / particular pond again," writes Levine. "Tell me about the woods again" (*TW* 45). This idea of an "again," divorced from a specific "before," links Levine to the surrealists in that the argument of evidence becomes inseparable from the argument of replacement. Throughout *The Wilds*, there are signs that figures have been traipsing through *The Wilds* before *The Wilds*. "Ontario," its first poem, confesses to "treads in the snow" (*TW* 4). In "Child's Song," the act of "shedding coal dust, bone dust, throat dust, marrow," later becomes "shedding stone dust, skin dust, speech dust, marrow" (*TW* 55–56). The sifted landscape reveals the sifted body. Even the titles in *The Wilds* often read like a stack of a child's alphabet cards referring to a shuffled world: "Document," "Hand," "Animal," "Insect," "Triangle," "Remember," "Song," "Poem," "Night." In "On Language as Such," Benjamin writes:

> After the Fall, which, in making language mediate, laid the foundation for its multiplicity, linguistic confusion could only be a step away. Once men had injured the purity of the name, the turning away from that contemplation of things in which their language passes into man needed only to be completed in order to deprive man of the common foundation of an already shaken spirit of language. *Signs* must become confused where things are entangled. The enslavement of language in prattle is joined by the enslavement of things in folly almost as its inevitable consequence. In this turning away from things, which was enslavement, the plan for the Tower of Babel came into being, and the linguistic confusion of it.[8]

What is startling about Levine's poetics is how precisely it recognizes this Fall as an interior debt that turns and returns into an ever-changing world of signs. "No tricks," writes Levine in "Ontario," "or intrigue, just a noisy / ineptness. // If that's a word. Beauty, dipped / in resin beneath its shag, / was always / ready with the right curse to / recite to our nature. It is / in us, it is, / in the smokehouse in the woods and the old man / looked away. Song of experience" (*TW* 3–4). Language is never free of its confusion. Experience means to "look away." The evidence is here, but what asks to be proven, what asks to be accounted for, is profoundly absent. In *Debt*, the "children," in "Work Song," "are always / drowning or falling through the cracks"

(*D* 17), while the multiple announcements of Henri read as much like birth announcements as they do like elegies. "You want so much to die," says Henri, "that you don't want to die" (*D* 18). By the time we arrive at *The Wilds* there becomes a splendid trace of Henri and these children always "falling through the cracks." They were here all along, but as an again divorced from a before. First, they slipped through the cracks as a loan to the debt of being. And now they have returned, if only as a trace, in a third collection. "Parents are distraught," "Work Song" continues, "but get over it. It's easy to replace a child. / Like my parents' child Henri" (*D* 17). Throughout *The Wilds* there is the sense that the shattered, fallen, drowned, and split figures of Levine's first two collections are what make possible the uncultivated sprawl of *The Wilds*, and its mingling of innocence and wisdom. Consider the second section of "Two Women":

> Something was inflicted.
> He was looking.
> The tiny cuts rained down.
> He wore an air of soiled gravity.
> Like a man on a child's train.
>
> And yet as he lay on the tracks
> as per novelistic instruction
> (German steel; crows pecking, biding it)
> he awoke less visibly severed than he ought.
> Pearly love bites by the dozen was all.
>
> He lay spanning and surveying
> (with the translator's detachment)
> the undercarriage and its skittering
> high gauge diagram, mosaic of pistons,
> drippings. And through the braying
>
> planks he viewed a scrim
> of scarved weepers gone shuttling by.
> Warm down there beneath the free-floating canopy.
> Wafts of mother's bodily perfume,
> Of dog hair.
>
> (*TW* 12)

Like Wallace Stevens, Levine's mastery of the chiseled, carefully measured line carves a highly believable dreamscape, one whose fundamental objective is not to mythologize but to remember, and through remembering enter into a relationship with a real, live, present world. The dreamscape here is thick with words that imply instrument: "cuts," "gravity," "steel," "pecking," "severed," "spanning," "surveying," "translator," "undercarriage," "gauge," "mosaic," "planks." There is a building going on. This is where Levine exits the surrealists' salon, because substitution or replacement, as in the associative gesture, for Levine, does not arise out of chance operation. It does not arise out of shenanigan, or subversion, or the drive toward "convulsive beauty."[9] It arises out of a measured necessity. And it arises out of a careful, almost anthropological gaze "through the braying / planks" (*TW* 12). Here is the poet at work cautiously peeling back the layers of the images he once laid down in order to see *again*. Through the planks, and the scrim, and the scarves, there is a weeping. Substitution and replacement, for Levine, is about a dislocation that mourns location. In *The Wilds*'s title poem it becomes impossible not to think of Henri and the slipped children when Levine writes, "You down there, old / child, you in your outgrown hobs. / I think I'll remember you / spilling your sense / where the earth things play" (*TW* 46).

In Levine's essay "Writing It: Some Observations on the Poetics of Territorality," he begins with Ashbery's "Pyrography" and the roaming territory of the "it." Levine writes:

> When Ashbery, in "Pyrography" opens by saying "Out here on Cottage Grove it matters," you've got to feel that Ashbery's "it" is tangled as much with the invoked presence of "here" as with the dizzy, dislocated problem of being on, and writing from the "outs," "the outhere"; and that the need to specify "Cottage Grove," a place named of two evocatively idealized place names, must in some way indicate a certain anxiety about its opposite, about losing the farm, about oblivion; and that "it" is therefore made of the pastness of the present, the presence of pastness, matter and immateriality equally; and that "it" is the matter and, indeed, "it matters."[10]

Levine has, in the past, been described as an "elliptical poet," who is always "hinting, punning, or swerving away from a never-quite-unfolded backstory . . . easier to process in parts than in wholes."[11] The implication is that the world, as it is understood, is whole and it is the elliptical poet who injects into it fragmented matter. Consider it, though, the other way around. Levine's obsessive attention to an anchorless, ever-changing "it," recognizes the world as it is actually experienced. And if this reads as obscure, or shifty it is because "it" is. In other words, when we look out that train window, we are in fact half of ourselves because, internally, we are also partially watching the train pass us by. Even Levine's Henri knows this. Even Henri knows "I am an astronaut / waving from my convertible at Henri" (*D* 17). He is the discoverer, the destroyer, and the spectator at once. And if the whole world is left out of "it," it is because the whole world is always left out of "it." Nevertheless, Levine knows this ephemeral "it" must be chaperoned back into the world. And he chaperones with irreverent audacity, as often as he chaperones with genuine awe. If Levine is to be nested in any poetic tradition, it is a tradition of resurrecting what is always swerving like a hollow in a hollow. What is never barely caught. He is as good with the net, as he is at writing coherence as a fine mesh of illusion. "Late night," writes Levine in "Self Portrait," "I crawl back into bed very slow not to hurt / the one lying there hard flesh and cold. / I turn him I open his gown I am gentle God I do love him. / We make love the two of me like a beautiful machine / we are the finished product" (*D* 29). Like the "I" (and like the lyric) the "matter and immateriality" of the "it" engenders itself as it recognizes its incompleteness. It falls from its own arms only to rise up again like erasure and like inscription. "How long ago," asks Levine, "was it that striving after impossible ideals was thought to be a humanizing impulse?"[12]

Throughout Levine's three collections, the "it" is everywhere, and is often unhinged. The "it" in *Debt* is often out of the question, or mostly dead, or denied, or with nowhere to go. In *Enola Gay*, "all the gods knew it" (*EG* 5), and "it" will often announce itself as a troubled mysticism. "It came to a halt—," writes Levine, "it studied us—it was less hungry then we thought" (*EG* 5). Here the "it" comes off as a lost restorer. In *The Wilds*, "it is in us" (*TW* 3), and "it suits you" (*TW* 52). "It" becomes like a traveling garb. In all three collections it is important to experience the character of Levine's "it" as an ever-changing figure that asks for a litany that refuses containment, as it tirelessly offers all the world's images up anonymously. It is as if Levine's "it" is stationed at the top of a Tower of Babel, inscribing the image with "its" entirety.

But what is "it?" It is often menacing, yes. It poses, and the pose is never the pose we quite expect. It is seductive, and actual, and wants, and keeps wanting. It calls to us. It makes us want to be for it a tender thing. It is everything and nothing at once. It is like being, becoming, and disappearing. It is like the nature of lyric. At the end of Levine's essay "Writing It: Some Observations on the Poetics of Territorality," he writes:

> A few years ago . . . I went to Bangladesh when the country was eighty percent covered in flood waters. People lived on their roofs; people lived in water; people slogged through chest-high water running with sewage and their skin would be discolored with infections. Though Bangladesh is theorizable, there was nothing theoretical about it, and to me it was an abuse and an evasion not to struggle with, and defer to, the referentiality of Bangladesh. I talked to a man whose shanty in the port city of Chittagong had been buried the night before in a mud slide. His two children had died, and he survived. He was digging through the muck to try and retrieve his cooking utensils. I asked him what he thought when he lay covered in the mud, waiting to be rescued. And he said: I thought that God had left the world.[13]

It seems inhuman and weirdly sterile to dissect this account in any way that does not simply repeat this account. At the same time, though, it is important here to acknowledge a critical guilt, because guilt is a necessary ideological constraint often found in Levine's poetics. What does it mean, really, to refer? It means to assemble and contain, but also inherent in reference is the replacement of a material. Reference explains a "here," by sending you over "there." Reference acknowledges the limitation of naming. For example, on one hand "Bangladesh" must be named, because "it" happened in Bangladesh. On the other hand, by naming the place where "it" happened as "Bangladesh," the word "Bangladesh" becomes a substitution for what actually happened, achieving an emotional distance. The nature of Levine's "it" allows his poetics to resist such a distance.

Enola Gay, Levine's second collection, flies through a war-torn landscape, dropping names ("Susan Fowler," "Jack and Jill," "Enola Gay," "John Keats," "Graham," "Jean Cocteau,") like bombs. The name ends at the moment it is dropped. Levine's poetics salvage what remains. "Enola Gay" is not a poem about an airplane or a bomb. "It is many years after the fact," writes Levine, "I send a squad car to gather data / from the sticky asphalt, and they / are far away and very quiet. I do / wish I had not surrendered my wings" (*EG* 43). Like the subject in *Debt*, who always reminds us that he too is a part of that guilty machine, who knows "I am not the man he used to be" (*D* 29), the subject in "Enola Gay" reminds himself that he too is implicated as he laments the surrender of his wings. He also knows that the attempt to collect makes him distant from the data to be gathered. Benjamin writes:

> What is decisive in collecting is that the object is detached from all its original functions in order to enter into the closest conceivable relation to the things of the same kind. The relation is the diametric opposite of any utility, and falls into the peculiar category of completeness. What is this "completeness?" It is a grand attempt to overcome the wholly irrational character of the object's mere presence at hand through its integration into a new, expressly devised historical system: the collection. And for the true collector, every single thing in this system becomes an encyclopedia of all knowledge of the epoch, the landscape, the industry, and the owner from which it comes. . . . He loses himself, assuredly. But he has the strength to pull himself up again by nothing more than straw; and from out of the sea of fog that envelops his senses rises the newly acquired place, like an island.[14]

It is in this "newly acquired place" where "The Great War" can be "seen through a glass horse balanced on a child's finger" (*EG* 9), where "Susan Fowler" is "the red stitching on the pocket of a man's shirt" (*EG* 8), where "Jack and Jill" "is rinsing his great surface / with heavy water and a drill" (*EG* 13), and where "The air was tilted at an awkward angle / and tasted, like lead, of the other side" (*EG* 55). Which is to say, to detach the thing from its original function, mystifies it. The great traipse through an untranslatable site makes language (and, concurrently, its images) strange. Levine, though, takes on even more burdens. For example, in "Bering Strait," when Levine writes, "his heels sticky with sighting land / his refrain the / hero's need to be unloved" (*TW* 7) one wonders: unloved by whom? By language? Is the unloved hero the poet who betrays language by using it to "sight land?" What, after all, is the difference between the collector of objects who collects in a "grand attempt to overcome the wholly irrational character of the object's mere presence," and the poet who uses language to overcome an inconceivable world? If the hero is unloved does this mean he has been abandoned by what he set out to rescue? Levine knows language is unhappy with him. He asks us to cheer for his demise, as often as he invites our sympathy. "He loses himself, assuredly." John Berryman, of course, led Henry (by the grouchy hand) into this poetic conundrum. Both Levine and Berryman know that to make the self evident to language, makes out of the self a poetics of vulnerability. "All the world," writes Berryman in his first Dream Song, "like a woolen lover / once did seem on Henry's side. / Then came a departure. / Thereafter nothing fell out as it might or ought. / I don't see how Henry, pried / open for all the world to see, survived."[15] Out of the poetics of vulnerability arises a poetics of responsibility. Once the poet pries open his subjects to enact a broken world, it becomes the poet's job to take care of his subject's slow disappearance, now strewn everywhere. Levine knows it is he who must clean this mess up. And this mess, this disappearing subject, is Levine's inheritance. And he knows this. Who, after all, is Henri if not Berryman's Henry started up again, like a sputtering machine, at the end of the twentieth century?

Levine's subjects hardly know how to address each other, as often as we hardly know exactly how to address Levine's subjects. Of the personages in *Enola Gay*, Stephen Burt writes, "they are persons of shaky and uncertain status—semi-generic, semi-universal, and self-consciously if unwillingly artificial. Like Henri, they have doppelgangers, or halves, or severable, willful, mechanical limbs; they are simultaneously a person and a place, or a person and an algorithm, or one person and several."[16] And so often they forget themselves. They forget their task. They wait in the dark to be reminded. They demand their return, and the return of their others. When "Jack and Jill" wonders about himself "Was he real? / Was he a rhyme? Was he a trace / of purple smoke escaped from base" (*EG* 12) we wonder too. When, in "Counting the Forests," "He set out in darkness. In darkness / we waited at the corner of the forest / for his reappearance" (*EG* 15), we wait too. We begin to trust the breakdown of the subject, and respond accordingly. Five of the poems in *Enola Gay* are named "Lyric," and in the first one Levine writes, "when I could watch no more / I undid myself and I watched" (*EG* 16). The human figure becomes a model of its own lack of evidence as it is revised, repeated, returned, and regretted. "At the very least," writes "Levine," in one "Lyric," "Lines circulated" (*EG* 22). And circulate they do. At the very least, they circle their lost inhabitants.

"She told me her story," writes Levine in "My Friend," "and while she told me her story I watched a shiny / beetle crawling through her hair. I didn't know what to do / so I kept watching" (*EG* 27–28). Here the argument of evidence becomes as inseparable from the argument of replacement as it does from the argument of forgetting. Her story (if heard) is forgotten inside the "shiny / beetle crawling through her hair." The beetle becomes the evidence of forgetting, as it crawls like a slow vehicle through the hair of a woman mistaken for the dead. Levine is the messenger of his strangers' forgotten testimonies. And the messenger is guilt-ridden. He knows he cannot but make a fiction out of what forgot itself. Like Krapp's fast forwarding, rewinding, playing, and pause, Levine's lines curl over, around, and back on themselves, sometimes enacting a refusal that resists then propels itself forward, stubbornly, carefully because there is a task at hand. "Twice I refused to visit your mother's / attic," writes Levine in "Two Springs," "but your mother would have it / no other way. She in her swimsuit / and red cap. Asleep and afloat / and the bathwater sticky with cold petals. // I went towards her as if pulled by a chain. / By then she had lost her gravity; and she softened / the air with blue kisses; and she sputtered / into the oncoming wave" (*EG* 32). The approach of the "I" epitomizes the dilemma of witness. To go toward the mother, "as if pulled by a chain," opens up for her a hole inside of which she can disappear "into the oncoming wave." To recognize the mother unplugs the drain that swallows her as she makes one last caress with her mouth to the air. To erase and inscribe, again, become a single act. Consider the double implication of wave: It is a gesture of existence. It is what takes the mother away.

"Levine is a collector," writes Stephen Burt, "of very strange objects."[17] "Event," for example, reads like a ledger, where number 10 is "Accordion, bamboo, crinoline, drift. / Burial, crabgrass, demonstration, edge." And number 12 is "The Women pretending to be crows, / The men pretending to be something else." And number 13 is "Bodies glossed by moonlight" (*EG* 37). "To read, to write," writes Blanchot, "the way one lives under the surveillance of the disaster: exposed to the passivity that is outside passion. The heightening of forgetfulness. It is not you who will speak; let the disaster speak in you, even if it be by your forgetfulness or silence."[18] As a way to enact "the way one lives under the surveillance," Levine writes two different kinds of list poems. One is a collection of disparate objects, like "Event." It refers us to what has already scattered. The other kind of ledger makes a scrap and scatter out of "it." "It," again, being the namelessness of *being*. In "The Fixed Wing," man begins in "strictest uniform; man in daylight. / Man in ill-starred tunnel, upright, chirping." "Streaks of man, the poem later continues, "on the so-called horizon; man robed in garish / sunlight; ink blots, ferment, silver holster, dog." And finally:

The combination of man and man in weedy gardens.
Man's footprint in disrepair. Man at odds
With salt-water and with the urgency of atoms.
Orbiting man. Man undone. Man in pursuit of the eel.
Man gathering shards of the withered fossil record.
Credit to man, to the winnowed breath of man,
Man's echo, man's stem, man's eager haunted remains.

(*EG* 71–72)

Man's survival becomes stricken by its surveillance. It's that old trick of repeating the word into oblivion. If the collector lived inside his lexicon, these could easily be his surrounding words: "fixed," "strict," "daylight," "blots," "footprint," "urgency," "orbiting," "pursuit," "gathering," "shards," "record," "breath," "echo," "haunted," "remains." Levine's poetics live inside a wired system of existence shattered by process. "Our machine / was wired," writes Levine in "John Keats," "with forgetfulness and failed to ease / the pressure in our mouths, the pressure of the / ground in prayer. Our machine coaxed us / with half-messages from the dying system; / and we saw the machine was weak, in need of rites; so we touched it" (*EG* 49). This system, overwhelmed by forgetting, bare echo, and stem, is the system Levine knows he has inherited.

In "W. G. Sebald: Other Places," Mark Levine writes about the "mordant scrapbook quality of Sebald's work," and what is found there: "poor-quality reproductions of postcards, family photos, architectural monuments, diagrams, drawings, handwriting samples, newspaper items, and, in one case, in *Vertigo*, the author's own passport photo, bearing a vertical black stripe down the center of the face."[19] This attention to "proof" is in direct conversation with Levine's project in that there is evidence, but it is saturated in interruption. It is even skeptical of itself. Levine goes on to say that the "receipt of identification papers . . . guarantees the sensation of dispossession . . . and that the fervent act of precise and detailed 'accounting,' which lends Sebald's work both the quality of a storehouse and that of a courthouse, spreads an uncanny sheen over 'the land of the living.'"[20] Also, a negative space, a "refined numbness," as Levine calls it, is disciplined through documentation. This procedure closely resembles Levine's poetics and its dialectic of inscribe and erase, distance and proximity. It reminds us of our dear friend Krapp who uses recorded evidence as an interruption not to lift, but to slant himself back into an existence that may have already forsaken him. Not only is the evidence insufficient—or, in Levine's case, not only is the image insufficient—but it reminds us how barely it remembers us under the guise of testament. Let's end with Levine "Counting the Forests," because "he had been there already and had taken count. / And he had counted the animal forest and the / smoldering forest and the weeping forest and the forest / of the forgotten tropics and the God-forest. What could he say to his accusers?" Let's end here because "Somewhere was a coldness with a rope in it / like a memory-braid or a pair of braids," and it is the task of poetry to remember not where.

NOTES

1. Samuel Beckett, "Krapp's Last Tape," in *Collected Shorter Plays* (New York: Grove, 1984), 55.

2. Emmanuel Levinas, "Nameless," in *Proper Names*, trans. Michael B. Smith (Stanford: Stanford University Press, 1975), 119.

3. Mark Levine, *Debt* (New York: William Morrow, 1993), 13. Subsequent citations to works by Levine will appear as follows: *D = Debt*, *E = Enola Gay*, *TW = The Wilds*.

4. Daniel Libeskind, "Traces of the Unborn," in *Architecture and Revolution: Contemporary Perspectives on Central and Eastern Europe*, ed. Neil Leach (New York: Routledge, 1999), 127.

5. Levinas, "Paul Celan: From Being to the Other," in *Proper Names*, trans. Michael B. Smith (Stanford: Stanford Univeristy Press, 1975), 44.

6. Levine, "W. G. Sebald: Other Places," *American Letters and Commentary* 14 (2002): 180.

7. Walter Benjamin, "Theses on the Philosophy of History," in *Illuminations*, ed. Hannah Arendt (New York: Schocken Books, 1968), 257.

8. Benjamin, "On Language and Such," in *Walter Benjamin: Selected Writings*, ed. Marcus Bullock and Michael W. Jennings (Cambridge, Mass.: Harvard University Press, 1996), 72.

9. Here I am referring to André Breton's concept of "convulsive beauty" as reality convulsed into representation.

10. Levine, "Writing It: Some Observations on the Poetics of Territoriality," *Iowa Review* (2002): 70.

11. Stephen Burt, "The Elliptical Poets," *American Letters and Commentary* 11 (1999): 45.

12. Levine, "Writing It," 71.

13. Ibid., 77–78.

14. Benjamin, *The Arcades Project*, trans. Howard Eiland and Kevin McLaughlin (Cambridge, Mass.: Harvard University Press, 1999), 205.

15. John Berryman, *The Dream Songs* (New York: Noonday Press, 1969), 3.

16. See Stephen Burt's review of *Enola Gay* at www.bostonereview.net/BR25.3/burt.html.

17. Ibid.

18. Maurice Blanchot, *The Writing of the Disaster*, trans. Ann Smock (Lincoln: University of Nebraska Press, 1995), 4.

19. Levine, "W. G. Sebald," 180.

20. Ibid.

BIBLIOGRAPHY

Books by Mark Levine

Debt. National Poetry Series Selection. New York: William Morrow, 1993.
Enola Gay. Berkeley and Los Angeles: University of California Press, 2000.
The Wilds. Berkeley and Los Angeles: University of California Press, 2006.

Selected Prose

"W. G. Sebald: Other Places." *American Letters and Commentary* 14 (2002): 180–83.
"Writing It: Some Observations on the Poetics of Territoriality." *Iowa Review* (2002):
   70–78.

Interview

Martinez, Martin J. "Interview with Mark Levine" *George Mason University's Nonfiction Universe*. http://nonfiction.gmu.edu/Visiting%20Writers/MLinterview.html.

Selected Criticism

Burt, Stephen. *Boston Review* (Summer 2002): http://bostonreview.net/BR25.3/burt.
   html.
———. "The Elliptical Poets." *American Letters and Commentary* 11 (1999): 45.
Darbyshire, Peter, and George Darbyshire. *Bookninja*. http://www.bookninja.com/
   reviews/Aug_2003/enolagay.htm.

References

Berryman, John. 1969. *The Dream Songs*. New York: Noonday Press.
Beckett, Samuel. 1984. "Krapp's Last Tape." In *Collected Shorter Plays*. New York:
   Grove Press.
Benjamin, Walter. 1999. *The Arcades Project*. Translated by Howard Eiland and Kevin
   McLaughlin. Cambridge, Mass.: Belknap Press.
———. 1996. "On Language and Such." In *Walter Benjamin: Selected Writings*, edited
   by Marcus Bullock and Michael W. Jennings. Cambridge, Mass.: Harvard University Press.
———. 1968. "Theses on the Philosophy of History." In *Illuminations*, edited by
   Hannah Arendt. New York: Schocken Books.
Blanchot, Maurice. 1995. *The Writing of the Disaster*. Translated by Ann Smock. Lincoln: University of Nebraska Press.
Levinas, Emmanuel. 1975. "Nameless." In *Proper Names*, translated by Michael B.
   Smith. Stanford: Stanford University Press.
Libeskind, Daniel. 1999. "Traces of the Unborn." In *Architecture and Revolution: Contemporary Perspectives on Central and Eastern Europe*, edited by Neil Leach. New
   York: Routledge.

Sebald, W. G. 2001. *Austerlitz*. Translated by Anthea Bell. New York: Modern Library.

Stevens, Wallace. 1990. *The Collected Poems*. New York: Vintage Books.

KAREN VOLKMAN

I won't go in today, I'll stay out today. I won't go home today, instead I'll go to sea. Today is a lot of work, yesterday wiser. Yesterday is a path made out of feet, today is a screwball alarmclock with a mawkish tick. Today offends everyone with nebulous gesture: "I think." "Yes but." "Still really." "Gee well." This becomes language you know becomes destiny, still you know that operator listening in on the phone? She of the darker stare and windy grimace? Yes she is writing every word, I wouldn't leave that blur too conspicuous, knapsack of roar. I wouldn't give just anyone access, but you know best. Seems to me you go out a little too spryly, hardly a step really more of a *sprawl*. You packed your bags reasonably enough, but what about all that dubious baggage from last fall? Seems we're in for shriller weather, your eye no more mild decries tornado and scar. Today needs a few more devotees lacking grace. But yesterday, imperious echo, knows who you are.

* * *

There comes a time to rusticate the numbers. The way the birds, jug jug, mount in steepleless processions, or the barely comprehensible division of our hands. Or the cliff with the face of a galled god, appalling. And these are boundable, we count them, each and each.

But my zero, windy and sleepless, how to teach it? It speaks to the rain, the spare precipitation—it says, Desert conditions, but I fathom the sea—and rain in its meticulous sermon mumbles back. Talk, talk, in shrill slaps, in strident speculations. As the almond trees flash the gold, precocious blossoms our cold maids call blind psyche. And this was me. I give you my digital, my radial, my baldest baby. While annul! cries the fitful keeper, who sears and scalds. But my zero, sum and province, whole howl, skies the all.

* * *

I never wish to sing again as I used to, when two new eyes could always stain the sea, of tangent worlds, indolent as callows, and the clock went backward for a skip, to rise, to set.

Some will twine grass to fit in a thimble, some will carve bread to mend a craggy wall, some in the slantest midnight cry for sleep. When the pitch-owl swallows the moon, what welt will show it? Sighing helps nothing, raspberries raw and green, in the form of a heart

imperfectly divided. A wave grows sharper close to the shore. Some own words like strips of scape and summon. It is possible to suffer even in the sun. And race the steep noon to its highest, hoary gate. Stares drop under the sky; silence of a windslap; and a scar drifts out of air to stand whistling:

She who listens poorly will always be calling. She who sounds silence drowns with the dumb.

She who cuts her hands off must drink with her tongue.

* * *

O verb, o void. Not more loose, but I kept a part back. I ogled the hostels, figured the fardels. My importunate frolic kept debtors at a dispatch.

Needing more hell, more harlot. Simple profit. I have a bank-robber heart in a felonious sling-back, and something in a Rubric lipstick would set you up.

Digital spine, maneuver, heart attack. Neon girls are chary, keep their lights on. Blue me a fugue and factor, future mark. It does the drum-roll when our $x2$ straddles,
   hex of my heart, blight of my thigh,
   my heat and light.

* * *

No noise subtracts it. It won't leave, or scatter jokes or fathoms, no tiny failing, or some short multitude impossibly, or now, it would certainly never scribble stanched fragments on this less. Noise is not, so words think, a complex logic, no one loses reason fast enough, or then. To murder sound, you must bleed the pastures, the so few animals and vapors, misread the minerals, or still the static the huge stones break when we close at night. You must never dream clouds in coils, convulsive weathers, or those greetings we never felt leaving: nights of adulthood whose boredom is forever explored.

A sorrow not meant for anyone, an ancient beneficence ending so softly, with such shallow and plain sustainings—days in the lavish spaces, nights in the desert, deserts, someone else—or is it too much to never sleep enough, to dream? There must be forebodings of a few dawns of contempt, none the same as any other, premonitions of a few men whispering from pleasure, or of loud leaping boys who have never touched death, and are opening this first time.

* * *

It could be a bird that says summer, that says gather no late failing harvest in a wealth of arms. Lost weed, still you remember, in a storm-suit, the sky came down to walk among us, oh to talk. Such grey conviction, cracked calculus, chasm. Black earth repeating, I was never him, and so many green words of schism, that and this. If a tree could say, if a tree could say, what are you? to my dim attention, to my wayward random shape. Suit, suit, you're a cold suit, your stitched rain shivers and splinters, what web is this? Unnumbered mesh of other, kill, kiss.

* * *

The first greeting on a bright sift, yes. And the less falls, a loss does. You will not be absent in the day's convocation, as a trickle wakes to find itself in the rift's mind. It drifts from the demurral in the clouds, cast off, to the uniform sameness of soil, a stream patiently distilling itself from stone. A blind culmination, at that trace where nothing stops being, no sweet surfeit—one could reject it, not from conviction, a less rational sorrowing strip from the sky, escaping when the stone falls.

It goes, straying from some refined mass of resistance. Something harder, one height against another, as the gradual, slow nourishment of artifice prevents you, unravelling, destroying no molecule in progress. Somewhere here on the firm ground you have pressed farther apart those ten tricks from the chaos which you rejected one by one—nothing to leave, worth stealing. It never meant to be casually accruing. Under the nothing of what decayed, or some scarcity, staying. Loss implies such rigid divisions. *Come in.*

* * *

Brown is the flat gestation of a maze,
grass-grown remembrance of a second look
the field holds open like a nascent book
in which the wind has written, Sudden strays,

sudden numbers beat—the roots of days
branched intangibles a stupor took
and slept and stroked and scattered in a shook
haze of wakenings, refracting rays

outleaping their seasons, daughters of a glance
ago-ahead, a retrograde advance.
Loving nothing but the fractal ways,

they gather flowers—pearl-petal, bitter blaze—
brilliant sisters in the infinite dance
at ardor's axis, integral of chance.

* * *

What is this witness, the watching ages,
yield of hours, blurred nights, the blue commerce
limned limpidities the skies rehearse
dreaming their seasons, raptured in their rages.

Eventless auction the sun screams and stages
for outered spectacles that bloom their source,
or eyes are mouths and utter tongued remorse—
read me, augur, from the wrists of sages

the shocks and tangencies strangled in their veins.
Or stars are livid links in lucent chains.
Heart will read its figure in its willing

or blinded needle the compass stains;
lidless volumes and vortices of pains
distinct the dolor, and kind the killing.

* * *

Grey airs, grey stirs. A form of flesh
nets its gray catch. The system swims.
Shibboleth synth, stanchions symptoms
effervescing to relinquish

rectilinears of rush and ash.
Grey gris, grau day, grisaille of sums,
gristle granular of stateless kingdoms,
spore and structure still distinguish

ghosts in spokes—the features flash,
the futures silver—spiral spumes
oceans of errata, columns

stutter, gray pearls that were his crash,
or fallow hull—greyness blooms
the no-wind its nightlessness consumes.

* * *

Reticulation of a premise
emerges in even harm
volitional as a storm
or stanching of plot and promise.

Latencies—the loss, the minus—
consider the song of the worm:
"am sightless as wing, leg, arm,
under my raw seeps the rawness."

How does a namelessness name?
Suppose it were better off dead.
Or its tongue were a species of beam

jouissance of the burning to seem
occult, aureate, aspect, thread,
not number that nevers the scheme.

* * *

Bitter seed—scarred semblance—Psyche
sows the portion of contagion, liberty
in nerve and number, Cupid's quiddity
who catalogues the adage, zed to z,

and spends the nothing lovers' numbing plea
It shall be if we kiss it. Stone can see
what factors fault its fathoms, ardor we
mistake for fracture. A split, a volt, a v

of vain misgiving, void's elected be
knowing no rapture but its own redundancy.
So vowels do not die. They scale and scree

and haunt the planets with a harmony
as the zodiac wheels its pale menagerie
of soundless animals no love can free.

* * *

The thing you do you keep or claim—
there was this reason, scattered squall
blurring its faces, random thrall
of crones and clones, replicate same

shatters its single, riven name.
Oh holy puppet, genius doll,
we like to touch it, call it all
the shunt of heartwork, lurid fame

some lucent lady cradles close,
and smiling, dimming, speaks one thin
immanent syllable, viral rose

hissing its petals, ciphered skin
no word will bleed, no wound you chose
deeps the speaking its noons begin.

* * *

Lifting whither, cycle of the sift
annuls the future, zero that you zoom
beautiful suitor of the lucent room
evacuating auras, stratal shift

leaping in its alabaster rift.
Lend the daylight crescent, circle, spume,
ether from your eye, appalled perfume,
ash incense to boundary when you drift

bluely looming—motion will be mute
season spooling its argent errant thread
endless loop and lavish as the dead

note resounding a transparent flute.
Tell the boys we're leaving—wind as red
event left at the altar—the bride is fled.

* * *

One might start here, with the blank specimen, not thinking too much or wanting to go home. Entrance is ample, the peak of the blank, a kind of acme in the ether. And what if you said No ceasing! No respite between night and pen. But it's not night yet, nor even crepuscular later, no haze blights the light, not yet, though the cycle progresses, you know it, contain it, know how it's measured in the movements of thought and body. Circadian authority, and also the way time breaks things, or is broken. Certain measurements portend that at such time in the morning. . . . So many voices of requirement, regiment, the authority of this or that strident device, fetters that tap on the skin's head and need an answer. Why such indignation in violation, old friend? Who is addressed with these questions. Ghosts of persons. Sometimes the desire for contact can be a certain color, transparent or opaque, or clearly clear. Is clearness a color, or another form of smudge? Ocular weather is every kind, all times. Power dreams in its frame. In a pasture, boys lost in the wheat, the high grown weeds. By land or by water. O Athena, Medusa, pick up the phone! There are ropes and routes and other things to hold. Avert your eyes, sweet sisters, call in phenomena with the medium in hand. Apparatus, deuce of minus. Too much has been left to the tendency, the message, the flowers bursting and bowing on the verge, allowing all their semblance of edge to flash and measure. But a plot, we want a story, a root to grow and figure. Let's see, she's asleep, in a bed so big one mistakes it for a sea. Birds beat at the window, holy hibou and humble alouette. Stars and birds bide their colors, weave them in the tapestry that is desire's web at evening, a dark blue hearkening inundates the land. One approaches, bearing lantern. Is it the monster or Psyche? Is our sleeping sister really a sinner, or hermaphrodite hiding the secret sex she dies in? All quiet, all sweet, all needle-bright and bleeding. That was what we came to, that land, that stain, that blissful kindness of a liquid called forgetting. From its insides, distill a new sequence, a process that pleasures its textures with a certain soothe. Or sooth, for we include bright wisdom in the process, not the one of the foolish harridan, her mouth a ruin, but that which springs from the thought's throat like a sheer shade of begot. And all those things, those times of the evening, collected in inkspots and nightbells, like a thread—keep saying, I am doomed in the stains I shall remember, they lay forgotten heads on the canopies, like a dress that spreads to every corner of the stage. Ring down the curtain, cold auditor, all is numen, an unctuous light activates the hand, and every act loves the strange blue weight of its attending. So far, so failing. What do we entail. A new contract or gambit, mask of antiquity with all its spectrum of stare and frown. And grin, the one hanging in the air like a lantern. Sometimes space needs a sectioning, a kind of break in the turbulence of its hastening, le vertige. Kiss the question, it's your long-lost sweetheart come to see you! I need a horse to escape, to bear me through the storm. I don't like the story, the end is too heavy, a child plays near the train tracks, make it stop! Some Russian catastrophe bearing all away. Mine would be the black bread havocked at evening, crude anchor of the norm. Five, six eggs in the basket, the hen is ailing. Rain eats the roof. Night spies land. It was sailing like a ship in a windy tinder, it lost its shore, now the black boat stays on course, the trip will finish, and what you find won't be worse than the event it was portending. What news of green? The stuff of light and issue. We lost day somewhere, in the ambiguity of twilight, smoke was solid in those heavy strikes, impermissable flowers bled and bloomed in heaps around us. But this was no grave, no petal or fragrant progress, it plumed its turn, a course of nuance and shyness, we held the tips of our tongues, alive with wonder! But shouldn't it be shrewder? Doesn't crude survival dictate? The talking waters with their eventual hands. But no one liked the weight, night's influx on the shoulders. Are we Atlas, do the skies resist our unrestraining flesh? She knew so much about bearing, the brightly borne. And are some things so light they can't anchor on any shoulder? Hence the unbearable is the levity that breaks and flies. No other woes but these, and the sun goes. But she feeds all who need her, or makes a kind nest for the vulture, with all her snows. Some nest, some frost, the place where the tongues rust. That wasn't a song, was a smite or incantation. As though war with the sun wouldn't break the darkest far. Roots bear, wind is rare in the forest of stasis. No more is a song mere breathing, smoke has shrouded any aptitude and cloud. Bird is a certain shade of whim, awake and inner. Network is the need's hurt, wounded, frail and spatial. Occasion, aureole. We return by runes, we know none free of symbols, we are a closed loop in the harm's heart, we don't forget. No leaps, no pipes, no happy forest gambol. Syrinx, you gave your bruised body for these sweets. As day never shed its many lights to be any person's present form. Sacrifice as a dream of freedom, but so is frame. No I can still or say it, bloodray, bright. Sometimes, some means, the eye grows weary, the fingers slur over keys, wounds, paper, the name of the topic was matter and all its ore. Or gold, or argent in the eyes' keep, saying never. Saying metal is precious which spills its ardent breath. Breathe but be not peaceful. Arcs decline in a curve, lovely and fatal. You are at every point, an actor, an archer, a specter spun and pensive. What night betrays you with its sentence, flight, thief, or barque of night traversing tarnished waters. So hum the spheres, alert with disappearance. So swells, dissembles. Core at the crux, indigenous, porous, as though green had a name for its tones, shapes, claims. A table will hold most anything you lay. A cup with its mouth saying fill me, faithful vessel. Are eyes just ruse, distorting every contact? Nothing helps, the mind is stained and will be its constant quotient of am-not. Rays rise and smite the outline, breeding flowers in the black benighted ground. So shall, so slow. A wheel is not an angle. Opaque erasures harmonize, where they absorb the frantic hammers, nothing will be like this light in its cloud of wild amber sifting, spreading. Sail, swirl, stall. Fearless candle, you are remedy and rule. This we knew, in our enfance, pale preliminary sounding. So far, so harm. Sometime there will be time, time less linear, more like the cloud with its clandestine take-me-hence. World implores, forebears, seeks its straying. There have to be these and those, swoops and frays. Colors there are no words for, opaque-clear, held in the eye like a stylus. Shine, inflection. So twines the name, soft fields of rumination, hard snows, bitumen littered in the loam. A coat, a wieldy blanket, some industry to glean. Leaf laws and freezes, summer of tabular data, where the blooming is doctored and discovered once and once. Bells, chimes, high buzz of fading flies, the city is called Aurora and you live there. You eat the flowers of its routes of leisure and cry Far. From this bench, at this moment the trees weep, bereft of season, the sermon you blur in your pocket is their mien.

POETICS STATEMENT

I'VE WRITTEN three books. Each has taught me some things about form. Thinking with and through form, whether set forms or broader formal concerns such as the dialogic dance of the book-length sequence, is an entry into what Anne Carson has called "the motions of the self" and the means by which that mutable, motile self is born of and into a thinking body. I'm intrigued by deformations of convention, ways in which traditional lyric gestures, embodying cultural codes, can be made malleable and strange; there is still tremendous power in these gestures, if they're understood as ceremonies of intensity, or maybe rituals of sensation—acts that strive to embody sensation but also represent gestures of awe or passion or longing—inviting, constructing, and containing those states.

Movement and constraint, impulse and impasse. Against the concision and angularity of my first book, *Crash's Law*, my second, *Spar*, is all excess, the overwhelmingness of emotion and sensation, conflict between resistance and abandon: the "I" becomes a locus of sensation that shifts and blurs, essentially an improvisation. The first human figure in the book is "someone," so anonymity, a permeable subject who is also a searcher, is the aleph term. When "I" turns up in the second poem, that term still holds—to be modulated or revolved in successive I's, according to the encounters staged, the phenomena called up in language. Despite the mobility, this speaker is boundaried to some degree by lyric tradition; the third poem in the book starts with an apostrophe to a star. It doesn't get much more conventional than that, but it's convention recast and reframed. The speaker exists in amorous relationship to words, in relinquishing at least partly the role of creator to become a created and stranger self—a submission to the unknown, including an unknown otherness of possible selves.

Such an excess finds breadth and boundary in the prose poem: while transgressing the line as inscribed limit, the poems establish new borders of sentence, paragraph, sound pattern. A seductive contradiction of the prose poem is its solidity of presence despite internal permutation and movement, the velocity of its disjunctive interior. Rosmarie Waldrop describes as "gapgardening" the way the prose poem "turns" on its inner disjunctions, as it lacks the more traditional turning of the line to effect that motion. Containment and movement find a balance. Motion within a visually solid frame (at least in my brick-shaped poems) grounds a sense of the contingent (however contradictory that may sound), of circumstances and loyalties in a necessary state of flux, the incompatible claims of restlessness and desire for change with the longing for stability, cohesion, immersion. "We love we know not what," writes Traherne, "and therefore everything allures us."

In my third book, *Nomina*, I use the constraint of the sonnet rhyme scheme as a different base for intuitive swerves. That strange machine, the sonnet, with its tension between nonrational relations of sound and the rationalizing structure of argument so crucial in its English tradition. Far from a tidy closed form, the sonnet strikes me as a volatile, sometimes violent instrument, resounding with struggle and shock. In its orientation toward argument, it is immediately a figure for the conflicted mind. The resolute character of its syntax and the fixed rigor of its rhyme scheme embody a passionate reaching toward a certainty that its conflicted stance questions and resists—in this, it strikes me as a form of anguish, longing for, but never fully believing in, the solace of its own intelligent system.

Despite their differences, my books have in common an organization that is to some degree dialogical, with poems juxtaposed to foreground tensions and contradictions, providing a kind of argument or conversation between tonalities and states. Again, motions of a self, or selves, re-formed, repositioned from poem to poem, with the nimble reader responding to, inhabiting, extending those gestures. I believe one of the jobs of poetry is to allow readers to discover different and more complex ways of engaging experience, including the experience of their own inner lives, by surprising them into developing new modes of response in their reading, new freedoms. And it's my hope that pleasure and intense sensation and a shock of strangeness will be part of the movement.

A SPACE FOR DESIRE AND THE MUTABLE SELF

Karen Volkman's Experimentations with the Lyric

Paul Otremba

BY THE TIME Karen Volkman's lyrical, debut collection of poems, *Crash's Law*, appeared as a National Poetry Series selection in 1996, the lyric mode had already spent decades under suspicion for being ahistorical and monological—the favored genre of mainstream poetry and the New Criticism.[1] By the 1990s, with the rise of feminist, Marxist, and poststructuralist theories, American poets were becoming self-conscious about the ideological implications of their medium, particularly lyric poetry's participation in upholding a patriarchal tradition and a belief in the "transcendental signified." In

"Ideologies of Lyric: A Problem of Genre in Contemporary Anglophone Poetics," Mark Jeffreys outlines various contemporary anxieties over and hopes for the lyric, noting that this materialist opposition comes from a perception of lyric's "imperial assertion of self, the programmatic exclusion of otherness or difference, and the logocentric quest for presence."[2] Nevertheless, many contemporary poets continue to explore this long-standing poetic mode; despite its suspect status the lyric can provide rich ground for interrogating subjectivity—and indeed, the representational aspects of language that Jeffreys points to. In response to this problem of voice and representational language, Susan Schultz has declared: "Lyric poets (because there are always such) must find ways in which to accommodate the lyric to the actual world, where voice does not denote mastery so much as conflict, identity so much as its confusions and contradictions."[3] To address this problem, Schultz imagines a kind of "voiceless lyric" that "acknowledges antihumanist critiques of the unitary self, while retaining a belief in the significant silences and spiritual and erotic desires traditionally expressed in lyric poems."[4]

Whether or not this "voiceless lyric" can be achieved, Schultz's prescription attests to the ongoing usefulness and desirability of the lyric mode. Karen Volkman's three collections—*Crash's Law*, *Spar*, and *Nomina* (this last, her most recent, is currently unpublished)—also confirm the staying power of the lyric and almost seem to respond to Schultz's notion of the lyric as a site of conflict and confusion.[5] Working from and against lyric convention to engage the conflicts, confusions, and contradictions of the self, Volkman develops a generative ethical approach to poetic tradition and convention, attempting continually to construct an identity out of a persistent intelligence and its articulation through lyric gestures and forms. Her poems give no illusion of finding resolution and certainty in an expressible, essential identity. Instead, the poems act as events, actively coming out of the experience they create from the materiality of language and the self-conscious employment of and experimentation with poetic forms. Inextricable from the self, desire—in all its permutations—is the great subject of Volkman's work. Whether destructive or creative (and often both), desire serves as a positive force, an opening into and from uncertainty. To accommodate the mutable desiring-self, *Crash's Law* uses techniques of parataxis, fractured narratives, and persona poems, as well as more conventional lyrics in dialogue with tradition. These poems are able to thematize and momentarily enact the self's creation, but they ultimately lack the sustainable, generative form of engaging the mutable self that is provided by the prose poems of *Spar*. While *Spar* continually asserts, makes, and remakes the lyric "I" in an ostensibly antilyrical form, Volkman's latest collection takes her experimentation to the opposite end of the formal spectrum. Even though *Nomina* is a lyrical sonnet sequence, the collection diffuses the "I" between the poles of semblance and the process of becoming, moving her poetry close to Schultz's vision for a "voiceless lyric."

Instinctual and compulsive, desire exists in Volkman's work, and its presence substantiates a location for that force, the desiring-self. The self comes into being by that other who attracts: in *Crash's Law*, which takes its title appropriately from Emily Dickinson's line, "Slipping—is Crash's Law" (no. 997), this relationship is complicated by the physical or emotional violence that the other is capable of inflicting or that results from misguided love. One argument made by these poems is that entering the space of desire or love means entering uncertainty. A causal relationship is even posited by a speaker who says, "It was love that shattered my compass—."[6] These poems face the challenge of not diminishing the self or desire because they can lead us to violence or "because we loved / inexpertly, inaccurately, / what would not stay" (*CL* 17–18). Reflecting this uncertainty, the self appears in *Crash's Law* as wounded, defiant, detached, or exuberant. Its relationship to the past is just as complex and shifting: the poems equally express an anxiety over loss, a fear of absence, a compulsive need to retell painful experiences, and a struggle to recover or let go of what are now only ghosts of a history. In the poem "Infidel," the speaker articulates the self's complex position as "I evade my history as one favors a damaged limb" (*CL* 22). The uncertainty of whom or what we should desire and the mutability of the desiring-self constitute the void these poems encounter. And the void is a concept to which Volkman is drawn. Discussing influence on her work, Volkman writes that she admires "Dickinson, Rilke, Celan, Traherne, Herbert, [and] Plath," who all "have a very personal relationship to the void, and all of these poets have that, whether this void takes the form of (to borrow the distinction Tomas Tranströmer makes in his poem *Vermeer*) the *empty* or the *open*."[7] The urgency and energy of *Crash's Law* results from the self's precarious position between accepting the void as empty or as open.

The self of *Crash's Law* manifests as the lyric "I," an internal voice given to sudden bursts of apostrophe or directly addressing a "you," who often takes the form of a previous lover. While a number of the poems in this collection participate in the presentation of a monological, expressive "I," the self resists fixity formally in other poems by parataxis, interrupted and fractured narratives, and the use of personae.[8] The book starts with "Infernal," a poem composed of discontinuous, closed couplets and shifting registers and qualities of diction. For example, the poem opens,

> Is it better to die by the hand of an intimate
> or to die by the hand of a stranger?
>
> The one with his pitchfork and the one with a wing of sorrow
> and the one with a shaky plow.
>
> > (*CL* 15)

Her motivation to use this technique is not overtly political, although a poem like "Infidel" does use it to disrupt authority in gender politics. A reader can gather a certain context out of this poem's series of isolated questions and statements, which use the sentence as the unit of composition instead of the line, many of which contain parallels. The poem begins,

> If the impersonal made personal isn't personal, then what is there?
>
> Removing one's trousers, as one acquires a taste.
>
> Do you prefer the sheets with the frilly edges or the black ones?
>
> (*CL* 22)

While no specific narrative presents itself, there is a scene, and it is identifiably the subject of many lyric poems: the domestic. The strategy of the sentences works to dismantle the fixity of a banal domesticity reduced to consumerism, which is implied by the question, "Do you prefer the sheets with the frilly edges or the black ones?" An example of Volkman's use of fractured narrative comes in the Ashberyesque "The Red Shoes," which collects bits of reported speech, utterances, parenthetical asides, and narrative details, with only the telling and associations holding the pieces together across the gaps. Both of these poems foreground process in a way that demands the reader participate in the construction of meaning, and they anticipate the direction Volkman takes in her later work.

The presentation of a mutable self also result from Volkman's use of persona poems. Like the masks in Plath's poems, the self ventriloquizes through biblical and mythological figures (Lot's wife and Persephone) who are sympathetic to the self's condition as victim of the violence of desire. In other poems, performativity asserts the constructed identity over the essential self when poems speak from the male voices of Casanova and the strange, macabre Dr. Feelgood. "Casanova in Love" provides a way for Volkman to simultaneously critique through mimicry this icon of male desire and reappropriate a position of power.[9]

The containment of the self's opposing positions finds its apotheosis in the figure of Persephone. This archetypal figure shifts between spring/winter, life/death, and "virginal abundance" and emptiness. She embodies *Crash's Law's* central concern with the void in the pull between *open* and *empty*. Even in the underworld, she stays close to water, the book's element for the self, walking the banks of Lethe, as "Queen / of this blasphemous backwater" (*CL* 45). Like many representations of the self, she is the object of desire and the victim of its inevitable descent into violence. The idea of inevitability is something the poem deals with directly. Persephone explains, "In the beginning— / such a child—I thought it punishment, / not fate" (44). She has not, however, internalized the power structure or accepted the rape. Nor is her stance resignation. Violence always remains a potential condition of desire. The only two bearable responses are escapist oblivion, "that blessed briny sip" from Lethe, or to create an inhabitable space out of the one that has been degraded. Creation is the only politically and psychological responsible choice. Persephone makes a home out of the constraints of her captivity, and her retelling the details of her violation leads to the conclusion, "I am alive" (45). The presence of violence brings the self into awareness of being alive, and so it is generative. The act of resolving momentarily the gap between the emptiness of uncertainty and the openness of possibility is also generative, an active making of the space the self can now inhabit.

"Persephone at Home" serves as a conceptual resolution, but the fact remains that for all of Volkman's attempts at openness in the lyric, the individual poems lack a form and method to create of themselves the needed, inhabitable space. "Chronicle" encapsulates the essential deficiency of *Crash's Law*:

> O lost regeneration!
> O saline amoeba! Elements
> and gods have no words
>
> for isolation,
>   (*CL* 32)

Volkman's experiments with the lyric might have found ways momentarily to deal with mutability, but what "regeneration" needs is a form of language that is as present, permeable, malleable, and capable of changing states as the elements. When Volkman moves to the prose poem in *Spar*, she is able to find the appropriate generative mode in the horizontal pull of the sentence and the materiality of language, with the word becoming the generative, volatile element.

Free from the obligations of line, narrative, and representation, *Spar's* untitled prose poems insist, turn, and accumulate meaning through the materiality of language and a logic based on sound, association, and accident. Compared to *Crash's Law*, the poems of *Spar*, for all their baroqueness and excess, are pared down to mere elements of lyric: intensity, music, and address. As a result of this intensification, the poems perform as gestures of tone and experience. Discussing *Spar's* "There comes a time," Volkman explains in an interview that she sees this prose poem working, "as a way of renewing . . . complex experience and communicating it intensely and viscerally to a reader. So, 'what happened' in the experience is the sensual/sensuous effect on the mind and psyche, a kind of compression of intensities at the level of language and sound—so the poem embodies an experience rather than describing it."[10] The "compression of intensities at the level of language and sound" manifests in *Spar* as rhymes within the sentences, alliteration, and shifts in registers of diction. A sense of play and pleasure attends this use of sound, but it is not separated from an intelligence actively at work in the poems, a kind of thinking through sound, where meaning is produced by associations and slippages. Rather, it is the intensity of sound combined with the "I" of direct address that give the poems of *Spar* their true, conventional lyric quality.

Volkman experiments with these conventions by bringing them into the horizontal space of prose. The shift to the sentence allows her to disrupt the "presentation" of either a coherent or fractured self. The sentence acts as a boundary for the self in flux, continually constructing and deconstructing a multifaceted identity. Volkman writes that her interest in the prose poem form lies in "the disjunctive moment between prose sentences as provoking the kind of leap or turn a line-break would in a lineated poem."[11] She ascribes this disjunction to what Rosmarie Waldrop has called "gap gardening" in her *Reluctant Gravities*.[12] As the poems move through their sentences, the mind tries to find structure, a meaning to the sound and connection across the gaps between sentences; the process leads to sudden associations, leaping into unexpected and unintended insights. These insights result partly from accident and misrecognition, but they can be intentional as are Volkman's use of juxtaposition, catachresis, and a recurring technique that could be called a propulsive series making.

By foregrounding language and bringing the lyric "I" self-consciously into the space of prose, Volkman places importance on process and composition. Composition makes her poems not representational but gestural, where signification works by context and performance. She does not seek a form to best express content, where form equals the organic extension of content. Formal elements take part in content in the active creation of an event, an experience's "sensual/sensuous effect on the mind and psyche."[13] In "Form and Discontent," Rosmarie Waldrop distinguishes between composition and organic form, or content made through the process of expression and content *finding* its perfect expression, saying that in composition: "transcendence is not upward, but horizontal, contextual. It is transcendence of language with its infinite possibilities, infinite connections, and its charge of the past. In other words, no split between spirit and matter."[14] In the organic form model, spirit articulates itself through matter, or content through form. In composition, spirit *is* its articulation through matter. Composition and its insistence on the materiality of language allow Volkman a way to reconcile moment to moment the split between "spirit and matter" that serves as the central tension of *Crash's Law*: the void as empty or as open. In *Spar*, the void is never empty. While it remains mysterious, violent, and ultimately irresolvable, it is sonorous and generative. The void opens for the self to make a space more inhabitable.

In making the void inhabitable, Volkman reconciles the anxieties over the potential violence of desire, unsustainable love, and the uncertainty of experience by giving over to the mutable self through a poetics of excess. In "Some Problems with Being Contemporary: Aging Critics, Younger Poets and the New Century," Charles Altieri discusses the draw toward excess in poets like Joshua Clover, Jennifer Moxley, and Karen Volkman, saying it is "rooted partially in a sense that nothing less ornately self-conscious could claim authenticity in a culture of spectacle, and rooted partially in the hope that only by fully playing out the energies of intelligence might we even glimpse what momentary peace and self-surrender could look like."[15] *Spar* opens with an epigraph from Thomas Traherne: "We love we know not what, and therefore everything allures us." The uncertainty and allure toward multiple others is not new to Volkman's work, but her approach toward them changes. The epigraph serves not as a warning but as a celebration of a fundamental condition of experience, of being a desiring-self. The poems in *Spar* argue that the only way to make excess bearable is to make the self out of excess. Such a proposition comes in the collection's first poem, "If they had more they would need less" (*S* 1), and in the poem that begins with the directives, "More feet on more legs, more hands on more wrists, more eyes in more . . . Directives fail me" (8). Even though the call for accretion admittedly fails here, the poem refuses closure, allowing the sentence to evade loss through another proposition, "it is safer to bail" (8). These poems don't fear but consume loss, just as they deal with the potential harm and disappointment of desire by actively engaging and transforming it.

This new position toward desire and the other finds expression in the poem, "What we know":

> What we know is too full of tremors. An ague takes me like a blade, glancing to futures not mappable as landscape. And you, whom I give my most infinite existence—the dream of a hand and its attendant caress—for this we are quiet, for this we veil our eyes.

> Which things will fulfill us? Time's tokens leave their lesions, night and rumor. Ecstasy, to be remembered. A coil of heartbreak in a handshake, a certain sigh.

> (*S* 12)

The speaker's address to the lover begins equally in uncertainty and possibility. Her "infinite existence" amounts to only the potential of contact, the "hand and its attendant caress," in some undefined future. When the image of hands returns, it appears as a potential past: "A coil of heartbreak in a handshake." The future caress could easily become the insincere "handshake" when the lover leaves. Instead of turning away and accepting a diminished conception of love, the speaker actively seeks out the potential harm if it means that love can exist, and she addresses the lover, "My predator, do no more leaving" (*S* 12). The poem ends with another imperative, "Drink the dark dram, lover, and be wine" (*S* 12). She invites the lover to take on the uncertainty of love by becoming it, being both container and the thing contained. Although this momentary balance is conceptual, the poem's language acts as a gesture of both the unsustainability and consummation of love.

"What we know" opens with the expectation of a complaint against fear and uncertainty; although metaphorical, the register of diction is, to a degree, poetically neutral. Instead of attempting transparency as an appropriate affront to being "too full of tremors," Volkman's speaker takes an aggressive position with the elevated, archaic, and metaphorically opaque, "An ague takes me like a blade, glancing to futures not mappable as landscape" (*S* 12). Assonance and shifts in diction make this sentence pleasing and plangent, but the sentence is not merely playing with language. The intellect pushes the reader through the complex of metaphors. "Ague" picks up the associations of "tremors," so what we know about love becomes a fever that the speaker then externalizes, giving it agency to take the self. Once externalized, the fever of that knowledge can be transformed by metonymy into the "blade," which introduces the ambiguity of "glancing." The horizontal aspect of the sentences asks us to go both forward and back along syntax to parse out meaning. Syntax tells the reader it's a blade moving off an object, but "glancing to futures" has its own connotations of looking ahead. Love's knowledge becomes an act of violence projected into the future, which refuses circumscription. Instead of bowing to the "tremors," the poem enacts them, and the aggressive catachresis simultaneously embraces and resists love's uncertainty.

In addition to meaning produced by the associative links of sound and catachresis, the other generative technique in *Spar* is the use of series that propel the poems into states or abstractions. The first strong example comes in "Shrewd star," the third poem of the book:

> Shrewd star, who crudes our naming: you should be flame. Should be
> everyone's makeshift measure, rife with tending—constellations called *Scatter*
> or *Spent Memory* or *Crown of Yes* or *Three Maids Slow in Pleasure*. Some days
> my eyes are green like verdigris, or green like verdant ardor, or like impair.
>
> (*S* 3)

The physical description of eyes as "verdigris" becomes the metaphorical eyes as betrayers of internal states, the "verdant ardor" being itself a metaphor, the green vegetation of inexperienced desire. So far the movement is dialectical, an easily mappable association. What follows, however, is not synthesis guided by the play of sound. Instead, the series disrupts its own established expectations and swerves into "impair." There is a conceptual association; betrayal and inexperience are forms of impairment. But what is important is the very disruption of expectations initiated by the etymological play and the movement into an indeterminately determined abstraction. There is no circumscribing article for "impair." This is not *an* impairment, the generic example implied by the indefinite article, and neither is it the representative example, that identifiable, metaphysical, and definite *the*. Volkman's use of "impair" is as the signified opened up and connecting simultaneously to all of its possible signifiers: the indefinite and definite momentarily collapsed. The materiality of the movement, the sudden leap to abstraction, resists dialectic's compromising and reinstating synthesis. The opposition to conventionality could be described as what Roland Barthes calls a *subtle subversion*. The subversion "is not directly concerned with destruction[; it] evades the paradigm, and seeks some other term: a third term, which is not, however, a synthesizing term but an eccentric, extraordinary term."[16] That the "eyes" should lead to this openness is no easy synthesis.

Spar is not exclusively composed of prose poems. The few lineated and titled poems offer moments of rest from the driving sprawl of text, but they also display a different approach to language within the constraint of the line. The prose poems introduce a poetics of elemental lyric gestures employed in the active construction of experience; they teach the reader how to release anxieties over the lack of narrative cohesion or a fixed "I" when Volkman does return to lineation.[17] One such poem is "Kiss Me Deadly":

> How do they get so close to the window,
> a tree in figment, arithmetic moon?
> Summer broke you, winter builds you—
> a lofty leafage in the prism, a pure
> empire. Where they've ghosted roofs
> on the drawings of infants—
> because I *did* leave a letter, a small map,
> semblance.
>
> (*S* 13)

This poem's title participates in the self's defiant, inclusive stance that is articulated in "What we know," which immediately precedes it. Although broken into lines, the sentence dominates the poem's direction and possibilities. The opening question leads to the oblique answer, "Summer broke you, winter builds you— / a lofty leafage in the prism," which is only cooperative if the reader cultivates the gap, working out the relevancy of the response. The tree and moon get close as a result of winter's "prism" effect on the window. In the next sentence of the poem, the use of a dash parallels the preceding sentence; this time, however, it does not signal an explanation but a swerving to a new idea. The exploration of syntactic possibilities generates new possibilities for meaning, just as experimenting with a series, "a letter, small map, / semblance," lets the poem move easily from the literal to the metaphoric and finally abstraction. When Volkman moves back into lineation for her third book, *Nomina*, she continues her exploration of the generative capabilities of a productive boundary, exchanging the prose poem's sentence and boxlike structure for the sonnet's architecture of stanza, rhyme, and argument.

Nomina takes Volkman's interest in working against and through lyric tradition and gestures to the opposite end of the formal spectrum. Whereas, on its surface, the prose poem signifies a defiance of the lyric mode, the sonnet stands as an institution within the genre. Given the sonnet's long history, even experimentation with the tradition has become itself a tradition. By choosing the sonnet as her form in *Nomina*, Volkman enters into a conversation with other contemporary American sonneteers, such as Ted Berrigan, Gerald Stern, and Stephanie Strickland.[18] All three of these poets push the sonnet beyond its conventional fourteen lines, while subverting and exploiting some of the other conventions in their attempts to recast the sonnet form, and poetry, itself, for contemporary experience. Berrigan sees the essence of a sonnet as a set of themes, a way of structuring units of meaning, a type of diction, and the interplay within a sequence. Strickland uses the turns and units of the sonnet to generate multiplicity; this generating, in addition to her interest in digital media, reorients how we view the text and how we read.[19] In his sonnets, Stern pushes the narrative possibilities almost to the point of leaving no traces of the form. Unlike her American contemporaries, Volkman does not experiment with the outward structure of the sonnet. Her innovations come at the level of language and speaker, introducing abstraction and stripping description and argument down to their most elemental states, as well as keeping the lyric "I" always in a state of becoming or materializing only as semblance.

Nomina is a sequence of forty-four untitled, almost exclusively Petrarchan sonnets. The poems follow the Petrarchan division between the octave (rhyming *abbaabba*) and the variously rhymed sestet, but Volkman doesn't always present an identifiable shift in the argument between the octave and sestet. The rhyme scheme, however, still performs the division as a result of the close relationship between thinking and sound in her poetics. Volkman brings into the boundary of the sonnet her interest in the materiality of language and its generative capabilities (explored so fully in *Spar*), and she still employs a similar element of accident and surprise within the lines themselves. The introduction of fixed rhyme, however, simultaneously opens her poems and leads them to constraint, which is evident in the book's first poem:

> Brown is the flat gestation of a maze,
> grass-grown remembrance of a second look
> the field holds open like a nascent book
> in which the wind has written, Sudden strays,

sudden numbers beat—the roots of days
branched intangibles a stupor took
and slept and stroked and scattered in a shook
haze of wakings, refracting rays

outleaping their seasons, daughters of a glance
ago-ahead, a retrograde advance.
Loving nothing but the fractal ways,

they gather flowers—pearl-petal, bitter blaze—
brilliant sisters in the infinite dance
at ardor's axis, integral of chance.

(*N* 1)

The poem begins with an abstract and metaphorical proposition about the color brown, and the speaker withholds a precise context until the third line, where the "field" appears, although "grass-grown" anticipates and carries the reader over into the "field." This sudden context gives the first line the characteristics of description and introduces an inductive approach. While stated with confidence, the first line retains an element of uncertainty, which becomes the driving force of the poem's argument. Conceptually and materially, the rhyme performs the mix of certainty and uncertainty, or constraint and boundlessness. "Maze" leads into "strays," which reinforces a sense of bewilderment, but it loses its implications of shape. The link to "days" is a little less expected, but shape returns, introducing a cyclical nature. The rhyme with "rays" is no more surprising, although it reveals another logic at work in the rhyme. Within their stanzas, "maze" to "strays" and "days" to "rays" break more general concepts into their less stable but integral parts. These movements enact the poem's central tension between desire and chance: "brilliant sisters in the infinite dance / at ardor's axis, integral of chance." Interestingly, the more surprising and self-consciously language-driven rhymes of the octave occur at the centers of the envelope rhymes, where memory becomes an act of reading with the linking of "remembrance of a second look" and "nascent book." This association takes a violent turn when connected with "took" and the more intense "shook." The poem's concluding couplet, which is not a closed-off Shakespearian couplet, encapsulates the way rhyme works in *Nomina*: it is both "dance" and "chance." The satisfaction the reader gets from the anticipated resolution of rhyme is always a self-conscious and precarious one.

The conflict between boundlessness and constraint represented by the rhyme scheme of the sonnet continues Volkman's obsession with uncertainty and the void. This conflict is carried out within the poems themselves in lines like "Border is the number of each thing" (*N* 24) and "vague body, unboundaried, portionless plot" (*N* 17). Images of shape and shaping appear continually in the poems. In "Brown is the flat," we are given "maze," "book," "numbers," "roots," "days," "fractal," "dance," and "axis" (*N* 1). An insistent de-shaping force is also at work in "strays," "intangibles," "scattered," "haze," "refracting," "outleaping," "infinite," and "chance." These two impulses are brought into conjunction with such violent conflations as "ago-ahead" and "retrograde advance." The tension between shape and dissolution is enacted by *Nomina*'s reflexive obsession with language and naming. The conflict of language appears in the modified repetitions of words like "ciphers," "vowels," "nomen" and the paradoxical signifiers, "null" and "zero." Or, as the speaker asks, "How does a namelessness name?" (*N* 19). Naming's attempt to contain uncertainty influences the quality of description in these poems. Anxieties over naming's efficacy reduce description to its most elemental: simple nouns, color, and movement. The sonnets recycle "trees," "sun," "sky," "flower," "ocean," and "seed," among others. Simple colors of "red," "green," "blue," "white," and "black," with the occasional "pale" or "dark," appear again and again as if they are all that is possible of precision. Because Volkman is a poet who believes the self is a thinking/feeling body, the mind and its abstractions also have a place in the project of naming in her sonnets. Of the numerous abstractions used in *Nomina*, "nascence" and "semblance" hold an important position, reflecting a shift in Volkman's approach to the mutable self and how that is influenced by the way the book works as a sequence.

Whereas *Spar* is all "I," with the self continually and aggressively constructing and asserting its shifting identity, *Nomina* sparingly presents an "I" or its possessive pronoun, "my." The poems retain the lyric gesture of direct address, but the quality of the voice changes. The self pushes its subjectivity to its boundaries by Volkman's use of social forms, the sonnet and argument. The book's opening poem establishes this shift with its presentation of the indistinct "daughters of a glance," "brilliant sisters" (*N* 1) as its subject. While the self is present in the second poem's lyric overflowing, "Oh the minus when it runed and roared" (*N* 2) and in the fourth poem's invocation, "read me, augur, from the wrists of sages" (*N* 4), a general "we" appears long before an "I": "The sky we bear on our shoulders" (*N* 5). The first time "I" is introduced is the opening of the fourteenth sonnet, which is one of the two sonnets that begins in this way, and both of these sonnets use the same opening lines: "I asked every flower I met / had they seen my palest friend" (*N* 14 and 25). The articulation of the self through the self-consciously lyric diction and the repetition between poems embodies both concepts of "nascence" and "semblance." Nascence, the act of being born or coming into being, reflects the biological and psychological impulses— or desires—coming into contact with social boundaries to produce the self. Across the poems, the self and its world are constantly in a state of becoming: "nascent book" (*N* 1) "nascent night" (5), "a nascent nought" (17), "My infinite late, dark nascence" (20), and "The soil that strains in the eye / breeding *nuance, nascence, name*" (25). This last example is important in that it equates *Nomina*'s concern with naming directly with the act of coming into being. Nascence also takes other forms, such as the reoccurring image of the seed, "gestation" (1), and the "Egg or pupa" (8).

While the self needs constraint to come into being, desire and social boundaries are also antagonistic, and they are ultimately irresolvable. The self of these sonnets expresses anxiety over "semblance," or the loss of identity, of being an empty reproduction, which results from being in a socially fixed form. The self's complex relationship to nascence and semblance is frequently asserted in *Nomina*, in lines like "sun's a semblance of a bled / blanched intransigence" (6), "the body-midwife with its semblant gloves / delivers the zero-baby" (12), and "Bitter seed—scarred semblance—Psyche" (40). Consistent with Volkman's earlier work, *Nomina* concludes that the self ("Psyche") is always frustrated desire ("the bitter seed") and desire breaking free of its containment ("the scarred semblance"). As in Volkman's other books, the dialogue between poems reflects this shifting relationship. The sonnet sequence works as "a retrograde advance" (*N* 1), a movement out of containment by moving back into containment, following the trajectory of the mutable desiring-self. This is not pessimism or resignation. It is how Volkman continually makes the void sonorous, provoking, and bearable.

NOTES

1. For a succinct, useful overview of experimental poets' concerns about lyric in late twentieth-century American poetry, see the opening to Lisa Sewell's "'Needing Syntax to Love': Expressive Experimentalism in the Work of Brenda Hillman," in *American Women Poets in the 21st Century: Where Lyric Meets Language*, ed. Claudia Rankine and Juliana Spahr (Middletown, Conn.: Wesleyan University Press, 2002), 281–83. For a more extended discussion of women experimental poets' response to lyric, see the introduction and first chapter of Linda A. Kinnahan's *Lyric Interventions: Feminism, Experimental Poetry, and Contemporary Discourse* (Iowa City: University of Iowa Press, 2003), xiii–40.

2. Mark Jeffreys, "Ideologies of Lyric: A Problem of Genre in Contemporary Anglophone Poetics," *PMLA* 110, no. 2 (March 1995): 197.

3. Susan Schultz, "'Called Null or Called Vocative': A Fate of the Contemporary Lyric," *Talisman: A Journal of Contemporary Poetry and Poetics* 14 (1995): 70.

4. Ibid., 71.

5. Charles Altieri's "Responsiveness to Lyric and the Critic's Responsibility," *Contemporary Literature* 32, no. 4 (Winter 1991): 580–87, which is a review of Marjorie Perloff's *Poetic License: Essays on Modernist and Postmodernist Lyric*, offers an interesting cultural reason for why the lyric is still a valuable and desirable mode: "it seems to me plausible that the more complex culture gets, and the more it tempts us to

distrust the mediations of language, the more important it is to preserve the classical sense of lyrical simplicity, that is, of a passion sustained not by its intricacy but by its capacity to stand as a surrogate for publicly sharable emotions which we might all want to utter" (586–87).

6. Karen Volkman, *Crash's Law* (New York: Norton, 1996), 69. Subsequent quotations from Volkman's work will be cited in the text using the following abbreviations: *CL* = *Crash's Law*; *S* = *Spar* (Iowa City: University of Iowa Press, 2002); *N* = *Nomina* (unpublished).

7. Karen Volkman, "Receptivity and Resistance," in *My Business is Circumference: Poets on Influence and Mastery*, ed. Stephen Berg (Philadelphia: Paul Dry Books, 2001), 254–55.

8. A traditional lyric "I" in a traditional lyric form doesn't enter *Crash's Law* until the sixth poem, "Equations." Conventional in approach and subject, the poem presents a speaker briefly meditating on the moon, metaphorizing and apostrophizing in her attempt to elicit some understanding about love. Even the hyperbolic epithets, "Stoic mathematician, / efficient wizard" (*CL* 24) are not without precedent, such as Philip Larkin's "Sad Steps" and Sir Philip Sydney's *Astrophil and Stella* (*CL* 31). This poem can be read, however, as challenging convention by opening up the patriarchal tradition. The speaker regrets, "A lover / is going, some lover is always // going" (*CL* 24); unlike the case in Sydney's or Larkin's address to the moon, the inconstant one is not a woman or the passion of youth but a male figure.

9. The image of the moon as an apt symbol to reflect love appears in this poem as well: "The moon's luminous suitors / throb and rise" (*CL* 27). With only one poem between "Casanova in Love" and "Equations," the hollowness of Casanova's sentiment is made more striking by the comparison.

10. Karen Volkman, "Chicago, Illinois," in *Poets on Place: Tales and Interviews from the Road*, compiled by W. T. Pfefferle (Logan, Utah: Utah State University Press, 2005), 32.

11. Karen Volkman, "Mutable Boundaries: On Prose Poetry," Academy of American Poets website, www.poets.org.

12. Rosmarie Waldrop, "*Prologue:* Two Voices," in *Reluctant Gravities* (New York: New Directions Books, 1999), 4.

13. Volkman, "Chicago, Illinois," 32.

14. Rosmarie Waldrop, "Form and Discontent," in *Dissonance (If You are Interested)* (Tuscaloosa: University of Alabama Press, 2005), 203.

15. Charles Altieri, "Some Problems with Being Contemporary: Aging Critics, Younger Poets and the New Century," *Paideuma: Studies in American and British Modernist Poetry* 32, nos. 1–3 (Spring, Fall, and Winter 2003): 411.

16. Roland Barthes, *The Pleasure of the Text*, trans. Richard Miller (New York: Farrar, Straus and Giroux, 1975), 55.

17. The linguistic play so essential to *Spar* does have precedent in Volkman's earlier poems. Perhaps the closest to the poems of *Spar* is "Primitives," which is broken up into boxlike stanzas. The poem focuses on process and language, and they do enact meaning. The lack of punctuation, however, is too self-conscious, resulting in fracture and disruption, not generation. "Primitives" lacks the productive boundary that can be found in *Spar*'s lineated poems.

18. The three collections these statements refer to are Ted Berrigan, *The Sonnets* (New York: United Artists Books, 1982); Gerald Stern, *American Sonnets* (New York: Norton, 2002); and Stephanie Strickland, *V: Waveson. Nets/Losing L'una* (New York: Penguin Books, 2002). While there are many poets experimenting with the sonnet, these three were chosen simply as representative of what has been happening externally with the form over the past few decades.

19. For Berrigan's own discussion of his sonnets, see "Sonnet Workshop," in *On the Level Everyday: Selected Talks on Poetry and the Art of Living*, ed. Joel Lewis (Jersey City, N.J.: Talisman House, 1997), 82–96. For information on Stephanie Strickland, visit http://vniverse.com.

BIBLIOGRAPHY

Books by Karen Volkman

Spar. Iowa Poetry Prize Selection. University of Iowa Press, 2002.
Crash's Law. National Poetry Series Selection. New York: Norton, 1996.

Selected Prose

"Angel, Interrupted." (Reginald Shepherd). *Boston Review* 22, no. 1 (February–March 1997): 41.

"August Zero." (Jane Miller). *Harvard Review* 6 (Spring 1994): 189–90.

"Autobiography of Red, On a Stair, Selected Poems." (Anne Carson, Ann Lauterbach, Medbh McGuckian). *Village Voice* (May 19, 1998).

"The Chime and Pity the Bathtub Its Forced Embrace of the Human Form." (Cort Day and Matthea Harvey). *Voice Literary Supplement* (Spring 2001).

"The Dream of the Unified Field." (Jorie Graham). *Harvard Review* 11 (Fall 1996): 148–49.

"Glare and Brink Road." (A. R. Ammons). *Poetry Review* (U.K.) (Spring 1998): 68–69.

"Gone." (Fanny Howe). *Boston Review* 29, no. 1 (February–March 2004).

"Green, Prickly Humanity: Lorine Niedecker's Collected Works." *Boston Review* 27, no. 6 (December–January 2002–2003). Reprinted in *A Poetry Criticism Reader*. Iowa City: University of Iowa Press, 2005.

"Isolato, Musca Domestica, Polyverse." (Larisa Szporluk, Christine Hume, Lee Ann Brown). *Poetry Review* (Summer 2000).

"The Lion Bridge: Selected Poems." (Michael Palmer). *Voice Literary Supplement* (October–November 1998).

"Mandelstam and Dante." *Crossroads: The PSA Newsletter* (Fall 2000).

"The Master Letters." (Lucie Brock-Broido). *Harvard Review* 9 (Fall 1995): 17–19.

"Memory At These Speeds: New and Selected Poems" (Jane Miller). *Boston Review* 23, no. 1 (February–March 1998): 41–42.

"New and Selected Poems." (Donald Justice). *Harvard Review* 11 (Fall 1996): 159–61.

"Poetry." *Encarta 2000*. Encyclopedia CD. Seattle: Microsoft Corporation, 1999.
"Receptivity and Resistance." In *My Business is Circumference: Poets on Influence and Mastery*. Edited by Stephen Berg. Philadelphia: Paul Dry Books, 2001.
"Soul Says." (Helen Vendler). *Harvard Review* 9 (Fall 1995): 186–88.
"A Wedding in Hell." (Charles Simic). *Harvard Review* 8 (Spring 1995): 145.
"The World Doesn't End: Charles Simic's Spectral Geography." *Harvard Review* 13 (Fall 1997): 51–54.

Interviews

With W. T. Pfefferle. *Poets on Place*. Edited by W. T. Pfefferle. Logan, Utah: Utah State University Press, 2005.
With Morgan Schuldt. *Cue: A Journal of Prose Poetry* 2 (Fall 2004).
"Octaves, Ovations." Interview with Ryan Murphy. Academy of American Poets website, www.poets.org (Spring 2003).
"On Spar, Sleeping Dogs, and the High Cost of Emotional Clarity." Interview with Nick Twemlow. *Direct Quote*, Poets & Writers Online Feature. www.pw.org/mag/dq (Spring 2002).

Selected Criticism

Altieri, Charles. "Some Problems with Being Contemporary: Aging Critics, Younger Poets and the New Century." *Paideuma* 32 (2003): 387–414.
Angel, Ralph. Review of *Crash's Law*. *Los Angeles Times* (April 13, 1997), 7.
Daly, Catherine. Review of *Spar*. *Sentence* 1.
Gordon, Noah Eli. "Bleeding, Beading, Trickling." *Boston Review* 28, nos. 3–5 (Summer 2003).
Hong, Cathy. "Manic Compression." *Voice Literary Supplement* (May 2002).
Muratori, Fred. Review of *Spar*. *Manhattan Review* (Winter 2003): 80–81.
Revell, Donald. Review of *Crash's Law*. *Boston Review* 21 no. 3 (Summer 1996).
Satterfield, Jane. Review of *Spar*. *Antioch Review* (Winter 2003).
Schuldt, Morgan. Review of *Spar*. *Cue* 1 (Spring 2004).
Shepherd, Reginald. Review of *Spar*. *Oyster Boy Review* 18 (Winter 2003–2004).
Sumrall, Daniel. Review of *Spar*. *Rain Taxi* 7, no. 3 (Fall 2002).
Yenser, Stephen. "Minutiae and Mysticism; or, Being Attention." *Yale Review* 91, no. 2 (Spring 2003).

D. A. POWELL

FROM *COCKTAILS*

[chapt. ex ex ex eye vee: in which scott has a birthday]

chapt. ex ex ex eye vee: in which scott has a birthday
[*many happy returns of the day*, says piglet]   & buys himself a puppy

soon the scent of burning leaves is too much.   hunting season
the crisp flannel air and hot oatmeal: instead of fishin'

crunching out through the yawping woods.   with his terrier
legs spindled as muskets.   his slight chest heaves.   his slender derriere

a pale chalkmark among the birches.   for a time he sits and smokes
scratching the curious brown dog behind its ears.—then snow

dusting down like dandruff on their collars.   they wait on haunches
listen for the woodchuck or roebuck: they have their lunches

and the whiteness covers them almost completely.   almost
far enough away from this moon and those rabbits and the geese

[when you touch down upon this earth. little reindeers]

when you touch down upon this earth.   little reindeers
hoofing murderously at the gray slate roof: I lie beneath
dearest father xmas: will you bring me another 17 years

you gave me my first tin star and my first tin wreath
warm socks tangerines and a sloppy midnight kiss
I left you tollhouse cookies.   you gave me bloody briefs

lipodystrophy neurosthesia neutropenia mild psychosis
increased liver enzymes increased bilirubin and a sweater
don't get me wrong: I like the sweater.   though it itches

but what's the use of being pretty if I won't get better?
bouncing me against your red woolies you whisper: *dear
boy*: unzip your enormous sack.   pull me quick into winter

[my lover my phlebotomist. his elastic fingers encircle my arm]

my lover my phlebotomist.   his elastic fingers encircle my arm
psychopompos: he guides me away from my worldly woes.   his prick
cutaneous → subcutaneous → intravenous.   an underground passageway

I rise to meet him: engorged.   I wear a negligee and surgical mask
he's fat with smalltalk: "this fog" he says.   and "keeping busy?"   I am
I say "sometimes seems like all you want is blood."   he's sheepish today

maybe he wants to hold me to his brutal chest.   wrap me in gauze
press his coffee breath into my mouth.   our tongues: snakes: caduceus
then quickly the affair is over.   out on the street: my feet are swinging

my bloody valentine.   *sweet comic valentine.*

stay

. . . .

[you'd want to go to the reunion: see]

Parting Glances (1986, Bill Sherwood dir.)

you'd want to go to the reunion: see
who got heavy.   who got bald.   see

who has ĸs lesions on the face and listen
to the same old tunes: there'll be a dj sure as anything

you'd want to show off your boyfriend who's spare
as a girlscout cookie.   who drinks to excess

who is immortal who has not tasted
blood from a chalice.   the vampyre's kiss

and whosoever drinks from the cup, they'll tell you
everlasting: they'll say

where did you go when you were lively?
zippers, faces, exile, jackhammer, rawhide, wreck room, the stud

you dress in black leather: color of a cormorant
shared wardrobe passed among siblings.   a masqued ball

lazy last nights on earth: how long has it been since you laid in bed
all day during the workweek.   spewing and rattling like a baby

wearing the loose shift of your skin: all hallows eve
you spook your parents and run through the husks of the fields

remember that once, sneaking out into streets
you sought beyond the boundaries of board games:

life & sorry.   aggravation & trouble (the milton bradley version)
you allowed men to manipulate you.   and were gifted

good boy collectible.   good boy swappable
good boy in a kit with moveable parts: turn him over

see where he's been made.   you laid
in their toy chests.   keepsies

kids everywhere are called to supper: it's late
it's dark and you're all played out.   you want to go home

no rule is left to this game.   playmates scatter like breaking glass
they return to smear the _____.   and you're it

[so the theatre dimmed and reclined. cramped balcony rubbed against my leg]
  Far From Heaven (2003, Todd Haynes, dir.)

> . . . leaving the movie before it's over
> with a pleasant stranger whose apartment is in the Heaven on Earth
> Bldg
>
> —Frank O'Hara, "Ave Maria"

so the theatre dimmed and reclined.   cramped balcony
    rubbed against my leg
nibbled popcorn from my buttery lap: what played
    that particular matinee?

not *les enfants du paradis.*   nothing noble: the re-release of *true grit*
    or *godzilla v. mothra*
it surprises me not that, years later, in a cassette of home movies,
    I see me skedaddling

eloped to the cinema—then: eloped *from* the cinema.
   how I tore my dungarees
my drawers my shirt my fleshy bottom delicate membrane heart and pouty
   lips

lime-scented boy of jadeite: the green son on a sunday.
   fruit of the hidden orchard
to swear off the bottle and onto a stack of *cosmo*s and *esquire*s that it's true

while I collected ribbons for bible verses [white ribbon = 5 verses,
   blue = 25 verses,
and 125 verses for red: color of the blood, my swollen mouth,
   my blushing penis]

the house teetered: whimpering for nails.   the wiring melted
   into a scouring pad
a spattering grease fire did what the termites couldn't:
   pickaxe, crowbar, battering ram

upstairs: the one parent slitting her skirt for sweet thing
   she brought back from market
the absent other: him at the oriental massage getting *jerkyjerky*
   and an icy finger up the bum

[I saw this movie twice.   both times I had to pee and missed this part:
   this parting]

now I wander into someone else's story: ghost light
   peering from the screen
a lambent young man opens his robe touching himself
   where he wants me to touch

take my hand and lead me stranger: hot, convulsing,
   delirious to taste of thy affection

[strange flower in my hands. porphyry shell. clipped wool]

a song of John the Divine with the Holy Prepuce,
as in the vision of St. Birgitta

strange flower in my hands.　　porphyry shell.　　clipped wool
all the dark caves that beckon and terrible mud chambers of the wasp

I touched the raphe of your skin where once it had seamed to you:
amethyst jewels on your crown.　　a skullcap upon the crozier of your loins

the old wet clothing of trees lies on the forest floor: naked world
spreading underbrush and tendrils of the new vines moist

once, I buried the soft body of you in my mouth.　　licked that hurt place
where they'd cut you [so long ago: you had put that infancy away]

you grew large inside me.　　gifted my lips and throat
　　with a swirling galaxy
milk of the nightsky.　　balm from the trembling branches of the poplar

explosion of pale confetti signaling the new year.　　the wine is bubbly
the bread, a generous slice.　　I will make a ring of this covenant.　　I will

bed thee down in a pasture and make a berm of your torso.　　I am the
　　marsh
above, a dipper pours thick liquid of your veins: cold now catch you I do

[listen mother, he punched the air: I am not your son dying]

a stabat mater

listen mother, he punched the air: I am not your son dying
the day fades and the starlings roost: a body's a husk a nest of goodbye

his wrist colorless and soft was not a stick of chewing gum
how tell?   well a plastic bracelet with his name for one.   & no mint
his eyes distinguishable from oysters how?   only when pried open

she at times felt the needle going in.   felt her own sides cave.   she rasped
she twitched with a palsy: tectonic plates grumbled under her feet

soiled his sheets clogged the yellow BIOHAZARD bin: later to be burned
soot clouds billowed out over the city: a stole.   a pillbox hat   [smart city]
and wouldn't the taxis stop now.   and wouldn't a hush smother us all

the vascular walls graffitied and scarred.   a clotted rend in the muscle
wend through the avenues throttled t-cells.   processional staph & thrush

the scourge the spike a stab a shending bile the grace the quenching
mother who brought me here, muddler: open the window.   let birds in

FROM *LUNCH*

[darling can you kill me: with your mickeymouse pillows]

darling can you kill me: with your mickeymouse pillows
when I'm a meager man.   with your exhaust pipe and hose

could you put me out: when I'm a mite a splinter a grain
a tatter a snip a sliver a whit a tittle.   habited by pain

would you bop me on the noggin: with a two by four
the trifle of me pissing myself.   slobbering infantile: or

wheezing in an oxygen tent.   won't you shut off the tank
mightn't you disconnect the plug: give the cord a proper yank

when I lose the feeling in my legs.   when my hands won't grip
and I'm a thread a reed a wrack a ruin: of clap and flux and grippe

with your smack connections could you dose me.   as I start my decline
would you put a bullet through me.   angel: no light left that is mine

—*for Sam Witt*

[when dementia begins: almost makes sense like hamburger translations]

when dementia begins: almost makes sense like hamburger translations
or the poems the body writes in its dysentery: explosions at either end
    and vile

my mind has many homes these days.   I have seen much of kitchen tile
much of the great round bowls.   in doorways I lose
    the heartbeat of decisions

me is no comfort place to be these days.   hang teeth and smiles
    in the windows
and fiddle fiddle with the thermostat.   but the mind don't stay:
    away to the mall

let the lookylous look: *rupt rush re so re bo re we re wa re you reat reali reall*
see streets of a lost city: the lights beyond keep blinking *how yet how yet*
    *how*s

[autumn set us heavily to task: unrooted the dahlias]

autumn set us heavily to task: unrooted the dahlias
lay wrapped in the cellar.   cider pressing time.   grain milling
time to pick persimmons.   time to fix the leaky hayloft

slaughtering time.   rendering time.   time to put up chokecherries
take the woolens from the cedar chest: britches mending time
rabbit hunting time.   tallow candle dipping time.   soap making time

count the butter and egg money.   count the diapers in the wash
time to split wood and clean the flue.   time that the pesky swallows
in the chimney took their leave.   molasses cooking time

kids sent to glean the fields at dusk.   yams laid out to cure
and the last huckleberries balljarred in the larder.   corn husking time
clay dull red in sunlight crumbling: abundant the harvest and the tithe

FROM *TEA*

[between scott's asshole and his mouth I could not say which I preferred:
perfect similes]

between scott's asshole and his mouth I could not say which I preferred:
    perfect similes
attention to cleanliness ran so deep.   I imagined a gleeming highway
    through the donner pass of him
a chill settling in his eyes: brown sierras.   I entered starving.
    I could eat my weakest daughter

I want to hold a past larger than his shoes.   I want to say
    that summit closed its ribs around me
a story that omits resorts.   denies progress.   forgets
    how easily I traversed his altitudes

the truth: he was no monument.   sockets I plugged into.
    warm circles I could make with my fingers
the truth: I have never left him.   I drive always toward california.
    not all bodies are recovered

[ode]

where have you gone blue middle of a decade?   the gates creak.
    a sigh is so vastly different
the diary is pure spine.   in the most gingerly way each leaf opened
    reveals the less of you

83, 84, 85: your relics in a converse box.   adoring letters from one
    upon whom you put the kibosh
shade trees bent to listen for a song.   [erasure?]   all of your best
    composing is lament

faithless time you steal the handsome petals for yourself.   a bruised fist
    of hyacinth becomes you
when the wind bears no whisper but alack: an eye fears you & distance:
    the short distance across

[who won't praise green. each minute to caress each minute blade of spring.
green slice us open]
    a song of mayflies

who won't praise green.   each minute to caress each minute
    blade of spring.   green slice us open
spew of willow crotch: we float upward a whirling chaff.
    sunlight sings in us *some glad morning*

when we are called we are called ephemera.   palpitating length
    of a psalm.   who isn't halfway gone
fatherless and childless: not a who will know us.   dazzled afternoon
    won't we widow ourselves away

POETICS STATEMENT

The Flesh Failures

WORDS ARE the way we call the world into being: "In the beginning was the word, and the word became flesh." The more words we have, the more ways of describing, the more exact, the more power over the world: when a child suckles, he begins to understand that what he wants, that milk, that sustenance, has a name. The first time he utters the name: "baba" for *bottle* (or, if not yet weaned, "mama" for *mother*), he understands the power of language: call for the thing by its name and the thing appears.

Intoxicated by the power of language, the child begins to play with words. He notices similarities between certain words, the way "mama" and "baba" rhyme off one another (though he doesn't yet know the word *rhyme*, he is aware of the condition of rhyming). He creates words for things for which he hasn't yet learned the names. He strings words together into song, gradually developing a syntax by which he might describe his experience of being (because he wants someone else to know that he has this power: *language*). And as he continues to grow, he continues to acquire the useful phrases. Perhaps he learns other phrases as well, but they have no practical application, and so he either stores them away or discards them.

Poets continue to suckle at the nipple of the world. They learn more names for more nipples. They hoard the power over all these breasts, feeding at their leisure, at their pleasure. They command an army of mammary, they store them in a box called *memory*, they bring them out like toy soldiers and let them do battle; they are rehearsing and nursing and breaking the rules of war with their words.

This is one way of thinking about why we're drawn to the material of language, as opposed to paint or music or photography or any of a number of other methods by which we might express our passions.

As for me, I know that I felt the power of language early, and I used it as a weapon. I wasn't always able to fight (though lord knows that didn't keep me from brawling) but I could probe someone with language, worrying their armor until I found the weak spot, then jab with a pointed phrase.

So why not become a critic, if all I wanted was to assault? Why write poetry?

Denise Levertov once said of the Language poets that they were taking "a private place on a public beach." True enough, I suppose. But isn't that why so many people are drawn to poetry, regardless of the aesthetic? Because it does have about it a feel of the private. Most poets I know discovered poetry around the same time they discovered masturbation. And probably for the same reason. Poetry gives us a place to explore our passions, to play with possibilities, to open ourselves up to the ecstatic.

And I think this is one of the reasons why we like to speak of poetry in terms of the body. Olson says that "the line comes (I swear it) from the breath." Pinsky says, "The medium of poetry is a human body: the column of air inside the chest, shaped into signifying sounds in the larynx and the mouth." I go back time and again to Longinus, who speaks of sublimity as corresponding to the collocation of the limbs in the body. Or to Whitman, writing that "wherever are men like me, are our lusty, lurking, masculine poems." The poem is the record of the body; how the body experiences the world. Rhythms correspond to breathing and to the systole and diastole of the heart. When Keats writes, "Bright Star! would I were steadfast as thou art," the falling away of "art" mirrors his own expiring breath. And when Whitman writes "sailing, soldiering, thieving, threatening, misers, menials, priests alarming—air breathing, water drinking, on the turf or the sea-beach dancing, cities wrenching, ease scorning, statutes mocking, feebleness chasing," the panting rhythm mirrors the erotic relationship of "We Two Boys Together Clinging." It doesn't have to be spelled out; the quickening breath tells us that this is a passionate embrace.

The body is the first writer of the poem. The mind is that caretaker who moves in to make order. Sometimes what the mind does to the poem is good. Sometimes, it's too much. "I am the enemy of the mind," writes Berryman, while Ginsberg insists that "mind is shapely." With whatever trust or mistrust we have of it, the mind works the poem in a different way. But let's be clear: intellects don't write poems. While they're wonderful to have, they are no substitute for the body's sense of the world. Because the body is *ir*rational, and the irrational is where the discovery happens. Keats calls it negative capability. García Lorca says it is the darkness, the *duende*, that it "is drawn to where forms fuse themselves in a longing greater than their visible expressions." Spicer says that we're like radios and the Martians are talking through us. By whatever metaphor we name it, we're listening to the voice beyond the edge of knowing. I say that it is the body, because I know that the body remembers and feels and expresses in a way separate from what the mind does.

Full stops. Broken phrases. Rising and falling rhythms welded within the same line. This is how I shape my poems. Because "silly" meant *blessed* before it meant *foolish*, I let the silly share space with the profound. Hell, I let the silly *be* the profound. We don't know where wisdom will come from; give an open hand to every utterance and let it weigh against every other. All of this voicing arises from the uncertain place that my body inhabits: medicated, rumbling, off-center, uneasy, failing. It's an instrument that needs, with its constant desire to eat, to shit, to breathe, to be cared for—and it is crude and unrefined. But I know by now how to play it, and I do.

"HERE IS THE DOOR MARKED HEAVEN": D. A. POWELL

Stephen Burt

IN FIVE and a half years D. A. Powell has achieved durable acclaim for three books whose topics, though not their techniques, permit quick summary. *Tea* (1998) used long lines and striking extended metaphors to describe Powell's own experience of gay America, including his own very early sexual encounters, his long, troubled romance with Scott Gulvas, and the loss of friends and lovers to HIV and AIDS.[1] *Lunch* (2000) gathered the short poems that prefigure his *Tea* style, including a sequence about his childhood in blue-collar, exurban California, along with a suite of poems about his own HIV-positive diagnosis. *Cocktails* (2004), the genuine sequel to *Tea*, returned to its settings and methods in the first of its three sections; the second rewrote Powell's sexual history through a series of films, most of them with queer plots or subtexts. The third and most original section of *Cocktails* took on biblical themes, finding versions of queer life, erotic devotion, and suffering in the Gospels and other early Christian writings. Powell has received, and surely deserved, attention as a voice of the HIV-AIDS crisis, and as a chronicler of gay life for his generation. His is hardly the only such voice. What has made Powell stand out in other poets' eyes is not his set of affecting subjects, but his invention of an original style.

Powell writes in the foreword to *Tea* that his work is "not about being queer and dying. It is about being human and living."[2] His style makes continuities and progressions, ongoing poems that represent ongoing lives, out of verbal and structural elements that look like termini, obstacles, premature closures. Powell's poems also flaunt, and sometimes quote, works of art and cultural codes created by gay American men; he likens his project to that of a DJ, who collects, sorts, mixes, and makes available for a community already existing songs. Powell's extended metaphors and double or triple entendres frequently link alluring, or highly esteemed, experience to things and actions rejected, degraded, debased. These figures, combining the stigmatized with the sacred, make his biblical sequence consonant with the rest of his poems: these songs of Saint John and Simon the Cyrene, like his earlier poems of hospitals, discos, and curious Boy Scouts, turn the abject into the exalted, keeping the Christian promise that the last shall be first, the rejected stone become the cornerstone.

Powell says he began writing *Tea* when he "turned [his] notebook sideways, pushing into what would traditionally be the margins of the page."[3] The long lines of *Tea*—replicated for most of *Cocktails*—remain Powell's most recognizable formal feature. These lines (and even the shorter lines in most of *Lunch*) make room for multiple caesurae, indicated by multiple em-spaces midline; often these caesurae separate nouns or noun-phrases with no corresponding verb: "the new seed germing: gifting in the storehouse. comb of honey / a jar of fragrant oil. physique rid from its abscess: robed in saffronia."[4] Powell's defiance of prose syntax also includes abrupt changes of verb tense and mood. He may shift from third-person, past tense indicative to second-person present, or from indicative to imperative, several times within one poem: "I saw this movie twice. . . . now I wander into someone else's story . . . take my hand and lead me stranger."[5]

What do these devices let Powell do? "The long lines of *Tea*," Powell has said, "are made up of short bits, of fragments. I felt like my life at that time was putting together the broken bits. Making a whole out of something that had been shattered."[6] Paul Monette opened *Borrowed Time*, billed in 1988 as the first "AIDS memoir," with a far gloomier statement: "the world around me is defined now by its endings and its closures, the date on the grave that follows the hyphen."[7] Powell's style begins by acknowledging such closures, many (though not all) due to HIV. The grammatical stutters and emphatic metaphors mean that almost any line in a typical poem of Powell's could be its last—and that most are not. Changes in verb tense, person, and mood make the poems seem immediate, unsettled, while also describing the way the poem coheres: "the ends I took up and selvaged. This veil shall not fray."[8] In "[remembering the taste of skin . . ." (from *Lunch*) any of its five lines could work as an ending:

> remembering the taste of skin: dim prehistory of dives
>
> secretions of the body: spume and seawater
> cells of the voluble tongue welcome old chums
>
> rapture of the deep: lungs fill with oceania
> rubber suit flops into the skiff. fins in the water[9]

This effect of hyperclosure or repeated false closure gives Powell's poems the sense of insistent continuance through obstacles: extended metaphors (here equating evolution, diving, drinking in "dive" bars, and sex—with a condom) seem to hold the poem together, while collapsing syntax threatens to break it apart.

Repeated efforts to overcome potential endings, to move past a break, define not only the structure of individual lines and poems but the structure of *Tea* as well. Punning on one of Robert Duncan's titles, *Tea* promises "to end and to open with a field," both the field in which Powell's friend Andy is "buried under a hunter's moon" and the scene of a car wreck in which Powell at age twenty almost died: "20. the year I went through the windshield"; "the crash divides my life."[10] Powell plays the resurrected survivor—"death puked me back out of its paunch"—committed to surveying the "field" of his friends' deaths; *Tea* not only begins with the crash but concludes with it, turning a symbol of auto safety into a symbol of sexual release: "the shiny buckle unfastens at last."[11]

Powell's corpus, especially *Tea*, tries to work both as art and as record, "trying to archive that period" of his life: "somehow, if I don't put all this stuff in it'll be lost."[12] No wonder collections, possessions, collectors—especially music collectors and DJs—play such a prominent role. Powell's collections show remarkable scope: Boy Scouts, John Waters, Air Supply, Häagen-Daz, Pushkin, Marvell, the disco producer Patrick Cowley. (High-culture touchstones crucial for a previous generation of white gay poets, such as Howard and Merrill, are notably absent.) Powell finds many uses for what he collects: song lyrics and song tunes can substitute for the metrical substructure his lengthy lines reject: " *tall and* thin *and young and lovely the* Michael with kaposi's sarcoma *goes walking*." More often Powell leans on proper nouns and song titles for their metaphors: "Eleven Disco Songs That Equate Sex and Death Through an Elaborate Metaphor Called 'Heaven.'"[13] Powell's world is full of figuration already; he shows himself not just collecting but documenting, advocating, demonstrating, bringing out figures already available in American culture (especially in its queer subcultures). Such collecting and demonstrating can take over whole poems: "[first fugue]," the last poem in *Tea*, uses three-part lines: the first part of each line quotes a gay male poet, the second a Sylvester track.

As late as 1979 (when Powell was entering high school) Robert K. Martin required a whole book to argue (what now seems beyond question) that "the sense of a shared sexuality had led many gay writers to develop a particular tradition, involving references to earlier gay writers," especially Walt Whitman and Hart Crane.[14] Poems like "first fugue" do not only place Powell in Martin's (and Crane's) "homosexual tradition"; they also, much more originally, expand that tradition far outside high culture, placing Whitman, Crane, Essex Hemphill, Merrill, and Sylvester in the same celebrated company. "The culture of disco," Powell explains, "wasn't just Gay culture, it was African American and Hispanic culture, too; it was a hybridization, but it was definitely distrusted and abused by the dominant white, heterosexual culture. And so disco went underground, and transformed and transmuted into all sorts of other musics. It survived. Queer people survived."[15]

Like the disco scene he describes, Powell's verse not only celebrates an identity but works to pluralize it. Movie protagonists, biblical characters, glimpsed counterparts in grocery stores, could all (for a few lines of poetry) *be him*. (Whitman's poems boast similar effects.) His project of representing *many* people—friends, dead and living; relatives; strangers; characters from literature, music, film—comes as a deliberate alternative to clearer autobiographical (not to say confessional) modes. Powell has been alternately laconic and explicit in describing his early years in the American South and then in Yuba City, California: that life includes time at Yuba College and at Sonoma State University (where he began to write seriously).[16] "There were times when I was younger," he has said, "when I had limited options and had to prostitute myself. It's something that is not very far beyond my life"; "believe me, I've had times in my life where I truly hungered and had nothing."[17] Such hints (combined with those embedded in his poems) suggest that his life story, told straightforwardly, could capture many readers.

Powell deliberately avoids such telling. Instead, the poems sketch and merge their episodes, often deflecting attention from Powell onto the other characters with whom he identifies (or whom he grieves). Rather than one life, or one life story, the poems offer sets of roles, all of which Powell inhabits, all of which are "real" and become part of him: he is not, so to speak, the dancer but the dance floor itself, and the DJ who keeps it alive. The DJ set, the one-time-only live mix for a particular place and occasion (rather than the rock album of discrete songs), also gives Powell a model for his forms. "He must have been a deejay this one" (in *Tea*) imagines "[the mix as a product of survival] pushing up to 144 bpm."[18] Matching beats, controlling tempi, turning discrete and preexisting units into continuous (and communal) experience, a club DJ constructs a set out of records very much in the way that Powell constructs lines, poems, sequences—and indeed books—out of events, references, preexisting pieces.

Where did he learn to write those fragments, those books? Powell remembers his "first foray into the genre of poetry" via Dudley Randall's anthology *The Black Poets*; he describes his earliest creative efforts as work "from the time when I was Black," and recalls, "It took me a long time to learn how to read white people's poetry. But I do now."[19] Other early models included T. S. Eliot, Gertrude Stein, and Powell's teacher at Sonoma State, David Bromige. What about Frank O'Hara: is *Lunch Poems* a source for *Lunch*? "As soon as I started reading Frank O'Hara," Powell told the *Harvard Crimson*, "I thought, this guy's ripping me off. Except he died when I was three." The same interview suggests that the long lines of *Tea* owe something to hip-hop: "Sugarhill Gang and Grandmaster Flash were as important to me as Gertrude Stein and John Keats."[20] Powell's comments elsewhere suggest a self-conscious San Francisco tradition—Spicer, Duncan, Gunn—in which he situates his own efforts. None of these writers except Gunn has any use for English meters and closed rhyming forms. Powell belongs, in fact, to the first generation of American poets who may have grown up without even a vestigial connection to the accentual-syllabic, rhyming English tradition; his inventive lines have this absence at their back.

"Before I wrote *Tea* I had written a collection entitled *Lunch*," Powell explained in 1998.[21] Interviews suggest that the earlier *Lunch* became most, but not all, of Powell's 2000 book; in it, we can see Powell's style take shape. "[sonnet]" looks like a prospectus for *Tea*: the poem offers "morsels of my lifeswork: the story of a professional party hostess," comparing itself to the music of the Eurhythmics and offering "newamericanwriting" its "nice mix of plights and music. boomerang boy and disco dollies . . . written in an enjoyable present: continuous. an unresolved work."[22] The poem gathers parts and characters in intimate earnestness; it assembles, too, a set of extended metaphors anchored by puns. ("Boomerang" and "dollies," for example, are types of microphone used in film work, as well as labels for dance-club habitués.)

Such extended metaphors and double-entendres seem even more fundamental to Powell's aesthetic than are his fragmented, extra-long lines. "A song of Sal Mineo" depicts, simultaneously, for six long lines, the poet receiving anal sex, key scenes from the last reel of *Rebel Without a Cause* and Persephone's abduction by Hades: "in the restroom at *the probe* I welcomed a sweet thrust   pomegranate droplets dotted the commode // he was the disembodied voice of the planetarium   I want to pretend it did not happen in the dark."[23] Jonathan Dollimore writes that "gay fiction from Radclyffe Hall onwards" presents 'the gay underworld as a place where the hero or heroine suffers into truth, and, by dissociating himself or herself from the tormented inhabitants of the place, writes of its tragedy."[24] Powell's double exposure creates a "gay underworld" but does not dissociate the poet from it at all: he "want[s] to pretend," not "that it did not happen" but that "it did not happen in the dark." (He is both a Persephone who enjoys her time in Hades, and a Sal Mineo who survives.)

One might object that such a passage wants to have gay sex (or a sex club) both ways, celebrating a descent it nevertheless views *as* descent, as shame or sin. Yet "having it both ways" is just what Powell's metaphors do. Often they make it hard to sort tenor from vehicle. One of the densest (and most anthology-friendly) poems in *Tea* carries a triple entendre through six lines, describing (a) a feigned tea service enacted by (b) boys camping in the woods (apparently Boy Scouts) who (c) engage in erotic play. All three situations become ceremonies of queer initiation. With its "floating" noun phrases, midline breaks, abrupt endings, and changes of verb person, tense, and mood, the poem makes the best brief example of Powell's *Tea* style:

> the merit of reading tea: gunpowder variety unfurls puptent green.   sleeping
>   bags zipped together
> all summer our mouths wore the parfum of shattered blossoms.   see: you
>   like butter your chin says

> in a clearing in the wood we were made to play nice & dainty: petite cookies
>   amid elegant service
> were we taught to rub two sticks together?   proper steeping.   poise and
>   balancing upon the knee
>
> our leaftips turn silver.   one would wander in search of cress: strangling in
>   the creekbed
> each discovery triggered by a broken cup.   using a trusty fieldguide to earn
>   badges: we identify[25]

Some of the visual puns are obviously sexual ("rub two sticks together"), some less obvious ("leaftips turn silver" with semen or pre-come), and some faint indeed: is the "broken cup" a teacup? A buttercup? The Grail, as parodied in Robert Frost's "Directive"?

If "[the merit of reading tea . . .]" relies on visual analogies, other poems unpack meanings inside key words. "They chose me for a host" brings in partygoers, wafers, and viral infection; "now I lay me down these fierce tracks" is at once a prayer, a DJ's statement of intent, and a promise to search for (human or animal) prey.[26] Other poems appropriate proper nouns, such as club names: "kenny lost in *the mineshaft* among silver stalactites. his irises bloom in darkness / the night is an open 'o.' he caverns and groans engulfing: largerbonessoulsweddingrings // leaking from the socket of his anus: cocytus. he stands apart involuntary. pooped himself."[27] The club's name already suggests the anus, but Powell goes further: almost every noun and verb here holds a pun. "Irises bloom," for example, means that Kenny's eyes widen in dim light, that he "flowers" sexually, and that other sphincters prepare to assume their receptive role.

Such extended figures (*Mineshaft* club = anus = actual mineshaft = classical underworld; tea party = scout camp = sexual initiation) serve as principles of unity, and as principles of entertainment, even comedy; they balance, perhaps, the fragmentation of Powell's grammar, and the seriousness of his subjects. In parts of *Tea* and especially in *Cocktails* the figures take on a grander goal: they redeem Powell's own, and his friends', suffering by linking stigmatized, even conventionally disgusting, experience to elevated or even holy states. One of the shortest and strangest poems in *Tea* appears to remember a pedophile uncle:

> when did the darkness climb on with its muscular legs pinning me under:
>   goodnight uncle boo
>
> giant teeth grazed me: he descended from the clouds.   wanting to explore
>   the downthere of me
>
> the biggest thumb.   I had to go bathroom but vines held me fast.   beanstalk
>   sprouting my pyjamas

at the foot of my trundle: magic beans could conjure him.   say it again: "I'll
    eat you up"[28]

Most of Powell's poems place their first lines in brackets to create their titles:
he calls this one "[untitled]" instead, as the child had no name for this con-
fusing, exciting experience, which seemed both to endanger him and to open
a magical alternate realm. (This child may not even have a name for the
penis, which he calls "the biggest thumb.") Again, the repellent (what is usu-
ally called molestation) is compared to the exalted, and the remembered
experience partakes of both: as Calvin Bedient put it, "the boy is not only
overwhelmed but hooked."[29]

Perhaps overwhelmed himself, Bedient called *Tea* "a book of abject self-
discoveries," comparing its sentence fragments to "seeds spat out in dis-
gust."[30] Yet Powell often invites us to link disgust with joy. "[college room-
mate gone . . ." shows Powell sorting the roommate's laundry: "piggish
delight the rooting after truffles. Whiff and snout."[31] "[dogs and boys can
treat you like trash . . ." seems to relish sexual self-abasement: "when a boy
goes away: to another boy's arms. what else can you do / but lie down with
the dogs. with the hounds with the curs. with the mutts."[32] Elsewhere the
humiliating images imply not sexual pleasure but medical difficulties, and
heroic survival: "I fear my mucus: its endless volume and amorphous shape /
a demon expelling from my lips. the moon wags its tongue."[33]

In "[untitled]" and "[college roommate . . ." the joyful side of the poem
remains secular: the otherworld of fairy tales; intimate knowledge of a
beloved (or at least of his laundry). Elsewhere Powell's paired opposites draw
on Christian belief. "Once I had really thought about it, I have all of the
Christian values that I was imbued with through my reading of the Bible,"
Powell says, "it's more radical for me to go back into the church and to say
'I am a Christian' than to just turn my back."[34] Reviewing the book, Joan
Houlihan found in *Cocktails* "an unexpectedly traditional, religious world-
view."[35] *Cocktails*—the whole book, but especially its last section—uses
extended metaphors to redeem (from homophobia, from physical pain, from
early trauma) experience we have been taught to view with disgust, and as a
way of using sexy tableaux and broken taboos to free (from its modern fun-
damentalist shell) what Powell sees as the core of Christian faith.

Christianity already has at least one ceremony whereby the prohibited
(the eating of flesh) becomes holy (the acceptance of Christ). Powell's met-
aphorical procedures in one sense simply extend the ideal of communion.
"Rather than drawing clear metaphorical equations," Powell has said, "I've
mixed up the sexual eating, the medical eating, the corrosive eating and the
ecclesiastical eating into a big, amorphous stew. Let god sort it all out."[36]
"[because as lives are aching . . ." (from *Lunch*) introduces the poet as both
saved and damned, his blood both poison and communion wine: "doing

all the poisoning myself // myself. need no wine to sanctify. as of the right now I am lucky: / need no litter bearer. children undigested I am able to throw back up."[37] (The last line, interviews make clear, refers to Powell's first months of taking anti-AIDS drug "cocktails," when he found himself vomiting pills he had to reingest.) In a poem about Christ's foreskin, circumcision, communion, winemaking (the communal trampling of grapes), sex, astrology (observation of Mars), and blood tests—all represent one another: "unsheathed the sword and cut the veil. visible the planet red / he wrapped in cloth: a loaf in offering. stained: they crushed his grape / now wine trickles from the vats and the barnfloor aches its charge."[38] Christ's foreskin—the only part of the Son that remained on Earth after His Ascension—stands for the interpenetration of transcendental with earthly concerns (as well as for penetration of other kinds).

Mary Douglas in *Purity and Danger* considered the "connection between dirt and sacredness" one of the founding problems of anthropology; "religions often sacralise the very unclean things which have been rejected with abhorrence."[39] We might (though Douglas does not) see the Eucharist, in which believers eat human-divine flesh and blood, as such a sacralization; Powell's figures work analogous transformation (from defilement to sacred mystery, *by way of* verbal blessing) on the rites and customs of gay men's subcultures and sexual practices. "[came a voice in my gullet . . .]" turns receptive oral sex into a kind of priestly blessing: "what had been circumcised fit me. the uncircumcised too / for nothing was given for my body which was not sacred / the seed the root the tongue and pure blood that cleanses."[40] The poems (like the bodies in the poems) take into themselves things and people previously considered defiling, and declare them clean.

Though Powell seems to compare himself to Christ on occasion, much more often he sees himself among the marginal figures, pariahs and former pariahs, whom Christ redeemed: "Lazarus the leper," the Magadalene, "Lazarus of Bethany." He has said that only in his dramatic monologues—not in his personal lyrics—do speakers deem themselves Christlike. Powell also emphasizes his indignities: "we was a beautiful lad once: not putrefactive nor foul / not blistering in the lips or nose."[41] Near the head of Powell's parade of New Testament surrogates stands Simon the Cyrene, who carried the Cross to Golgotha (Mark 15:21, Matthew 27:32). Powell's song of Simon the Cyrene begins: "because I were ready before destruction. bearing the sign of his affliction / in my laggard arms: the sign was made as the stretching limbs of him." Like Simon, Powell is now a "carrier": " 'the carrier' I was called. so did I carry: my hand did not defect. my sores / who can tell us all about love: a flaying."[42] Gnostic Christians such as Basilides believed that this Simon was crucified in Christ's stead. Another tradition emphasizes African origins: the biblical scholar Boykin Sanders considers Simon "a native North African Black person who was commandeered by the Roman authorities."[43] "In modern times," adds the *Oxford Dictionary of the Christian Church*, "Simon the Cyrene has been claimed as patron by groups of people working among outcasts."[44] His blackness, his outsider status, his role as "carrier"—sharing the *physical* pain of the Cross—and his relative obscurity all make him an especially appropriate mask for Powell.

Nor do the resemblances stop there. "I am writing the spiritual self through sexuality," Powell says of the last part of *Cocktails*; "There's a long tradition of that going back to the Song of Solomon, and the odes that are attributed to Simon of Cyrene."[45] Usually called the Odes of Solomon, these poems are early Christian (Jewish-Christian) lyric works modeled on the Song of Songs and on the Psalms; the most remarkable among them express a homoerotic devotion to the crucified, resurrected Savior. The Third Ode, for example, begins (in Willis Barnstone's translation) "I clothe his limbs, his own limbs / and hang from them. / He loves me," and continues "to love the son / I become a son." In the Sixteenth Ode, "His love feeds my heart, / his sweet food reaches my lips"; in the Nineteenth, "The Son is the cup / and he who was milked is the Father / and he who milked him is the Holy Ghost."[46] These odes recall in their blend of erotic and sacred the odic ambitions of poems in both *Cocktails* and *Tea*.

They also suggest a serious aim toward which almost all Powell's techniques point. Club nights, backroom sex, church services, even perhaps hospital visits—all become in *Tea*—as cinemas, bars, supermarkets, and Christian rituals become in *Cocktails*—*communal, ritual experiences* where *performative language exalts a vulnerable (gay) male body*, confirming rather than countering its erotic charge, and rendering desirable, or honorable, its experience of disgust and pain. As his "Eleven Disco Songs" suggest, Powell takes on what Dollimore calls "the age-old connection between death and sexuality," and "the association" (fueled by, but far older than, HIV) "between homosexual promiscuity and death."[47] Rather than offer a safe, clean description of gay male desire, one designed to dissociate it from dirt, mortal danger, corruption, and infection, Powell's double meanings, and his willingness to describe taboo topics (child molestation, feces, sores, nausea) offer gay persistence and gay pleasure as a triumph over the corruption they appear to incorporate.

In this sense Powell writes what Julia Kristeva calls "literature of the abject." "Abjection," Kristeva avers, "transforms death drive into a start of life, of new significance"; "The abject is perverse because it neither gives up nor assumes a prohibition, a rule, or a law, but turns them aside, misleads, corrupts, uses them . . . the better to deny them." Literature of the abject imagines "a crossing over of the dichotomous categories of Pure and Impure, Prohibition and Sin, Morality and Immorality."[48] One precedent for this project is Jean Genet, a writer Powell never quotes, but does know well: the poems that merge or reverse degradation and holiness, ecstasy and sadness, revulsion, or grief, invoke the problem at the core of Genet's writings whereby "a certain feeling . . . is obliged to borrow its expression from the opposite feeling so as to escape from the myrmidons of the law."[49]

Genet has become the patron saint, so to speak, of critics, such as Dollimore and Leo Bersani, who see in queer sex and in its depictions—especially in anal sex between men—a mortal blow (no pun intended) to humanism and individualism. These critics praise "a sense of a sexual pleasure that crosses a threshold, and which shatters psychic organization," "a radical break with the social itself" in a "celebration of pure destructiveness."[50] Yet Powell is no antihumanist, no eraser of character and social relations. Instead, his poems present a series of metaphors in which the dynamic equilibrium linking disgust and delight, shame and pleasure, need not displace (as Bersani thinks it must) "objects" in the psychoanalytic sense, attachments to a cast of characters. Powell's ambition to gather and speak for a broad array of people does not compete with, but reinforces, his boundary-breaking, sexualized pairings of the sacred and the profane: he calls his mouth "a tiny neon lounge," where characters ("like my lovers") congregate.[51] Some of those characters hail from Powell's life (Scott, Kenny, Victor), others from twentieth-century popular arts (Sal Mineo, Patrick Cowley), and others still from the early Christian church.

I have tried to describe how Powell's works (especially *Tea* and "Bibliography") not only exhibit distinctive forms but use the forms to register ideas and emotions. Their project is not only celebratory, not only memorializing, but charged with a Christian ethics as well. Future critics can look more closely at the disco tracks, singers, and producers Powell names, and to whom he compares himself. They will look at the other New Testament characters in "Bibliography" and at the movies in "Filmography." And they will certainly look in greater detail at the links among (and at psychoanalytic claims about) shame, dirt, sexual excitement, and ecstasy or religious transport that Powell's poems instantiate.

And yet critics who investigate only those serious topics might miss one of the best things about Powell's work. If *Tea* flaunts disgusting details and retains its serious purposes (mourning, celebrating, promising) it also flaunts comedy, calling the now-deceased "nicholas the ridiculous" "nick at night.   tricky nick.   nicholas at halloween a giant tampon." "We toy in earnest," a later poem insists.[52] Powell's forms make room for excess, for frivolity, too, boasting mordantly comic sound effects: "we slip and slop and spill our soup—we pop our rocks—droop and droplet / flung over the back of the sofa: limp as a cashmere coverlet damp as a bloodclot."[53] Powell works hard to reject any kind of decorum: neither light humor nor repellent detail nor the conventionally beautiful will be left out. (He rejects, instead, ironic distance, balance, "maturity": "don't make me mature by myself."[54]) To sound fun, sexy, flirtatious, voluble are not, for Powell, opposed to memorial or sacral purposes: indeed, to repudiate one of those ways of being is to dishonor them all.

Conversely, to recognize their interdependence is to enter the gathering that Powell wants his fragmented, populous poetry to create. We might say that these poems of parties and mourners, of cinemas and the primitive Church, "can render the experience of desire as also an experience of grieving," as Dollimore wants gay radical writing to do; we might say with equal truth that Powell's remixes, long likenings, and juxtapositions "involve . . . a recognition, implicit in the expression of every experience, of other kinds of experience which are possible."[55] "[coda & discography]"—which closes *Cocktails* as "first fugue" closed out *Tea*—suggests that Powell's antinomian redemptive project has at last been accomplished, the strands of queer heritage, personal experience, elegy, blessing and purgation all complete: "the garment the tore: mended.   the body that failed: reclaimed." Echoing Whitman (and Lorca) he invites a series of agents to find fulfillment in his poem: "voyeurs, passion flowers, trolls, twinks, dancers, cruisers, lovers without lovers // here is the door marked HEAVEN: someone on the dancefloor, waiting just for you."[56] What follows is not more language of Powell's invention but a list of important disco tracks, including Patrick Cowley and Sylvester (the tutelary artists of *Tea*) but also many other singers and groups: the "HEAVEN" whose verbal figures Powell assembles belongs to them too—it is not, cannot be, Powell's alone.

NOTES

1. Powell himself did not test positive until after completing *Tea* and leaving Iowa. Sam Witt and Sean Durkin, "Turning the Paper Sideways: An Interview with D. A. Powell." *Poetry Flash* 284 (February–March 2000), www.poetryflash.org/archive/284Witt.html, 23. Page numbers for this interview reflect the Web format, viewed and printed September 1, 2004, rather than the print version of the magazine.

2. D. A. Powell, *Tea* (Middletown, Conn.: Wesleyan University Press, 1998), xiv.

3. Ibid., xi.

4. D. A. Powell, *Cocktails* (Saint Paul, Minn.: Graywolf, 2004), 52.

5. Ibid., 39.

6. Witt and Durkin, "Turning the Paper Sideways," 15.

7. Paul Monette, *Borrowed Time: An AIDS Memoir* (New York: Harcourt Brace Jovanovich, 1988), 2.

8. *Cocktails*, 45. "Selvage": "to form a boundary or edging to" (*OED*). (The *OED* lists the verb only as transitive, though.)

9. D. A. Powell, *Lunch* (Middletown, Conn.: Wesleyan University Press, 2000), 26.

10. *Tea*, 3, 14, and 58. Duncan entitled his 1969 volume of poetry *The Opening of the Field*.

11. Ibid., 3 and 63.

12. Witt and Durkin, "Turning the Paper Sideways," 18.

13. *Tea*, 9 and 11.

14. Robert K. Martin, *The Homosexual Tradition in American Poetry*, expanded ed. (Iowa City: University of Iowa Press, 1998), xv.

15. Witt and Durkin, "Turning the Paper Sideways," 19.

16. Powell (born in 1963) later lived in San Francisco, in Iowa City (where he attended the Iowa Writers' Workshop) and in the Boston area while teaching at Harvard.

17. Witt and Durkin, "Turning the Paper Sideways," 20; Matthew Cooperman, "Between the Brackets: An Interview with D. A. Powell" (unpublished ms.).

18. *Tea*, 23. "bpm": beats per minute. We might also say that Powell's poetry—like the queer punk fanzines discussed by Matias Viegener—"stages or rehearses the kinds of contradictions endemic to postwar Western urban culture, particularly to youth": "grow up / stay young, sex is good / sex is bad, be nice / be cool, follow upward mobility / go slumming, be modest / be shameless, be private / be public." Matias Viegener, "Kinky Escapades, Bedroom Techniques, Unbridled Passion and Secret Sex Codes." In *Camp Grounds: Style and Homosexuality*, ed. David Bergman (Amherst: University of Massachusetts Press, 1993), 234–58 and 243.

19. Witt and Durkin, "Turning the Paper Sideways," 4 and 16; Jascha Hoffman, "'Cocktails' for Two: Interview with D. A. Powell." *Harvard Crimson*, November 9, 2001. www.thecrimson.com/article.aspx?ref=122140, viewed September 1, 2004.

20. Hoffman, "Cocktails."

21. *Tea*, 13.

22. *Lunch*, 49. "new american writing" refers to a Chicago-based magazine edited by Paul Hoover and Maxine Chernoff, long hospitable to very difficult poems.

23. *Tea*, 17.

24. Jonathan Dollimore, *Death, Desire, and Loss in Western Culture* (New York: Routledge, 1998), 296–97.

25. *Tea*, 61.

26. Ibid., 18.

27. Ibid., 6. The poem both delights in its puns, and preserves gay history: the Mineshaft (in New York) was "a club legendary for its extremism." As Jonathan Dollimore quotes Rupert Haselden: "I had never seen anything like it: fist fucking, racks, and the stench of piss and poppers . . . and I remember . . . thinking, 'This is evil, this is wrong.' I remember being very frightened; it seemed so extreme. But . . . the next thing I knew I was back there and within weeks it felt like home." Jonathan Dollimore, "Sexual Disgust." In *Homosexuality and Psychoanalysis*, ed. Tim Dean and Christopher Lane (Chicago: University of Chicago Press, 2001), 367–86 and 378.

28. *Tea*, 30.

29. Calvin Bedient, "In Search of the Torturer's House." *Parnassus* 24, no. 2 (2000): 315–30 and 316.

30. Ibid., 315.

31. *Cocktails*, 30.

32. Ibid., 14.

33. Ibid., 49.

34. Witt and Durkin, "Turning the Paper Sideways," 16–17.

35. Joan Houlihan, "A Terrible Beauty: D. A. Powell." *Contemporary Poetry Review* (August 2004); www.cprw.com/Houlihan/powell.htm. Viewed September 1, 2004.

36. Cooperman, "Between the Brackets."

37. *Lunch*, 59.

38. *Cocktails*, 46.

39. Mary Douglas, *Purity and Danger* (New York: Praeger, 1966), 7 and 159.

40. *Cocktails*, 61.

41. Ibid., 51.

42. Ibid., 56.

43. Boykin Sanders, "In Search of a Face for Simon the Cyrene," in *The Recovery of Black Presence: An Interdisciplinary Exploration*, ed. Randall C. Bailey and Jacquelyn Grant (Nashville, Tenn.: Abingdon, 1995), 51–64 and 51.

44. F. L. Cross and E. A. Livingstone, eds. *The Oxford Dictionary of the Christian Church* (Oxford: Oxford University Press, 1997), 1503.

45. Witt and Durkin, "Turning the Paper Sideways," 25.

46. "Odes of Solomon." In *The Other Bible*, ed. and trans. Willis Barnstone (San Francisco: Harper and Row, 1984), 267–85, 268–69, 276 and 279. Powell has confirmed to me that by "odes attributed to Simon of Cyrene" he means the Odes of Solomon, and that the Barnstone translation is one he used.

47. Dollimore, *Death*, xxx and 294.

48. Julia Kristeva, "Approaching Abjection," trans. Leon S. Roudiez, in *The Portable Kristeva*, ed. Kelly Oliver (New York: Columbia University Press, 1997), 248–267, 241, and 242.

49. Jean Genet, *Our Lady of the Flowers*, trans. Bernard Frechtman (New York: Grove, 1963), 117. Powell has confirmed to me (via e-mail) his early and strong interest in Genet's writings, especially *Our Lady* and *Prisoner of Love*.

50. Dollimore, *Death*, 303; Leo Bersani, *Homos* (Cambridge, Mass.: Harvard University Press, 1995), 176 and 168.

51. *Cocktails*, 3.

52. *Tea*, 5 and 67.

53. *Cocktails*, 23.

54. *Tea*, 5.

55. Dollimore, *Death*, 327; T. S. Eliot, *Selected Prose of T. S. Eliot*, ed. Frank Kermode (London: Faber and Faber, 1975), 170.

56. *Cocktails*, 65.

BIBLIOGRAPHY

Books by D. A. Powell

Cocktails. Saint Paul, Minn.: Graywolf, 2004.
Lunch. Middletown, Conn.: Wesleyan University Press, 2000.
Tea. Middletown, Conn.: Wesleyan University Press, 1998.

Interviews

"Between the Brackets: An Interview with D. A. Powell," by Matthew Cooperman. Unpublished.

"'Cocktails' for Two: Interview with D. A. Powell," interview by Jascha Hoffman. *Harvard Crimson*, November 9, 2001. www.thecrimson.com/article.aspx?ref=122140,

"Turning the Paper Sideways: An Interview with D. A. Powell," interview by Sam Witt and Sean Durkin. *Poetry Flash* 284 (February–March 2000), www.poetryflash.org/archive/284Witt.html.

Selected Criticism

Alexander, Jonathan. "O Camerado." *Lambda Book Report* 12.08–09 (March–April 2004): 13–15.

Bedient, Calvin. "In Search of the Torturer's House." *Parnassus* 24, no. 2 (2000): 315–30.

Bedient, Calvin. "Desire's Nemesis." *Boston Review* 29, nos. 3–4 (Summer 2004); http://www.bostonreview.net/BR29.3/bedient.html.

Dressler, Adam. "Veritas in Vino." *Perihelion* 3, no. 9 (2004); http://www.webdelsol.com/Perihelion/powell.htm.

Houlihan, Joan. "A Terrible Beauty: D. A. Powell." *Contemporary Poetry Review* (August 2004); www.cprw.com/Houlihan/powell.htm.

Manguso, Sarah. "Cocktails." *The Believer* 2, no. 9 (September 2004): 42.

PETER GIZZI

BEGINNING WITH A PHRASE FROM SIMONE WEIL

There is no better time than the present when we have
lost everything. It doesn't mean rain falling
    at a certain declension, at a variable speed is without
purpose or design.
    The present everything is lost in time, according to laws
of physics things shift
    when we lose sight of a present,
    when there is no more everything. No more presence
in everything loved.

In the expanding model things slowly drift and every-
thing better than the present is lost in no time.
    A day mulches according to gravity
    and the sow bug marches. Gone, the hinge cracks, the
gate swings a breeze,
    breeze contingent upon a grace opening to air,
    velocity tied to winging clay. Every anything in its
peculiar station.

The sun brightens as it bleaches, fades the spectral value
in everything seen. And chaos is no better model
    when we come adrift.
    When we have lost a presence when there is no more
everything. No more presence in everything loved,
    losing anything to the present. I heard a fly buzz. I heard
revealed nature,

cars in the street and the garbage, footprints of a world,
every fly a perpetual window,
   unalloyed life, *gling*, pinnacles of tar.

There is no better everything than loss when we have
time. No lack in the present better than everything.
   In this expanding model rain falls
according to laws of physics, things drift. And every-
thing better than the present is gone
   in no time. A certain declension, a variable speed.
   Is there no better presence than loss?
   A grace opening to air.
   No better time than the present.

REVIVAL

for Gregory Corso (1930–2001)

It's good to be dead in America
with the movies, curtains and drift,
the muzak in the theater.
It's good to be in a theater waiting
for The Best Years of Our Lives to begin.
Our first night back, we're here
entertaining a hunch our plane did crash
somewhere over the Rockies, luggage
and manuscripts scattered, charred fragments
attempting to survive the fatal draft.
To be dead in America at the movies
distracted by preview music in dimming lights.
I never once thought of Alfred Deller
or Kathleen Ferrier singing Kindertotenlieder.
It's good to be lost among pillars of grass.
I never once thought of My Last Duchess
or the Pines of Rome. Isn't it great here

just now dying along with azaleas, trilliums,
myrtle, viburnums, daffodils, blue phlox?
It's good to be a ghost in America,
light flooding in at this moment
of never coming back to the same person
who knew certain things, certain people,
shafts of life entering a kitchen
at the end of an age of never coming back now.
To hear reports on the radio,
something about speed, they say, accelerated history.
It's good to share molecular chasm with a friend.
I never once reached for Heisenberg
or The Fall of the Roman Empire.

On this day in history the first antelope was born,
remember The Yearling, like that,
but the footage distressed, handheld.
A hard, closed, linear world at the edge
of caricature, no memory now of the New Science
or The Origin of the Species.
It's good to feel hunted in America.
To be the son of a large man who rose out of depression
and the middle world war, poverty and race
to loom in mid-sixties industrial American air,
survived classic notions of the atom,
to think to be. The official story walks
down the street, enters bars and cafés.
Plays. Airs. Stars. To sing a song of industry,
having forgotten Monty Clift was beaten
for reading Ulysses. It's dark in a theater,
hoping to say never return to the moment
of return, as a hollow ring from Apollo 13
sinks back to burn into the atmosphere
which made it, huh. How come all the best thoughts
are images? How come all the best images
are uncanny? What's the use of The Compleat Angler,
searching for effects at the bottom of a lake

next to a shoe slick with algae, at the base of a cliff
with pine needles and a rotting log?

I was talking about rending, reading, rewriting
what is seen. Put the book down and look into the day.
I want an art that can say how I am feeling
if I am feeling blue sky unrolling a coronation rug
unto the bare toe of a peasant girl
with vague memories of Jeanne d'Arc,
or that transformation in Cinderella.
Where is your mother today?
I think of you, soft skin against soot.
How much has the world turned
since you were a girl in Troy?
In these parts both widow and banker are diminished,
something outside the town defeated them.
In these parts neither possessed their life.
This pageant demands too much,
that we work and not break, that we love
and not lie, and not complain.
It's good to not break in America.
To behave this time
never once looking into Chapman's Homer,
or quoting the Vita Nuova translated
by Dante Rossetti. No, I am thinking
blurry faces, a boy, girl, looking
at New York harbor for a first time,
soil in pockets, missing buttons,
needing glasses, needing shoes.

It was war. A capital experience!
Investing in narratives of working up
from the mail room, basement, kitchen.
It's good to believe in the press kit
sailing away from rear-projection tenements
like a car ride after a good fix,
offset by attractively angled shots,

neo-cartoonish, with massive distorting close-ups,
part lockdown, part interest rate,
part plant, part machine. Part dazzle?
Lulls and high sensations.
I always wished I could be funny ha-ha,
instead of "he's a little funny," if you get my drift,
just courage to accept the facts
that poetry can catch you in the headlights
and it's years refocusing the afterimage,
the depth and passion of its earnest glance.
This part untranslatable, part missing line,
feather in the chest. A description
to account for the lack of detail
the Wealth of Nations conducts on the organs.
We look forward to serving you here
at Managed Health Network.
Thank you for calling, call volume
is still exceptionally heavy. If this is an emergency . . .

All the codes have been compromised.
This is why the boy can't fathom polar lights,
liberty, merry dancer.
Ineluctably the privileged nostalgia of a toy boat.
In the diagram did the vessel survive?
Like an old book, even a beloved book,
its pages give way to a good sneeze.
What have they done, I sit here thinking
of your monuments, trophies, hahahaha.
"Here are my flowers,"
what do they smell like? "Paper."
This is why athenaeum joy, why shiny pathos
intoning the letters, prance and skater,
o say, can you see?
What does it mean to wait for a song
to sit and wait for a story?
For want of a sound to call my own
coming in over the barricades,

to collect rubble at the perimeter
hoping to build a house, part snow, part victory,
ice and sun balancing the untrained shafts,
part sheet music, part dust, sings often—
the parts open, flake, break open, let go.
Why so phantom, searching for a rag
to embellish the holes in my sonnet,
no tracks leading beyond and back,
no more retrograde song cycle tatting air.
These parts wobble, stitching frames
to improvise a document:
all this American life. Strike that.
All our life, all our American lives gathered
into an anthem we thought to rescue us,
over and out. On your way, dust.

TO BE WRITTEN IN NO OTHER COUNTRY

Now it is time for the scratch ticket
to bruise the inner wishes of single moms,
for night to be enough for the pensioner
and his "buster" in TV light.
If we were to answer the geese overhead
would we ever find a home
lost as we are in the kiddy section of Wal-Mart?
As a youth did Grant wonder
that he would become both a drunk
and president and die like Melville, forgotten,
buried under ambition and guilt.
It is a sorry day for the pollster and body electorate
for the mildewed pages of a wound dresser.
And when and whenever past Saturdays
of adolescents in faded Kodak
enter the discourse of politicians

know you are not alone and your scrapbook
will be enough in talk of resolutions
and what you plan to do this weekend
to the garage and to the porch.

PLAIN SONG

Some say a baby cries for the life to come
some say leaves are green 'cause it looks good against the
blue
some say the grasses blow because it is earth's instrument
some say we were born to cry

•

Some say that the sun comes close every year because it
wants to be near us
some say the waters rise to meet it
others say the moon is our mother, *ma mère*

•

Some say birds overhead are a calligraphy: every child
learning the words "home"
some say that the land and the language are the father
some say the land is not ours
some say in time we'll rise to meet it

•

Some say there are the rushes the geese the tributaries
and the reeds

•

Some say the song of the dove is an emblem of thought
some say lightning and some the electric light some say
they are brothers

•

Some say the current in the wall is the ground
some say the nervous system does not stop with the body
some say the body does not stop

•

Some say beauty is only how you look at it and some
beauty is what we have some say there is no beauty some
truth

•

Some say the ground is stable
others the earth is round
for some it is a stone
I say the earth is porous and we fall constantly

•

Some say light rings some say that light is a wave some
say it has a weight or there is a heft to it

•

Some say all of these things and some say not
some say the way of the beekeeper is not their way
some say the way of the beekeeper is the only way
some say simple things all there are are simple things

•

Some say "the good way," some "stuff"
some say yes we need a form
some say form is a simple thing some say yes the sky is a
form of what is simple

•

Some say molecular some open others porous some blue
some say love some light some say the dark some heaven

CHÂTEAU IF

Usage is more powerful than reason.
—Castiglione, *The Courtier*

If love if then if now if the flowers of if the conditional
if of arrows the condition of if
    if to say light to inhabit light if to speak if to live, so
    if to say it is you if love is if your form is if your waist
that pictures the fluted stem if lavender
    if in this field
    if I were to say hummingbird it might behave as an
adjective here
    if not if the heart's a flutter if nerves map a city if a city
on fire
    if I say myself am I saying myself (if in this instant)
as if the object of your gaze if in a sentence about love
you might write if one day if you would, so
    if to say myself if in this instance if to speak as another—
    if only to render if in time and accept if to live now as if
disembodied from the actual handwritten letters m-y-s-e-l-f
    if a creature if what you say if only to embroider—a city
that overtakes the city I write.

IN DEFENSE OF NOTHING

I guess these trailers lined up in the lot off the highway will do.
I guess that crooked eucalyptus tree also.
I guess this highway will have to do and the cars
    and the people in them on their way.
The present is always coming up to us, surrounding us.
It's hard to imagine atoms, hard to imagine
    hydrogen & oxygen binding, it'll have to do.
This sky with its macular clouds also
    and that electric tower to the left, one line broken free.

UNTITLED AMHERST SPECTER

a sound of open ground having been taken

now a silver wisp winking on the roof

silver imp waving from a long shaft ago

I am a leaf storm night

I have seen the long file of mule trains and metal

the cavalry

these sounds we live within speaking to you now

sir, I was a soldier in these woods

LAST CENTURY THOUGHTS IN SNOW TONIGHT

This is winter where light flits at the tips of things.
Sometimes I flit back and glitter.

Too much spectacle conquers the I.
This is winter where I walk out underneath it all.

What could I take from it? Astonishment?
I wore an extra blanket.

This is winter where childhood lanterns skate in the distance
where what we take is what we are given.

Some call it self-reliance. *Ça va?*
To understand our portion, our bright portion.

This is winter and this the winter portion
of self-reliance and last century thoughts in snow.

POETICS STATEMENT

Extract from a Letter to Steve Farmer

(From a talk at the Kelly Writer's House at the University of
Pennsylvania, 1999.)

As I listen to a poem unfold in my ear it becomes clear that for every line
I hear there are more lines resonating in the same field of meaning. Listen-
ing is everything in poetry: to the silences, the pauses, shifts in syntax, tone,
and content. Always for me a poem is about tracking what is not said and the
particular place I can go to know what that is by what is stated. As if there
are always two poems in my ear. What amazes me is how specific the "other"
or phantom poem can be, and it occurs to me how language, when arranged,
manipulated, built, or what you will, is saying both readings—together and
separate. I imagine that the lyric is next to my life, but it isn't my life at the
same time that it is real. Think of breath on a mirror. Sometimes, if I'm
lucky, I can record this "other" poem and make it my own. But mostly it is
a fragment felt and struggled with. I find myself left to develop the ruins of
what did not come through. These hours spent listening, however, are what
I believe to be the exceptional experience of poetry. The same way nightin-
gales inhabit Romanticism and are unsupported by any real concrete image:
"birds as words," Zukofsky would say. They are an experience in the mind
both heard and as Cavalcanti would suggest, "'tis felt I say." The problem
with trying to risk something, articulate something larger, is that it's bound
to failure, and the problem with taking on something stable is that it's bound
to succeed but it's ultimately unsatisfying. It's more complicated to use intui-
tive thought toward repair.

. . . I want the field of my work to also include other works, displacing con-
text to create narrative, emotional, psychological, and formal turbulence. I
think of these gestures of narrative disturbance, this quoting out of context,
this bending and borrowing and blending of tradition as musical notations
to create depth, emotive effect, even sincerity. I am interested in nostalgia
but I would renovate its use: it's not just a return to home (or origins, the
texts that inform me) but a survival of home (a process of individuation).
For an artist it means to survive the poems, texts that compose one—the
awesome ground (power) of Modernism. We are the children of Modern-
ism much in the way the ground for the troubadours was classical literature.
And there's an exhaustion to this process, this movement, because there is no
actual site to return to. As Steve Farmer puts it: a movement "from a desire
to critique/dismantle to a desire to rebuild." How to at once accommodate

the gorgeous traditions of poetry and the fact that we are also simply "folk"? To build a comprehensive music. . . .

. . . I guess what I'm after is closer to an environment, an experience of structure that collects in me. This condition of openness also figures a constant grappling with absence and lack. In a sense all my work is about this reckoning and displacement, enacted through an experience of lyric possession. A form of animism, but in it I would replace essentialism or soul with aesthetics or an empty core, a kind of holding open to allow tendencies of cadence, form, tone, coloring to move through the space of writing: a force that is both a construction of self and an emptying of self. Not autobiographical but autographical: flexible enough to accommodate figures, things, voices, documentation; to combine, build and dissolve being, boundaries—to somehow let the poem become itself.

PETER GIZZI'S CITY
The Political Quotidian

Cole Swensen

SINCE WHITMAN and Baudelaire, the everyday has increasingly been modern poetry's territory, revealing our conviction that art can live a daily life, and that art has a role in our daily lives. The fusion of art and daily life quickly became a cliché of the early twentieth-century avant-gardes, but it was also a concrete goal, and one with a political impetus. Once daily life was executed along artistic principles, they felt, the general populace would be released from the lethargy of dead-end materialism, and culture would no longer be co-optable as a simplistic index of class distinction.

The quotidian and the political are inherently connected, but while the daily has stayed in the foreground of European and North American poetics, politics has not always been so prominent. For several reasons—not the least being the number and urgency of current global political crises—poets are again putting the two together, but searching out ways to do it differently, to do it subtly, using the arts to refine and enlarge the definition of the political.

Peter Gizzi achieves this, not in only in his poetry, but in every aspect of his life. His various facets—writer, editor, critic, publisher, teacher, traveler, citizen—cannot be separated from one another, nor any of them seen apart from his poetry. They function as a single gesture, one that is political in the deepest sense: it brings the other into the everyday.

For Gizzi, the political starts with the very word and its root in the polis. His individual poems are sited there, in the city, which he sees both as a dense heterogeneity and as community. Though those two views may seem contradictory, bridging contradiction through language is what Gizzi does. He makes his poems into cities themselves; they are diverse but synchronized collectivities. The long poem "Etudes, Evidence, or a Working Definition of the Sun Gear," from his most recent book *Some Values of Landscape and Weather*, is such a collectivity, but it also brings us to a real city, Marseille, and to human confluence and community in general.

Stylistically, the poem is representative of much of his work in that it blends three tendencies from three historic periods: a twentieth-century fascination with the daily, manifest in both language and content; a late twentieth- early twenty-first-century aesthetic of fragmentation that implicitly explores the distinction between juxtaposition and disjunction; and an early nineteenth-century Romantic appreciation of loss.

Gizzi's engagement with the daily parallels those aspects of American society that are increasingly secular and committed to the immanent as opposed to the transcendent, trends that date back to the early nineteenth century. In Gizzi's work, however, it's more immediately rooted in American Modernism from Pound and Stein through Williams and on up to the New York School, whose writers had an eye for the poetic within the everyday to the highest degree.

Gizzi's poems are full of objects we see every day: freeways, flagpoles, birds, bricks, and clouds. They evoke familiar situations that take place in recognizable surroundings, and he presents them in speech-based phrasing: "How come all the best images are uncanny?" (49); "Spider webs are scarier / when you have a mortal disease, / or just creepier, more final / somehow" (44). "How come," "scarier," "creepier" are not only mundane, they're aggressively casual; they belong to the ephemeral world of passing conversation, so their appearance on a page has a startling incongruity.

The Varied Fragment

Because such terms are ephemeral, we get them only in pieces, glimpses. It's as if all the things his swift language brings us were caught in the corner of the eye, in turn suggesting that fragmentation—that hallmark of the postmodern—is based in part in a fascination with motion. In Gizzi's work, the motion is usually double: both the thing seen and the seeing thing are moving, requiring a sort of perceptual calculus that poetry, with its tendency to keep language itself in motion, is particularly good at. Formally, Gizzi's normally correct syntax breaks down rarely enough to keep its ruptures startling, yet often enough to establish fragmentation as an aesthetic and philosophic choice.

Aesthetically, fragmentation accentuates edges and, like the high-contrast shots of film noir, gives an attentive, almost nervy feel, counteracting the complacency that his often homey imagery and phrasing might otherwise invite. Gizzi is an avid film buff, and his work is full of just this sort of oblique adaptation of cinematic principles. Philosophically, fragmentation opens up abysses that implicitly question the balance of absence and presence: is what is *not there* more powerful in its absence and insinuation that what *is* there? Fragmentation tests our intuitive notion that there's a hollow at the core of things. Is it a hollow? Or is it a bit of anti-matter to match every bit of matter? Either way, the fragment is demanding. It requires the reader either to "tread water in mid-air" or to complete, at a split-second's notice, this incomplete thing.

On a more abstract level, any fragment questions the very concept of completeness, just as it questions the concept of the incomplete; it asserts the validity of all those anarchical things that cannot be made into parts of some larger whole. Any fragment allows the essentially heterogeneous nature of the world to show through. Gizzi's poems are, in this respect, realistic: he doesn't use grammatical or imagistic fluidity to create the illusion that the world out there is itself a smooth flow.

Gizzi's fragmentation also highlights a play between juxtaposition and disjunction. These two appear similar, but imply radically different approaches to and assumptions about connection. They both startle, and they both split the mind's attention—a little like a stereoscope fitted out with two different images. But while juxtaposition makes us aware of the immense potential for connection across physical and conceptual distances, disjunction raises the possibility of irreconcilable difference. Using both, as Gizzi does, guarantees a dynamic restlessness throughout the text.

More important, however, using both makes us consider their very distinction and query our own sense of the world's integration. Is this a world with sufficient inherent connectivity to allow almost any two things to shed some kind of light on each other (as juxtaposition argues)? Or is it one that features a "center that will not hold," generating perspectives that can't be reconciled (disjunction)? Each view has its political ramifications, and while neither is "true," there may be a truth revealed by the alternative one chooses. Gizzi, for the most part, chooses juxtaposition, in keeping with the many other bridging activities built into both his poetry and his life.

Juxtaposition can also be seen as a version of the reconciliation of opposites so important to the Romantics. And in many ways, Gizzi's work is firmly rooted in the Romantic tradition: his are, for the most part, first-person lyric poems focused on the emotions as experienced by a integrated and consistent subject, with love as the ruling sentiment. That love often takes the form of longing, which by extension becomes a love of longing itself. And the longing is *for* the self; it's a nostalgic glance backward by an "I" that can't quite believe in the ideal, consolidated subject and the coherent world that such a subjectivity constructs, even as it speaks from that subject position.

THE DESIRE FOR LOSS

"I want an art that can say how I'm feeling," Gizzi states in "Revival"—in a context shot through with the unattainability of both the "I" and the art. A later line in the poem, "For want of a sound to call my own," is equally ambiguous: is it the "sound" or is it the "I" behind the "my" that's missing? Or both? And to what degree are these losses interdependent, with the "I" disappearing for want of a vehicle of expression? The slightly tongue-in-cheek opening of another poem, "A history of the lyric" ("I lost you to the inky noise") shows that he's aware of his investment in loss, and aware that it's bound up with writing, thus with representation, thus with doubling. It's a loss we're all refusing to let go of in this society increasingly invested in representation.

On the other hand, throughout Gizzi's work, other lines and passages adopt the Romantic posture without apology or other subtext. "Desire rose in the lofty tree of those evenings" (31) states one, with the single word "those" making the evenings impossibly distant, as inimitable as the originals are unattainable. Gizzi uses loss/longing to establish something analogous to atmospheric perspective—a series of receding tones that draw the reading mind further on—which allows him to go beyond the modernist immanence-of-the-daily without encountering the problems of hierarchy imposed by transcendence.

He also uses loss to record and explore a very real, acute sensation, one that is both personal and political. The entire long poem "Revival" is about the loss America has made of itself, and about the dangerous way that we compensate ourselves for that loss by enjoying it. It's the principle that drives an Edward Hopper painting, and we keep updating it everywhere from popular songs and Hollywood movies to the "retro" craze in home decorating.

THE URBAN WALKING POEM

These three stylistic principles—the quotidian, fragmentation, and longing—come together in the theme of "Etudes, Evidence," as signaled by its epigraphs: "Many elements are common to many things, as letters are to words" (Lucretius), and "The organization of movement is the organization of its elements, or its intervals, into phrases" (Dziga Vertov).

In the broadest sense, the question that both haunts and drives Gizzi's poetry is "How are things put together?" Which quickly extends to "And how do they hold?" "Etudes, Evidence" adds another layer to these questions by asking how deep the structural parallel between language and the physical world goes. Is there any accuracy—and/or is there any point—to asserting that the elements of the world are arranged according to a kind of syntax? And what kind of order does that syntax demand? Is it a restrictive one or a generative one?

Early on, Gizzi establishes a parallel, not only between language and the physical world, but specifically between language and the city, and he does it through simple splicing, using the same kind of juxtaposition that characterizes the urban landscape. The phrases "full, volumetric night, scribbling streets," "the color blue today has 26 hues," and "the shaped light is making the curve of an *s*, / loop of *e*, the crown of *a* as boats / in spilled ink sway" (69) all occur in the first page.

"Etudes, Evidence" is an urban walking poem, in the family of Apollinaire's "Zone," and the journey is a true one in that the "I" emerges change. At the same time, however, because it's an urban journey, it's circular; it leads nowhere. There is no distance covered, only ground. This is also true of another, much shorter poem in the book, "It was Raining in Delft." The way that the "I" walks that city, recording impressions and his reflections on them, suggests a causal relationship: the things of this world cause the things of the mind. It's a subtle demonstration of Williams's "no ideas but in things."

The world, then, walks into the person, rather than the other way around. This view of the human/world interface is particularly apparent in a cityscape, which, unlike a landscape, has no horizon pulling one along a progressive, linear path; instead, it constantly mirrors itself, as well as your own face, back to you in buildings and windows; its roads keep turning corners; urban public transportation runs in circles, and more and more, cities are bounded by ring-roads, more effective barriers than ancient city walls.

These poems model not traditional extensive walking, but rather an intensive kind, which serves as a metaphor for poetic rather than discursive uses of language, in that both intensive walking and poetic language work by building up layers on a predefined and limited surface, compressing and complicating it. The sun in the "Etudes, Evidence" title is emblematic of this for Gizzi, who has commented that the Mediterranean sun feels so intense and so ancient that it resembles a *nihonto*, a Japanese sword made by pounding the metal out and folding it back upon itself time and again.

"Etudes, Evidence" is a poem of arrivals; it operates as a gate, taking in whatever comes, and taking it as it comes, making no comparisons, value judgments, or distinctions of scale or importance. This discourages relationships among the poem's (and the city's) elements, on the one hand, but on the other, it encourages us to see each element in its own right. Gizzi has created a poem-as-receiver along Spicer's radio model, taking the city's dictation.

Deregulating the Senses

Just as Gizzi's perceptions are not arranged hierarchically, neither are his senses. Gizzi has inherited from Rimbaud a recognition of what a "dérèglement de tous les sens" can do, and he uses the principle to create certain effects, particularly a synesthesia that operates as an equalizing force—"the chubby honk of tugs by the pier" (70), "a ricochet of boys in the street" (72), "The big green day is peeling" (72). While keeping the elements themselves distinct, he suspends our habit of privileging certain senses over others, which keeps his sensual evocations bright and alive.

Gizzi uses "senses" in the widest sense, too—in short, he adds a few. Color, for instance. For Gizzi, color is another channel through which we acquire raw data on the world. By presenting it in unexpected places (green day, blue-hued letters), he augments the information imparted by each object. Color also exists as an element in its own right: the boats in spilled ink, for instance, sway "from indigo to silver." Color-as-element holds true throughout Gizzi's work; further, a line in "The Quest" ("I want you / muted in the overall chromo") suggests color as a principal medium of daily life.

Another of Gizzi's extra senses is language. And it's a pro-active sense; it doesn't wait for stimuli, but instead moves through the world, actively seeking the raw material of its sensations. Thus, Gizzi makes language into a kind of human sonar, projected ahead of us to take soundings of the world. Like color, language isn't only a sense, but is also a thing among the things of this world. "Between buildings and sky is a GULF / and CINEMA" (70)—among the things of this world, are words any less real than their referents?

Part and Whole

Lines such as the one above also point to the larger question of representation, which Gizzi raises in the opening line of "Etudes, Evidence": "In the picture of a thought the *f*-stop opens" (69). He soon reinforces it by mentioning "lens" in the third line. We're immediately reminded that "all seeing is seeing as." And as such, is all seeing equal? About halfway through the poem, Gizzi begins to describe a postcard reproduction of Trevor Winkfield's painting *Still Life*, and yet the frame is left unclear. Where do the objects listed stop being those represented in the painting and go back to being those represented in the poem? And is one more mediated than the other? And, again, would that make it any less (or more?) real?

Through such blurred framing, Gizzi addresses the relativity of representation and underscores the volatility of any given point of view. Ambiguous frames also make us aware of how arbitrary such delimitations always are. They invite analogy with conceptual frames such as the one that keeps language apart from the world, or the one that separates inside from outside, or nature from culture. As he says a little further on, "if you step back is it all nature?" (73).

And how far do we have to step back before this essential kinship is recognizable? Do we keep stepping back until we see a whole? And are we ever likely to encounter one in this work in which, as mentioned above, almost everything occurs in fragments? This poem, like many others, is composed of brief images caught in accidental and momentary frames that dislocate them from their contexts, and clips of overheard language similarly removed from a larger sense-field. Even his inner mental reflections seem to be only the most current word on much longer considerations or speculations. This compositional strategy frees things from their narrative and dramatic histories, allowing them to mingle with each other and with our own associations. It effectively makes the reading mind into the support for a vast collage. And yet his poetic form undercuts and complicates this conceptual form, for the poem is written largely in complete sentences. This silent contradiction makes us reexamine our notion of "a whole." To what degree is our sense of the whole in all aspects—visual, sensational, situational—based on the grammatical definition of a whole? A complete sentence is "a complete thought," we're taught. And we take the abstract and unrealizable ideal of "a complete thought" as a model for completeness in other aspects of life.

Gizzi often uses variations on this compositional scheme. "Revival" offers a particularly rich part/whole dynamic. Here, too, he frequently uses complete sentences, but he mixes in others that begin normally and then gradually break down. For instance:

> To be the son of a large man who rose out of depression
> and the middle world war, poverty and race
> to loom in mid-sixties industrial American air,
> survived classic notions of the atom,
> to think to be.
>
> (48)

While it flows unimpeded, it's actually composed of the fragments of at least three different complete sentences. Its subject matter is equally clipped, a mix of shorthand ("mid-sixties industrial American"—a phrase that captures so much more than a place and time) and half-formed ideas ("to think to be"—who's thinking? to be what? pointing to Shakespeare? or Descartes?). This emphatic play between parts and wholes suggests that fragments are wholes in their own right, based not on grammar, but on availability— whatever your eye grasps, whatever your ear catches is always, in itself, an entirety.

The concept of wholeness, too, has political ramifications, and "Revival" touches on these toward the end of the poem, where he begins listing parts:

hoping to build a house, part snow, part victory,
ice and sun balancing the untrained shafts,
part sheet music, part dust, sings often—
the parts open, flake, break open, let go.

(52)

These lines suggest a different kind of whole, one that is not necessarily seamless or homogeneous, one that, in fact, echoes contemporary American demographics, modeling a kind of diversity on the page. Gizzi doesn't confine it to the page, though; for him, the polis of poetry is linked to a living community, one that has little to do with the local, or with likeness, but that responds to our increasing need for the arts to show a larger international front.

INTERNATIONALITY

"Etudes, Evidence" participates in such a front by crossing borders into another country and another language without capitalizing on or fetishizing their differences. The dual-language title is emblematic; the beginning assonance links the two words despite their belonging to different linguistic systems, effectively creating a new system to which they both belong. His use of French expressions and phrases throughout this predominantly English-language poem operates in the same way; it unites languages' differences without diminishing them. In addition, because the title's second word "evidence" has meanings (albeit slightly different) in both French and English, it disrupts the notion of a language as a self-contained system that is the property of a particular people or region.

Gizzi's work has been influenced by the internationalism inherent in early Modernism as well as by examples much closer to home, particularly the internationalism of Rosmarie and Keith Waldrop and their Burning Deck Press with its two series of works in translation, Série d'écriture and Dichten=. Over the years, he has been involved in a number of projects that use poetry to de-nationalize language.

At the Fondation Royaumont in 1990, *o·blēk*, the journal Gizzi cofounded and coedited with Connell McGrath, was the focus of a three-day conference, and he returned there a few years later to take part in an international translation conference and a French-American colloquium. He has also spent time at the Centre Internationale de Poésie Marseille, in 1998 for both a seminar with Un bureau sur l'Atlantique, a project run by Emmanuel Hocquard to foster French-American poetic exchange, and a seminar on poetics and film. He returned in 1999 to spend the fall in a residency at the center, where poems from *Some Values of Landscape and Weather*, including

"Revival," were translated into French and published in a chapbook titled *Revival*. And most recently, he spent the summer of 2004 in residence at an international center in Madrid. As the term "residency" implies, everywhere he's stayed, no matter how long, he's done so, not as a visitor, but as a resident, simply living the local and the daily.

Because Gizzi is always simply living and never visiting, he can write about various places without becoming scenic, didactic, or exotic. By its very nature, the mundane cannot be other. But Gizzi fits well into other cultures in part because there's an aspect of alienation inherent in his relationship with himself: he can, and often does, take himself as other, which drives many of his poems in which the I or the self is questioned. This is not the disappearing "I" mentioned earlier, but an "I" that, despite (or perhaps even because of) an intense presence, has become alien.

In "It was Raining in Delft," he observes, "I am far and I am an animal and I am just another I-am poem" (81). "Take the 5:10 to Dreamland" opens, "Sometimes I am so far from myself" (36). Other entire poems, such as "Wind" (31) are largely about this self-distance. Beginning with the direct, "Who isn't a stranger collating stones," the poem ends with reentry, but it's not into the self; instead, it's into "the song, the street, the house, the shower." The self is continually moving away from itself, becoming other.

TROUBADOUR

Poetry is a mode of travel for Gizzi, and it has taken him elsewhere in time as well as in place. In Provence in 1999, he began a study of the Troubadour poets, a tradition that took him back to the twelfth century. It's a tradition that, in turn, incorporated several others, creating a cosmopolitan mix from the Catalan, Celtic, Arabic, and Latin influences on Provençal. Yet what the Troubadours did with the lyric was wholly new, and some, including Nietzsche in *Beyond Good and Evil*, place them at the root of contemporary European culture because of their revolutionary concepts of romantic love and the role of the individual.[1] Gizzi, recognizing the Troubadour tradition's historical force as well as its key position in the development of the lyric, wanted not only to embrace that tradition as a reader, but also to respond to it in his writing. His response became the chapbook *Fin Amor* (later reprinted in *Some Values of Landscape and Weather*).

"Fin amor" is the Troubadour expression for ideal love, a purified emotion distilled from time and place, and a concept central to and unique to the Troubadour poets. Again, Gizzi's title functions as a bridge. It links the present (through the contemporary French words "fin/e" and "amour") with the ancient (through the old Provençal words "fin" and "amor"). All French speakers and most English will instantly recognize the title, but may not recognize that they are spanning centuries to read a language that hasn't been in daily use for generations.

The "fin" of the title can also be read as "end," thus offering a second title with an opposite meaning, which lets it function as an autoantonym or Janus-word, those words, such as *cleave*, that have two opposite meanings, and that, by encompassing both what they are and what they are not, manage to grasp an uncanny entirety. Throughout the collection, we constantly feel both the great span of time and a haunting timelessness.

The title of the first poem in the chapbook, "Château If," sends us firmly into the past with its allusion to the sixteenth-century castle in Marseille harbor, the Château d'If of Alexander Dumas's *The Count of Monte Cristo*, and yet the poem keeps us in the present with postmodern punning and contemporary syntax and form. "An Allegory of Doubt" also spans time, reaching back to the beginning of the twentieth century and Giacomo Balla's Italian Futurist experiments with motion in painting, and from there, even further back to colonial times—all reported in the present tense. Another poem, "Plain Song," achieves this span through form, using the eerie and echoing voice of proverbs. The anonymity, or even communal nature, of proverbs is underscored by the recurrent "some say," which seems to gather generations of disparate speakers all into its sweep.

THE CANTE JONDO

Gizzi's poetry is rooted in the lyric tradition; indeed, *Some Values of Landscape and Weather* opens with a series titled "The History of the Lyric" (3). He is interested in maintaining a connection to song, but in doing so through exclusively poetic means rather than by borrowing music's signature devices, such as foregrounded rhythm and rhyme-based sound relationships. Two of his methods are anaphora, the litany-like repetition of opening words or phrases, and nonce structures, formal structures created for a single use.

The seven-part poem "Masters of the Cante Jondo" (57) takes a third approach. It roughly follows the course of a flamenco song through its denser and lighter modes and its passages of call and response, introspection, and passionate outburst. Rather than translate music into words, Gizzi aims for the force behind it.

The question underlying this serial poem is a version of his larger question, "How are things put together?" And the answer begins (again) in the title: in evoking the Cante Jondo, or deep song, made widely known by Lorca in his essay on the *duende*, Gizzi is seeking the connective principle that distinguishes the arts from other modes of expression. He pushes the question further, past what the arts have in common, to explore how poetry might bring into its own body the "other" of the other arts (in this case, music)—and, by extension, how it might incorporate the other of outside experience in general. Such incorporation is precisely *not* translation, which would change one body into another; instead, it involves a kind of possession of the sort Lorca claims is an integral aspect of flamenco.

But, as Lorca goes on to say, the only guarantee of such possession is its untraceability, so Gizzi can't approach his project directly. He does, however, incorporate the body of this other art, in part, by taking its voice, by mouthing its words in this new context. This is the essence of tradition. Building off of Spicer's ideas in his letters to Lorca, Gizzi sees tradition not as an accumulation, but as repetition: we are all playing the same song, writing the same poem, and the artist's challenge is to re-create the enabling conditions. In "The Masters of Cante Jondo," Gizzi finds the enabling conditions in the city; two lines in particular, "and the shape of our walk become pages / become pavement underfoot" (62) reinforce the city/poetry/walking equations cited earlier. But they also augment the walk with the turns of the dance, suggesting urban density in the form of a human body, winding itself always more tightly. By the end of section 4 (song), he is able to say:

> By the time of this speech
> the original has vanished
>
> without promising emancipation
> The sound is a body
>
> This sound is my body
>
> (61)

While the Troubadours allowed Gizzi a deeper encounter with Provence, flamenco allowed him an entrance into Spain. In each case, he has used a traditional mode of song to deepen his understanding of the specific lyric qualities indigenous to an area, both for the formal and conceptual models it offers him as a writer and for all that it tells him of the otherwise inarticulable aspects of the region and its poetry.

Spicer and Atemporality

Gizzi inherited not only his take on tradition from Spicer, but also his notion of the necessary atemporality of poetry. Materially, atemporality is inherent to poetry; though rhythm may be language's timekeeper, it is syntax that keeps that time in order, keeps it consistent and unidirectional. Even poetry such as Gizzi's, which makes much use of the full sentence, takes syntactic liberties that disrupt the uniformity of time and contribute to a general temporal suspension.

More important, however, conceptually, atemporality is entwined with tradition. Only by denying time through rewriting an earlier poem (in some nonidentical way, of course) can a poet of today converse with poets of earlier eras without reducing the earlier poet to the terms of the present. In this way, atemporality guarantees the survival of difference.

Gizzi's ongoing conversation with Jack Spicer is an excellent case in point. Through editing Spicer's lectures for his book *The House that Jack Built*, writing the book's afterword, and now editing his previously unpublished last poems, Gizzi has come not only to understand but also to experience Spicer's concept of atemporal conversation. It's less an exchange of ideas than a matter of sharing a space—the space of the poem.

Contemporaneity has nothing to do with time; one's contemporaries might be centuries in either direction. Rather, it's based on a slippage of ideas, which is itself made possible by alignment—again, a spatial rather than a temporal issue. Gizzi seeks out his contemporaries, but particularly enjoys finding them in other countries and other centuries because the need to span such distances increases the space his poetry occupies.

THE COMMUNITY OF US AND THEM

Gizzi always parallels what he's doing in his poetry with activities in the public sphere. The parallel to this poetic exploration of other countries and other times is in his editing and publishing. *o·blēk* magazine, which he cofounded and coedited from 1987 to 1993, routinely presented work that crossed national, linguistic, and genre boundaries, and included, among others, pieces by Claude Royet-Journoud, Emmanuel Hocquard, Edmond Jabès, Anne-Marie Albiach, Georg Trakl, Jean Grosjean, and Isabelle Baladine Hovald. And among the very few books that *o·blēk* published were Emmanuel Hocquard's *Theory of Tables* (translated by Michael Palmer), and a visual/verbal collaboration between Clark Coolidge and Philip Guston titled *Baffling Means*. This cross-media work comes out of a lifelong interest in the visual arts that stretches from painting to film and includes the book, which he views as a unique and complex object rather than as a container for otherwise disembodied language.

His 1995 anthology for Exact Change Press, *The Exact Change Yearbook* was guided by the same border-crossing principles, and gave him the opportunity to emphasize both the visual and the international.[2] In that volume, he gathered poets, translators, and commentators and created separate sections of work from France, China, Germany, Canada, the Carribean, the United Kingdom, and Ireland into a volume that demonstrates the international influence of literary Modernism and the diverse experiments it spawned.

In 1992, with Julianna Spahr, Gizzi organized and produced a large national conference that brought more than a hundred poets together to discuss new directions for experimentation.[3] Held at the State University of New York at Buffalo, the conference's three days of papers, roundtable discussions, and readings marked the opening of a generalized discussion about post–L=A=N=G=U=A=G=E experimentation that embraced the earlier movement's political emphasis while addressing additional and differing goals, including a return to the "I"—though kept under scrutiny, and in fact, often used as a tool of scrutiny, as Gizzi does.

The one common denominator among all Gizzi's projects is their focus on community. Together, they form a body of work that makes readers and listeners consider just what community means. Perhaps at its most basic, it simply means "us"—an equally slippery, but less abstract term, for while the referent may slide, it's always composed of tangible bodies. And in asking about us, we must also ask about "them." In its vagueness, "they" often has an ominous aura; it is, at its most basic, "what is not us." Gizzi, curiously enough, has almost no "they" in his poetry; instead, it's full of "I," "you," "we," and "us," which amounts to a radical assumption of responsibility and a refusal to see anyone as categorically other. Such usage is consistent with his attempts to build community through an exploration and eventual retrenchment of the self.

For the most part, he uses the terms "you," "we," and "us" in both an intimate and an open-ended, inclusive way. Anyone is welcome to step into the "we" of a line such as "if we ask that every song touch its origin" ("A Panic That Can Still Come Upon Me") or "The difficulty of being here is what do we transmit of ourselves that we can ever really know?" (33). Gizzi's pronouns not only welcome everyone, they assume, even require, everyone's participation.

Reading Gizzi's work makes you a member of a community. And though it's true that all acts of reading create community, because Gizzi is particularly focused on this role of literature, access to community through his work is unusually heightened. You enter these pages and become a word: "you" or "we" or "us," or even, through empathy, "I."

Thus, Gizzi's poetry constructs a community of words, a city of words. But it's not the famous city of words that Plato discusses in the *Republic*, that just city that exists only in the mind or soul; it's a city of words that can and *does* exist on earth, and that can, through its dedication to the polis, have a political effect in the world.

NOTES

1. Friedrich Nietzsche, *Beyond Good and Evil*, trans. Walter Kaufmann (New York: Random House, 1989), 208.

2. Peter Gizzi, ed., *Exact Change Yearbook* (Boston: Exact Change, 1995).

3. Peter Gizzi, ed., *Writing from the New Coast* (Stockbridge, Mass.: Garlic Press, *o·blēk* Editions, 1993). This two-volume issue presents creative and critical works by the conference participants.

BIBLIOGRAPHY

Books by Peter Gizzi

Creeley Madrigal (on handmade paper by Pam Rehm). Providence, R.I.: Materials Press, 1991.
Music for Films. Providence, R.I.: Paradigm, 1992.
Periplum (with artwork by Trevor Winkfield). Penngrove, Calif.: Avec Books, 1992.
Hours of the Book (with artwork by Antoni Tapies). Gran Canaria, Spain: Zasterle, 1994.
Ledger Domain (with artwork by Trevor Winkfield). Providence, R.I.: Timoleon, 1995.
New Picnic Time. Buffalo, N.Y.: Meow Press, 1995.
Artificial Heart. Providence, R.I.: Burning Deck, 1998 [2000].
Add This to the House. Cambridge: Equipage, 1999.
Château If (with artwork by Anne Slacik). Paris: Anne Slacik Editions, 2000.
Revival (with artwork by David Byrne). New Haven, Conn.: Phylum, 2002.
Fin Amor (with artwork by George Herms). Oakland, Calif.: Tougher Disguises, 2002.
Some Values of Landscape and Weather. Middletown, Conn.: Wesleyan University Press, 2003 [2005].
From a Cinematographer's Letter (with artwork by Tom Raworth). London: Tolling Elves, 2004.
Periplum and other poems, 1987–1992, Cambridge: Salt Publishers, 2004.

Other Publications by Peter Gizzi

o·blēk: A Journal of Language Arts (coeditor). Stockbridge, Mass.: Garlic Press, 1987–93.
Exact Change Yearbook (editor). Cambridge, Mass.: Exact Change / Manchester, U.K.: Carcanet, 1995.
The House That Jack Built: The Collected Lectures of Jack Spicer (editor and author of afterword). Middletown, Conn.: Wesleyan University Press, 1998 [2005].

Selected Prose

"An Occult Circuitry: Jack Spicer and Poetic Dictation." *The Recovery of the Public World*. Edited by Edward Byrne and Charles Watts. Vancouver: Talonbooks, 1999.
"A Note on James Schuyler's 'February.'" In *Dark Horses: Poets on Overlooked Poems*, edited by Joy Katz and Kevin Prufer. Urbana: University of Illinois Press, 2005.
"*The Bernadette Mayer Reader*." *The Poetry Project Newsletter*, No. 146 (September–October 1992).
"Blaser and Prynne." *Lingua Franca: The Review of Academic Life* (May–June 2002).
"*The Collected Poems of James Schuyler*." *Lingo*, No. 2 (1993).

"Correspondences of the Book" (a meditation on John Ruskin and Emily Dickinson). In *The Poetics of Criticism*, edited by J. Spahr, K. Prevalet, M. Wallace, and P. Rehm. Albany: State University of New York Press, 1994.

Foreword to *Writing from the New Coast: Presentation. o·blēk*, No. 12 (1993).

"For the Time Being." *Writing from the New Coast: Technique. o·blēk*, No. 12 (1993).

"*Gnomic Verses*." By Robert Creeley. *Washington Review* 18, no. 4 (February–March 1993).

"In Lieu of an Introduction for John Yau." *Talisman*, No. 5 (1990).

"Introduction to *The House that Jack Built*." *American Poetry Review* 27, no. 1 (1998).

"Jack Spicer and the Practice of Reading." In *The House that Jack Built: The Collected Lectures of Jack Spicer*. Middletown, Conn.: Wesleyan University Press, 1998.

"Leon-Paul Fargue." Preface to a collection of Fargue's poems translated by Peter Thompson. Lewiston, N.Y.: Mellen Press, 2003.

"*One Big Self: Prisoners of Louisiana*." Photographs by Deborah Luster and text by C. D. Wright. *Rain Taxi: Review of Books* 9, no. 3 (2004).

"On the Conjunction of Editing & Composition." *Review of Contemporary Fiction* (Bradford Morrow Issue). Edited by Jonathan Foer. 2002.

"Out of Time: Bruce Conner 2002 B.C." *Modern Painters* (London) 15, no. 3 (2002).

"Poetry & Politics: The California Lecture of Jack Spicer." *American Poetry Review* 27, no. 1 (1998).

"*Potential Random* by Keith Waldrop." *Washington Review* 18, no. 4 (February–March 1993).

"Richard Linklater's Film *Waking Life*." *Modern Painters* (London) 15, no. 1 (2002).

"*The Selected Poems of Ron Padgett*." *Small Press Magazine*, Providence, R.I.: Moyer Bell Press, 1996.

"The Serial Poem and *The Holy Grail*." *Boxkite: An International Journal of Contemporary Poetics*, No. 2. Sydney, Australia, 1998.

"Textual Mirroring." Special Feature on the Poetry of Jack Spicer. Edited by Chris Alexander. *Jacket: international poetry on-line*, No. 7 (April 1999).

"*The William Corbett Issue of Lift*." *Small Press Magazine*. Providence, R.I.: Moyer Bell Press. 1995.

Interviews

Hammer, Mark. 1992. Interview and profile of Peter Gizzi. *Art Voice* (September 23, 1992): 28.

Kane, Daniel. 2001. "Poets Chat: Poets on Poetry." Interview with Peter Gizzi. *Teachers & Writers* (May–June); online.

Kunin, Aaron. 2003–2004. "In the Moment of Looking." Interview with Peter Gizzi. *Rain Taxi* (Winter): 20–22.

Selected Criticism

Anderson, Beth. 1998. Review of *Artificial Heart*. *Poetry Project Newsletter* (June–July): 4–5.

Andrews, Ruth. 1999. Review of *Artificial Heart*. *Rain Taxi Online Edition* (Spring); online.

Boughn, Michael. 1993. Review of *Periplum*. *Poetry Project Newsletter* (February–March): 19–20.

Davis, Jordan. 1995. Review of *Exact Change Yearbook*. *Poetry Project Newsletter* (April–May): 22–23.

———. 2004. "Gizzi's Lyrical Sublime." Review of *Some Values of Landscape and Weather*. *Village Voice* (January 7–13): C75.

Foust, Graham. 1998. Review of *Artificial Heart*. *Washington Review* (October–November): 28–29.

———. 2004. Review of *Some Values of Landscape and Weather*. *Verse* (December); online.

Gilbert, Alan. 1994. Review of *Periplum*. *Denver Quarterly* (Spring): 111–13.

———. 1998. Review of *Artificial Heart*. *Chicago Review* (Summer): 197–200.

Gonzalez, Ray. 2004. Review of *Some Values of Landscape and Weather*. *Bloomsbury Review* (March–April): 12.

Green, Joshua. 2002. Review of *Artificial Heart*. *Boston Review* (April–May): 69–70.

Henry, Brian. 2004. Review of *Some Values of Landscape and Weather*. *Times Literary Supplement* (February 27): 30.

Joron, Andrew. 1998. "After Spicer." Review of *Artificial Heart*. *Hambone* (Fall): 207–12. Reprinted, 1999, *Jacket* 7 (April); online.

Kinsella, John. 2004. "A Spot of Wordplay in Clement Times." Review of *Some Values of Landscape and Weather*. *Sydney Morning Herald* (April 9–11): 12.

McLane, Maureen N. 2003. "Poets of Our Climate." *Boston Globe* (April 13): E2–3.

Mills, Bronwyn. 2004. Review of *Some Values of Landscape and Weather*. *Talisman* (Winter): 126.

Olson, John. 1999. Review of *Artificial Heart*. *American Book Review* (January–February): 4 and 10.

Palattella, John. 2004. "A Delicate Balance." Review of *Some Values of Landscape and Weather*. *Los Angeles Times* (March 21): R16.

Perloff, Marjorie. 1995. Review of *Exact Change Yearbook*. *Sulfur* (Fall): 245–48.

———. 1998. Review of *Artificial Heart*. *Boston Book Review* (July–August): 34–35.

Peterson, Tim. 2004. Review of *Some Values of Landscape and Weather*. *Harvard Review* (Spring): 195–97.

Philips, Brian. 2005. Review of *Some Values of Landscape and Weather*. *POETRY* (February): 392–93.

Powell, D. A. 1993. "Tight Pants." Review of *Periplum*. *San Francisco Poetry Flash* (July–August): 28.

Riley, Peter. 2004. "A Skateboard on a Ridge." Review of *Some Values of Landscape and Weather*. *P.N. Review* (July–August): 76–77. Reprinted, 2004, *Jacket* 25 (February); online.

Tejada, Roberto. 1998. Review of *Artificial Heart*. *Sulfur* (Fall): 201–203.

Tost, Tony. 2004. Review of *Some Values of Landscape and Weather*. *Octopus Magazine* (Spring); online.

Tursi, Mark. 2004. "Dotted Archipelagoes of Language." Review of *Some Values of Landscape and Weather*. *English Studies Forum* (Summer); online.

Vetock, Jeff. 1993. Review of *Periplum*. *Washington Review* (April–May): 23–24.

Zawacki, Andrew. 2004. "Poetry in Motion." Review of *Some Values of Landscape and Weather*. *Boston Review* (Summer): 64–66.

JULIANA SPAHR

GENTLE NOW, DON'T ADD TO HEARTACHE

I.

We come into the world.
We come into the world and there it is.
The sun is there.
The brown of the river leading to the blue and the brown of the ocean is
        there.
Salmon and eels are there moving between the brown and the brown and
        the blue.
The green of the land is there.
Elders and youngers are there.
Fighting and possibility and love are there.
And we begin to breathe.
We come into the world and there it is.
We come into the world without and we breathe it in.
We come into the world.
We come into the world and we too begin to move between the brown
        and the blue and the green of it.

II.

We came into the world at the edge of a stream.
The stream had no name but it began from a spring and flowed down a
        hill into the Scioto that then flowed into the Ohio that then flowed
        into the Mississippi that then flowed into the Gulf of Mexico.
The stream was a part of us and we were a part of the stream and we were
        thus part of the rivers and thus part of the gulfs and the oceans.
And we began to learn the stream.

We looked under stones for the caddisfly larvae and its adhesive.

We counted the creek chub and we counted the slenderhead darter.

We learned to recognize the large, upright, dense, candle-like clusters
of yellowish flowers at the branch ends of the horsechestnut and
we appreciated the feathery gracefulness of the drooping, but
upturning, branchlets of the larch.

We mimicked the catlike meow, the soft quirrt or kwut, and the louder,
grating ratchet calls of the gray catbird.

We put our heads together.

We put our heads together with all these things, with the caddisfly larva,
with the creek chub and the slenderhead darter, with the
horsechestnut and the larch, with the gray catbird.

We put our heads together on a narrow pillow, on a stone, on a narrow
stone pillow, and we talked to each other all day long because we
loved.

We loved the stream.

And we were of the stream.

And we couldn't help this love because we arrived at the bank of the
stream and began breathing and the stream was various and full of
information and it changed our bodies with its rotten with its cold
with its clean with its mucky with fallen leaves with its things
that bite the edges of the skin with its leaves with its sand and dirt
with its pungent at moments with its dry and prickly with its
warmth with its mushy and moist with its hard flat stones on the
bottom with its horizon lines of gently rolling hills with its
darkness with its dappled light with its cicadas buzz with its trills
of birds.

III.

This is where we learned love and where we learned depth and where we
learned layers and where we learned connections between layers.

We learned and we loved the black sandshell, the ash, the american
bittern, the harelip sucker, the yellow bullhead, the beech, the
great blue heron, the dobsonfly larva, the water penny larva, the
birch, the redhead, the white catspaw, the elephant ear, the
buckeye, the king eider, the river darter, the sauger, the burning

bush, the common merganser, the limpet, the mayfly nymph, the
cedar, the turkey vulture, the spectacle case, the flat floater,
the cherry, the red tailed hawk, the longnose gar, the brook trout,
the chestnut, the killdeer, the river snail, the giant floater, the
chokeberry, the gray catbird, the rabbitsfoot, the slenderhead
darter, the crabapple, the american robin, the creek chub, the
stonefly nymph, the dogwood, the warbling vireo, the sow
bug, the elktoe, the elm, the marsh wren, the monkeyface, the
central mudminnow, the fir, the gray-cheeked thrush, the
white bass, the predaceous diving beetle, the hawthorn, the
scud, the salamander mussel, the hazelnut, the warbler, the
mapleleaf, the american eel, the hemlock, the speckled chub, the
whirligig beetle larva, the hickory, the sparrow, the caddisfly larva,
the fluted shell, the horse chestnut, the wartyback, the white
heelsplitter, the larch, the pine grosbeak, the brook stickleback, the
river redhorse, the locust, the ebonyshelf, the giant water bug, the
maple, the eastern phoebe, the white sucker, the creek heelsplitter,
the mulberry, the crane fly larva, the mountain madtom, the oak,
the bank swallow, the wabash pigtoe, the damselfly larva, the pine,
the stonecat, the kidneyshell, the plum, the midge larva, the
eastern sand darter, the rose, the purple wartyback, the narrow-
winged damselfly, the spruce, the pirate perch, the threehorn
wartyback, the sumac, the black fly larva, the redside dace, the
tree-of-heaven, the orange-foot pimpleback, the dragonfly larva,
the walnut, the gold fish, the butterfly, the striped fly larva, the
willow, the freshwater drum, the ohio pigtoe, the warmouth, the
mayfly nymph, the clubshell.
And this was just the beginning of the list.
Our hearts took on many things.
Our hearts took on new shapes, new shapes every day as we went to the
stream every day.
Our hearts took on the shape of well-defined riffles and pools, clean
substrates, woody debris, meandering channels, floodplains, and
mature streamside forests.
Our hearts took on the shape of the stream and became riffled and calmed
and muddy and clean and flooded and shrunken dry.
Our hearts took on the shape of whirligigs swirling across the water.

We shaped our hearts into the sycamore trees along the side of the stream
and we let into our hearts the long pendulous polygamous racemes
of its small green flowers, the first-formed male flowers with no
pistil and then the later arriving hairy ovary with its two curved
stigmas.

We let ourselves love the one day of the adult life of the mayfly as it
swarms, mates in flight, and dies all without eating.

And we shaped our hearts into the water willow and into the eggs spawned
in the water willow.

Our hearts took on the brilliant blues, reds, and oranges of breeding male
rainbow darter and our hearts swam to the female rainbow darter
and we poked her side with our snout as she buried herself under
the gravel and we laid upon her as she vibrated.

We let leaves and algae into our hearts and then we let mollusks and
insects and we let the midge larvae into our heart and then the
stonefly nymph and then a minnow came into our heart and with
it a bass and then we let the blue heron fly in, the raccoon amble by,
the snapping turtle and the watersnake also.

We immersed ourselves in the shallow stream. We lied down on the rocks
on our narrow pillow stone and let the water pass over us and our
heart was bathed in glochida and other things that attach to the
flesh.

And as we did this we sang.

We sang gentle now.

Gentle now clubshell,

don't add to heartache.

Gentle now warmouth, mayfly nymph,

don't add to heartache.

Gentle now willow, freshwater drum, ohio pigtoe,

don't add to heartache.

Gentle now walnut, gold fish, butterfly, striped fly larva,

don't add to heartache.

Gentle now black fly larva, redside dace, tree-of-heaven, orange-foot
pimpleback, dragonfly larva,

don't add to heartache.

Gentle now purple wartyback, narrow-winged damselfly, spruce, pirate
  perch, threehorn wartyback, sumac,
don't add to heartache.
Gentle now pine, stonecat, kidneyshell, plum, midge larva, eastern sand
  darter, rose,
don't add to heartache.
Gentle now creek heelsplitter, mulberry, crane fly larva, mountain
  madtom, oak, bank swallow, wabash pigtoe, damselfly larva,
don't add to heartache.
Gentle now pine grosbeak, brook stickleback, river redhorse, locust,
  ebonyshelf, giant water bug, maple, eastern phoebe, white sucker,
don't add to heartache.
Gentle now whirligig beetle larva, hickory, sparrow, caddisfly larva, fluted
  shell, horse chestnut, wartyback, white heelsplitter, larch,
don't add to heartache.
Gentle now white bass, predaceous diving beetle, hawthorn, scud,
  salamander mussel, hazelnut, warbler, mapleleaf, american eel,
  hemlock, speckled chub,
don't add to heartache.
Gentle now stonefly nympth, dogwood, warbling vireo, sow bug, elktoe,
  elm, marsh wren, monkeyface, central mudminnow, fir, gray-
  cheeked thrush,
don't add to heartache.
Gentle now longnose gar, brook trout, chestnut, killdeer, river snail,
  giant floater, chokeberry, gray catbird, rabbitsfoot, slenderhead
  darter, crabapple, american robin, creek chub,
don't add to heartache.
Gentle now king eider, river darter, sauger, burning bush, common
  merganser, limpet, mayfly nymph, cedar, turkey vulture, spectacle
  case, flat floater, cherry, red tailed hawk,
don't add to heartache.
Gentle now black sandshell, ash, american bittern, harelip sucker, yellow
  bullhead, beech, great blue heron, dobsonfly larva, water penny
  larva, birch, redhead, white catspaw, elephant ear, buckeye,
don't add to heartache.
Gentle now, we sang,
Circle our heart in rapture, in love-ache. Circle our heart.

IV.

It was not all long lines of connection and utopia.
It was a brackish stream and it went through the field beside our house.
But we let into our hearts the brackish parts of it also.
Some of it knowingly.
We let in soda cans and we let in cigarette butts and we let in pink tampon
        applicators and we let in six pack of beer connectors and we let in
        various other pieces of plastic that would travel through the
        stream.
And some of it unknowingly.
We let the run off from agriculture, surface mines, forestry, home
        wastewater treatment systems, construction sites, urban yards, and
        roadways into our hearts.
We let chloride, magnesium, sulfate, manganese, iron, nitrite/nitrate,
        aluminum, suspended solids, zinc, phosphorus, fertilizers, animal
        wastes, oil, grease, dioxins, heavy metals, and lead go through our
        skin and into our tissues.
We were born at the beginning of these things, at the time of chemicals
        combining, at the time of stream run off.
These things were a part of us and would become more a part of us but we
        did not know it yet.
Still we noticed enough to sing a lament.
To sing in lament for whoever lost her elephant ear lost her mountain
        madtom
and whoever lost her butterfly lost her harelip sucker
and whoever lost her white catspaw lost her rabbitsfoot
and whoever lost her monkeyface lost her speckled chub
and whoever lost her wartyback lost her ebonyshell
and whoever lost her pirate perch lost her ohio pigtoe lost her clubshell.

V.

What I did not know as I sang the lament of what was becoming lost and
        what was already lost was how this loss would happen.
I did not know that I would turn from the stream to each other.
I did not know I would turn to each other.

That I would turn to each other to admire the softness of each other's
   breast, the folds of each other's elbows, the brightness of each
   other's eyes, the smoothness of each other's hair, the evenness of
   each other's teeth, the firm blush of each other's lips, the firm
   softness of each other's breasts, the fuzz of each other's down, the
   rich, ripe pungency of each other's smell, all of it, each other's
   cheeks, legs, neck, roof of mouth, webbing between the fingers,
   tips of nails and also cuticles, hair on toes, whorls on fingers, skin
   discolorations.
I turned to each other.
Ensnared, bewildered, I turned to each other and from the stream.
I turned to each other and I began to work for the chemical factory and I
   began to work for the paper mill and I began to work for the
   atomic waste disposal plant and I began to work at keeping men in
   jail.
I turned to each other.
I didn't even say goodbye elephant ear, mountain madtorn, butterfly,
   harelip sucker, white catspaw, rabbitsfoot, monkeyface, speckled
   chub, wartyback, ebonyshell, pirate perch, ohio pigtoe, clubshell.
I replaced what I knew of the stream with Lifestream Total Cholesterol
   Test Packets, with Snuggle Emerald Stream Fabric Softener Dryer
   Sheets, with Tisserand Aromatherapy Aroma-Stream Cartridges,
   with Filter Stream Dust Tamer, and Streamzap PC Remote
   Control, Acid Stream Launcher, and Viral Data Stream.
I didn't even say goodbye elephant ear, mountain madtorn, butterfly,
   harelip sucker, white catspaw, rabbitsfoot, monkeyface, speckled
   chub, wartyback, ebonyshell, pirate perch, ohio pigtoe, clubshell.
I put a Streamline Tilt Mirror in my shower and I kept a crystal Serenity
   Sphere with a Winter Stream view on my dresser.
I didn't even say goodbye elephant ear, mountain madtorn, butterfly,
   harelip sucker, white catspaw, rabbitsfoot, monkeyface, speckled
   chub, wartyback, ebonyshell, pirate perch, ohio pigtoe, clubshell.
I bought a Gulf Stream Blue Polyester Boat Cover for my 14–16 Foot
   V-Hull Fishing boats with beam widths up to sixty-eight feet and
   I talked about value stream management with men in suits over a
   desk.

I didn't even say goodbye elephant ear, mountain madtorn, butterfly,
      harelip sucker, white catspaw, rabbitsfoot, monkeyface, speckled
      chub, wartyback, ebonyshell, pirate perch, ohio pigtoe, clubshell.
I just turned to each other and the body parts of the other suddenly
      glowed with the beauty and detail that I had found in the stream.
I put my head together on a narrow pillow and talked with each other all
      night long.
And I did not sing.
I did not sing otototoi; dark, all merged together, oi.
I did not sing the groaning words.
I did not sing otototoi; dark, all merged together, oi.
I did not sing the groaning words.
I did not sing o wo, wo, wo!
I did not sing I see, I see.
I did not sing wo, wo!

POETICS STATEMENT

I LOVE reading all those optimistic things that people say about poetry. Those sweeping statements about poetry being all about love or poetry being all about countering the oblivion of darkness or poetry being the genre to comfort in times of trouble. They make me feel good about poetry.

But poetry really doesn't work that way for me. For me, poetry is a troubled and troubling genre, full of desire and anger and support and protest, primarily useful because it helps me think. Lyn Hejinian's essays, her explorations of inquiry, have been really helpful to me on this. My theory is that poetry helps me think because it is a genre that is so open right now. There are so many rules about how to write poetry that there might as well not be any at all. Poetry moves words around. It rearranges them from their conventions. It re-sorts them. It uses more than one language. It repeats. It pursues aconventional language and divergent typography. It often experiments. It can be ephemeral and occasional. It often uses pleasing patterns as it does all this. And all that helps me think.

And yet . . . it isn't only the way that poetry moves words around that makes it matter to me. There is something deeper also. Whenever someone like my uncle, the university professor in engineering, asks me as he does every holiday, why are you interested in all this poetry stuff and why does it matter? I want to answer as Gertrude Stein did when asked how she felt about modern art: "I like to look at it."

But if I really want to figure out why poetry helps me think, there is also another story, this story: The town I grew up in was ugly and dirty. The town was dirty because it had a barely environmentally regulated papermill. It had a barely environmentally regulated papermill because nothing else was in the town. It was a one-industry town. Nothing was in the town because it was in the middle of nowhere. What had once been a thriving crossroads and trading spot that the Shawnee Indians built on the Shawnee River, a spot once called something like the Chauouanons, was no longer an active trading spot because of nineteenth-century globalism aka European expansion and then those related tools of globalization like airplanes, which made the town part of what coasters call flyover land. Because the town was dirty, whenever I read poems about the beauty of the English countryside or New England woods, they made little sense to me. So then I went and found by accident this stuff by Gertrude Stein, and because I was looking for something that didn't seem to be some sort of weird lie, and because this stuff by Stein was so weird it at the least didn't seem to be lying in the usual ways, I clung to it. And that began an interest in stuff, in poetry.

"It's an exciting time to be a poet" Lisa Jarnot was once quoted as saying in *Glamour*. It *is* an exciting time to be a poet. It is *always* an exciting time to be a poet, the genre of all people at all times. There has never been a culture without poetry. And that has to tell us something about how deep our roots are with this genre. It is always an exciting time for poetry because poetry feels like the moment when the knot finally comes untied after appearing to be impossibly tangled. Or the moment of being aware of the exact meaning of words and of all the changes that occur in the exact meanings of words in thoughts and sensations, the difference between feet and feat, between there and their, between red and read. A moment of coming to the end of the road, pulling up right in front of the concrete bunker that symbolizes the end of the road, getting out, climbing over the bunker, walking out into the grass of the field, slowly and steadily. And poetry feels like the springing off the diving board and moving into the part of the dive that feels aerodynamic and smooth, feels just right to the body, the feeling of moving through the air, and then the feeling of entering into the water as if in slow motion, as if floating but really with a certain quick sensation of smoothness. And it feels like what the inner smoothness that moves plovers, monarchs, whales, garden snakes, herds of walking animals from one place to another must feel like. The feeling of being set in motion, a feeling that moves one to another place, a place of water perhaps or a place of dryness or a place of coolness or of warmness. Or it feels like beginning to walk up several long flights of stairs, letting the intenseness of breath and the tightness in the legs develop while knowing at any moment you can just turn around and walk back down and then turning around and walking down them quickly and easily. Or suddenly noticing a clenched fist and then unclenching this fist and how this sensation of unclenching travels up the hand and into the chest and into the breath. And the reverse, clenching the unclenched fit and noticing how this sensation travels up the hand and into the chest and into the breath. Or just spreading hands wide and putting them on the floor and then kicking up into the air and balancing there. I guess what I mean is that it is always an exciting time to like to look at it, to like to look at poetry.

ALL TOGETHER/NOW

Writing the Space of Collectivities in the Poetry of Juliana Spahr

Kimberly Lamm

AT THE CLOSE of her essay "Poetry in a Time of Crisis," Juliana Spahr calls for "more poems dealing with these difficult moments of how we talk to each other that acknowledge how difficult it is. More outward turns."[1] Spahr composed "Poetry in a Time of Crisis" in the aftermath of September 11, when familiar forms of individualized expression were insisted upon rather than relinquished or reimagined.[2] Historical events that traumatically punctuate time remind us of the collective dimensions of experience; but when readers enter the space of poetry, still fixed by the model in which a reader encounters the writer's lyrical expression, this knowledge is difficult to sustain.[3] "Poetry in a Time of Crisis" argues against reducing historical crises to private, subjective renditions, while also acknowledging the difficulty of doing otherwise; it argues for "public declarations of collective culture and connective agency," that is, "[m]ore outward turns."[4] Engaged in conversations about the difficulties and possibilities of talking to each other within and across languages, war zones, beds, televised events, streets, discourses, and continents, Spahr's own poetry is full of outward, inclusive turns, and calls attention to the collectivities that emerge through connective agency.

Shaping and tracing the connections within collectivities is the core ethos of Spahr's work. It informs her poetry, literary scholarship, and activist practices.[5] Without relinquishing poetry's tie to intimate encounters, Spahr prioritizes the need to imagine and communicate with collectivities. In "Poetry in a Time of Crisis," Spahr articulates the need for "models of intimacy that are full of acquaintance and publics."[6] Compelling for its brave simplicity, Spahr offers an observation that emphasizes the importance of collective imaginations that are composed with intimacy and widen in connection: "All I can figure out with any certainty about recent events is that the reason two airplanes slammed into two buildings and these two buildings collapsed had something to do with groups of people on both sides having trouble thinking about people on the side they were not on."[7] Spahr identifies the ethical challenge posed by the contemporary historical moment: resisting habitual perceptions and retraining the imagination—what Gayatri Spivak describes as "the great inbuilt instrument of othering"[8]—to see and respond to a planet increasingly split and homogenized by globalization, marked and mapped by capitalist expansion and exploitation. Spahr's call for new collectivities composed in and through language aims at countering the divisive forms of collectivity globalization imposes. Spivak might say Spahr evokes "planetarity," which works against globalization's capitalist abstraction; that is, she moves responsibly toward the planet and its "alterity," which is "an experience of the impossible."[9] The call of Spahr's work—"all together/now"—is a call to collectivities that are resistant and responsible, open to the alterity of the planet and the ethical impossibilities it demands.

Spahr's work distinguishes itself because she writes the poems for which her critical work calls. The opening poem of *this connection of everyone with lungs* (2005), entitled "poem written after September 11, 2001," destroys the spatial and imaginative impasse of "both sides" by following the rhythm of the breath's migrations as it links the interior of the body to ever-wider layers of space:

> everyone with lungs breathes the space between the hands and the space
> around the hands and the space of the room and the space of the building
> that surrounds the room and the space of the neighborhoods nearby and the
> space of the cities and the space of the regions and the space of the nations
> and the space of the continents and islands and the space of the oceans and
> the space of the troposphere and the space of the stratosphere in and out

In unpunctuated lines that render the world's continuous, quiet, but incantatory rhythms, Spahr builds an argument for recognizing the collectivity of spaces we already inhabit and the connections already threaded by the body's necessary breath. Connection is this poem's theme, and space, its refrain. "poem written after September 11, 2001" attests to the fact that any story of "collective culture and connective agency" involves thematizations of space, as it is the fundamental medium through which collectivities are formed. In the penultimate stanza, Spahr traces the elements of the air everyone shares, including traces of disaster: "minute silicon particles from pulverized / glass and concrete." The last line underscores the stakes in these connections: "How lovely and how doomed this connection of everyone with lungs."[10]

This commitment to collectivities is the impulse shaping Spahr's lucid style, her inventive compositions, her experiments interfacing literary spaces and cultural topographies, and her willingness to write love poems that move beyond the sanctity of the heterosexual couple and into the multiplicity of queered spaces.[11] Because it is attentive to the contingencies of context, her commitment to collectivities has not developed in direct lines. In *Choosing Rooms* (1995), Spahr examines a collectivity's repressions and exclusions, and theorizes an image of community that is always consciously inside space, representation, and language. In *Response* (1996), Spahr surveys an unresponsive repertoire of aesthetic representations, their political effects, and the imaginaries emerging in reaction to them. In *Fuck You—Aloha—I Love You* (2001), Spahr links a critique of American colonization to erotic encounters. And in *this connection of everyone with lungs*, Spahr creates a supple vision that can link the doomed beauty of global politics to a lover's discourse. Through all its variety, Spahr's commitments remain clear. She calls for collectivities that have a responsive and responsible relationship to the worlds within and around them. These lines from *Response* articulate her work's variety and consistency:

> while the ways that we encounter relation are various
>
> we remain
>
> searching [searching
>
> we question, respond[12]

For Spahr, poetry is not an activity cordoned off in private spaces; it should instead participate in the various ways "we encounter relation." "We," the pronoun of both collectivities and intimacies, appears often in Spahr's work as a shifter anyone can inhabit. In her spare lines, "we" becomes a space open to multiple identifications. Writing within and at the edge of "we" certainly pushes poetry beyond the hand-held mirror of the Western lyric, but "we" is not necessarily inclusive. Collectivities are contested as much as they are shared, and Spahr works with poetry's plasticity to explore the difficulties and possibilities of their making. Who constitutes the "we" of collectivities and what role do poems play opening or policing the gates of "we"? How can poetry defamiliarize the process through which "we" emerge into visibility? These are the questions that make Spahr's poetry move; the cultural, political, and ethical imperatives within these questions become the poetry's destination. As the language poet Lyn Hejinian writes, "Make it go with a single word. We."[13]

Spahr's work emerged out of Language poetry's provocative and utopian claim: poetry can become a means for creating collectivities rather than solidifying the particularities of the individual voice.[14] In "After Language Poetry," Spahr delineates both the collective project and the individual contributions of Lyn Hejinian, Ron Silliman, Susan Howe, Bruce Andrews, and Joan Retallack to highlight their generative effect on her own work:

> I found value in the retreat from individualism and idiosyncrasy and in works that instead pointed to heady and unexpected and yet intimate pluralisms. And in writing that helped me to think of culture as large and connective. And in writing that comments on community and that moves poetry away from individualism to shared, connective spaces. And in writing that reveals how our private intimacies have public obligations and ramifications, how intimacy has a social bond with shared meaning. The tendency in language writing that writing not be given up to aesthetics *only* or aesthetics *mainly* means a great deal to me.[15]

Rather than asserting poetry's traditional alignment with the individual's creation and experience of beauty, the Language poets stress its capacity to inspire critical thought about culture, ideology, and community. This emphasis does not mean a rejection of intimacy or response, as Spahr's phrase "intimate pluralisms" makes clear. Developing the insights of the Language poets, Spahr renders the public dimensions of intimacy, and in turn, highlights the intimate dimensions of public life.

Spahr's poem "switching," from *Fuck You—Aloha—I Love You*, grapples with the compelling paradoxes of "intimate pluralisms." "switching" renders the limits and possibilities that emerge when a "we" attempts to make the physical configurations of erotic encounters an analogy for communication and negotiation. "switching" exemplifies Spahr's talent for rendering scenes that suggest both personal intimacies and "public obligations and ramifications." The poem begins with sturdy, deliberately built lines:

> In a room we sit around a table.
>
> The table is dark wood.
>
> It has thick legs.
>
> It is a space for gathering with a
> boundary of wood.

"Dark wood" and "thick legs" are common phrases, but become defamiliarized through bare sobriety of these lines, their careful inscription into the wide space of the page. This defamiliarization extends to the "we" of the poem. Who are the "we" sitting around this table, and how do we, as readers, imagine them? The table is space that separates and joins; it links the table's human purpose—"gathering"—to its material limitation: "a / boundary of wood." On the following page, there is a quick switch into another space: "In another room, in a hotel room, / we hurriedly undress." The hotel's standard, anonymous spaces and its associations with sexual privacy make it perfect for exploring "intimate pluralisms." From a hotel room's clean anonymity, Spahr moves to the bed, and the poetry thickens with sensual textuality:

> A bed is soft and we, the two
> people in the hotel room, run our
> hands over each other's bodies
> while reclined upon it.

Table, hotel room, bed: each space intensifies the we's physical proximity. The bed is a space of sensual pleasure: "We like the feel of each other's / bodies." It is also the space of communication: "This is also speaking." "switching" highlights different forms of speaking and the various spaces in which speaking takes place. Around the space of the table, the individuals of the "we" are the same; their communication is rational and direct: "We are similar to each other. We / look like each other. We understand / each other even in argument." In the hotel room, however, the physical distinctions among the members of the "we" become clear:

> One of us is lighter, one is darker,
> one is paunchy, one is thin, one is
> wrinkled, one is resilient, one is
> hairy, one is smooth.

As Spahr intersects the space of the table and the bed, the more complicated the composition of the "we" becomes. "I / am confused," the speaker states, "I am part of a we and then no / part of a we." "switching" seeks to connect the kinds of communication that take place in bed and across the table, but this is not easy. The following passage reveals why this "switching" might be desired. Here, bodies are not represented through gendered demarcations, but instead resemble sentences that are placed together awkwardly but equally to figure for expressions of desire that do not reinforce uneven power relations:

> The problem is how to we all
> together now.
>
> How to speak around a table as if
> one leg is on one shoulder and
> then the other is stretched out or
> twined around the other person.[16]

In Spahr's work, relations between people—sexual, intersubjective, and political—are not only negotiated through language but assume its pliable forms. "switching" reveals that collectivities are shared and contested, and Spahr employs the malleability of poetry to explore the difficulties of their making. Notice in the lines above, line breaks split "all" and "together," which suggests the contingency of collective forms. Moreover, Spahr leaves out the verbs that we might expect after "how to"—speak? see? create?—which makes the line work against idiom. These subtle choices bring hesitancy to the imperative "all together now," which is usually confident and unquestioned.

Though attention to collectivities aligns Spahr's work with political concerns, she does not necessarily write to retool existing policies and institutions, but rather to rethink poetry's relationship to readers emerging into visibility. In the last lines of *Choosing Rooms*, Spahr writes: "behind the darkness are the voices of a crowd / this crowd chants [respect] / who is listening?"[17] Increasingly, Spahr's work has become attuned to the voices of emergent subjectivities hinged between particular histories and the homogeneity of globalization. Her immersion in Hawai'i's colonial history has made her work attentive to the global inequities produced by colonialism and imperialism, inequities that now feed globalization even as they are exacerbated by it. And yet, like so many other artists and thinkers of this moment,[18] Spahr seeks to render the traces of new collectivities' imminent emergence—what Giorgio Agamben calls the "coming community," and what Michael Hardt and Antonio Negri describe as the "multitude."[19] In the concluding chapter of *Empire* (2000), Hardt and Negri enumerate the revolutions that have erupted in the twentieth century to call attention to the possibility that they have "pos[ed] the conditions of new political subjectivity, an insurgent multitude against imperial power. The rhythm that the revolutionary movements have established is the beat of a new *aetas*, a new maturity and metamorphosis of the times."[20]

Attentive to and part of this new *aetas* (which means lifetime and generation in Latin), Spahr's work reimagines the poem's relation to readers by opening up the directions through which one can approach the poem and enter its production of meanings. It is Spahr's clarity that makes this entrance possible; the work's shrewdly composed and emotionally resonant lines reach out to readers and blur their distance and difference from writers. In "localism and or t/here," the opening poem of her collection *Fuck You—Aloha—I Love You*, Spahr problematizes the center/periphery model that sustains spatial hierarchies and uneven power relations by playing with the arbitrary, necessarily contextual distinctions between "here" and "there," and then folding these designations into a poem unsettled by Steinian repetitions: "There is no there there anywhere. / There is no here here or anywhere either. / Here and there. He and she. There, there." Reaching for the yet-to-be-determined reader, Spahr demonstrates that poetry can productively unsettle distinctions among readers, writers, spaces, and genders. Here Spahr's lines open out into gestures of desire, toward the space the writers cannot yet see: "And we are arrows of loving lostness / gliding, gliding, off, and off, and off, / gliding." Gliding off and away from contemporary poetry's solipsism, Spahr's poetry finds its heart in the languages and spaces we may collectively share. "localism or t/here" ends with a stanza in which selves and their locations abundantly proliferate: "And you and you and you are here and / there and there and here and you are / here and there and tear."[21]

This tear introduces a note of sadness to *Fuck You—Aloha—I Love You*, a critique of America's colonization of Hawai'i. Hawai'i appears in this collection as a complex political, cultural, and emotional terrain. The title alone makes the emotional ambivalence within Hawai'i's emblematic gesture of hello and goodbye quite clear, and the poems delve into specifics. In "gathering paolo stream," Spahr examines how the rights of people indigenous to Hawai'i to "gather plants, harvest trees, and take game" have been "eroded" and undercut by property owners. Paolo stream flows openly through the beginning of the poem, and Spahr draws from the rich repertoire of words for Hawai'i's natural resources to describe the stream's meanings. The stream "Is mongoose and freshwater / Is 'awa and kukui." Access to the stream and its plenty, however, has been impeded: a parking lot and a rental space business, fences, and buildings have been built around it. "This is about how certain of we / have rights on paper yet not in / place," Spahr writes, making the meaning of the poem and the situation to which it refers quite clear. Colonization is a claiming and remapping of space that enforces cultural hierarchies, and Spahr's work seeks to reveal how literature and language can implicitly reinscribe those hierarchies. In the last part of the poem, Spahr links the barriers the parking lot represents to the power of those who create language's figurations and meanings: "certain of we are driving the / metaphor."[22]

No doubt Spahr's work was developing in political directions from the start, but living in Hawai'i, witnessing and participating in its struggle against cultural and linguistic hegemony, inscribed the quest for social justice and resistance into her work. "things," the book's second poem, explores the political inventiveness of "da kine," a pidgin word that is malleable and multivalent and therefore resistant to the homogenizing fixities of colonialism. "[D]a kine," the poem suggests, is figure for pidgin itself. By naming this poem "things," Spahr calls attention to the materiality of language, and, in turn, language's tie to material conditions. At the opening of the poem, Spahr presents da kine's multiplicity:

> There are these things and they
> are three fold at least.
>
> They are da kine.
>
> They are things; they are more.[23]

In an essay on the work of poet and political activist Haunani-Kay Trask, Spahr argues that Trask's choice to italicize Hawaiian words in his poetry "mark[s] not a foreignness but an emphasis on the history of how the Hawaiian language was outlawed in Hawai'i from 1896 to 1970."[24] In "things," the word "da kine" creates a similar point of emphasis. Spahr aligns "da kine" with the tear that appeared at the end of "localism or t/here"; they orbit through the poem and in relation to each other, together becoming signs of sadness, error, and resilience:

> The tear refers to an ideal circle that is
> not met.
>
> The tear is not right or circular.
>
> Yet it is capable. It is da kine.

Da kine's elasticity, its pragmatic capability, make it a means to connection:

> Da kine for me is the moment when
> things extend beyond you and me
> and into the rest of the world. It is
> the thing.

Most prominently, da kine is a space of connection that is both expressive and resistant. In the following passage, Spahr literalizes the space of collectivity da kine makes possible by aligning it with the mosh pit and making both an expression of the anger and tenderness of the book's title:

> Da kine is the mosh pit at the fuck-you-
> aloha-I-love-you show.
>
> The mosh pit is thrashing about in
> masking tape.
>
> Everyone is connected in the thrash,
> everyone taped together in the fuck-
> you-aloha-I-love-you.

The angry thrashing of the mosh pit is a form of "reaching out for others," and the masking tape becomes a figure for this gesture's embeddedness within by language: "The more thrashing, the more sticking."[25]

Fuck You-Aloha-I Love You makes the strong case that poetry's attention to language can contribute to political critique. But one might ask: aren't there louder, brighter mediums—television commercials, billboards, newspapers, films, and brand names—that address and shape collectivities much more explicitly than poetry? Spahr's work shows collectivities emerge in the vicissitudes of language and cultural imaginaries, and the words and images through which their intelligibility congeals can never be wholly determined or predicted. So it is precisely poetry's ostensible distance from more visible cultural forms that allows for the possibility of reflecting upon how collectivities are formed in and through language. In *Publics and Counterpublics*, one of many recent scholarly texts that align with Spahr's work, Michael Warner writes: "[P]ublics exist only by virtue of their imagining. They are a kind of fiction that has taken on life, and a very public life at that."[26] Collectivities are imaginative fictions that become visibly embodied in public life, and the malleability of Spahr's poetry allows readers to trace and participate in the tenuous, compelling process of collectivities' imaginary fictions becoming lived and public actualities.

For Spahr, reflecting on how collectivities are formed has ethical and political consequences, and should be considered with care. The opening lines of Spahr's collection *Response* map the questions motivating the book's formal and thematic details. Notice her choice to write every letter in lowercase makes this line of questioning appear to be a thoughtful pause just at the edge of the not said:

> how to tell without violating?
> how to approach mass thought
> > as history?
> > as opportunity?
> > as truth?
> > as art?[27]

Reflecting upon the ethical dimensions of the representational act is crucial to Spahr's poetics, more important than developing a particular voice or an intricate stylistic signature. Spahr writes poems that question the writer's power to depict. In the lines above, the pronoun "I" is conspicuously absent, and is coincident with questioning the writer's authority. The choice to erase the most expected and explicit sign of the writer's presence underscores the work's collective gestures, and makes the questions she poses open to the reader's participation. Without an "I," Spahr lets the long history of poems that speak from and focus on the contours of individual subjectivity slide away. Her poems analyze "mass thought," shared discourses, cultural perceptions, as well as their historical determinations and reverberations. Spahr builds her poems with the quotidian language of "mass thought" to see the strange and rich artistry at work in cultural expression. "how to approach mass thought," Spahr asks, "as truth / as art?" This crucial question comes from Spahr's unique talent for clearing the poem of the extraneous, carving it down to the process through which thought appears.

In *Response*, Spahr develops an ethical vision that emerges from the fragile space between a detached and inflexible cultural symbolic and a supple imaginary that testifies to the need for connection. "responding," the book's first poem, restages familiar cultural tableaux to expose their fixity in cultural perception. In the following passage, the unspecified subjects and pronouns are placed in brackets to solicit the reader's imaginary participation—and yet the scenes through which these openings appear are so familiar, so "universally" recognized, they suggest that reimagining art's relationship to politics requires much more than allowing the reader to enter the available syntax of visibility:

> we know art is fundamental to the [New State] as is evidenced
> in village scenes, majestic ancient views, masses and
> masses of [generic human figures] marching in columns,
> swords coded as plowshares, image as spectacle

Whereas this scene restages the rhetorical platitudes, genres, and spectacles associated with the Russian Revolution, in the following lines, Spahr aligns a tableau of international multiculturalism in line with propagandistic clichés of a leader's aura:

> it is a ride in the country, the car crowded with children
> > [each child represents a different
> > ethnicity of [name of nation]
>
> it is a moment of standing with light resonating around [major
> historical figure[28]

By presenting these tableaux with such flat clarity, Spahr calls attention to their fixity. The subsequent poems "testimony" and "thrashing seems crazy" map illusory worlds that seem to be reactions against the tableaux's detachment. In both, discourses of victimization and violence haphazardly mend split selves and fractured identities, what Spahr astutely describes as "attempts at comfort from those without the vocabulary of / comfort." "testimony" assembles statements of people who believe they have been abducted by aliens. Their words bear witness to individuals attempting to see themselves within large ideological systems that occlude their participation: "'they close our eyes' / 'our voices are silent.'"[29] "thrashing seems crazy" restages the testimony of Ruth Finley, a woman with "dissociative personality disorder" who testified on *Oprah* that she was "stalked by a male persona of herself." In the opening poem of "thrashing seems crazy," the repetition of the phrase "this is true" emphasizes the need to be believed and recognized within the frame of a recognizable story.

> this is true
> a man in an alley grabbed my arm
> this is true
> someone called me and left the phone dangling at the post office
> this is true
> a man stalked me
>
> someone tells a story

Indirectly, Ruth Finley's testimony attests to multiple truths: the self is an other one cannot see or communicate with easily; gendered polarizations split the self unnecessarily. "[T]his is true," Spahr writes, "a woman is at times a man." Telling a story is an attempt to mend those splits, and reveals what we do not know about ourselves. Spahr implicates the poet in this scenario of self-detachment. Not only does she write, "a woman calls her stalker The Poet" (notice the strategic use of capitalization) but describes the process of entering the story to rearrange its meaning, and resorts to repeating declarations of truth: "someone tries to enter into the information / to pass words back and forth that have meaning / fails, resorts to this is true."[30]

Spahr is present in *Response* as an arranger of various citations that testify to an unsettled cultural landscape. In a section of "testimony," she arranges quotations from renditions of alien abductions across the page, which creates a landscape of both atomized dispersion and potential connection:

> 'I did not choose to join'
> 'I do not know why I kept waking'
> 'I think I'm floating out a closed window'
> 'I wake up invaded'
> . . . .
> 'I have recurring nuclear war dreams'
> 'Who analyzes like that? It's just something new'

Together these statements attest to a panic about disaster and a desire for connection to things outside the borders of the body: "[S]he finds herself drawn towards the light and enveloped by it."[31]

These themes—desire, disaster, and transcendence—come together in the last poem, "witness." In "witness," Spahr reveals how an unresponsive cultural repertoire alienating people from themselves and each other changes, partially, in response to AIDS. Blood is the chapter's witness: it makes visible the invisible stories of linked bodies. But the possibility of collectivity is impeded by social isolation, denial, and shame. In a section entitled "attempts at witnessing," Spahr creates a list of individuals connected primarily through isolation: "a person waits in a darkening room for a phone call / . . . a person has a dream and discounts its validity / . . . a person agrees to have sex with another person in the back of / a car on a deserted road." In response to these scenes that speak to the need for connection, public images and discourses emerge. Here is a wall of graffiti that displays a grow-ing list of people lost to AIDS: "Gloria Ed Junior Ken 8Ball Diamond Tony S Lou 8Str Emily." A few pages later, Spahr represents various attempts to distribute safe sex information to others, which connects to the work of the writer: "a person drops off books everyday at various bars on his/her way home from work."[32]

Central to Spahr's work of moving the poem away from poetry's implicit emphasis on individuals and toward collectivities is the understanding that collectivities are often composed against a constitutive outside. In *Choos-ing Rooms*, Spahr grapples with the ethical questions this dynamic poses by placing images of suffering (and particularly gendered forms of suffering) at the book's elusive center. Crucial to this process is highlighting the spa-tial dimensions of the poem, the page, and the stanza, and making them representations of social spaces in which interactions take place and ethical choices are made. Intersecting literary and social spaces allows the gendered metaphors invisibly sustaining both to emerge into visibility. In one poem's opening lines, the figure of a woman becomes a site for demonstrating the ethical complexities of a collectivity's vision, the place where the sight lines of complicity and witnessing cross in confusion.

> things tease
>
> we are told: your sight is exposed as complicit
>
> we sit in hard wood chairs before a blackboard
>
> we watch
>
> a man pries open a woman's eyes before us
>
> once her eyes are open
>
> she sees things we wish we hadn't

"things tease," the poem's inaugural line, hinges the poem to the material objects beyond the page, making the stanza float in brackets to the side of the constellation of signs that compose reality. Moreover, the poem's detached tone and defamiliarized atmosphere makes the space in which the "we" gather a site of questioning rather than certainty. The blackboard sug-gests that the anonymous "we" gathers for a lesson about sight's complicity. A woman's sight is a passageway to this insight, but also becomes the image of actual and bodily witnessing that deflects the "we's" responsibility.

Spahr develops this idea in subsequent poems to reveal the gendered unconscious of collectivities:

> in the room where we sit there are no answers
> but a corridor of live wires
> four metal rods mounted on wooded crosses
> batteries
> woman
>
> a naked woman enters this room but is contained between
> the wires attached to the battery.

Here a woman has been listed, after the batteries, as part of an exhibition's components; she thus becomes part of the conduit necessary for the circulation of energy, not part of the "we" looking for answers. In *Choosing Rooms* Spahr examines the way in which woman becomes both an abstraction and an emblem of recognizable meanings that collectivities make into a passageway that connects members to each other and to the reality outside their collective form. *Choosing Rooms* foresees the fact that in Spahr's representations of collectivities, spaces between individuals, and spaces between actualities and imaginaries, are not impediments to ethical connection, but sites of its possibility. Here Spahr offers an image of space that serves as a compelling ideal that one, and many, can imaginatively pursue:

> so in memory, what remains most important, is the mind's
> eye crossing the empty room slowly but irregularly
> to focus on a postcard of waves scotch taped to the
> wall[33]

The postcard of the waves is not an unmediated space of the natural, nor is it a personification of raw energy that must disappear for connection to be actualized. It is a picture that provides a passageway out of, but also back into, the space of collectivity. Spahr revisits the image of the postcard in *this connection of everyone with lungs*. These postcards create a visual and thematic echo across the arc of Spahr's work and suggest her commitment to developing the implications of her own poetic repertoire.

this connection of everyone with lungs was not only written in response to September 11, but to events that exacerbated global crises: America's invasion of Afghanistan and Iraq. Reflecting the attempt to understand, the poems list the wars, violence, and injustices that sear each day into a historical scar: "When I wake up this morning the world is a series of isolated, / burning fires as it is every morning."[34] The litany of daily disasters inspires the speaker to look for images of hope. "December 8, 2002," begins with images of the planet, seen and photographed from space, and the feelings they inspire: "something in me jumps when I see these images, jumps toward / comfort and my mind settles." This jump into comfort and out toward the planet inspires the speaker to revisit the moment when she bought a post-card of Ḥawai'i:

> Beloveds, when we first moved to this island in the middle of the Pacific I took comfort from a postcard of the islands seen from space that I bought in a store in Waikīkī. There was no detail of the buildings of Waikīkī in the islands seen from space. No signs of the brackish Ala Wai that surrounds Waikīkī. Everything looked pristine and sparkled from space. All the machin-ery, all the art was in the pristine sparkle of the ocean and its kindness to the land. The ocean was calm.[35]

Later in the book, Spahr contrasts, but also links, this calming image of Hawai'i to the images of protestors writing the planet with dissent. The calm "sparkle" of the ocean connects to the busy "glimmer" of idiosyncratic detail: "These images of the protests are busy, detailed with all the glim-mers / of individuals."[36]

In *this connection of everyone with lungs*, Spahr does not speak to crowds or politicians, the mourning or the dead. Each poem is addressed to her "beloveds." The sensuality of their care and domestic pleasures emerge, at first, as a counterpoint to "the spinning / earth, the gathering forces of some sort of destruction that is / endless."[37] In "December 1, 2002," Spahr cites the day's death count: "I speak of the forty-seven dead in Caracas / And I speak of the four dead in Palestine. / And of the three dead in Israel," which contrasts so sharply to a space that beloveds share: "we sit in / our room in the morning and the sounds of the birds are outside our / windows and the sun shines."[38]

What is even more haunting, and what Spahr renders with brave inven-tion, is that the apparatuses and discourses of war become part of sensual and caring encounters: "When I wrap around yours bodies, I wrap around the USS *Abraham* / *Lincoln*, unmanned aerial vehicles, and surveillance."[39] While this strange synthesis foretells of doom, there is also the possibility that tying the language of war to the bodies of her beloveds makes the stakes of war, and the necessity of collective resistance, clear. Making the bodies of her beloveds the figurative sites of destruction, Spahr offers a compelling image of globalization's and neoimperialism's violent encroachments into intimate, subjective spaces; in turn, she makes intimacy part of war's public discourse. "Globalization," as Spivak defines it, "is the imposition of the same system of exchange everywhere."[40] War is the most explicit expression of this impo-sition. Spahr's examination of collectivities is a call to resist globalization's violently enforced homogenization and to see that it enforces collectivities premised on severing ethical connections to others. No doubt the future will provoke Spahr to continue pursuing these themes in the name of resistance, but there is also no doubt that future readers will look to her work to see what we could not afford not to read.

NOTES

1. Juliana Spahr, "Poetry in a Time of Crisis," *Poetry Project Newsletter* 189 (2002): 8.

2. Spahr writes, "When *USA Today* turned to the poet laureates and asked them 'to select a piece of their work that they believe has a message for these difficult times,' the poet laureates did not choose poems about collective, connective necessities and difficulties" ("Poetry in a Time of Crisis," 8).

3. In Juliana Spahr's scholarship, the lyric poem is often a subject of critical inquiry and contestation. See "'Love Scattered, Not Concentrated Love': Bernadette Mayer's *Sonnets*," *differences: A Journal of Feminist Cultural Studies* 12 (2002): 98–99. See also the introduction to *American Women Poets in the 21st Century: Where Lyric Meets Language*, ed. Claudia Rankine and Juliana Spahr (Middletown, Conn.: Wesleyan Univesity Press, 2002), 3.

4. Ibid. It is clear that Spahr does not insist upon strict definitions of "the public" and "collectivity"; rather, she uses them interchangeably. Spahr's use of the word "collectivity" aligns with Raymond Williams's definition of "collective" in *Keywords: A Vocabulary of Culture and Society*, rev. ed. (New York: Oxford University Press, 1983). Williams writes that the word "collective" developed from the Latin word *collectus*, which means "gathered together" (69).

5. See Spahr's *Everybody's Autonomy: Connective Reading and Collective Identity* (Tuscaloosa: University of Alabama Press, 2001). *Everybody's Autonomy* defines "connection" as "works that present and engage with large, public worlds that are in turn shared with readers" (4). Spahr participates in Sub-Poetics, a publishing collective. She also edits, with the poet Jena Osman, *Chain*, an award-winning journal devoted to newly emergent forms and concepts in contemporary poetry and visual arts; the journal attempts to expand beyond Western avant-garde traditions and the exclusive selection process of many poetry journals. See <http://www.temple.edu/chain/>. See also Spahr's essay, "Poetry, Academy, and Anarchy," *Poets & Writers Magazine* (November–December 2000): 21–25; and "Editing and Community," <http://people.mills.edu/jsphar/essay.html>.

6. Spahr, "Poetry in a Time of Crisis," 8.

7. Ibid.

8. Gayatri Spivak, *Death of a Discipline* (New York: Columbia University Press, 2003), 13.

9. Ibid., 102.

10. Spahr, "poem written after September 11, 2001," *this connection of everyone with lungs* (Berkeley and Los Angeles: University of California Press, 2005), 7 and 10. My understandings of space have been informed by *Space, Gender, Knowledge: Feminist Readings*, ed. Linda McDowell and Joanne P. Sharp (London: Arnold, 1997).

11. Spahr's poems often address lovers rather than singular entities. This is most noticeable in *this connection of everyone with lungs*, as the poems are addressed to

"beloveds," and she pluralizes the second person possessive, "yours." In her analysis of Bernadette Mayer's sonnets, Spahr draws from the work of Michael Warner and Lauren Berlant to define *queer*. Although queer draws and develops from gay, lesbian, and feminist theory, Spahr explains that "the term 'queer' works best, as Lauren Berlant and Michael Warner have pointed out, if not taken to be synonymous with gay and lesbian studies but rather to describe those sexualities that are inclusive of, but do not fit strictly into, gay, lesbian, or straight categories." See "'Love Scattered, Not Concentrated Love,'" 110.

12. Spahr, "responding," *Response* (Los Angeles: Sun & Moon Press, 1996), 31.

13. This line is from Lyn Hejinian's *My Life* (Los Angeles: Sun & Moon Press, 1987).

14. These cursory definitions of Language poetry have been informed by *The Politics of Poetic Form: Poetry and Public Policy*, ed. Charles Bernstein (New York: Roof Books, 1990); and *In the American Tree: Language, Realism, Poetry*, ed. Ron Silliman (Orono, Maine: National Poetry Foundation, 2002).

15. Spahr, "After Language Poetry," <http://www.ubu.com/papers/oei/spahr .html>.

16. Spahr, "switching," *Fuck You-Aloha-I Love You* (Middletown, Conn.: Wesleyan University Press, 2001), 35, 36, 38, 39, 43, 47, and 49. The desire to bring sex and sexuality to more "public" forms of discourse and communication aligns with many of the formulations in Michael Warner and Lauren Berlant's essay "Sex in Public." *Publics and Counterpublics* (New York: Zone Books; Cambridge, Mass.: MIT Press, 2002), 189 and 193.

17. Spahr, *Choosing Rooms* (Norman, Okla.: Texture Press, 1995), 31.

18. There are too many artists and thinkers that share Spahr's interest in collectivities to enumerate here, but I shall mention a few. Fredric Jameson argues that theorizing "collective subjectivities" is on the intellectual horizon. See "Symptoms of Theory or Symptoms for Theory?" *Critical Inquiry* 30, no. 2 (2004): 406. See also Katy Siegel's "All Together Now: Crowd Scenes in Contemporary Art," *Artforum* (January 2005): 167–71; Stephen Burt's "'September 1, 1939' Revisited, Or, Poetry, Publics, and the Idea of the Public," *American Literary History* 15, no. 3 (2003): 533–59; and Jonathon Monroe's "Index and Symptom: 'Connective' Reading, (Post) Language Writing, and Cultural Critique," *Contemporary Literature* 44, no. 4 (Winter 2003): 748–70.

19. Giorgio Agamben, *The Coming Community*, trans. Michael Hardt (Minneapolis: University of Minnesota Press, 1993).

20. Michael Hardt and Antonio Negri, *Empire* (Cambridge, Mass.: Harvard University Press, 2000), 394.

21. Spahr, "localism or t/here," *Fuck You-Aloha-I Love You*, 3 and 4.

22. Spahr, "gathering paolo stream," *Fuck You-Aloha-I Love You*, 31, 22, 26, and 29.

23. Spahr, "things," *Fuck You-Aloha-I Love You*, 7.

24. Spahr, "Connected Disconnection and Localized Globalism in Pacific Multilingual Literature," *boundary 2* 31, no. 3 (2004): 76.

25. Spahr, "things," *Fuck You-Aloha-I Love You*, 12, 8, and 13.

26. Michael Warner, *Publics and Counterpublics*, 8.

27. Spahr, *Response* (Los Angeles: Sun & Moon Press, 1996), 9. My reading of *Response* has been influenced by Raymond Williams's chapter "Dominant, Residual, and Emergent," in *Marxism and Literature* (Oxford: Oxford University Press, 1977), 121–27.

28. Spahr, "responding," *Response*, 14 and 16.

29. Spahr, "testimony," *Response*, 60 and 63.

30. Spahr, "thrashing seems crazy," *Response*, 34, 35, 40, and 39.

31. Spahr, "testimony," *Response*, 61 and 55.

32. Spahr, "witnessing," *Response*, 82, 87, and 88.

33. *Choosing Rooms*, 7, 15, and 25.

34. "March 5, 2003," *this connection of everyone with lungs*, 56.

35. "December 8, 2002," *this connection of everyone with lungs*, 35.

36. "March 5, 2003," *this connection of everyone with lungs*, 60.

37. "December 8, 2002," *this connection of everyone with lungs*, 36.

38. "December 1, 2002," *this connection of everyone with lungs*, 19 and 20.

39. "March 27 and 30, 2003," *this connection of everyone with lungs*, 75.

40. Spivak, *Death of a Discipline*, 72.

BIBLIOGRAPHY

Books by Juliana Spahr

2199 Kalia Road, with Candace Ah Nee. Honlulu, Hawai'i: Subpress Self-Publish or Perish Project, 2003.

American Women Poets in the 21st Century: Where Lyric Meets Language. Edited with Claudia Rankine. Middletown, Conn.: Wesleyan University Press, 2002.

Asking. Buffalo, New York: Buffalo Vortex, 1994.

Choosing Rooms. Norman, Okla.: Texture Press, 1995.

This Connection of Everyone with Lungs. Berkeley and Los Angeles: University of California Press, 2005.

Dole Street. Honolulu, Hawai'i: Subpress Self-Publish or Perish Project, 2001.

Everybody's Autonomy: Connective Reading and Collective Identity. Tuscaloosa: University of Alabama Press, 2001.

Fuck You-Aloha-I Love You. Middletown, Conn.: Wesleyan University Press, 2001.

Gentle Now, Don't Add to Heartache. Oakland, Calif.: Subpoetics Self-Publish or Perish, 2004.

Identifying. Elmwood, Conn.: Potes and Poets Press, 1994.

Live. Sausalito, Calif.: Duration Press, 2000.

Nuclear. Buffalo, N.Y.: Leave Press, 1992.

Poetry and Pedagogy: The Challenge of the Contemporary. Edited with Joan Retallack. New York: Palgrave Macmillan, 2006.

Powersonnets. Honolulu, Hawai'i: Subpress Self-Publish or Perish Project, 2000.

Response. Los Angeles: Sun & Moon Press, 1996.

Spiderwasp Literary Criticism. New York, N.Y.: Spectacular Books, 1998.

Things of Each Possible Relation Hashing Against One Another. Long Beach, Calif.: Palm Press, 2003.

Unnamed Dragonfly Species. Honolulu, Hawai'i: Subpress Self-Publish or Perish Project, 2002.

We Are All, Some of We Eating Grapes Some of We and the Land that was Never Ours While We Were the Land's Sparrows are Pecking at it Eating to Push Far What is With. Brooklyn, N.Y.: Subpoetics, Self-Publish or Perish, 1999.

Selected Prose

"A, B, C: Reading Against Emily Dickinson and Gertrude Stein." In *A Poetics of Criticism*, edited by Juliana Spahr, Mark Wallace, Kristin Prevallet, and Pam Rehm, 281–92. Buffalo, N.Y.: Leave Press, 1994.

"After Language Poetry." <http://www.ubu.com/papers/oei/spahr.html>.

"Astonishment and Experimentation." (Book review). *American Literature* 44, no. 1 (2003): 172–75.

"Connected Disconnection and Localized Globalism in Pacific Multilingual Literature." *boundary 2* 31, no. 3 (2004): 75–100.

"Editing and Community." <http://people.mills.edu/jspahr/essay/html>.

"Greening the Lyric." (Book review). *Landfall* (2002): 200–202.

Introduction to *American Women Poets in the 21st Century: Where Lyric Meets Language*, edited by Claudia Rankine and Juliana Spahr, 1–17. Middletown, Conn.: Wesleyan University Press, 2002.

"'Love Scattered, Not Concentrated Love': Bernadette Mayer's *Sonnets*." *differences: A Journal of Feminist Cultural Studies* 12, no. 2 (2001): 98–120.

"Poetry, Academy, and Anarchy." *Poets & Writers Magazine* (2000): 21–26.

"Poetry in a Time of Crisis." *Poetry Project Newsletter* 189 (2002): 6–8.

"Sista Tongue." (Book review). *Contemporary Pacific* 16 (2004): 211–12.

"What Anti-Colonial Poetry Has to say About Language and Why It Matters": <http://people.mills. edu/jspahr/anticolonial.html>.

"If Writing is Written." *West Coast Line* 26, no. 1 (Spring 1992): 51–60.

Interviews

Adolf, Antony. "Poetry Without Borders: An Interview with Juliana Spahr." In *Voces de América / American Voices: Entrevistas a escritores americanos / Interviews with American Writers*, edited by Alonso Gallo and Laura P. Cádiz, 397–414. Spain, Aduana Vieja, 2004.

Selected Criticism

Lamm, Kimberly. "Writing 'Becoming-Woman': The Movement of Deleuzean Thought in Contemporary American Poetry." *theory@buffalo* 8 (2003): 42–67.

Monroe, Jonathon. "Index and Symptom: 'Connective' Reading, (Post) Language Writing, and Cultural Critique." *Contemporary Literature* 44 (Winter 2003): 748–70.

Ngai, Sianne. "Bad Timing (A Sequel). Paranoia, Feminism, and Poetry." *differences: A Journal of Feminist Cultural Studies* 12, no. 2 (Summer 2001): 1–46.

Wallace, Mark. "A Reading of Against: Juliana Spahr as Poet, Editor, and Critic." *Tripwire: A Journal of Poetics* 1 (1998): 110–41.

JOSHUA CLOVER

Baader Meinhof Three-Person'd God

walking around with heavy manners, you're going home in a fucking ambulance

Batter my heart, three person'd God: for, you As yet but knocke, breathe, shine, and would be loved faine, But am betroth'd unto your enemie: Divorce mee, untie, or breake that knot againe, Take mee to you, imprison mee, for I

Yet dearely I love you, and proves weake or untrue. Yet dearely I love you, and would be loved faine,

mee should defend, But is captiv'd, and proves weake or untrue.

— the one he didn't paint. This is how we have her now, not the model-actress with the band, not the model-actress with the band, too sexy for mere appearance, not the model-actress with the band, jut, side glance — the one he didn't paint. This is how we have her now,

He made three paintings from the four shots of her perp. walk, ... of her perp. walk, hippiechick smock and sandals, wan angularity and bones;

— Richter's Ensslin, the aura of erotism nowhere visible amidst

Pictures on the Run 67-77 (Astrid Proll)

The pic in which she shows even the least attitude, jut, side glance

rueful grin. The pic in which she shows even the least attitude

too light to hang, out of the courtroom photo and into the year, too sexy for mere appearance,

too light to hang; she pops bloody and amazing, out of the courtroom photo and into the year, then we proceeded forth but the princes of appearance would allow only traces that faded rather swiftly. Sensation. Come with me inside the black poppy

With each iteration Meinhof withdraws from us (We slept in the State and dreamed against it)

We lived but nothing happened. In our time — in here —

the black poppy of this blast radius —

that the mechanical eye is not the eye of the people?

And who should say

Stern, Der Spiegel, etc

the whole world turns out to be ideology — well, lives were measured by traces left on the ideology — well, — lives were measured by traces left on the labyrinth

5:50 AM: a lilac-colored Porsche pulls up outside of the garage

COLLECTIVE THIS IS THE HATE SOCIALIST

sleeping and dreaming are dialectical)

That's right, process. It's hard being death. On trial for arson four years earlier; then we proceeded forth

Gerhard Richter: October 18, 1977

baader meinhof (baader meinhof 1996)

I, like an usurpt towne, to another, due, Labour to admit you, but Oh, to no end,

Your force, to breake, blowe, burn and make me new. I, like an usurpt towne, to another, due, Labour to admit you, but Oh, to no end,

Except you enthrall mee, never ever chaste, Nor ever chaste, except you ravish mee.

That I may rise, and stand, o'erthrow mee, 'and bend Your force, to breake, blowe, burn and make me new.

AT THE ATELIER TELEOLOGY

The sun tutoyers me! Adrift beyond heroic realism
In the postmodern sublime where every window can lie
Like a priest, adrift in the utopia for bourgeois kittens
Having of late learned the trick of how to listen to two
Songs at once—double your measure double your fun!—
It seems to defy death and the still the commodity
Is not cast down. I say Frank O'Hara was an anarchist,
Nothing else explains all that joy. Exclamation point!
He was not a systems guy. At the end of Beckett's version
Of "Zone" the new century rips the head off the old
And calls it the sun and that's joy too, the anarchic sun
Leaping out of a fin de siècle type of sparagmos
So it can make with the rendez-vous a century later
And greet me all casual as if we were old friends,
Where did you get those shoes, how's Rodefer doing,
Who's sleeping in their warehouse studio and oh
By the way Joshua why are you so obsessed with the modern
And its endnotes, what about going to bed in the sensuous
Now and Here, you know, the *sublime* sublime. These are all
Good questions, which explains how you got to be the sun,
And I know it's not an easy job, knowing everything
Half the time or half of things all the time, melting
Everybody's cacao whisky, being called names by poets,
And other tasks and tribulations, this world,
This half-read hebdomaire, this jacquerie of knick-knacks.
All in a day's work, sun sez, adopting a comical Bolshevik
Accent, but please, tell those boys to stop writing poems
For Lili Brik, it doesn't get more homosocial than that.
So I am wondering if the sun is the last soviet, the self-
Sustaining factory of the sun, but just as I begin to wonder
Into the old haunts under the scarlet letter *H*, the cold
Afternoons of Vitebsk and the Dziga Vertov, Dziga Vertov,
I recall my new friend and shout over my shoulder
Thanks for the advice! Anytime, after all, it's free,
Say hello to the generation that burned itself in effigy.

It turns out everything is the world in miniature and this was not good news

In the magazine racks in the downtowns in the video arcades while the band danced in a café in two suits and a dress

I turned twentyone in parole doing prison without life

It is a beautiful night we live in the world

Of the antilyric and the train that bears money into the city

Where it is at its happy-go-luckiest after a season socked

Away in the cabinet of a country house bordered on all sides by the austere cinematic light of mid-century

When the money arrived it leapt the canals gracefully sometimes in the skins of men

And sometimes leaping more abstractly through the city

Between bare consciousness and the bourse of basic beliefs

Where as the pocket philosophes often say "everything is connected"

An idea that casts the Janus-shadows of paranoia and mysticism and still is not mistaken

We could not understand until we had been there in the long hallways in the passages in the upstairs windows low under the glass roofs

We survive in the speech of what voices

We the alphabet present in a purely spoken language

Ah America you have got worn thin
Plus unable to hold Americans

In the morning citizens loiter on the little bridge beneath the latest
    billboards
Talking on mobile phones in popular modern languages and the jargon
    of birds

All the Futurists are in the past giving the sense history
Really has ended sometime around El Lissitzky

In the evening one is always coming upon some square
Where meaning has already congealed amidst architecture students
    and beer

You love one of them from a shy distance
As melancholy Albania loves indifferent France

It seems important to have a theory of
Writing based on Giorgio the painter de Chirico

Lest a leisurely debate on dreams brawl into the street
And occupy our attentions until it's time to sleep

There is no pleasure like wasting time in your city divided into quarters
    sisters and zones
Beneath the clattering gears of the moon and the sun

Oh most industrial and beguiling of lullabyes
Heard at the wedding of Sonia Terk and Robert Delaunay

It is a beautiful night we live in the world
Of the antilyric that is still sung in the city's dominated sectors

The Blue Bar is closing and the Orange Bar is closed
I wonder how friends are while walking home

Sleeping and dreaming are dialectical dear
I have a fragment in my head Guillaume Apollinaire

You go to the black suburb, *Et in arcadia ego*. Past Arrival Street, you
is ambiguous. Many things are music of which some [*six or seven words
struck out and illegible*] for me as he was to almost all the younger ones,
a stranger, *Et in arcadia ego*. The art of the present comes down to four
discrepant images of B.B. turning toward us, toward our shared machine
eye, our deep disfluency. Out past Arrival Street we go to the black
suburb, we are buried in Grant's Tomb, *Et in arcadia ego*, we walk in the
garden of his turbulence, *Et in arcadia ego*, we are in a station of the metro,
we are lost in the editing of July, we too lived in arcades in arcades you
will find us.

POEM

We always send it to the wrong address
And now that buoys even our most impersonal days. Everyone is
    beautiful!
And then almost everyone. *C'est cool-ça*, the shift that enchants the world
Or at least the afternoon of the world before it's off
To meet Chris and all at glimmering Colleen's
Arriving southside early and so twenty min for Lyn's *The Fatalist*
Amidst the superlit video store on the corner. It's funnier
In French: *superlit* but not much else. One is haunted
By the suspicion that one is in a society
Composed of people one will never meet for example
The Society That Thinks About Someone Named Anne-Lise
Occasionally. So I walk back around and up
The stairs and Chris puts on *either/or*. Elliott Smith 20th Cen. American
Is nonetheless a star in the constellation
Our Romanticism and we have been hanging out
A lot there recently. A keener melancholy

About the music for a week or two afterward may be obvious
But something has to be done with the excess flowering inside death
Or is it just apotropaic? We'll see. The most awful thing
About the phrase "Every Germinal must have its Thermidor"
Is that one never gets to say so anymore
And really mean it. We lie down in categories
And wake up in concepts but must there be so much of the day spent
Tracking stray remarks and others' hearts
And maintaining a casual balance between OxyContin and "poetic prose"
So new sensations emerge? Meanwhile but I am happy
To see you! It's enough but not of anything.

CHREIA

At this time there was an expectation of terror meaning cops in kevlar and the green civic garbage cylinders sealed with discs of steel.

At this time the new train ran to an underground forest sheathed in books.

This time many years after the towers near the sex of the city were found to be twin cruets of jizz and sang.

We all floated with the same specific gravity in the constantly moving stream of money as of this time.

As in time of strike there was quite a bit of garbage loose in the street not like an Ourang-Outang in the Rue Morgue but it eddied and whorled at the edges of the seductively weeping stream.

I was riding a swan to the underground library or having sex with a swan under a shroud of words.

As of this time we kept a copy of the city in the library and another in the ether.

Constantly offered as a time of therefore but with a feeling of as.

Kevlar and carbines and garbage reduplicating into the quotidien in the time of the Plan Vigipirate.

Not more people in the street but more intensely as in the time of a transit strike promenading behind the veil of speech.

Around this time we thought of the skyline as new nature.

And through it flowed the invisible milk as through the ether and the sewers the milk of capital.

There was an expectation in everyday life.

It gathered in the dead spaces beside the endlessly grieving stream.

Of milk jizz and sang in the time of garbage in the vale of lang.

The shining order the burning simulations there are more of it.

WHITEREAD WALK

Vertigo Europa austere museum sex hotel record shop Odeon neon breath isolations in the vale of lang climbing the Whispering Gallery doing the Strand glad girls paper wedding painted retina crosses a small continent between two bars colored rays of visible things in the Spring in the superlative Hotel Europa Drag the light of the past tense falls from an iron hotel railing a long skirt drenched in lassitude all Polaroids are out of focus felt anagogic the taxi came thwack we drove into a book

WHITEREAD WALK

Monumental the lacunae between illbiquitous promenaders down to
the Square past the Open 24 Hours as social forms of grieving we are
prohibited this is the remix the new glitch has been recalled melancholy
of luscious Pictober the fall of the phenomenon into the iris back with
another one of those Return of the Flaneur as hardcore Autumnophage
echolocation always places you in a different country the cure is beats per
minute bad year in Brooklyn Bombs Over Baghdad the negative needs no
introduction and/or here we go!

CERISERIE

Music: Sexual misery is wearing you out.
Music: Known as the Philosophers's Stair for the world-weariness which
    climbing it inspires. One gets nowhere with it.
Paris: St-Sulpice in shrouds.
Paris: You're falling into disrepair, Eiffel Tower this means you! Swathed
    in gold paint, Enguerrand Quarton whispering come with me under
    the shadow of this gold leaf.
Music: The unless of a certain series.
Mathematics: Everyone rolling dice and flinging Fibonacci, going to the
    opera, counting everything.
Fire: The number between four and five.
Gold leaf: Wedding dress of the verb *to have*, it reminds you of of.
Music: As the sleep of the just. We pass into it and out again without
    seeming to move. The false motion of the wave, "frei aber einsam."
Steve Evans: I saw your skull! It was between your thought and your face.
Melisse: How I saw her naked in Brooklyn but was not in Brooklyn at the
    time.
Art: That's the problem with art.
Paris: I was in Paris at the time! St-Sulpice in shrouds "like Katharine
    Hepburn."

Katharine Hepburn: Oh America! But then, writing from Paris in the thirties, it was to you Benjamin compared Adorno's wife. Ghost citizens of the century, sexual misery is wearing you out.

Misreading: You are entering the City of Praise, population two million three-hundred thousand . . .

Hausmann's Paris: The daughter of Midas in the moment just after. The first silence of the century then the king weeping.

Music: As something to be inside of, as inside thinking one feels thought of, fly in the ointment of the mind!

Sign at Jardin des Plantes: GAMES ARE FORBIDDEN IN THE LABYRINTH.

Paris: Museum city, gold lettering the windows of the wedding-dress shops in the Jewish Quarter. "Nothing has been changed," sez Michael, "except for the removal of twenty-seven thousand Jews."

Paris 1968: The anti-museum museum.

The Institute for Temporary Design: Scaffolding, traffic jam, barricade, police car on fire, flies in the ointment of the city.

Gilles Ivain: In your tiny room behind the clock, your bent sleep, your Mythomania.

Gilles Ivain: Our hero, our Anti-Hausmann.

To say about Flemish painting: "Money-colored light."

Music: "Boys On The Radio."

Boys of the Marais: In your leather pants and sexual pose, arcaded shadows of the Place des Vosges.

Mathematics: And all that motion you supposed was drift, courtyard with the grotesque head of Apollinaire, Norma on the bridge, proved nothing but a triangle fixed by the museum and the opera and St-Sulpice in shrouds.

The Louvre: A couple necking in an alcove, in their brief bodies entwined near the Super-Radiance Hall visible as speech.

Speech: The bird that bursts from the mouth shall not return.

Pop song: We got your pretty girls they're talking on mobile phones la la la.

Enguerrand Quarton: In your dream gold leaf was the sun, salve on the kingdom of the visible.

Gold leaf: The mind makes itself a Midas, it cannot hold and not have.

Thus: I came to the city of possession.

Sleeping: Behind the clock, in the diagon, in your endless summer night, in the city remaking itself like a wave in which people live or are said to live, it comes down to the same thing, an exaggerated sense of things getting done.

Paris: The train station's a museum, opera in the place of the prison.

Later: The music lacquered with listen.

YEAR ZERO

The clock into which you stared as into a mother's face now seen as a time-factory under winter.

Year Zero the mistakes have yet to be invented and music—well it comes down to inventing flowers.

This they do down at the flower factory over the bridge from the factory where cherries tumble from the cherry-making machinery.

Nothing is true everything is the case.

Paused at the edge of the tub turning away wanting to be seen.

Morning apartment where the light has lost its yellow at the moment of the sign.

Turns away wants to be seen.

Just then you turned to look—a sweetness with a hook on either end.

Surely it is the century of clouds?

A long walk across town with your social realist overcoat turned up: citizens yawning on the passing train.

The train windows blurring past like movie frames run sideways starring our exhausted revolutionary sweetheart whose head cracks open to swallow the day.

We have made the world flat once again.

Meetings in the cold warehouse on the outskirts of the Year Zero.

In the red suburbs of the Year Zero.

In the other night on the other side of permission you could have her or a police car on fire if you preferred the second you wore a black square on your jacket or in your hair.

The machine flower the machine music blotted out all other sounds still you could not get it loud enough.

Needs to know looks back.

Wants to be seen turns away.

Had meant to write the century of crowds.

And beneath it the gear-rooms of the calendar where tiny cracks have been discovered in every hour time has started to trickle staunched with grease and sweat a shudder a sadness at waking.

Now must begin again it must be new time.

In the morning of the sign lying in bed in cold Utopia and alone under the black square.

Your ears swelled with flowers a corpse in your mouth.

You are free though a freedom with its ribs showing.

POETICS STATEMENT

Once Against (Into the Poetics of Superinformation)

SUPERINFORMATION doesn't abandon the territory. Superinformation is neither primitive erudition nor sophisticated accumulation. Superinformation is the set of relations through which—within the excess of signification, the immanence of actual life and its frantic dissimulation—we live more, not less. Looking at Gursky's photos of architecture and spectacles that present themselves as purely optic I have the sense that the personal eye can't see everything—that the scene is beyond a lone viewer. This is superinformation's signal affect; it implies the plural, the collective consciousness. So does *Wedding Feast at Cana*, five centuries old: not just a crowded picture, but one that needs a crowd. It takes a riot to see it. History finally caught up, late cap, sprawl cities, global markets, the disavowal of individuality. Even negation, the ecstasy par excellance of the first person, must escape into the plural. One Mao, many Maos (rhymes with *chaos*). Standing around talking to everyone isn't poetry, but I like a poem that makes that seem like a good idea. Superinformation is the excess of signification turned on itself as a strategy. Whose Too Much? Our Too Much! A poem could be a direct communication between you and me, Frank, except the blond I am in love with has very dark hair and I have a mobile phone. So there we were chatting away but poems really are poetic, otherwise we would just work for software. The day has integuments and superinformation is always trying to fill them, to live without dead space; austerity is a lost art, and phew! One can relax inside superinformation, but autonomy that ain't. Superinformation admires the pure singularity of Dickinson and Rimbaud, and so waves goodbye to them from the far side of a great divide, a billboard flying the tattered half-tones of ten thousand publicity cycles. I stole that from Jacques de la Villeglé, do you think he'll mind? Do you think Hains will mind that I credited someone else? Superinformation doesn't read the billboard for the secrets of the lost world, nor as the sign of its passing; it's just a name for how the last evening of summer etches itself there, a sense that everything the sign can't contain is present in the catastrophe of its reading. The fluctuations of interest rates take us as the object of their speculations, while architecture finally seems indifferent to us. Data is a phenomenon of life organized by survival; superinformation hangs out near where the waves of data crash against the seawall of the sublime, mixing metaphors in the infinite. Superinformation is a manifesto; the manifesto is the most passionate hoax. Categories are preparation for thinking, but the mighty superinformationists are no Boy Scouts.

THE PLEASURES OF NOT MERELY CIRCULATING

Joshua Clover's Political Imagination

Charles Altieri

JOSHUA CLOVER'S first book, *Madonna Anno Domini*, presents an intriguing challenge to its readers. On the one hand Clover's modernist credentials are everywhere present in his refusing traditional expectations about the pleasures available in lyric poetry. These poems obviously will not settle for orientations of the psyche eager for identification with exercises in delicate sensibility straining to locate exemplary qualities within personal experience. Nor do they content themselves with any kind of realism, presentational or narrative; the path to pleasure requires paying careful attention to the intricacies of the poems' constructedness. The play of intelligence bound only to elaborate formal constraints is their fundamental source of lyric value. Yet this intricacy is not at all an end in itself. In fact Clover is intensely anti-aestheticist. Often art seems a handmaiden to popular culture, as if the resources of poetry were necessary to save popular culture from the culture industry. Elaborate patterning and dense impasto effects become a measure of poetry's distinctive claims on social life.

By his second volume, *The Totality for Kids*, the struggle to reclaim the popular takes on a more explicitly political edge. By aligning with what we might call a Situationist-inspired realism, Clover attempts to establish pleasure as a politically charged dialectical force. Traditionally poetry eager to make claims about society has depended on a logic of mimesis: what engages the real world depends on representing it by depiction. Clover explores instead the Situationist idea that we should begin with the imagination of what is possible, then understand reality as an effect of probings directed by such possibilities. In other words, his basic concern is not how poetry might fit into the real but how poetry at its fullest may establish pleasures that provide standards for what one is willing to live as real. And that project interprets pain as the enforced realization of the failures discovered as one's efforts confront yet intractable aspects of social reality.

One cannot quite say that Clover "believes" in Situationist hopes, just as one cannot quite say that Yeats "believed" in the arguments of *A Vision*. But one can say that he is passionately committed to the possibility that life would be much diminished if we were content to function as convinced non-believers. Even if Marxist stances cast a somewhat jaundiced eye on the most radical Situationist attitudes toward play, it remains also the case that Marx (through Adorno) helps historicize those stances so that one can enter fully into both their pathos and their critical potential. Clover is particularly astute on how Situationist values project modes of agency and identification capable of resisting the impact of the culture industry. He shares with the Situationists an interest in how affects can be explored that are not narrowed to individual subjects. So the adventures within his lyrics are not concerned with dramatic events or with political agendas but with how a fundamental alienation can be rendered and its pressures made a dialectical measure of underlying social structures. And then the treatment of our limitations as individual subjects becomes the condition for acknowledging our inescapable bonds to large social units, especially with regard to how we experience pleasure.

I

I want to study how pleasure negotiates such alienation in Clover's second volume. Clover shares with Stevens the sense that the imperative "it must give pleasure" is closely tied to two other imperatives: "it must be abstract" and "it must change." But Clover does not share Stevens's sense that abstraction can directly mirror the real in the same way that the idea of the sun supplements the felt pleasure of sunlight. Rather, he seems to think abstraction is necessary because our historical condition leaves only the abstract as a potential source of freedom: all the rest, all the "empirical content of experience," is caught in the logic produced by the domination of the commodity. Abstraction now cannot be the work of pure idea because such work has been fatally compromised by the instrumental criteria developed for it by Enlightenment thinkers. Instead, lyric poetry must follow the lead of modernist artists in pursuing modes of abstraction that focus on elemental concrete forces within the relevant medium. Then the poet can envision expressing what seems the emergence of thinking before it turns into familiar thoughts. Form becomes an elemental feature of content because it is capable of directly modifying our sense of what counts as possibilities for action, and luscious excess then serves as one possible means of breaking the hold of a psychological economy based on the commodity.[1]

I shall distinguish modes of pleasure deriving specifically from the poet's formal activity from the tensions between pleasure and alienation effects that constitute much of the drama in Clover, although the two are clearly connected. Then in relation to form I shall isolate four distinctive ways the poet's constructive activity calls our attention to the work pleasure has to do thematically and emotionally on the discursive level of the work. There are experiments in continual enjambment like "Alas, that is the name of our town: I have been concealing it all this time," while making it seem that every line could also be end-stopped. There is in "An Archive of confessions, a genealogy of confessions" an emphasis on various forms of rhyme as the materializing force at the end of the line. In a different register, Clover's marvelous "The Dark Ages" plays on rules about line length; the poet can chose when to break the line so long as there is not room in the line for what proves the next word:

> Many people had candles and torches were a dime a dozen. "You Light Up My Life" was one of the most popular songs. What about illuminated manuscripts and those lightbulbs every time they had an idea—imagine how that must have been in the Dark Ages! Stealth would favor the village idiot, but a wise man would be as a strobe light in a rain storm. Once in the Dark Ages, believing the precinct to be deserted, I wandered as one lost. Then the beams of a passing car would light the street for some distance, all the other faces flashing here, here, here like terrible saints. . . .
>
> . . . In poetry the line is something like a lamplit way onto which you have just turned, nodding lilies and a couple of desperadoes under the eaves. The line break we would call darkness, for there the street ends, the lamp fails, and all is occluded. . . .

In this case the spirit of formal play is necessary to counter the utter bleakness of the situation. The human scene invoked is basically one of terror, the boys attending each other's wounds and the blue chalk outlining where bodies fell. Playfulness will not transform such a scene, but the background that playfulness provides will enable one to engage the scene without succumbing to its morbidity and the accompanying sense of desperation. The point is not to evade the desperation but to encounter it on a different level, at the margins of history (and at the margins of the line) where perhaps the poet can confront his own murderous reactions to the violence.

Finally notice how the introductory section in "Antwerp rainy all churches still haunted" generates tension by having each line an end-stopped sentence that nonetheless blends into larger semantic units:

> My name is Ferdinand the Word.
> I have lived apart from the other words.
> In the afternoon towns in the gray towns in June's fall.
> Among the shadow-shaken riders of the yellow streetcars.
> On their iron course past housing blocks and the rail terminal.
> And the gothic panopticon of Cathedral Eleven.
> The streetcar line a phrase which turns back wholly upon itself.
> Being constructed letter by letter like a labyrinth.
> Curtain of post-war reconstruction over the old town.
> Electronica of the present humming behind the curtain.

Two pulls are obvious—toward the world through description and toward emphasizing the chains of signifiers where landscape turns into wordscape. One could escape nominalism if one could substitute expressions like "I am

Ferdinand the Word." But Clover recasts that as "My name is Ferdinand the Word" in order to make us aware by contrast how the more obvious formulation asserts subjectivity and hence treats predication as a simple unfolding of identity by clarifying how one experiences the world. As Clover puts it, there is no projection of subjectivity in his rendering because it is names, not conditions of experience that provide terms for identification. And this nominalism becomes a troubling reminder of the inadequacy of *any* description: there must always be prior terms that enable the description to count as description.

This war on description is constant in Clover. But "Antwerp" will have to stand as representative for the ways his constructive activity works thematically. In this poem the challenge is not to provide an alternative to nominalism but to materialize the practices that constitute its effectiveness. Hence the streetcar line forms a palindrome, its going out of the city a mirror of its ways of coming in. Analogously, the idea of the labyrinthine ways of the old city seems directly borrowed from an understanding of linguistic structures. Then there is the beautiful last stanza's efforts to envision how landscape can appear as language, as well as in language, because the description also parallels what the language is taking on materially:

> Antwerp rainy all churches still haunted.
> Each thing saying itself into the scribble and whisper.
> Words on the yellow streetcars riding their one empirical sentence.
> We turn round and round in the night and are consumed by fire.

The first line of this last stanza returns to the title, its combination of vowels an evocative reminder of literariness at the core of the emotional center of the poem. And by echoing the introduction this line returns to the palindrome of the streetcars, while preparing for the literal palindrome in the last line. Yet this intensification of the signifying dimension of the poem also offers probably the most evocative representation of the landscape by fusing it with two elemental material features of language—the scribble and the whisper (which also correlate the visual and aural). The last line then assumes a collective responsibility for that repetition, while also yielding completely to the transformations that make the now collective situation overtly merge with the constructedness of language effects. The night skies even blend into memories of the war that give the evening such power as threat and as consummation.[2]

II

Obviously one could go on at length reading Clover primarily for how his dizzying formal intelligence secures a stance that can express profound alienation without entirely succumbing to rage. But that mode of reading generates too narrow a conception of form, reducing it to technical devices. The concept of form ultimately involves projections of an ideal reader, responsive ultimately to the full panoply of satisfactions afforded by the poet's efforts to realize his or her commitments. In Clover's case those commitments are primarily to embody strange conjunctions where the work of negativity opens into realizations that social change might be possible, despite the reification and alienation produced by an increasingly globalized capitalism. Clover explores what can be made of Situationist hopes that by pursuing our less alienated pleasures we make guerilla raids on the habits accommodating ourselves to dominant social practices. One does not have to believe utopian thinking in order to manipulate the pressure points that it exposes.

Clover clarified his relation to Situationist theory in a talk he gave on the modern city at the Modernist Studies Meeting in Madison, Wisconsin, in 2002:

> One of the things one might suppose about a labyrinthine poetics is that it would be, at least at times, hard to read, what with its dead ends, blind peregrinations and doublings back, its frustrations and the necessary duration of any traverse. It's a form of real contingency—not, that is, the limited set of formal choices afforded at every intersection of the grid city, but moments of both choice and necessity which will have unknown consequence for the course of circulation. Baudelaire, in one of his best-known passages, made the connection explicit: "Which of us, in his moments of ambition, has not dreamed of a poetic prose, musical, without rhythm and without rhyme, supple enough and rugged enough to adapt itself to the lyrical impulses of the soul, the undulations of reverie, the jibes of conscience? / It was, above all, out of my exploration of huge cities, out of the medley of their innumerable interrelations, that this haunting ideal was born."

By foregrounding these moments of choice, Situationist thinking simultaneously honors and transforms the constructivist impulse in modernist art. Art's basic task becomes to put contingency at war against "its dialectical double reification":

> Here the modern and Modernism part ways, for Modernism (at least at its best) meant to undo, or at least argue against, reification. . . . Each of these [modernism's formal strategies], in its own way, responds to or enacts formal qualities of the grid city with its brute regularities, its short blocks and quick turns, its dense cultural agglomerations spilling into each other. It's a poetics of quick, unceasing circulation; as a Modernism, it's a contestation of the modern insofar as it proffers a control over the circulation which is not the control of capital. . . . If we are to find the Modernist city, it will be at the very moment when art escapes into practice when it stops being a form of, a mimesis of, or

a critique of the urban, but becomes an urbanism itself. The art of the future will be the overturning of situations or nothing."[3]

At stake then is the possibility of reconfiguring our ways of valuing imagination. Rather than treat social judgment as primary and honor the art that best reflects the values in such judgments, we can envision having what satisfies as art provide these terms for social judgment: "When a poem by Mallarmé becomes the sole explanation for an act of revolt, then poetry and revolution will have overcome their ambiguity." Analogously, by taking Situationist claims as literally as possible (which is also to take them as figuratively as possible), one establishes a sense of demand for oneself to explore how art might inform social change. Such change will be extremely difficult to realize because of the embeddedness of habits of living shaped by capitalism. But at least one can make the difficulties clear by following Raoul Vaneigem's dictum that such an art can "continually raise the question brutally ironic? brutally hopeful?"

III

Situationism's major vehicle for such ironies and such hopes is the principle of détournement, the pleasures of perversities that have the interest of the polis in mind. But Clover's fealty to Situationism emerges less in any specific device borrowed from the past than in the pursuit of a commitment he shares with Debord: that art cease being "a mimesis of, or a critique of the urban," so that it can live an ideal of urban life and of what urbanity contributes to life. That is why the Mallarmé passage on revolution is so important to him. Such an ideal is doomed to fail, doomed to generate brutally ironic disappointments. But the disappointments can be factored into the poet's social vision so that there is also considerable room for a brutal hopefulness: predictable disappointment can be treated as a perennial reason for refusing to make the compromises that will prevent both the disappointment and the possibility.[4]

In order to demonstrate how such commitments to social relations operate in Clover, one has to be careful to avoid the discourses about history dominant in the past two decades. Talk of witnessing sounds hollow to him and talk of causality crude. Worse, talk about witnessing presupposes powers as agents that are exactly what he thinks our experience of history calls into question. If there is to be lyric that can accurately capture contemporary conditions of social agency, it will have to render the strange impersonal or transpersonal dependencies that bind us to our cultural moment. And it will have to recognize the partial blindness of the damaged subjects who are working their way toward expressing their situations. Therefore Clover cannot simply project a poetry that is the continuation of social theory by other means. Poetry for him must begin by asking how one might get any hold at all on what reification and alienation make of our psychic lives. So at best this poetry has to pursue the sense of placed displacement that makes it conceivable one's experience could be interpreted as an aspect of social totality. One begins with the desire to make, not to know; then one pursues the shaping of immaterial thoughts and feelings to see how they might attach to the insistences of the world.

That commitment to making allows Clover an indirect but deeply engaged response to what I have to call our historicity. Our historicity emerges primarily in those seemingly inescapable attachments generated by a collective feel of the symptomatic and the enigmatic. For then we have to take account of what separates us from ourselves as subjects and forces us to attempt seeing ourselves, despite the fact that we know we can grasp at best a partial view. Identification then is a fundamental concern in his poetry, but almost never in ways that can reinforce us as subjects. As in Ashbery, we are always already coming upon the identifications that shape us. But unlike Ashbery, Clover rarely finds cause for celebrating the distances that seem to allow lyric energies to attach to social forms. The festive is always in the background, always something that seems already reappropriated within structures of control. Analogously Ashbery's fluidity among personal pronouns becomes in Clover a constant sense of how weak a hold we have on the various permutations of self-reference. Ashbery's fluidity becomes a measure of the impotence felt when one looks at the many ways individual subjects become utterly bound to their roles and narrow interests. No wonder that Clover's formal strategies are less a foregrounding of mastery per se than a rendering of efforts at expressivity that is at odds with objective conditions.

IV

These topics are important enough, and Clover's work good enough, that I shall now address two somewhat different poems exploring what poetry's pleasures can do to convey a distinctive contemporary sense of historicity. The first is "No More Boffins," a poem where Clover's sense of alienation is fully on display. Then I shall only have time to briefly indicate how in "Chreia," Clover marshals the pleasures of lyric to define possible ways that consciousness can seek alternative spaces within a commodified world.

"No More Boffins" concentrates on how lyric can render the sense of inhabiting the symptomatic conditions that make us historical beings:

> We were drinking gin and tonics on the terrace when the midi skirt
> Came back into style. At this time movies were extremely popular
> Although no more than usual, after which many people stopped in
> At the Liberty Equality Fraternity Café for ice cream,

The ice cream of novel thoughts. Everyone was wearing
Those sunglasses everyone's wearing. Just a few felicities
Make a movement, the kind that should really have its own comic book
Exploring the great issues of the age but still with boffo action
And a speaking part for the lightbulb.
And so the crowd promenaded, lacking a manifesto,
Yet to have condemned the passésists or started the exclusions,
Scarcely aware they were (in the words of Archigram—
Clever boys, give them their own terrace immediately!)
A moment-village. They goeth abroad in the land.
How long have we been discussing whether we are a part
Of what passes by, and at what point did that become
The main conversation, replacing the summer, our cadastral survey
Of its many crowded quarters, its tuned suburbs and departments,
Its way of being a different sort of parade,
The kind which can be conveniently depicted with a spectrum?
Paint samples from Jane's Hardware will do in a pinch.
Already the fete is erasing itself from the popular memory
Like exploding instructions, leaving stained confetti as a reminder
You were supposed to get something done. Little tasks,
Large problems, philosopher say: Who will do the laundry
Now that history is coming to an end? What advantage
Would someone have over me who knew a direct route
From blue to yellow, far from this shady way-station
Where we dream aimlessly of love in the afternoon,
The post-historical kind? However big you grow in my estimation,
You will always be a dwarf compared to these buildings,
Their skins glassy and inviting as that lake just to the west
Of wherever we grew up, you remember, Something Lake.
The information lurks in the shoals in forms by now
Almost unrecognizable. Now if only you could dive sideways.
When is the real holiday, the one for which everyone gets a sharp haircut,
Cruel atonal singing seeps from the crypt and the meaning of objects
Is once again up for grabs? Even bricks were once straw.

The title is especially appropriate now because "Boffin" is a British term
for experts—no more talking heads, especially those who wear stars on
their shoulders. Getting adequate social analysis requires a quite different
approach. So the poem begins by quickly surveying several social locales,
including a quotation comprising the first line that makes Ashbery a funda-
mental aspect of the cultural geography. In effect the poem wants to work
out what kinds of information might sustain and give substance to its own
desire to speak as and for the first-person plural. Then one might be capa-
ble of shifting identifications from the ironic observing "we," up on the bal-
cony to the social collective "we" down in the street, and one might do so
without being recuperated by controls that make one walk this way and that,

imagining one is free. Clearly such conditions are too dispersed to allow an "I" to emerge, except in the form of lamentation for all that it cannot possess about its own social conditioning. Even the initial "we" comes to our attention as states of consciousness where the festive flow of possible identifications has no anchor, no site where examination and judgment can take hold. Ironically it is only the material fact of movement that by route of pun calls up the possibility of a manifesto. And that possibility is quickly dismissed because this is a "moment-village," united not by ideas but by these proliferating processes.

Lines 15 and 16 change the tone by shifting to explicit self-consciousness about consciousness: "How long have we been discussing whether we are a part / Of what passes by." On one level this question thickens the poem's obsession with information, with how one comes to terms with all the ways one registers oneself part of a world—or, in our post-Stevensian climate, parts of worlds. But the poem also helps show how our media become blocks to our ever gaining the necessary information. Notice how this sentence intricately places time elements against space elements so that geography and history pull against each other. Each dimension is necessary for grasping the "now," but each involves different kinds of measurements, and each seems to demand different kinds of self-consciousness. Positioned in time, we have to work our way through narrative forms; positioned in space, we find the movement conditioned by the many crowded quarters through which the parade passes. No wonder the poem is driven to surreal notions of how depiction might take place.

The sense of festival made us attend to our social place. But as that sense explodes, the feeling of sociality takes on content primarily as a set of questions that come to structure the poem. Here two interesting aspects of the social come to the fore. First, second-person and first-person pronouns now enter the poem because the issue of person is inseparable from these questions about what kind of place the individual might have in this effort to work out the consequences of the initial attention to festival. Second, as the poem enters this questioning phase, the speaking voice becomes increasingly locked into the postures basic to capitalist society. The speaking presence becomes insecure about the possibility that others might find ways to have advantages; at the other pole, there emerges what Adorno and Horkheimer called the negative subject of capitalism seeking an existence apart from social relations.

I am not sure how to read the last section. But I think the difficulty is not so much a problem with the poem as a problem for the poem—given the situation that has been depicted. Trapped by what we might call the historical geography shaping cultural identities, the speaking presence wobbles between a tentative, unrealizable lyricism addressed to "you" and an unbearably clear awareness that the facts involve forces with more determinative power than the positioned intellect has the resources to grasp. And when the speaking tries to be expansive about the "you," it is instantly forced to recognize how pathetic the human seems in relation to the buildings that frame the scene. But, good interpellated subject that it is, the speaking figure also lets its fascination with the buildings provide a lyrical hope of reconciliation with the environment. The terms of reconciliation, however, depend on fantasized memories of the kind of lake that dwells for most of us in the remote shoals of memory. Here is our festival, yet we have no way to gain access to it as a vital social or personal force.

So while the imagination may be willing, the poem proves weak. It can envision the possibility of diving sideways in order to gain access to the lake through the reflecting presence of the buildings. But that action is so unlikely that the poem opts instead for the prospect of a holiday, only to bring into the present the sounds of an atonal operatic funeral procession. Dreaming and dying have far too much proximity. Yet even if persons cannot dive into the lake-buildings, the dream of revolution remains: meanings reduced to straw can still become the bricks that get hurled against the dominating glass. The poem is left in the horrible position of refusing to give up on the dream of revolution while it has to recognize how this dream makes every present attachment to the social a source of alienation.

Were an individual expressive subject to offer this account of alienation, many of us would find the pathos self-indulgent and somewhat suspect. However, if poetry can imagine itself into the symptoms, into an abstracted and nonsubjective version of the pains and uncertainties that shape our relation to our own sense of what the social might be, the dream of revolution, sufficiently tempered by despair, might seem itself an ineluctable part of our geography. Theory can explain why revolution may be necessary and analyze what constrains us. But perhaps only poetry can show how that cry emerges from modes of awareness more intimate, more widely shared, and more desperate than theory can develop.

VI

One reason I need a second poem is that "No more Boffins" seems to sell poetic agency a little short. At least that seems the case from the perspective provided by "Chreia." That poem's dissatisfaction with the symptomatology of "No More Boffins" generates the need to explore how an individual lyric can engage Marxist concerns with totality while retaining a distinctive sense of poetic agency. This is the first half of the poem:

> At this time there was an expectation of terror meaning cops in Kevlar and
> the green civic garbage cylinders sealed with discs of steel.
>
> At this time the new train ran to an underground forest sheathed in books.

This time many years after the towers near the sex of the city were found to be twin cruets of jizz and sang.

We all floated with same specific gravity in the constantly moving stream of money as of this time.

As in the time of strike there was a quite a bit of garbage loose in the street not like an orangutan in the Rue Morgue but it eddied and whorled at the edges of the seductively weeping stream.

I was riding a swan to the underground library or having sex with a swan under a shroud of words.

As of this time we keep a copy of the city in the library and another in the ether.

Constantly offered as a time of therefore but with a feeling of as.

"Chreia" are pregnant sentences borrowed from some author then appropriated by certain rules. In this case the relevant sentence is a proposal by Breton that Paris would be improved if Notre-Dame were to be rededicated as a home for virgins, with its two towers replaced by containers of blood and semen. Then, figuratively, chreia become aspects of the city of Paris itself, sentences that become embedded units of meaning endlessly recombining as they echo one another. For Clover the modern city effectively speaks because of its regulatory designs and because of the history of signifying acts that become objective features of life for a contemporary flaneur. But the very fact that it speaks with so many tongues means that such cities cannot quite be described. The relations they have to an overall sense of totality can at best only be glimpsed. And even those glimpses depend on our capacity to envision their various aspects as participants in a complex code that emphatically resists interpretation on more local scales.

Clover's treatment of the details embodying our alienation risks a fatal opaqueness. But facing that risk makes possible two exciting features of the poem: it presents a daunting effort to find the level of abstraction on which the signs *do* make sense, and it can recombine the chreia to constitute one possibility of using something like a formal plenitude to exemplify how our reading of urban simulation need not devolve into passive complicity. This poem is as densely layered as *The Waste Land*, and as dependent on cadence; yet it offers a very different sense of history and of possible redemption. In effect the internal parallels among the four-line units set up virtual squares that give the poem an almost literal three-dimensionality.

The most overt feature of the patterning is the repeated mention of "this time," providing a sense of urgency and testing the powers of agency that the readers can bring to bear. Seen in this light, the "we" of the fourth line takes on considerable significance. That "we" cannot refer to preexisting conditions but seeks a form of agency that can encompass the impact of all the occurrences comprising "this time." "We" then becomes a possible figure for the agency accompanying what Clover calls a "time domain," a structure by which anticipating time spatially makes possible a coherent stereo-effect. "WE" is the site for responding to the overall stereo effect established by the many echoes within the poem.

This stereo-effect consists primarily of two noise-sequences; one expressing the causal effects created by historical forces, the other a range of immediate feelings intensified in the concluding stanzas:

Kevlar and carbines and garbage reduplicating into the quotidien in the time of the plan Vigipirate.

Not more people in the street but more intensely as in the time of the transit strike promenading behind the veil of speech.

Around this time we thought of the skyline as new nature.

And through it flowed the invisible milk as through the ether and the sewers the milk of capital.

There was an expectation in everyday life.

It gathered in the dead spaces beside the endlessly grieving stream.

Of milk jizz and sang in the time of the garbage in the vale of lang.

The shining order the burning simulations there are more of it.[5]

It is clear that as the poem becomes more intimate and more capable of lyricism, it also grows more desperate. That may be why the concluding section seems so elegiac. The lines are stripped of detail so that in effect they present raw and elemental feelings. We are told that there was an expectation in everyday life, but we are not told the nature of the specific expectation. Perhaps that is because in retrospect that expectation has lost any distinguishing quality except the fact that a kind of agency existed. And perhaps the expectation cannot be qualified further because Clover wants us to recognize the close connection between hope and despair when we look back on expectation. Just consider the origin of the expectation in the "dead spaces beside the endlessly grieving stream." The stream is in one aspect the Seine; part of its grieving the sense that it longs for the company of the New Bibliothèque that is unfortunately being constructed underground. Architecture itself serves primarily to nourish dreams that only haunt what could be a sense of presence.

The third line in effect extends that grief to the major details in the poem—not by metaphoric amplification but rather by reducing the figures to impotent echoes of Breton's fantasy. So the fourth line's emphasis on phenomenological affect now can do nothing but repeat that spirit of reduction in three distinctive registers. There is the surface appeal to the "shining order" of the modernist city; there are the burning simulations that this shining order becomes to the alienated eye; and there is the simply prophetic abstraction promising only repetition, all images spent.

Depressing as they are, however, these lines establish a strange dignity, perhaps because they function almost as the coda to a villanelle. Each line quietly and abstractly and untheatrically marshals the information from the preceding stanzas as if, taken together, the lines could exemplify the plight of a civilization. It becomes difficult to tell whether the aura of acceptance involved is the taking of responsibility for the citizen's plight or the utter evasion of the sense of responsibility it would take to organize frustration and act upon rage. The utopian potential of the Arcades project now is only faintly traceable in our resisting the fact that the only mode of order here is poetry approximating elegy. But the reminder that "there are more of it" also suggests that the brutal ironies continue to be tempered by brutal hopes. To recontextualize a line from "Return to Rue des Blancs Manteaux": at least we can send "our imaginings ahead to do the dirty work." Clover is not so utopian as to believe the dirty work will be followed by a architectural project responsive to that weeping river, although the poem does suggest there is no more important fantasy than that such work might be possible.

NOTES

1. Compare Mallarmé's famous statement that he rejects the "erroneous aesthetic . . . which would have the poet fill the delicate pages of his book with the actual and palpable wood of trees" for the forest's shuddering or the silent scattering of thunder through the foliage. Clover shares the resistance to realism, but his abstraction does not have the same confident route to reference. For Clover the idea of the shuddering is always shrouded by what commodification can do to nature. So the relevant abstraction is an effort to capture at once the distortion and the intended referent by having language at once prepare a path for thinking and deflect from what seems the original impression.

2. I do not know what the empirical sentence is that is referred to in the penultimate line. But probably that empirical sentence has something to do with "tracking," with linking what follows a program to the program itself. Even the possibility of that probability is sufficient to flesh out the second meaning of *sentence*: the sentence

is empirical in part because it shares in the repetitiveness that has been the defining quality of the material landscape.

3. This Situationist vision of poetry manages to honor modernist art and writing because it sees that work struggling to escape the effects of modernization. Yet this vision also affords a clear difference from how these writers and artists pursued their ambitions. Situationist values project an aesthetic opposed to any distinctions between styles within art and ways of engaging life. Rather than establish separate domains of play or *Schein* and social forces, Situationists treat play as precisely what art contributes to our resources for engaging the real. Art can transform urban space into a ludic field in the hope that it can create alternatives to the banalizations basic to modernity. Hence Guy Debord's ideal of drifting "through the city, allowing its signs to divert, to 'detourn,' your steps, and then to divert those signs yourself, forcing them to give up routes that never existed before—there would be no end to it. It would be to begin to live a truly modern way of life." These routes make visible "sites where capitalism is unstable and the architectural complex it controls modifiable. Its aspect will change totally or partially in accordance with the will of its inhabitants." (Guy Debord, quoted in Greil Marcus, *Lipstick Times* [Cambridge, Mass.: Harvard University Pres, 1990], 170.)

4. Clover then takes on the difficult task of preserving Debord's sense of play while also stressing how a Marxist perspective explains the perennial disappointment of Situationist ambitions. So Clover is willing to be much more analytic about the limitations of social life than any Situationist work with which I am familiar. In fact the richest source of pleasure for me in reading Clover is his ability to absorb that Marxian sense of limitation while refusing to have it justify submitting to a theater of alienation. Perhaps his success stems from his refusing to reduce a Marxist perspective to a few ideas by which to beat other academics. Instead his is a poet's Marx, a Marx that has to accommodate to the formal demands of poetry and the strategic pleasures that give the soul a feeling of control over circulation that is not the control exercised by capital. Clover's is a poetry that explores basic psychological consequences of living under the law of the commodity, and hence it has to grapple with the impotence of individuals in relation to historical forces.

Clover is never unaware that such questioning is rife with problems—largely because of the formal expectations within the question-answer pattern. Formulating questions produces expectations that knowledge is the product sought. But knowledge is a tricky property when one is dealing with social conditions. What we often come to know is only how remote are the possibilities for meaningful political action. So it is all too easy to decide it is more prudent to cut one's losses than persist in what may be hopeless pursuits of social change. Yet that stance ignores the possibility that desires for change, or even desires for some kind of striking out, can be sufficiently strong to challenge the stances produced by "knowledge." Marx's insistence on the priority of practice was not an insistence on reasonable actions measured by risk-managers. Analogously, many feelings about social relations that submit to conditions of knowledge are likely to generate despair. But perhaps such despair about social justice is best seen as a historically conditioned phenomenon making it possible for capitalist world visions to thrive.

5. The first lines in each of our two "stanzas" render the city in crisis by concen-

trating on how its garbage becomes a signifier. These are not standard lyrical feelings but embedded states of terror and frustration, with their own possible fascinations as the garbage becomes a "seductively weeping stream."

There is no weeping in the much quieter second lines that seem driven by private experiences rather than overtly public ones. But these lines express similar frustrations, now in the form of the sterility of the new Paris Bibliothèque, its underground stacks probably a symbol for the shrouding of words in cultural life.

The third lines put the city itself within the library, for good and for ill. Breton's sentence shapes the relevant line of the first stanza; the burying in the library of Benjamin's original manuscript for the Arcades project stands behind the second. Finally, the fourth line in each stanza provides something like the phenomenological feel establishing an affective register for the previous details. Reading arrives at a sense of collective agency, as pathos and as hope, through a recognition that we all participate in Simmel's "constantly moving stream of capital." The second stanza names that sense of agency by repeating "constantly," then beautifully rendering feelings abstract and elemental enough to bind that sense of agency. Our sense of time is "therefore" because one can only interpret the stream of capital as a model of causality. But when we look for causality, we only find simulation: the feeling of "as" must suffice for our sense of substance.

I think the poem becomes more lyrical as the details gather energy from repetition and as the patterning grows more evocative. Now there can be an explanation for the connection between expectations of terror in the city and the inundation of garbage "at the time of the strike." The plan Vigipirate is the city of Paris's model for public security in a time when the threat of terror is substantial. (They seem to know when that occurs without our color coding.) Among its details is the sealing of the public waste cans so that bombs cannot be deposited there. Everyone is asked to suffer a little so that no one will lose a life, a version of socialism without economic justice. But the very rationality of the plan abstracts from the details and reveals the strangely organized discomforts to which city life is subject. In the second line the expected reference to the library now extends to a veil of speech manifesting a possible life in the frustrated crowds. And the poem now offers a correlate of that frustration by replacing specific references to the city with a reference to an overall effect of the skyline. That skyline now appears as "new nature" because nature itself becomes continuous with urban life: at best, a new source of energies; at worst, a spreading of simulation and reification. So the fourth line's phenomenological self-awareness returns to figure of flowing streams, but only to register the absorbing of sensation into the effects sustained by the flow of capital.

BIBLIOGRAPHY

Books by Joshua Clover

Madonna Anno Domini. Baton Rouge: Louisiana State University Press, 1997.
The Totality for Kids. Berkeley and Los Angeles: University of California Press, 2006.
Their Ambiguity. Oakland, Calif.: Quemadura, 2003.

Critical Book

The Matrix. London: British Film Institute, 2004.

Selected Prose

"The End of the Experiment." *Village Voice* (Voice Literary Supplement) 47, no. 1 (October 9–October 15, 2002): 76.

"Good Pop, Bad Pop: Massiveness, Materiality, and the Top 40." In *This Is Pop: In Search of the Elusive at Experience Music Project*, edited by Eric Weisbard, 245–56. Cambridge, Mass.: Harvard University Press, 2004.

Museum catalog, Walker Arts. Minneapolis, Minn.: Walker Arts, 2004.

"The Rose of the Name: A Genealogy of LANGUAGE Poetry." *Fence* 1, no. 1 (Spring 1998): 35–41.

Selected Criticism

"Active Magic." By Laura Mullen. *Colorado Review* (1999).

"Channel Surfing." By Edward Dougherty. *American Book Review* 20, no. 2 (January–February 1999).

"Cyan Ideas." By Geoffrey G. O'Brien. *Iowa Review* 28, no. 3 (Winter 1998): 162–69.

"Rogue Clover." By Cal Bedient. *Poetry Flash*, No. 276 (April–May 1998): 1.

"Strange and Admirable." By Wayne Koestenbaum. *Parnassus* 24, no. 2 (2001): 297–311.

[Untitled review]. By John Yau. *Boston Review* (December–January 1997–1998).

KEVIN YOUNG

FROM *TO REPEL GHOSTS*

DEFACEMENT
(1983)

Acrylic & ink on wallboard
25 × 30 in.

Basquiat scrawls
& scribbles, clots
paint across

the back
wall of Keith Haring's
Cable Building studio—

two cops, keystoned,
pounding a beat,
pummel

a black face—scape
goat, sarcophagus—
uniform-blue

with sticks. The night
Michael Stewart snuck
on the tracks

& cops caught him
tagging
a train—THIRD RAIL

DANGER LIVE
VOLTAGE—
taught him better

than to deface public
property. Choke
hold. Keep NEW YOKE

CITY Clean.
Give those men
a PABST BLUE

RIBBON, a slap
on the wrist
a meddle

of honor. Basquiat
produces *Beat
Bop*, black

on black
vinyl—VOCAL.
TEST PRESSING.

INTESTINES.
TARTOWN
RECORDS. EAR.

All revolutions
33⅓
When Haring moves

up & out, he'll tear
down that wall
careful to get

Basquiat out intact—
in Haring's
bedroom modeled

after the Ritz
¿DEFACEMENT?
sits, saved

like a face, framed—

FAMOUS NEGRO ATHLETES

B anomaly—
anomaly he be—
caught between

a hock
& a hard race—
From the peak

you can almost see

the far
side of the river
Lights stretch

out suburban
satisfied
Black is this

season in
It goes
with everythin—

They know not
who he is because
he is not like

what ever they know—

Lashed
to the mast
the hero rides

past, ignoring
the sirens
steering by stars

& desire—
Only he can hear—
The others' ears

stuffed w/ cotton
so's not to listen—
What leads us

into the water we
inhale
as if air, smiling

whiles we die—
Bliss is this—
Is not his

luxury, no matter
how heavy
his pockets, how full

no one will let
Gentleman Jack
Johns'n board this Titanic—

O how the ship will rock
when it meets
that giant block

of ice—doing
the Eagle Rock—
it's not what

you can see
—the white—
that kills, but what you cannot

FROM *JELLY ROLL*

FISH STORY

For you I would give up
God—repeal

once & for all, unkneel—
you are beautiful,

little devil—redboned
rusted.
        I trust

you take my soul
someplace I don't want

to know—
dance me round

till dawn. I sleep
long & wake with a crick

running down my neck

to remind
me a you—find

my top drawers empty
my eyes watery

& wind & when
will you again—

To repent I wander
down to the forgetful river

—wait for you there—
& wonder

if the uncaught, low-
down fish know

how lucky they are

NOCTURNE

I have other names
for you—sin, cobalt

blue, whatever fits
& is not too French.

Forget. Foaming
the mouth, I bark

out commands, cat-
calls. Wolf-tickets—

I call you Paris,
Telemachus, whatever

that means. I mean
sweet hijacker, you make me

want to make you
mine, to kidnap

ourselves & fall
in love with our

captors. My kisses
the prayers a hostage

makes—holy, please,
begging be saved.

FROM *BLACK MARIA*

NIGHT CAP

He loves me slow
as gin, then's out

light-switch quick.
The moon's burned-

out bulb in a blackened sky,
I lie in the dark & want

his name to be mine—
or to be alone—

Wish I could walk out
this overheated railroad flat

& everyone on the street
knew me, home, & he'd wake

in bed alone & wonder
where I'd gone. Instead,

his unsteady snore—
calling the hogs, sawing.

Sleep, for now, is almost
enough—want it to start

in my toes & tingle
upward, then explode

behind my eyes, closed—
Said start down in my toes

& explode behind
eyes now closed

like the pawnshop
across the street, its sign

blaring all night what
only daylight

can buy. Up
& down the block

you can hear the dogs talk—

never us—till the pigeons
pace the ledge

outside my bedroom & strut
like the painted girls down

on Twilight Avenue,
moan the morning blue.

THE HIDEOUT

Woke up dead

tired, in my arms
an empty

an instead. Tried
sleeping it off,

my hangover of her,
wishing for some hair

of the dog—or slow purr—

The light my eye hurts

My tongue
white, eyes red.

I am in chalk, an outline,
a back-alley body—

afraid his face
in the mirror (that hides

my strychnine mouthwash)
may be the only one left.

Do I need again

to lose my skin, start
a new town, man?

Grow a beard,
or become one?

I'm sick of taking

it on the chin, of waking
gimlet-eyed from the gin—

Shoe soles like carpet,
or excuses, grown thin.

Cloudy tap water.
One dusty aspirin.

Outside my newsprint
curtains—the black

& white of words,
yellowing—

What I can no more weather

I watch till I'm sure
no light remains

Night staining the streets clean

POETICS STATEMENT
from Deadism

IT HAPPENS every few years, perhaps oftener: we get the article, widely and usually well-published, that declares poetry dead. Often the accompanying sound is less a lament for this premature pronouncement than a jig on poetry's pre-paid grave. Rarely do I hear such an essay sound more like an Irish wake or a New Orleans jazz funeral, two sounds I think poetry should aspire to more often. A raucous solace.

Instead, poetry is dead.

I disagree; I plan wild essays; I respond point by point, debunking and spelunking.

But tonight, why not—poetry is dead. Let it be dead then, let us write as if we are already dead. If poetry is dying, than let's just write a poetry pronounced DOA.

Perhaps it is just because I have witnessed too many deaths these past few years, but I have tried since to write a poetry of life, against those deaths and even Death in general. Maybe. But it also seems to me some of the same folks who think poetry is dead, or proceed without it, turn to poetry in crucial moments: at a death, or a wedding. Poetry as invocation, as ceremony.

I want an afterparty poetry, a poetry that sings a bit off key, drunk or I never touch the stuff, but sings anyway.

For years I've felt poetry was not ceremony, but the daily thing. The dirt. It is an everyday, not an occasionally. I still think this. But perhaps the only way to make this truly true is to write a poetry that is not like death, but is death: surprising yet inevitable, everyday yet far-off in the future, an ever-present that we still manage to forget. In this, it may resemble jazz—or is this simply because, as Ralph Ellison says, "life is jazz-shaped"? Death may be jazz-shaped too, just ask Gabriel and Satchmo in their cutting contest.

The only way to find out is to write a dead poetry.

I am not taking this lightly: I am not suggesting a poetry of suicide (don't do it), or of homicide (give that up); I am not suggesting a poetry celebrating war, or ignoring war, or a poetry of a war that we celebrated too early our victory in, and now cannot ignore. (The deadening of poetry is celebrated too early and often too.) A dead poetry does not believe in "-icides" of any kind; it believes in insides, in soul and sorrow, in silence and also the singing that is against such silence.

Deadism believes that poetry should capture a living language, it just knows that we should write in dead languages too.

Write not like something endangered—not like a spotted owl—or reintroduced into the wild, but dead already. (The poetry of "they're coming to get us," the poetry of the horror movie I've seen too much of, the poetry of lament, of victimization, or worse, of declaring the various and nefarious threats to freedom, equality, blackness, or justice seems to take too much pleasure in watching the killer even as it's shouting out warnings in the theater. This poetry is over, but not yet dead.) Write not like a coming extinction, but like the extinction already. That said, do not write like a dodo, something rare and flightless—but like the passenger pigeon, a poetry once plentiful and ever-present and so therefore killed off.

Do not write a poetry of rarity, or of rarification, but of *never again*.

Do not even write this poetry, but find it, come across it, and step over it. The helpless ant that in the end can lift more than ten times its weight: that is a poetry.

Maybe what we need is an undead poetry—not to take death back from poetry, but to take death back from death itself. A poetry of shambling power, devouring everything in its path. A vampire poetry that will live forever, sexy and dangerous and immortal, shapeshifting when necessary.

That bat in my friend's toilet (true story) a poetry. That dog. That mewling cat caught under my house that left sometime in the night a poetry. It is hard to find, and harder to coax out, but will one day on its own.

In the meantime, a poetry that speaks from the mouths of those gone that aren't really gone, a poetry of ghosts and haunts. Of haints; not ain'ts. Dead is something you can be, after all, is not itself an *ain't*. The ain'ts I'm afraid are here, among us living.

Instead there's the haints, which our poetry should be: haunting, hard to pin down, glimpsed yet believed. That's a poetry I believe in. A poltergiest poetry that moves things, and us, when we least expect.

Deadism: I did not invent it, it invented me. Paul Celan, Gwendolyn Brooks (*We Real Cool*), Fenton Johnson ("I'm tired of civilization"—throw the children in the river), the exhaustion of Bob Kaufman who wrote in order to be forgotten, the ghostly poetry of Larry Levis. The poetry of Alan Dugan seems dead already, a voice from beyond. Toni Morrison's *Beloved*. Kenneth Koch writing a poetry of life that is in the end death. I used to hope for a poetry of preserving; in my first book, this is what emerged, writing to try and capture the voices of the life I saw that was rapidly disappearing. That of the black rural South of my parents and grandparents.

Some would say they were happy to see it go; what I saw were the good things going too. And worse, nowhere a poetry of it, no poetry either marking or mourning the passing of a way of life—a way folks I knew seemed to mark and remark on, mostly by humor. This was not to me a contradiction, but the paradox back of existence: mournful laughter.

At the same time, my first book seemed almost dictated to me by the ghosts of my family—but a set of ghosts that were my family. My job, in part, to conjure them up—even when they were still alive, as my grandfather (rest in peace) was then. In order to write about him, I had to write about his death, which hadn't happened yet but I knew would; I had to write his funeral, and had as witnesses folks imagined, some remembered and some who were already dead, like my young cousin who'd recently killed himself. The poem then is for the real him, but the living him, made by the poem, also speaks and tells of the funeral of our grandfather, still in real life alive.

While in one way this is preserving, and in another it is merely an insufficient explanation of the vagaries of the imagination, in the main it is to say that I have been a Deadist longer than I remember. So too William Carlos Williams in *Spring and All* and *The Descent of Winter*: how in the former he must destroy everything before rebuilding, before spring.

Rebuilding is more difficult than we thought.

But if we write a poetry not of ending, but of end, a poetry that is itself unmoving, we may actually move. A poetry not of *if*, but of *when*.

Deadism like those movies with voiceovers that sound not only dead, but by the end you find out are from a dead man: not ready for my close-up, but the one floating in the pool, the one who knows what he can't know but tells us anyway. A poetry not of witness, or of victimhood, or one of experience or innocence, but of the moment after: write like a saint, not the picture of a saint. Write like the bone in the box, the relic to be kissed. Better yet, write like the saints that have been officially declared saints no more; write like something once holy, now decanonized and attempted to be forgotten. Write not like remembering, but the forgetting.

This does not mean writing erasures, which has been done (but not, unfortunately, to death). Do not write like the *Erased DeKooning Drawing* by Robert Rauschenberg, brilliant as it is; do not write like the once beautiful thing, ancestral, now gone. Instead, write like DeKooning picking not the ugliest of his drawings for the kid with the good idea to erase, but instead picking a really nice one: write like something you don't mean to be erased but one day know will; then let them try.

MIXED-UP MEDIUM

Kevin Young's Turn-of-the-Century American Triptych

Rick Benjamin

AMONG CONTEMPORARY poets, no one's more in tune to his diverse subjects or more mixed-up in both his craft and mass media than Kevin Young. He is a maker of old-school and of-the-moment modes and forms, a serious practitioner and technical innovator. Since 2001 Kevin Young has composed three volumes that not only offer up a new and rich blend of both ancestral and contemporary consciousnesses, but also a diverse and wide-ranging poetics that is this new century's *Montage*. Referential and reverential, equal parts throwback and visionary, Young's a hybrid of the known and new. In his long-book meditation on the artist Jean-Michel Basquiat, for example—*To Repel Ghosts* (2001)—he employs a version of Dante's terza rima and the hip-hop or pop artist's approach to archiving history. In *Black Maria* (2005), film noir meets mock-heroic couplets, a bittersweet coupling figured through film. In his third book, *jelly roll* (2003)—a National Book Award finalist—the blues form's stretched, in this case to joy and back. Even his first book, *Most Way Home*, a National Poetry Series winner in 1995, is an audibly lyrical meditation on lineage and cultural heritage. With his latest book, Young completes a sustained cultural critique through the lenses of major African American artists and art forms. Together, the three volumes mark the emergence of a major voice in American poetry.

To Repel Ghosts is a major retrospective, a deep drop into American hell-realms: racism, consumerism, fame, and addiction. The book is presented as a series of "discs" that, while reminiscent of vinyl and CDs, are also more wild, unwieldy, and sustained versions of these musical wraps. Young's discs have two or three sides and countless songs of which to keep track, signaling extended listening of this one, prematurely ended, black artist's life.

"Campbell's Black Bean Soup," is just the first of hundreds of Young's plumbing, punning, stripped-down terza rimas:

> . . . Bartering work
>
> for horse, Basquiat churned
> out butter, signing each
> SAMO©. Sameold. Sambo's
>
> soup. How to sell out
> something bankrupt
> already?[1]

This is Dante's stanza in more short-limbed, downbeated form, harboring at once the audible labors of a poem like Hayden's "Those Winter Sundays" and the jumpy play of Hopkins's language and sprung rhythms in a poem like "Pied Beauty." I reference a mid-twentieth-century American poet and nineteenth-century English poet deliberately, because every deft move of Kevin Young's suggests apprenticeship to both traditional and contemporary forms. Just as Hopkins bent and truncated the sonnet to his exuberant and quirky telling, so Young means to retune the thirteenth-century terza rima for a more headlong and plummeting twentieth-century descent.

It's a fast-paced, freestyle world we've stumbled into, and Young himself enters it in a first-line gallop, all trochees, followed by resonant downbeats. Slant- and off-rhymed, heavily stressed, no more than two or three beats per line, language here is commensurately stretched, pressed. The double duty of words like "lofty" and "sell out" and "bankrupt" testifies to both crass commercialism—embedded in the puns—and also to more valuable currencies, the duplicity and double entendres suggesting an alternately playful and edgy representation of the neo–pop cultural moment seen in retrospect:

> . . . Basquiat stripped
> labels, opened & ate
> alphabets . . .
>
> . . . he smacked
> the very bottom, scraping
> the uncanny, making
>
> a tin thing sing.
>   (*TRG* 5)

Getting under the conceptual frame for this artist means getting under the skin: the cost of seeing through and living past "labels." The sound of banging pots, the poet's trochees and dactyls, eat up Dada's premises, leaving only the sound, the song of "a tin thing": this Campbell's soup can's sentient. In the rhymed and hard-driving closing can also be heard the insidious melody of the quick fix, the promise of freedom through metamorphosis—but the arch of this illusion of transcendence will be decidedly downward, toward "the very bottom" of human experience.

And so ensues a kind of "portrait of the artist" from five "sides." Some sides, like this first one, called "Bootlegs," are excavating, explicatory: they cover Basquiat's time at the experimental City As School, his stint hawking postcards for heroin on St. Marks, his early shows and collaborations. These early poems more or less take for granted the knowledge that Basquiat was addicted to heroin, that his graffiti tag, SAMO, stood for "same old shit," that neo-pop in the hands of Warhol was the bright surface of a soup can.

But one of the great achievements of *To Repel Ghosts* is its persistent historicizing: one comes out of the book considerably more educated about Basquiat, his artistic and cultural milieu, about the perverse and myriad ways America reifies race. As historical document, biography, as self- and other-conscious meditation on the life of the black artist in America—on all these levels, *To Repel Ghosts* succeeds brilliantly.

Young's wildly associative three-line riffs sound the strange, appropriating American arts establishment in which the young black artist has found himself. Part virtuoso performance, part warning label, poems like "Dos Cabezas" are songs toward setting the record straight:

> . . . the gap
> in Basquiat's teeth
>
> *What me worry?* . . .
>
> Warhol with hand raised
> pensing or perhaps
> picking his nose . . .
>
> the pair, returning
> to Andy's Factory,
> the canvas still wet
>
> as a kiss. A gift. Sold
> at auction their faces fetch
> five times the asking—
>
> feeding frenzy . . .
>   (*TRG* 55)

Young's poem has all the pleasures of Dada/pop/late *beat*: *Mad* Magazine's Alfred E. Neumann inhabits Basquiat's own gap-toothed smile long enough to suggest the generational difference between "B" and Warhol; Warhol is either deep in thought or "picking his nose." Art here is one person's gift and another's fix. The lines skillfully sound the connoisseur-consumer's appetite, high-bidders devouring at a gallop. Without explicitly saying so, Young refers here to the fact that Basquiat provided Warhol with a second wind; their collaborations on large canvases relied upon the younger artist's energy and vision. The older, white artist, however, disproportionately profited from their convergences in the auctions that followed their two-headed compositions. Friendship or exploitation? the poem asks.

"Amateur Bout," the twenty-fourth and one of the longest of the twenty-seven "songs" on this first side of disc 1 embodies and sounds all of the contradictions of the young black artist making art in the belly of a beast whose appetite for new blood seems bottomless. Young's figuring of this embattled terrain as a boxing match—punch-drunk, hyped-up prowess circumscribed by a roped-off ring—is brilliantly rendered:

> Blood in his mouth
> this morning, high
> cotton, a prize
>
> fight—trying
> to beat this thing,
> breathe easy
>
> as money.
> THIS IS NOT
> IN PRAISE
>
> OF POISON
> ING MYSELF . . .
>   (*TRG* 57)

"High cotton" here is both in the mouth and speaks of the cotton field where slaves pick (off) the fashion statement someone else wears. Dante's stanza is put to great use, as Young demonstrates the purgatorial nature of this fight, fought against multiple opponents: the "poison" of Warhol's "strictly cash," art awash in money; any addiction—whether drug- or desire- or fame-induced—that throws its own hooks; "THE UGLY, FAT LIKE A PIG" art establishment and the all-consuming culture of which it is a spectacle or centerpiece, apple in its mouth. It's a setup, dehumanizing traps masquerading as riches. And this consuming bout with addiction, co-optation and commercialism is, to Young's perfectly pitched ear, all pop-punned, run-on:

> He's off
> like a bet—dime
> bag, training
>
> bag, punch
> drunk & judy—
> a hit—
>
> THE CUSTOMER . . .
>
> ●
>
> JUNK AND CIGARETTES
>   (*TRG* 61)

Young's extraction of Basquiat's capitalized words from the canvas for integration into the language of his own poem is deft, connective: heroin and consumer culture are one. In Young, Basquiat has a loyal transcriber, a twenty-first-century interpreter of maladies for both the young, late twenti-eth-century black pop artist and contemporary poet.

Young easily and opportunistically borrows others' words to fill in blanks and for purposes of transition. Poems about the dropping of the atomic bomb on Hiroshima ("Gringo Pilot"), the Negro Leagues and the breaking of the color barrier ("Monarchs" and "3 Kinds of Fences"), and urban devel-opment ("Man-Made")—all based on paintings—are dropped in by way of representing more fully the range of Basquiat's catalogue. This is a country-sized canvas, a large-scale book of poems. "Gringo Pilot" is an early poem in *To Repel Ghosts* that demonstrates Basquiat-Young's uncanny ability to sing the saddest stories of America while representing simultaneously the bomb-like quality of SAMO's© sorties as he tags the city:

> Trinity
>
> Test, Fat Man,
>
> Little Boy—unstable
> isotope,
> fissionable core—
>
> Rita Hayworth taped
> to the bombshell. Exit
> Row. Do not write
>
> on the back. Write
> English with all capital
> letters. Keep form
>
> until departure from
> U.S.—deported, interred,
> Interrogated . . .
>   (*TRG* 21)

The "labeling" here is breathtaking, unexpected: Young black artist with a blond Mohawk ("English with all capital / letters" his tagging medium) renders as aircraft the heart of white America. "Little Boy"—with its pic-ture of a bombshell pasted to the bombshell—renders sex and slogans as lit-eral tags marking the imminent depopulation of Hiroshima. Like Basquiat, Kevin Young can't *not* make connections: deportation, internment, interro-gation (race matters) the extraordinary marshaling of artlike energy in mili-tary projects like Trinity, identity of the perp hidden in a plane's black box.

When it comes to identities, *To Repel Ghosts* performs multiple acts of excavation. One of the best of these acts is side 2's twenty-two-page revision-ist project on the boxer, Jack Johnson (**29.** Jack Johnson). Young's three-line stanzas are punctuated by statements from Du Bois, Booker T. Washington,

Jack London, Miles Davis, among others. The effect is collage, crescendo, collapse; that is to say, all of the effects one might see also on Basquiat's canvas representing the same subject. Young charts the rise and fall of the artist-icon with a montage that reads like a history lesson, a cautionary tale, the boxer accounting for himself at the same time that others speak both for and against him. Segregating the icon from the iconography surrounding him, he finds the boxer's stance and pulls out all the stops. Lyrical and muscular, this telling goes the distance, fifteeen rounds mixing first-person singular and secondhand accounts:

> That fight with Willard was a fix
> not a faceoff. Out of the ring
> three years, jonesing
> for the States, I struck a deal
> to beat the Mann
> Act—one taste of mat
>
> & I'd get
> let back home . . .
> ***
> Down, I counted too, blessings
> instead of bets. Stretched
> there on the canvas
>
> —a masterpiece—stripped
> of my title, primed
> a return to the States.
>
> Saved. Best
> believe I stood up
> smiling.
>   (*TRG* 80–81)

Young underscores the hypocrisy, racism, and corruption informing this bout, while the voice of the now former heavyweight champion is a kind of chilling play of puns and double entendre. The great irony of "I struck a deal / to beat the Mann"; the relentless, downbeated punning in the verbs "down," "stretched," "stripped," "primed," and "saved"; the sound of both triumph and a sigh of relief in the words "Best / believe I stood up / smiling" —all testify eloquently for victory in defeat, for the willingness to play a game in order to get out of one. Young's own virtuoso performance here is in signaling fully the nature of Johnson's cultural disaffection and defection. I can only begin to hint at the myriad pleasures and pressures of this important poem. May these few lines serve as a call to reading!

The movement from the painterly, biographical *To Repel Ghosts* to the second part of Young's trilogy, *jelly roll*, is a "giant step" between idioms. *jelly roll* is loose and liberating, swinging between "songs" that sound, to use Young's own words from the epigraph poem, "Epithalamion," both "eagled" and "unsettled" states. This is "A Blues" that has neither the gravity nor density of the earlier book's three-line drops into Dante-like hell-realms. Instead, this book's idiom is so sensuous that, even when giving voice to suffering it wallows in a pleasurable languor just beneath pain's surface. A common practice in both *To Repel Ghosts* and *jelly roll* is "taking culture, both black and popular," in order to "make it sing" (*GS* 8). Young has said that he and other poets of his generation are apt to "find ancestors anywhere the ghost takes them," and in the blues form, of course, he has many predecessors.

With a few notable exceptions, *jelly roll* is a slow dance of couplets, a fluid back and forth of love lost and gained, dying or becoming. This "blues" is as much about pleasure as pain. Many of the earlier poems read like an Elizabethan sonnet sequence, celebrating boundlessness and abundance even as there is the implicit awareness, as in "Cakewalk," that these are transitory accumulations:

> Baby, you make
> me want
> to burn up all
> my pies . . .
>
> sink some peach
> cobbler. See, to me
>
> you are a Canada
> someplace north
>
> I have been, for years,
> headed & not
>
> known it . . .
>
> you are a found
>
> fallen thing—
> a freedom—not this red
>
> bloodhound ground—
>   (*JR* 7–8)

The sound of the blues is in the sharply stressed awareness of what we will "burn up" for love. There's no getting around the sensuality of Young's language, the almost visceral attraction to something that's both life-giving and destructive. And this kind of blues, of course, also charts a trajectory of creative progress and disintegration: language itself here—as in the self-conscious sonnet sequences of Sidney or Shakespeare—is the fuel as well as the hand that extinguishes. An early poem like "Siren" signals this doubling of desire and its singular expressions, whether heralding a new spark or a dying ember:

> On the fire throw
> another can of sterno
>
> that hiss is
> flame finding
>
> the wood wet...
>
> I mean, darling,
> to be an ABC
>
> extinguisher, kept
> handy, kitchened, a six-alarm
>
> APB . . .
> 　　　(*JR* 10)

Like what it describes, such language has the power to suffocate as well as suffuse; in the agile rhymes, in the alliterative and sprung rhythms, in the associative, quick-stepping thought is an undercurrent of "bad luck & / heart." What's carnal can't last.

In the very next poem, "Rhythm & Blues," Young manages at once to surface the sound of emancipation, containment, and a self-conscious wistfulness:

> Through the wall
> I hear them
>
> again—the couple—
> not fighting
>
> but doing
> the other thing—
>
> his cat-cries
> as if a trapped beast . . .
>
> her quiet—my own
> eavesdropped breath—
> 　　　(*JR* 11)

This couple's contained in and circumscribed by their couplets, of course, the "trapped beast" still aspiring toward something surpassingly sacred: what's transcendent and transitory are one. And the poet, no mere interloper, also drops the breath of his own expression from the eaves, another fallen thing. Even first-person can't stay this tide, as in "Etude":

> I love making
> love most just
>
> after—adrift—
> the cries & sometime
>
> tears over, our strong
> swimming done—
>
> sheet wreck—
> mattress a life-
>
> boat, listing—
> > (*JR* 14)

The moment after lovemaking is a "sheet wreck," conceived here as the bed-boat about to go down. Despite the the quick-stepping, tenderly associative riffs of this tongue, love's adrift. Yet so much of the first part of *jelly roll* is about love's spark, the fire, even if what fuels it is also what burns it up, as in "Song of Smoke":

> . . . you stir
> me like coal
>
> and for days smoulder.
> I am no more
>
> a Boy Scout and, besides,
> could never
>
> put you out . . .
> > (*JR* 46–47)

The second part of *jelly roll* is where Young enters more familiar blues terrain, love going and gone bad, the self hurt hard but still half-longing for what's been lost. Like the first and third parts of the book, this midsection is composed of thirty-some poems, most of which stick to Gwendolyn Brooks's epigraph at the outset: *You are the beautiful half / Of a golden hurt.* "Sorrow Song" hits just the right note:

> . . . on the subway
> home, her mouth still
>
> on my mouth
> like the gospel

        (thick as a cough
        or its syrup) hummed

        by a woman on the loud
        orange seat beside me.

        What else besides us
        is this? working

        down bone, a bright
        hymn—asking, asking.
                (*JR* 69)

I love the way the balanced choriamb, "thick as a cough," with its hard kiss
of sound on each side, gives way to the softer anapest, "or its syrup" (malady
muffled by cure) and that the woman humming on the subway is similarly
almost free of stress (soft-stepping anapest followed by the almost inaudible
pyrrhic foot and a closing iamb). That's the more harmonious sound at play
here. But the rest is strongly stressed loss, as if the word "loud" sounds some
kind of percussive cue. I count thirteen stresses in the last four lines; almost
every word is a point of emphasis: the sadness of goodbye is the "working /
down bone." And, make no mistake, it is heavy, hard work.

    Young's flow, his style, his play with rhyme and sprung rhythms—these
pronounced and audible inflections just under the form—are the sounds of
our own contemporary musical-poetic cipher. This poet loves his elders but
he's also of and in the moment. In *jelly roll* form's not fixed: this book is "*A*
Blues," not *the* blues. And Young stretches the genre into places it hasn't been
before. This is particularly evident in the third section of *jelly roll*, where
the poet greets loss through an almost visionary lens. Love, gained and lost,
stretches, conceives (of) possibilities that simply did not exist before. The
first poem in this last section, "Envoy," reads like a defection from "business"
as usual even as it affirms breathing into a new instrument:

        I quit. Resigned
        from your company

        entirely—I walk
        like paper. Short

        notice. Mama,
        boss lady, I'ma

        miss you—so too
        the trees. Time

```
now to get down
to brass, to this

bidness—of breathing—
        (JR 123)
```

This summing up, the dedicatory poem of the last section of the book, is also a beginning, signaling a new way of singing. Nothing unusual in the quitting: successive iambs sound the normative, everyday. What's striking are the heavy stresses: "miss you—so too / the trees. Time," sadness pressing, pent up, practically every word emphasized—*that* kind of missing. But the last sound, though equally short-limbed, is a different kind of breathing. "Now to get down"—well-balanced choriamb—is both an enjoinder to settle down to the "real" work and an urging to jam(b), to make something vibrant and energetic from the old "job" left behind. There is, to put it another way, an opportunity for spaciousness inside sadness to which the artist now turns. No accident that the last sound is another choriamb, balanced but still trailing off with an extra, muted syllable. A faltering utterance to be sure, but also the sound of something (*dash*) continuing. It's a Dickinsonian maneuver, both explosive and unfinished, a primer for reading the last fifty-plus pages of this "blues."

What follows are poems with titles like "Ramble," "Anthem," "Honky Tonk," "Saxophone Solo," "Slide Guitar," "Plain Song," and "Lyre"—song types, instruments, voices, versions, that speak eloquently of loss's double edge. If the habit of heartbreak is like a chain gang, throwing it off can feel like finding freedom, as in "Anthem":

```
. . . the chain gang

breaks rocks out
of habit—hunh—does not

look up to see
one man—hunh—chains

trailing—hunh—broken
as the jailbird's

wing, fleeing the field—
back stripes—hunh—stars
        (JR 130)
```

Young pays tribute to ancestors and genre—blues seeded and sung by others in cotton fields, in slavery and while incarcerated—while also breaking free of the conceptual frame of both the singers and their songs. So much of the breathing in this final section's toward "stars," toward a "sight" that "spirits into flame" ("Tacit"), disembodied "wind," ("Saxophone Solo") even though this blues remains grounded, embedded in tradition. Another way of saying this is that Young stays steeped in a blues idiom, while nevertheless falling into language that hasn't yet been heard, as in "Tacit":

> Even language
> leaves us—even the train . . .
>
> . . . the ants
>
> who my house invaded
> heading everywhere, hungry
>
> for what is not there.
>
> Since you, honey,
> my cupboards being bare . . .
>   (*JR*, 131)

It's Rilke, in his third Sonnet to Orpheus, singing toward the emptiness human suffering engenders. Nothing in the cupboards, but bareness still offers something that ants find before they catch fire.

A few poems later in "Deep Song," such inquiry is couched in terms of self-immolation and salvation, dive and leap:

> Belief is what
> buries us—that
>
> & the belief in belief . . .
>
> plunge in
> —the lungs . . .
>
> high ledge
> the leap—a breath
>
> above the lip of the abandoned
> quarry—belief . . .
>   (*JR* 144)

Again, the almost gravitational pull here is toward what's earth-bound; "belief" is the ground that claims us but also the "plunge," or countermove-ment, toward ecstatic leaps and depths. Young puts his faith in what's most elusive, nearest places to which love and love lost take us. Pain as both source and salve drives this book to its bittersweet closure. Colloquial, casual, these poems are nevertheless pleas for release from pain. Shut down, all signs sig-naling "closed," yet open to the last, bitter sweetness, as in "Rock":

I swing shut . . .

. . . get drunk on little
things . . .

. . . The rocking chair don't

by itself rock—
If only she

was here to tell me
shut up, quit

complaining, to kiss
my mouth closed.

(JR 149)

The hard, alliterative sounds at the end of this poem ("quit," "complaining," "kiss," and "closed") are an audible dissonance, but they are also the lover's soothing *shushes*, fingers to mouth, lip-locked end to querulousness on the singer's part. What spurs this blues can also stop it more or less on a dime. The suffering's deep but also, in a moment, mutable, subject to an almost immediate turnaround. No wonder there's so much pleasure in the singing, then, in the hearing.

The last book in Young's important American trilogy, *Black Maria*, sustains precisely this blues sound as well as its themes of love lost, departed and gone bad, but film noir is its foregrounded stage. Also composed primarily in couplets, the book moves in slow dance between private eye and femme fatale, stepping languidly through conventional noir plotline: set-up, seduction, sleuthing, double-crossing, betrayal.

In obvious ways, it's the same old story; the novelty is that this time it's being told in verse. All the energy and sweep's in the language, in the agile, associative riffs, the elaborate collocations and contexts of the detective, the chanteuse, the femme fatale, and the private dick. Young has the genre down cold, the types, their lingo, the fogs in which they, furtively, duplicitously move. The effect is not quite so deep as in the earlier two volumes of the trilogy, but the surface play here's breathtakingly swift, supple:

. . . in the deep end

I could not swim,

we kissed & my bow tie
turned a whirligig, lifted

me high among the trees
till I could see

how far I'd fall, that between us
air was all

we had left. My eyes oysters

pried open—
shucks.

> (*BM*, 176–77)

She wore red like a razor—
cut quite a figure . . .

dividing day
from night, there

from here. Where
I hoped to be is near

her & her
fragrant, flammable hair—

> (*BM* 12)

"The Hunch" gathers evidence audibly in terminal rhymes, springs rhythms like sudden surprises for the sleuth. The language is slippery, seductive, sure, perfectly pitched to its subject. I love the dropping onto the word "shucks" in the first poem. Nothing is quite as it sounds, which is to say it's more than that. Enjambments are extensions into new sensations and pleasures. All the suspense is poetic, as in, *what will he think up next?*

It's not surprising that technique is front and center here, that the stage-hand's craft, the elaborate effects and machinations of poetic noir, are obvious as studio sets. The self-conscious artifice that is both this book's sleight of hand and stock-in-trade suggest a virtuoso performer at the top of his game. But also under the weather: this atmosphere's thick as self-deception. Despite the trappings, poem noir cuts to the bone:

I'm tired of the city
telling me what it needs

isn't me—that mist is more
necessary to the picture

than I am. Pay
the man. Head outside

where the dark gathers round

fires built in the empty
barrel of the moon, men holding

their palms to its light
as if warmth . . .

. . . tonight I'll wander home
to sleep a few
hundred years & hope

her poison kiss might
slay me at last awake.
                    (*BM* 154–55)

Lines like "that mist is more / necessary to the picture" are so pyrrhic and
understated because his presence now seems to mean so little! Later, the six
successive iambs of "a stone—tonight I'll wander home / to sleep a few," with
their comforting, familiar poetic rhythm, is disrupted by the unexpected and
rather jarring line drop on "hundred" (trochee simultaneously breaking the
beat and sounding the depths and length of this dull fatigue). Like the barrel
of fire, writing itself offers some kind of warmth and transient comfort. But
the poet's tired and this form, like elegy, won't ultimately heal or hold.

   In all of Young's books, so much depends upon that familiar American
idiom that frames our history and that at once testifies to and witnesses in its
many voices, versions, and vernaculars: heartbreaking losses and betrayals;
unspeakably sweet stays against such experiences; deep repositories of exploi-
tation and brutality; freedom, as it always is in America, a dream deferred, yet
also, perhaps, just around the bend; impermanence itself the promise of an
end to suffering (but also, of course, to joy)—a rich, complex, contradictory
idiom and legacy to be sure. The great achievement of Kevin Young's trilogy
is that it speaks to all of this. While his early twenty-first-century blues calls
up, pays tribute to, poets like Gwendolyn Brooks and Langston Hughes, as
well as countless singers and musicians; while his aspiration to capture his
cultural moment is reminiscent of Walt Whitman's stretch to document his
day; while his loose, freestyling language and syntax reverberate back to Clif-
ton, Hayden, Dickinson, and Hopkins even as they reach, wild and improvi-
sational, toward the prophetic—while all of this is unmistakably true—when
either entering or leaving a book by Kevin Young you are also in the pres-
ence of something unmistakably *new*. This work is a jam session in progress:
Coltrane out on a limb for thirteen minutes with that familiar melody of
"Favorite Things," but in a way you've never heard before, dropping finally,
but only for a moment, on dogs barking and bees stinging. He's playing our
song: set ariff by reading; hanging on the next note.

NOTES

1. Kevin Young, *To Repel Ghosts* (South Royalton, Vt.: Zoland Books, 2001), 5. Subsequent quotations from Young's work will be cited in the text using the following abbreviations: *TRG = To Repel Ghosts*; *JR = Jelly Roll* (New York: Knopf, 2003); and *BM = Black Maria* (New York: Knopf, 2005).

BIBLIOGRAPHY

Books by Kevin Young

Black Maria. New York: Knopf, 2005.
Blues Poems (editor). New York: Everyman's Library / Knopf, 2003.
For the Confederate Dead. New York: Knopf, 2007.
Giant Steps: The New Generation of African American Writers (editor). New York: Perennial / HarperCollins, 2000.
jelly roll. New York: Knopf, 2003.
Most Way Home. Hanover, N.H.: Zoland Books, 2000; New York: Morrow / Quill, 1995.
To Repel Ghosts. South Royalton, Vt.: Zoland Books, 2001.

Selected Prose

"The Black Psychic Hotline; or, The Future of African American Writing." Introduction to *Giant Steps: The New Generation of African American Writing*, edited by Kevin Young, 1–12. New York: Perennial / HarperCollins, 2000.
"One Big Thing: An Exchange." Dialogue with Adam Kirsch on Howard Nemerov and contemporary poetry. *Poetry* 183, no. 3 (December 2003).
"Responsible Delight." On the poet John Berryman. *Kenyon Review* (Spring 1999), 160–61.
"Six Uzbek Poems by Langston Hughes." *Callaloo* (Fall 2002).

Interviews

Callaloo. Interview with Charles Rowell. Emerging Male Writers issue (Winter 1997).
Indiana Review 23, no. 1 (Spring 2001).
Poets & Writers. "'A Short Distance to the Blues': An Interview and Conversation with Colson Whitehead." Vol. 31, no. 1 (January–February 2003).
Bookworm. Interview on National Public Radio, produced by KCRW in LosAngeles, September 2003.

Selected Criticism

Brouwer, Joseph. "Black Maria: Verse Noir." *New York Times Book Review* (May 22, 2005).

Caldwell, Heather. "Why Poetry Still Matters." *Town & Country* (July 2003): 47–49.

Dove, Rita. "Poet's Corner." Two poems from *Most Way Home*, discussed in *Washington Post Book World* (August 13, 2000).

Hirsch, Ed. "Poet's Corner." Article on *Blues Poems*. *Washington Post Book World* (February 1, 2004): 12.

Thomas, Lorenzo. Discussion of poems "Jack Johnson" and "Everywhere Is Out of Town." In *Extraordinary Measures: Afrocentric Modernism and 20th Century American Poetry*, edited by Charles Bernstein and Hank Lazer. Tuscaloosa: University of Alabama, 2000.

TRACIE MORRIS

POETICS STATEMENT
Sound Making Notes

I STARTED working toward sound poetry, consciously at least, through hip-hop. I made awkward associations between rhyme schema in hip-hop and other things I was studying, such as code switching in the Puerto Rican community, which I was learning about in my Black and Puerto Rican Studies classes at Hunter College. This association between "Black English"/Ebonics and code in the African diaspora began swirling around in me before I formally began my creative writing life.

There was something hidden within the rhyme I was hearing as a teenager and young adult, and I was trying to articulate what it was, operating from an essential premise that there was nothing wrong with the way people in my neighborhood spoke.

Eventually I began to work more and more with the sound itself (trying to tease it away from literal meaning) and started to feel it in the body and adjust it within the body. This led me to make physical not just conceptual segues, uttered and nonuttered choices. (At a certain point, it's impossible to distinguish between the two.)

This way of working with the body started with a hip-hop poem called "Project Princess," and I first began deconstructing it in 1993 at a reading at the Apollo Theater for a special youth-oriented program. My formally distinct sound poems were influenced by that pivotal moment as well as three other influences: (1) the deconstruction of standards in jazz that I had heard growing up; (2) the work of the Four Horsemen in Ron Mann's "Poetry in Motion" video that I saw at the Action Poetry retreat in Banff, Canada—particularly the work of sound artist Paul Dutton (one of the Four Horsemen) who also presented work at the retreat and with whom I've had the pleasure of conversing; and (3) the work of Kurt Schwitters, a contemporary of the Dada movement, which I first heard of via Edwin Torres (who also introduced me to his take on experimental poetry). The first time I heard Edwin read was when we read together at the Knitting Factory circa 1991. I had no idea what he was talking about but I think I was encouraged.

Another important early experience was volunteering for a tribute to the "people's historian," Dr. John Henrik Clarek, a black nationalist, chair emeritus of the Department of Black and Puerto Rican Studies at Hunter, and self-described socialist thinker. It was there I first heard the work of Sonia Sanchez and I think it subconciously pushed me along the sound trajectory. I didn't know what her sounds meant for sure and I wasn't writing poetry at the time, but I think that I was encouraged to make variations on conventionally uttered sounds later because of that forum. I also wasn't culturally/politically raised to think that the avant-garde was somehow an unapproachable area for Afrocentric people, that there was a collective continuity to tap into and embrace. I think that the concept of coding in our tradition (for aesthetic and safety reasons) encourages us to construct our own avant-garde.

Nowadays I'm not only trying to figure out how to make more poems (and in fact I've come to love the distinct forum of the page even more than I had before working with sound) but how not to exploit the poems I've made so far. I have an aversion to being stereotyped, pigeonholed (though I have no problem with specific identities) but I also feel that the topics that drove me to work primarily with sound (to the exclusion of description, imagery, etc.) were those that affect the body and not the head. In my work, the response has to be as visceral as the call: Stereotypical expressions circumvent visceral sensibility.

The first sound poem I wrote was "A Little." I heard it while I was walking from the subway to my house. Within a block I knew what the poem was about (sexual abuse of girls) but struggled with how to get at the heart of the character's transition and adjustment, as well as her feelings of inarticulateness and isolation. Six or so blocks later when I got home, I realized that there were no words other than "I am just a little girl." And I decided not to create cognitive-inducing text. I came up with the notion (for myself) that the physicality of words would drive the poem, not the text, not even the context. Without thinking of the words, the hearer is with the body and since in this poem, the body of the subject is the focus of impact—where the story is—the inability of the listener to escape into the mind underscores the character's vulnerability, her inability to escape. Description can often be overemphasized and overprivileged, which prevents the words from expanding, from doing as much work as they can. A simple detail can intellectualize the poem, allowing for an escape route from the central trauma of the event. (It is possible that a poem could contain joy as a central element. But at this point I haven't written a sound poem with joy as its nexus; the closest I've come is irony in an unpublished poem called "Procrastination/Self-Flagellation.") I believe that any depictions beyond "I am just a little girl" would just get in the way. The five words and their variations were all that could be said.

Some of the other sound poems I've composed, "The Mrs. Gets Her Ass Kicked" (aka "Heaven") and "Chain Gang" refer to stories that were created around popular songs (such as Fred Astaire's version of "Cheek to Cheek") and other songs, including Sam Cooke's "Chain Gang." They usually have a cultural resonance that gives them more currency, more value than the literal meaning as well as a physical premise. I didn't reference the songwriters (Berlin; Cooke and Cooke) because I think it's the deconstruction of the version as sung, the particular sound of them even more than the text (in terms of visceral recognition) that determines thei value. I had used songs as introductions to poems in some of my earlier efforts but had not fully integrated them into the poem as with those two sound poems. One such example of song lyrics used as introduction: "The Old Days," published in *In Defense of Mumia* as a predictor/critique of the nomination of someone like Clarence Thomas after the retirement of Thurgood Marshall, used a section of "It Ain't Necessarily So" (the version rendered by Sammy Davis Jr. in the film *Porgy and Bess*).

This level of sound incorporation links directly to the blues, jazz songs, gospel songs, and ring shouts, which all convey more than one meaning at a time. I guess what I'm trying to identify here is how something that sounds so "out there" is actually a natural progression from concepts that have always been a part of African/African American and American aesthetics.

This reflection on my personal aesthetics, as well as my multiyear ongoing conversations with Claudia Rankine, prompted me to recognize that two of my fully realized sound poems are based on young females who are somehow negotiating impending adult situations. The variations in tone may have been subconsciously inspired by vocal changes that occur during puberty. In reaching back to discover sounds to adjust in my throat, I discovered that one memory embedded in the larynx is the transition between "little girl voice" and "woman voice."

Often, a poem will evolve through repetition and performance. "Chain Gang" began its improvisational life with primarily masculine-oriented sounds and male expulsions but later took on polyphonal qualities of various ages, genders, and lifetimes. Although, oddly enough, I haven't used Cooke's "Hoo, Hah!" from the recording—the exclamatory sounds in the original haven't found themselves into my text (yet)—"Chain Gang" was the first time I added words outside of the text that weren't extrapolations on the original words. At the first New Ark reading I attended (out of two as of this writing) at Amiri and Amina Baraka's home in Newark, New Jersey, the words, "n****r," "Kunta," and "Kizzie" came up. I think they may have made an appearance in "Chain Gang" because (1) they were "slavery words" that were not supposed to be spoken (I still do not use the "n" word except if the poem requires it for this reason; and (2) I felt the pressure (self-imposed) to approach the language with new ideas in this particularly intimidating setting. I mean, no way was I tryin' to be corny at that moment!

I don't ever try to be "good" but I do try to get out of my way (that's where I think the corniness comes, from "blocking" the poem) but there are times when the pressure to expel (however one may mean it) the internal build toward the combustion of the poem forces the mind/body to work out a new something. On the other hand, at this point I'm wondering how not to exploit my work. I have two concerns regarding this. The first is its exploitation in pop culture terms, the voyeuristic, Jerry Springer–like "poor abused woman, let's watch" approach, which affects how people experience performed work. Similarly, I was concerned about the work and the process being exploited in the "high art" context: the Saadje Baartman/Venus "death under the glass" objectification of the work with the dead recording that is understood as object. I consider these poems to be living entities that invite a live moment between the listener and utterer. It is a challenge to keep engaging the audience in this experience if either of us intellectualizes the poem by objectifying it.

This worry was heightened when I was invited to contribute work to the 2002 Whitney Biennial. I should say at the outset that Debra Singer (the curator I worked with at the time) invited me to contribute work to the Biennial but it was my choice to determine what that work would be. Because the environment was so foreign to me anyway, I figured I might as well contribute my most experimental work. So the pressure to put the sound poems "in a box" was my decision, ultimately.

I had to figure out how to put the pieces in the museum in a way that kept the integrity of the process and the poems as intact as possible. I chose my sound engineer, Val Jeanty (an electronica musician and Haitian drummer) because we had worked on a sound recording together on slavery a year before (her composition and my improvisation). I knew that she was very attentive to the dynamics of living sound and the way in which it can be disembodied yet have a corporeal texture. I did want a woman to be represented in this particular project besides myself, particularly in a technical field where women and people of color are underrepresented. And as she is an up-and-coming artist, I thought the experience would be helpful to her. She's also well versed in Pro Tools software and is very generous with her time. I knew this recording project would take a moment to figure out. We had to edit the poems down with the sound software because the live built-in dynamics—the poet's effect on the audience's energy—could not be improvised in that installation setting. I couldn't feel the listener and respond on the spot. (Could the call be living without a live response?) So we created a more economical build through Pro Tools. I had one quirk, though: in order to maintain my sense of honesty with the poems, I insisted on reading them live, for myself, with the dynamics as edited. In other words I had to be able to "do" the edited version live. These exercises weren't recorded. I had to hear the sounds coming out of my mouth as edited. If I didn't think I could do that, with the dynamics feeling organic to me, I wouldn't keep the version. I rarely deleted any, thank goodness, but it was a real concern. If it didn't feel real when I did it after the version, then it couldn't live in the recording and I couldn't live with it. It had to feel as if I *could have* improvised it.

We recorded at Val's home studio and one thing I wanted to make clear to the listener in the museum—especially with "A Little" and "The Mrs. Gets Her Ass Kicked"—was the inability of the utterer to leave the situation. I wanted the room in which the traumatic event occurred to be the head of the listener. The head is an inescapable place in that you can't just walk out of it. One could certainly center an experience in another part (say, the viscera of the body), but then the head becomes part of the body, not something that one leaves behind. So the sound had to facilitate the notion of enclosure.

Val and I recorded the sound in a small vestibule between the rooms of her apartment that let out into the living room where she could cue me. The sound would bounce off the closed doors, creating an undertone of echo without the echo effect. In one's head this sounds closer to the sound one hears when one speaks to oneself. The headphones used by the Whitney were perfect because they completely enclosed the ear, so there was no out-side bleed-through and the experience could be more alive and personalized. They also had a wooden bench bolted to the wall so that what seemed like a place of respite on the upper floor of an extensive exhibit actually presented some jarring, dramatic material. This place of respite that really wasn't a respite was just great for the sound poems. That was the Whitney's call and an excellent choice. (I didn't see the installation until the opening.)

There was one point at which the museum and I disagreed on aesthetics about what seemed to be an incidental item: the choice of whether or not all the poems would be put on a continuous loop. I knew as an improvisational artist that the poems had to be segmented. If the poem about sexual abuse resonated with a particular listener, she or he may have needed to focus on that piece. (I don't think I have ever done one public reading of "A Little" without at least one woman coming up to me to tell me that she was sexually abused as a child. Often when I read "The Mrs. . . ." particularly at affluent colleges, the children's faces betray their mothers. With "Chain Gang" there is, depending on the group, anger, sorrow and/or embarrassment.)

The museum was concerned with the visual aesthetics of four bulky play buttons on a console. But I was adamant about letting the audience hear and rehear what they may have needed at the time. This was a way of letting the hearer, to a certain extent, improvise their experience with the poems. The museum let me have my way, and one of the comments I received from a listener was that she appreciated knowing that there were finite parameters to the poems. In other words, that it wasn't a continuous stream of sounds. Even in improvisations there needs to be discrete edges; otherwise, the integrity of the experience is lost, its corporeality can be compromised. In a different way, this listener addressed one of the distinctions I had made in constructing the work, between my sound poems and those of Kurt Schwitters: that the sound be improvised but with a guided hand for interpretation.

The issue of avoiding exploitation, whether in the museum or a live context is still a question for me. I also don't want to have a knee-jerk reaction of abandoning these poems for the next new idea I come up with. I don't want to make a fad out of the poems: "Oh, sexual abuse was so 'last year!'" That's part of the art scene, too. I became aware of that danger when I circulated, briefly, with the "high art" world.

My personal queries include all these things as well as how (if it's possible) and if I should combine my sonically driven writing with the type of experimentalism/minimalism I use in my written work. This might mean another conscious performing of it that I don't engage in now.

IMPROVISATIONAL INSURRECTION

The Sound Poetry of Tracie Morris

Christine Hume

TRACIE MORRIS conceived her first sound poem while walking down the street. Imagine: the rhythm of walking replicates unwilled rhythms of her body—breathing, beating heart—and paces a limbo between being and doing, idling and vigilance. Walking home drives her outward. A sentence catches the rhythm and repeats itself as the sensorimotor connectivity of walking repeats. Each city block is an imbrication of familiar terrain and unscreened encounters that the sentence strides through, shifting with minute perceptions and their thresholds. Language walks itself out of habitualized routes. Sounds pace through the body; the body paces through landscape. Walking makes a single chord of mind-body-world out of which Morris makes oral poetry in tour-de-force performances that send language-as-we-know-it out for a hike. Her sound poems strip language down to its acoustical-rhythmic potencies and potentialities to engage with the world while traveling in it corporeally.

Morris made her artistic debut in the spoken word scene of the 1990s—garnering championship titles in the Nuyorican Grand Slam and the National

Haiku Slam—where the premium is on performance, especially "authenticity" of emotion and tone, and improvisation, especially audience responsiveness. Her poetry's musical influences run deep, though in style, technique, and attitude rap has cleared a definitive space for the spoken word culture on which Morris cut her teeth. Both antecedents are predicated on a paradigm of improvisational (re)iteration and autobiographical narrative that gravitate toward themes of cultural and physical abuse. "Project Princess," one of Morris's signature poems, packs a fools-not-suffered political audacity; inventive rhyming; vernacular swagger and playfulness; amphetamine-driven, balladic rhythm; and the mobile facial expressions and bodily gestures that we might expect from a winning slam poem.[1] The poem is an ode and rallying cry addressed to young black women, like Morris herself, from Brooklyn's housing projects. In this, as in Morris's later sound poems, which tend to be more explicitly protest poems, we hear an effusive jocularity and a delight in pleasurable pathos that bolsters the confidence of its political power. "Project Princess" hints at the half-spoken, half-sung recitative style that will go on to inform her sound poems, yet the intonation patterns and rhythms exist so fully within a predetermined slam style that the work comes close to feeling commodified. If it's true, as Icelandic singer–songwriter Björk says, that "every genre has these mechanical clichés that get implanted in the voice and start to hide the power of words," then much of Morris's accomplishment in sound poetry is to break away from those clichés, while retaining the riveting intensity and renegade virtuosity of her earlier feats.[2] And "Project Princess" provides a good measure of just how much pressure she has put on ratified modes of expression in order to fabricate entirely new ones. Though her spoken word poetry in many ways anticipates her sound poetry, the latter amplifies the techniques and goals of the former to such an extent that it now travels in "experimental" and high art venues. By existing between easy definitions and within a wealth of osmotically integrated sources, Morris's new work swims in the wide ocean of sound poetry. This work bypasses the more programmatic features of the two poetic praxes she has been associated with, slam and contemporary avant-garde, by standing against reified notions of authenticity and sincerity as well as ready-made loopholes of indeterminacy and alienation.[3] It also, as Harryette Mullen laments, strains critical narratives of representative identity: "'Formally innovative minority poets,' when visible at all are not likely to be perceived either as typical of a racial/ethnic group or as representative of an aesthetic movement."[4] No matter how far her work cuts across the twilight zone of poetic alliances and artistic disciplines—Morris has collaborated in theater, dance, music, and film, as well as written books—we want to stay within earshot.[5]

In a series of sound poems that she performs live and records for museum installations, Morris fuses illocutionary and theatrical aspects of performatives to create spells of somatic and social impact. "Illocutionary performatives," as defined by J. L. Austin, are statements that perform, rather than describe, an action: *saying* is in effect *doing*.[6] Usually her sound pieces begin with an illocutionary performative that quickly gets restless and distends—amending and appending itself—into a theatrical parade of mobile meanings that leaves behind any empirical descriptives or expository elaborations. By inhabiting and improvising within one sentence, Morris releases the physicality of words, plays with sonic associations, and funnels the referential residue of language into more visceral, more estranging, and ethical functions. Familiar speech sets in motion something close to glossolalia by way of accent, slur, stutter, backtrack, striation, and telescoping tempo. Performativity in the piece "The Mrs. Gets Her Ass Kicked," for instance, renders the effects of the title true the way a judge levels convictions. As a protest against domestic violence, the poem might seem at odds with the title's cynicism, but, it's that very shock—one that uses humor to show horror—and disjuncture that drives the relentlessly visceral work. Expect no familiar or flinching treatment of this social ill. The title provides the narrative context and brutal tone; the words are recycled from the Irving Berlin song "Cheek to Cheek"—"I'm in heaven, and my heart beats so that I can hardly speak"—lending an ironic counterpoint. From this linguistic minimalism, the piece uncorks an excess of mind-carbonating expressivity, eschewing semantic strategy in order that aural alterity might regrain the texture of spousal abuse. That is, words decompose into chokes, hyperventilations, and galloping chest and throat slaps. Morris's riffing dismembers "describe" into "scratch" and remembers "heart beats" as "hard beats." These words magnetize and pull together recombinatory sounds, carried by the force of their own impulsive impetus, in a process that fuses emotional speech with syntactic elaborations usually associated with its opposite, propositional speech. Morris's shifting intonations of the "same" words reverberate multiple codes that feed off each other's feedback. Compare Paul Dutton's formal technique in his sound poem "Reverberations," in which Dutton seems to be playing verbal catch with the words "gong" and "going."[7] In differing pitches and tones, he lobs the words back and forth. Their phonetic likeness exploits subtle performed differences and sets up a resonant field between the two.

The power of reiteration forces each next moment in language, yet Morris takes advantage of the interstices between these moments, as if she were showing us a CAT scan of how language gets generated, including the parts usually kept invisible or inaudible. She makes a three-dimensional experience out of reiterating restless reinscriptions. The torrential cascading of a single moment creates the felt-time of a protracted and panicked present tense. The slight variations in repeated phrasing—what Gertrude Stein calls "insistence" or "emphasis," Henry Louis Gates Jr. calls "play of differences," and Amiri Baraka calls "the changing same"—in which language is troped and transformed, *propel* Morris's language within an illusory stillness of one spinning sentence.[8] As in Beckett's short play *Not I*, fragments ceaselessly added to and subtracted from the interior of a phrase break open otherwise imperceptible understandings. In Beckett's and Morris's pieces, cinematically fast cuts are strung together with ellipses (in Morris's case, *heard* ellipses) that syncretically concoct an identity without contextual props; isolated segments allow for unexpected adhesions and apertures. All of Morris's pieces to date exploit the gaps in speech in at least two ways. By conjuring word constellations based on alliteration and assonance, the poet provokes memory and emotional narrative without recourse to time markers or hypotaxia. In doing so, she trains the audience to listen within patterns of rhythmic phrasing. We then learn the gestalt listening of Morris's endlessly concatenated and abridged new language.[9] As we complete phrases and register half-heard words, we are loaded into the rhythm, where we live as her most important collaborator.

What Morris's presentational vocal mode—performing, rather than representing—makes clear is that minimalism, at its most astonishing, tightly contracts an excess of ideas, be they intellectual, spiritual, or emotional. Exactitude and procedural dissolution are the front and back side of her style. This is a coup of exhaustive, minimalist performative poetics, one that is based on a conviction to continue to upset social codes in more confrontational ways. All of Morris's sound poems reference, echo, mirror, revise, and respond to some scrap of common cultural currency, such as a "found" line of speech, a name, or song lyric. This kind of intertextuality—"signifying" in the tradition of African American art—takes a radical turn (both moving forward and looking backward) in its formal innovation. According to Gates, "The more mundane the fixed text ('April in Paris' by Charlie Parker, 'My Favorite Things' by John Coltrane) the more dramatic the Signifying revision."[10] This is certainly true of Morris's work at the Whitney Biennial in 2002, which uses deceptively simple sentences, in language often so familiar as to sound ritualistic, as their departure points. "A Little," which begins "I am just a little girl," works through a synecdochical process of remotivation in the implied context of an extreme social power imbalance. The girl narrator digs her teeth into the vocabulary available to her, granting it an omnipresent and somological capacity to mean, making it perform actions beyond semantics.

The initiating text might be compared to the mask—described by Gates as "the essence of immobility fused with the essence of mobility, fixity with transience"—encoded with meaning through rhythm.[11] By putting on a mask of ritual identity, Morris dramatizes a girl's trauma of sexual abuse: extreme mutation and disarticulation of the original language, guided by a nearly mystical rhythm, evoke an ecstatic state of anguish. Given the situation, the poem's tonal range—from playful and celebratory, to pissed off and terrified to demanding and pleading—brilliantly challenges convention and infuses the piece with psychological astuteness as it builds a narrative of abuse. As "I am just a little girl," the galvanizing statement, is put through a series of spooked and spooky intonations, the words become so simultaneously loaded with and bankrupted by the force of their apparent intentions that they explode into a rhythmic spray of screams, grunts, rasps, throat clearings, unexpected enjambments, and stammered phonemes, which act as even sharper instruments of perception. The initial strict illocutionary performative (where saying is doing) migrates to and merges with the theatrical performative (where vocalizations enact saying), compounding effect and affect. An audible breath begins the piece. The iambic performance quickly defibrillates into a jagged isochronicity, a derangement of the refrain, as it evolves and dissolves in our ears as language dwelling in the crisis of communicating beyond its usual means: "Just a little. Just a little. I am just a lit-it-ittle girl and. I am just a little and I am just a. Just a little. It-tle."[12] Morris's nimble voice punches holes in the surface reference, creating a kinesthetic texture and depth. Extremities of sensation overwhelm word boundaries, which become like the girl, violated objects. The girl's objectification, her imposed "itness," resounds as Morris extracts "it" from "little" and scats "it" into its most concrete incarnations. At another point, Morris works the word "leet-tle" into a siren sound, alerting us to the dangers of littleness—of mind (adult perpetrator's) and body (child victim's). "Leet-tle" is a call to awaken language's resources and rally them in the service of the girl's ethical and epistemological questing. The oxymoronically loud assertion of the girl's littleness signals an untenable juxtaposition between her childhood age and her "adult" situation. The performance of "little," belittled into "it" then extended into a siren sound, emblematizes the gamut of conditions and comprehensions expressed as the girl searches for ways of being heard, even to herself.

Morris does violence to the words, performing the girl's visceral reactions in an extensive mimetic process operating phonologically, morphologically, and syntactically. The piece's shifting tempo often kicks into a barely audible rapid-fire delivery that actualizes a pulse gone faint but furious. Intense fragmentation and condensation elide narrative into an enactment of the girl's isolation. The pressure Morris exerts on the sentence to account for complex modalities of identity forces a palimpsestic text to emerge. With each listening, new sounds and words leap out at us as if auditory ghosts were spilling from the wounds of words in search of inoculative knowledge. Crypt words, or elliptically heard words, such as "sex," "unjust," "injure," "undress," and "night" subliminally persuade us to understand the context without quite knowing why.[13] This puts us in a similar situation to that of the girl, who comprehends the facts of her abuse, but is stymied in her ability to articulate it conventionally. Instead, a language invents itself as it goes, defamiliarized enough to instantiate a forceful materiality. This defamilarization alchemizes an almost hallucinatory listening experience, drawing our own hearing into question and disrupting the boundary between orality and aurality. Morris's sound work encourages mishearings that dilate our engagement with its ideological imperatives. As listeners, we hitch a ride on a slurred, speedy phrase repeated with differing intonal insistences to hear a simulacra of new language. "I-am Just" might distort into a near hearing of "Aunt Jemima," icon of black female exploitation and servitude, furthering the frequencies of the piece's political pitch.

According to linguist Reuven Tsur, when we hear a sound, our minds categorize it and process it as either speech or nonspeech: "We seem to be tuned, normally, to the nonspeech mode; but as soon as the incoming stream of sounds gives the slightest indication that it may be carrying linguistic information, we automatically switch to the speech mode."[14] Poetry, in Tsur theory, usually relies on some "precategorical sensory information" that stimulates an attention to the mystery of sound, the nonspeech mode.[15] Though Tsur's account might be somewhat oversimplified, listeners to Morris's sound poems will recognize the cognitive stuttering of trying to double process. With both auditory and phonetic centers perked up, a neural crosstalk concentrates the richness of active listening. By immersing us in prelinguistic and extralinguistic dimensions of sound and sublimation, Morris draws the listener into an intimacy of immediate experience, one that is coextensive with improvisation. We track allomorphs tumbling into anagrams. We startle as noises of dissent (unt-ugh) and surprise (ut-oh, egh) break out of haplology. Nonreferential sounds and phonetic substitutions blot out words in the radical cacophony of a mind caught in cyclic rhythms that seem arrested in time as they break down mechanistic traps of conventional language use.

Morris foregrounds the epistemology of vocalizations here; the girl's sounds, like those of anyone, constitute a piece of autobiography, the interior life stealing in on the public. Though not strictly formulated, the piece first refigures the predicate "little girl," then attends to the first-person subject; this inversion of the inaugural script indicates a movement from identification with a category, "little girl," to an investigation of the self, the "I am." Repetition establishes the equivalences of these terms but motivates an essential ungrounding of received identity. This shift in the course of the piece is reinforced by a vibratory sibilance that introduces self-consciousness in the form of "I was just" and "I said," phrases broken off and synonymous, as slips into past tense, where deed ("I was just" [minding my own business]) and word ("I said" [no]) are equally ineffective defenses. The sentence—in both senses of the word—cannot be contained. In and through it, the phonetic intensive "i" proliferates as "ice," "Isis," "is," "lit," and "eyes"— words suggestive of self-assertion, witness, and rage—and "nice," "quiet," and "quite"—words suggestive of diminutive girlishness). Sound symbolism splits into competing networks, though Morris's voice is anything but limited to chiaroscuro delivery. These words take up a multitude of relationships and codes that play with notions of escape and discovery; the "I" seesaws between absence and presence in an elaborate game of self-naming. The rich, volatile tradition of naming in African American vernacular is turned inward, spinning out a taxonomy of improvisational figurations and impersonations that rely on irony to mobilize identity.[16] Morris's quicksilver tonal changes—from gleeful to grave, tough to vulnerable—show the deeply psychotic ravages of child abuse and Morris's ability to convey pathos through the concatenation of syllables. Not only do the runaway mood shifts *show* these effects, they make us *feel* them physically and psychologically. Sounds drift into words and words into cognates as if the speaker were in a fugue state, trying out modes of national, neighborhood, and private broadcasts, testing alliterative ramifications, in search of herself or a way out of "herself."

There's no sidestepping the corporeality of Morris's voice. Her pitch and dynamic ranges display merged subjectivities of expression with culturally informed iconicities of sound. High vowels, usually associated with littleness and belittling in English, are delivered often at full volume, compacting the effect of the piece's mixed messaging. Before we come to our intellectual senses, a Western association of high vocal pitch with untrustworthiness and hysteria has its way with us. Morris drives the upper registers to compound the sense of the girl's disturbance and to expose a possibly sexist response. Crash gutturals, raw lower vowels, and syncopated throat noises punctuate those flights. At other moments, the piece demands intense concentration from the listener, who must strain to hear the almost whispered syllables. The effect arrests our capacity to respond in the familiar passive way: both critical and transcendent listening habits compete for full engagement as the audience oscillates between a stiff-arming distance and gut identification. Each is a relief from the tyranny of the other.

When Morris performed "A Little" at Barnard College in 2002 and at Eastern Michigan University in 2004, some members of the audiences found the piece funny—a response that encourages self-reflection, but one that also betrays the piece's power to suspend the listener between deep empathy and defensive discomfort. After all, the diction might catch in our ears as absurd given the excesses of outrage it has been grafted onto and the adult it is being performed through. This is precisely the position of the girl, being enormously little: her boast shoots down powerlessness by aggressively claiming it. If surprise and incongruity are at the root of humor, then our first impulse just might be gallows laughter. Think of Kurt Schwitters's *Ur Sonata*, which strikes listeners as funny because the rigorous formal structure seems wildly incongruous with the carnal play of pure sound.[17] By flaunting vulnerability, the girl exposes and denaturalizes its violence and also suggests that her helplessness is also our own. The girl's voice possesses us: the voice bleeding its repository of the body's memory, the voice that grinds between child and adult, the voice threatening to subsume our own.[18] Conversely, we might also feel the urge to titter nervously at our own position as audience to the implied accusation. Witnessing puts us in a position of responsibility, allowing a vague, confusing guilt to creep in. The boon in this kind of jaded humor is that it can do the work of resignification. The dynamic of name and named thing is a prophylactic against paralysis, where irony is the rhetorical form of self-reflexiveness. "A Little" ends, almost under the breath, with the initiating sentence boiled down and its ethical imperatives siphoned off: "I am just; I adjust." Yet how might the speaker adjust? Given the ambiguity of prospects, this uncertain resolution leaves us reeling out of the poem's mighty momentum into the air of our own naked inquiry. The unfinished quality of the sentence, Morris's refusal to cinch the point, frustrates the telos of hearing in favor of irresolution. What we lose in the satisfaction of knowing, we gain in the impact of the scandalized friction. Morris revitalizes the postmodern cliché of dwelling in impossibility by infusing it with real stakes and real risk.

As "A Little" demonstrates, reiterating a small pool of words in the process of repetition and revision draws our attention to subtle distortions and slippages. This open display of the procedural nature of language allows a rare simultaneity of intricate apprehensions that seem more available to the ear than to the eye. Consider an unscored "transcription" of the first thirty seconds of "slave sho' to video a.k.a Black But Beautiful," which uses motivated repetition to volley between two ready-made discursive universes, both riddled with syntactic and lexical ambiguities that allow Morris to expand their reaches. Morris begins with a call ("Ain't she beautiful") and response ("She too black"), then moves quickly into a rhythmic echo chamber of erasure and expansion, sounding out a spectrum of emotional shadings. One typographic rendering, albeit provisional, might run:

> Ain't she beautiful / She too black / She too beautiful / boot-booty-ful / she too black / ain't she ain't she boo-boo-beauty-ful ain't she / she ain't beautiful she too black / too too beautiful tutu tu-tu beautiful / she ain't ain't she she ain't ain't she she ain't / is she ain't she beautiful / e-sh-she too black too beautiful ain't she / she ain't she ain't / anxy she too black too beautiful too b-b-beautiful butt-beautiful butt booty full booty too black

Once beached on the page, the words flatten and forget their flexibility. They no longer bodily manifest all the symptoms that Paxil wants to save us from. The sounds are full of decisions that one need not make while listening: "tutu" or "too too?" "But" or "butt?" "Bootyful booty" or "booty full-booty?" In addition, many of the sounds hover between two words in their actual articulation, so that a composite listening is the only accurate experience.

This piece animates and mobilizes contradictory cultural discourses loaded into the words "black," and "beautiful." The subject "she" is posited at the crossroads, poised between an under-the-breath assumption that "black"

and "beautiful" are antonymic, or self-canceling, and a self-conscious asser-
tion that "black" and "beautiful" are synonymous or twin categories. Each
term is used to judge the other. The historical auras around words become
part of their schema—here designing a false binary that Morris restages and
ultimately reserves, as well as a false tautology that Morris references and
ultimately rewrites. She takes up Sonia Sanchez's challenge from within the
Black Arts movement:

> who's gonna take
> the words
>   blk / is / beautiful
> and make more of it
> than blk / capitalism.[19]

Morris animates psychological dimensions and synaptic firings as she
becomes a vatic mouthpiece through which language splits apart and spits
back. She rescripts "black is beautiful," mindful of the often masculinist and
materialist agenda of the organization responsible for its genesis. The Black
Power slogan of the 1960s and 1970s, though never uttered in the piece itself,
is on trial, as its key words participate in a *sentence* that gets a good re*hearing*.
Not only is the slogan "on trial," but also this metaphor reminds us that key
members of the Black Power movement were subject to unjust sentencing
and state-sponsored assassinations. Morris may be challenging the sexism of
the movement, and commodification of the slogan as much as she is chal-
lenging the forces it was protesting. To listen to the piece is to be swept into
a hypnotic process that eschews product, a performative dialogue opposed to
empirical descriptions or discursive authorizations. Morris makes that inter-
nal dialogue audible as she moves from the initial conflict, "she beautiful; she
too black," through a proliferating rhythm of sonic associations that uncover
tangled semantic liaisons, to the final statement, "beautiful and black." By
talking out the triggering citation, she performs a ritual chain of resignifica-
tions that break down oppositions of mind/body and matter/language.

"Slave sho' to video a.k.a Black But Beautiful" is built entirely on the
pyrotechnic repetitions of the sounds of the opening five words, letting
the sounds of these words slip into what Morris calls "sonic puns" and the
"almost heard."[20] One of the most illuminating slippages in the piece moves
"aint she" to "anxy," literally infusing the question with "anxiety." The neol-
ogism "anxy" then evolves into "and she," allowing the introduction of the
positive conjunction "and," which effectively replaces the negation "aint"
by the end of the nearly four-minute piece. This process—question, crisis,
affirmation—finally fosters a Boolean marriage of the two terms ("beauti-
ful *and* black") that began as "opposites" ("black *but* beautiful"). Conjunc-
tions and connective words figure largely, creating out of sound itself a new
syntax, and out of syntax, an unforgettable music. "Beautiful" fractures into

"but," and "but too," reinforcing the titular tension ("Black But Beautiful"). This conjunction also puns on its homophone, "butt," in order to explore the objectifying force of beauty itself. "Butt," of course, is the fetish body part often cited in rap songs, indicative of its special place in the black urban psychosexual pathos. Notice that Morris's alliteration, like the best of rap, uses two warring strategies: staccato syllable pileup and a delayed teetering elongation of syllables. This device compounds the time of rhyme as it cuts our expectations both ways: uncertainty about whether rhyme will materialize in a predictable manner ballasts uncertainty about where its arrival will throw the meaning. Words in this piece hatch into hearings and peripheral hearings of "booty," "bait," "butterful," "booby," "bound," "bounty," "sheep," "ample," "Bantu," "tutu," "Tutu," "cute," "tootable," "chichi," "ain't shit," and "taint." These words explore the faintly diabolical machinery of "beautiful" and "black" as static cultural categories.[21] Morris combs received messages about black women's bodies and endemic bifurcated constructions of "black woman" as object of repulsion and appeal.

The subject "she" is a symbol so powerful as to be eligible for the conceptual absorption, containment, and representation of the collective body of the African American woman. Morris speaks for, through, and to this subject. Signifying here starts with the title, "slave sho' to video a.k.a Black but Beautiful," which foregrounds race, self, and presence—and its own history, its own revision. The work is a sound portrait of a woman made vivid to herself through contradictory historical messages about her body as spectacle—slave auction capital, breeder, worker; music video dancer, singer, performer—and builds into a critique of that objectification.[22] The title signals the ensuing investigation of how speech acts out on its subjects. Judith Butler speculates: "I am led to embrace the terms that injure me because they constitute me socially. The self-colonizing trajectory of certain forms of identity politics is symptomatic of this paradoxical embrace of the injurious term."[23] Morris has given us a release from this embrace of internalized racism, one that goes beyond "blk / capitalism" by way of deliberately flaunting the injurious idea and employing a linguistic jackhammer to crack open its words, whose sounds will find their way to alternative meaning. Racist speech, as Butler argues, works by invoking convention, one that lives in and through language itself, and repeats the trauma through signs that both obscure and restage the subjugation.[24] Directed repetition and reverse citation here not only repeat the anguish of racist speech but rip it away from the historicity that keeps it alive. Morris's rechanneling of injurious speech works like a spell, "translat[ing] experience into meaning and meaning into belief."[25] As words scratch and reverberate they retune language and the consciousness of that language. Meta-English intersects with para-English, creating an acoustic conundrum that underscores language's propagation of corrupt power dynamics.

Morris employs the kind of fierce, active repetition that might make even veteran Stein readers dizzy, but she does so with electric phrasing, lightning-fast tonal shifts, an uncanny sense of time, and a stampede of ligatured sounds that provides a literal vocal bridge between musical improvisation and poetry. In this regard, "slave sho' to video . . ." is clearly drawing from rap and jazz traditions, both of which foreground the musical physicality of words. Morris's piece also plays on the jazz-inflected sermon in the prologue of Ralph Ellison's *Invisible Man*; both polemics ride on rhythmic repetition and elliptical phrasing directly linked to an African American musical tradition. Ellison's narrator, absorbed fully into Louis Armstrong's "What Did I Do to Be so Black and Blue," hears a call-and-response–style sermon that swings between contentless assertions of "black is . . ." and "black ain't . . . ," "it do . . ." and "it don't . . ." The heavy ellipses in this text suggest both the emptiness of these propositions and the given nature of what and how "black will make" or "unmake you."[26] Morris also banks on aural ellipsis to suggest words and encourage the listener to imagine connections. In the work of both Morris and Ellison, racial essence is the target of a parody that mocks the logic of essentialism itself, that "black" can be signified in any transcendent way. However in "slave sho' to video," of the two verbs employed, both marking epistemological status, "ain't" by far outnumbers "is," which, when it is used, always comes in the form of a question. "Ain't" functions doubly, flip-flopping as a stand-in for "is" as well as its negation. This flickering circuitry underscores the struggle to be seen, to be present at all, ironically set against the struggle to be seen as something more capacious than a sign. In this sustained ambivalence, the collocations of "is" and "ain't" as well as "black" and "beautiful" perform the crisis of linguistic limitation. Listening to the piece, we confront the mental contortions of double-talk and the rhetorical arabesques of circular reasoning necessary in the cultural persistence of race as an oppressively defining trope. The high-pressure scrutiny Morris applies to inherited structures of thought and feeling pushes language to unsettle the totalizing myths of language and blackness.

As a consolidated portrait, "slave sho' to video a.k.a Black But Beautiful" deploys puns, intonation fluctuations, and syntactic play reminiscent of Stein's sound-driven portraits. Stein's "If I Told Him. A Complete Portrait of Picasso" begins by holding a mirror up to the first sentence, reversing the dependent clauses: "If I told him would he like it. Would he like it if I told him."[27] Morris uses this mirroring strategy prolifically, reversing the syntax of "black" and "beautiful" as well as "aint" and "she" in exhaustive, percolating scats. So doing, she holds up a mirror to interpellation, enacting the necessary "double consciousness" of inhabiting white culture. Chiasmus here is not only structural but conceptual, verbal, and phonetic.[28] For both Stein and Morris, words live inside other words. Released and multiplied, words become self-regarding and, rather than superseding their components, enter into dialogue with themselves. The repetition as such is never blind or mechanical but metonymically suggests and sounds out other words that act as "portals of discovery."[29] Simultaneously conflicting and cooperative assertions about beauty call its definition into question. They rattle any sense of its objective status and unravel a sure sense of identity. With its ontological status of project and postulate, identity behaves verblike, morphing from one permutation in Morris's language to the next, crosscutting between erosion and vexation. Morris reorders syntaxes—rewiring language and identity—until the words evacuate their signifying functions. Instead of maintaining delight in a pleasurable chaos of echoes and linguistic destabilizations, she moves us through the wreckage to reconstitute language and thus identity into a state of nonessentialist inclusivity. The poem's final words, "beautiful and black," cannot be heard in isolation, but rather packed with the dialectical performance of their interpretation and reinvention as they update the famous Black Power dictum.

Morris effectively valorizes somatic experience to dispossess and repossess the language of identity. This is no hairsplitting intellectual argument, nor is it political sloganeering; it's music forcing itself into articulate spoken magic. Morris's approach departs from those who *point out* that language teaches violence and self-hatred; her language use is a theory in living practice.[30] Signifying, in Morris's mouth, is an analogue to the verbal actions of charms or spells. According to Andrew Welsh, a charm (like Austin's performative speech act), is a magic incantation, a vocal staging of an efficacious action: "At the roots, the words of a charm are themselves magic actions." With the charm, however, words carried on a rhythmic vocalization generate their own irregular, internal rhythm; the charm rhythm "developed by the assonances, alliterations, rhymes, and word-repetitions in the language of the poem" is dictated by the rhythm of the words themselves as they recur and reorganize in the course of the poem. Welsh contrasts this rhythm with that of a song or chant, in which the words are subordinate to the external, regular music. As in Morris's sound pieces, most charms involve unusual phonological and grammatical forms galvanized by "repeat[ing] a few words or a single line over and over as often as is necessary for the charm to work its effect."[31] The melopoeia that engineers them directs the bearing of their meaning. By harnessing the rhythmic shape of language, Morris transforms the voice into an enchantment, where sound is kinetically apprehended. When we hear Morris's works as spells, we are not engaging in magical thinking but recognizing of the persuasive force residing in rhythm, a language-derived rhythm that communicates before it is understood.[32]

Welsh discusses charm as a global, ancient form that charges language with the power to drive away an evil force by naming it or to superimpose good by way of renaming. "slave sho' to video a.k.a. Black But Beautiful," like all of Morris's sound poems, is propelled by a necessity of incantatory webs of textured sound that invoke, work over, then dismantle cultural curses. Instead of ignoring stereotypes, for instance, Morris acknowledges them, injecting a small amount of their disease into the listener's ears to produce an inoculation against franchise identity and habitualized consciousness. The antidote to venom is venom; the injuring name is deployed against its user. The spell's double articulation provides us with synchronously valid etymologies: as we adopt our mother tongue, our individual feeling for a word alongside historical linguistics. Performed by Morris, sentences like "I am just a little girl," "I'm in heaven," and "She too black" atomize a fecundity of implicit and explicit meanings. In Renaissance incantation, spells were thought to be words ejected by the imagination to form themselves as solid things. In Morris's work, a recovery and a manifestation are equally present. Some of the undoing of language sounds like an effortful recovery of words momentarily suppressed on "the tip of the tongue" and trying out ad hoc vocabularies, as if the body were offering up its own speech. Though the refrain might be an echo from the world, the echolalia that ensues reanimates and subjectivizes the reiteration.

Morris infuses improvisation into the somewhat predetermined sound patterns of traditional spell: "Stuff comes out that I am not prepared to utter . . . ," she says, "Almost all the time, sounds come up that never have presented themselves [to me] before."[33] Morris produces a sound embodied —and bound to exceed the body—with memory, prophecy, and rapture. As in the blues, the music generated by verse is a pan-rhythmic "explanation" of the words, meant to extend and to problematize them. There's simultaneously a trust in the inherent intelligence of language itself (as alliteration, assonance, and rhythm draw out latent meanings) and in her own individual ethical and aesthetic intelligence, which may "correct" or expose language's less admirable cultural baggage. Language acts as an inspirer and irritant, unraveling a repertoire of purposes that follow the compass of Morris's own excitement. The work's improvisational nature ties it to musical traditions such as jazz and hip-hop, and to spiritual traditions such as speaking in tongues and African diasporic ritual possession. All of these cultures embrace the rapture of inspiration that manifests as possession at a metaphoric or literal level: something beyond the pale of consciousness, and almost beyond containment, enters and speaks through the host. By entering a rhythm-induced trance, the medium accesses cultural memory—evoking synæsthetic spiritual, metaphysical, and emotional states that produce an urgent surfeit of responses. In Morris's sound poems, the mesmerizing, muscular rhythm becomes a force that distracts the listener from a frustrated sense of the language and lets it exist between consciousness and sentience. By unsheathing meaning to a state of sensations and drives, the rhythms sensitize our awareness of the moment; we are both asleep and awake in its lulling monotony and arousing variety. When improvising, the mind is liberated from the demands of the will. The eroticism of giving ourselves up to another's authority—the character that's speaking through Morris—is predicated on and intermingles with our own anxieties about self-control and power.

As listeners, we are transported into Morris's trance, tapping into what Julia Kristeva calls "chora," or "a rhythmic space," that precedes spatiality, temporality, and verisimilitude; it is a prelinguistic rhythmic language, untranslatable and anterior to judgment.[34] In psychoanalytic terms, language regresses in order to be translated. Through "linguistic overcompetence," an "experimental psychosis" emerges to reach into "the hazardous regions" where the writer's sense of psychic unity degenerates (30). As it moves through the mind and body without fixed orientation, language triggers the improvisational nature of memory and imagination and becomes pathologized: an oral disordering symptomatic of a psychic one. A compulsion for repetition brings a spontaneous rhythm to the fore. Spontaneity doesn't necessarily guarantee, as Kristeva wants to claim, access to the primal, authentic, unexpected, or subversive; our ideas about what's "authentic" are often just as culturally engineered and rehearsed as that which we name "artifice." However, in Morris's work, rhythm *moves* us to access otherwise incommunicable realms of experience. It is the organizing system in a theater of correspondences that forces a trust in elliptical and peripheral perception. Language germinates rhythm; thereafter Morris relies on the stringencies of the simultaneous. That is, language and rhythm exist in a carnal stereophonic relationship, each motivating and investigating the other.

In the symposium "What's African About African American Poetry," Morris claims that her investment in Africanized words has "become a form of ancestral worship."[35] Most of her sound poems harvest Africanisms in both African American English and standard American English: "bad," "boot," "boo," "boogie," "Bantu," and "tote," for instance, from "slave sho' to video." The word "boot," for example, might reference the contemporary idea of being under the boot or being given the boot, as well as its slang meanings, circa the Harlem Renaissance, "to give," playing on the stereotype of woman as service provider; "to explain or tell or listen," and "the making of exciting music," culling out self-referential emphasis; and especially "a black person," a definition that comes from the black color of boots.[36] The lexical genealogies here channel origins and authoritative meanings at the same time they violate those historicizing tendencies by insisting on temporality and contextuality. Not only does Morris compost phonemes to hothouse new meanings, but she breathes multiplicity into words and phrases. They "gesture toward an anarchic and generative meditation on phrasing" and "mark the generation of or from a lost language," a limbo, a gateway, a threshold.[37] The word "bounce," wells up in "slave sho' to video" like a sonic aftershock. Clearly the word resounds with context-appropriate expressions, (1) as a verb: to bully or bluff, to recover from a blow, to scold, to boast, to expel, to walk with a springy step, to dismiss; and (2) as a noun: resilience, verve, a style of jazz. These definitions, from *Webster's Third International Dictionary*, overlook one of the most obvious meanings in the urban black vernacular of Morris's piece—that is, to fuck. The contraction of "bounce" into "bow(n)" provides a basal link between sound and sense, if we hear the contraction as vocal impersonations of bass notes that anticipate heated scenes in porn movies. The word's euphemistic power and its pandemonium of inflections marshal visceral effects and psychosocial resonances that make it impossible to hear singularly. Yet Morris isn't simply celebrating language's interpretive branchings. By relying on clustered reduplications that spiral into abiding uncertainty and auditory ephemerality, words seep, at once provisional and whole, into our consciousness and assume unpredictable powers there. These words are at once provisional and whole; their cross-purposes, repressed identities, and secret narratives emerge, thereby connecting linguistic practices with social formations. Her designs arouse questions about power and memory and their relationships to language's regulatory function. In this poem, Morris destabilizes assumptions about objectification and delivers the concepts "beauty" and "black" into a matrix of complex states and attitudes.

Paul Miller's (aka DJ Spooky) notion of sampling as a harnessing of the uncanny gives us another way of reading Morris's use of language and rhythm. Samples invoke memory at the same time that they drastically recontexualize it, seamlessly reprocessing it to create a sense of estranged familiarity. Out of preexisting recordings, sampling orchestrates a new music; the stolen sound returns as a hallucinatory presence, haunting the current with associative histories. Sampling becomes an enactment of metaphor, yoking the known and the new in a dialectical process that never resolves: each import maintains equal reference to the original and to the new composition. Miller's syncretic reading of sampling and dub suggests that its invocations and quotations extend the ancient traditions of improvisation and possession: "Dub speaks from erasure, the voice fragmented and left to drift on the shards of itself that are left when its [original] body is taken away."[38] The soundscape encourages play reminiscent of the griot's wordplay, the Jamaican dub master's "versioning," and the "archive fever" of the era of live jazz and blues sessions, "where everyone had access to the same songs, but where they flipped things until they made their own statement." Though the current smackdown on sampling—the copyright cordons are tightening around the legal use of samples—suggests that all samples are implicated in Jameson's postmodern pastiche, Morris (as well as anyone who uses sampling well) demonstrates that her use of samples is not just another capitalist co-optation, but rather a citation and transformation of the original. Compare her version of Sam Cooke's 1960 song "Chain Gang," for instance, with the rapper Shinehead's contemporary rendition or most of the nearly one hundred borrowings of the song found on Napster.com that are clearly fueled by a desire to cannibalize the song's cultural prestige.[39]

In vocal ecstatic traditions, the tongue might be thought of as sampling equipment—with five connective points to the nervous system and an innate rhythm—that channels found texts into collaborative context. This lineage becomes direct in Morris's sound piece "Chain Gang," which borrows a line from Cooke's song, which itself was the result of heavy improvisation in its origin and in the studio.[40] Morris summons the restiveness and physical toil embedded in Cooke's refrain, "That's the sound of the man working on the chain gang," and adrenalizes it to signify alienation, exhausted patience, anger, and threat. Morris's piece specifically protests the reintroduction of chain gangs in the United States: "It was like a physical blow. Looking at my people working for free, with chains on in public."[41] Morris uses the uncanny echo of Cooke's song as an homage, but the recontextualization, forty years later, renders it bitingly ironic.

In the course of "Chain Gang," Morris radically unhinges the original: she lets loose invocations of African deities Ogun and Agun, the gods of mask and theater as well as ironwork and metallurgy, further seeking a sense of spiritual recovery. The deep, percussive pronunciation of the names of these Yoruba gods help the piece to dramatize blues experience in deeply physical terms. Sounds of ancestral agency combat sounds of enslaved working; these two "characters" rip the idea of the chain gang away from its supporting conventions and confound its offense. "Freestyling," or improvising rhymes to an established rhythm, sends the song even further into other histories and contexts: "sane" and "insane" as well as "devil" and "angel" extend the narrative subtext and its simmering insinuations. The implied and actual erasure here serves as a reminder of how memory keeps recrystallizing and recontextualizing. As Morris builds in a sense of stricken inarticulation, her vocal expressivity irrupts into thundering grunts and raw-throated expirations. This loosening of word from meaning, of sound from word is part of Morris's process of generative de/re-construction as if the rest of language's resources had been abandonded. The body's pain, as Elaine Scarry claims, disables language, and it is just this unrepresentability of physical pain that Morris presents.[42] The demonic discharges of "ch" and "ga" seem to be a sonic emblem of the exhaustion of words themselves.[43] They manifest a sonic narrative of train chugging, worker grunting, rail splitting, and clock ticking. Thus Morris skewers the economic implications of the chain gang and revises the longing of Cooke's song into retributive threat. Is the "tick-tock" at the piece's end a bomb's timer? Does it signal an exhaustion of the possibility of words, or talk, to change calcified racism? Does the ticking point toward an impending outbreak of violence or the violence of continued racism itself? Say that the clock's onomonopoeia points to the future or to the past and you won't be wrong. The poem's immersive lingering refuses to let us out of its all-encompassing present, which is a sounding board for ideological and material struggles relating to race.

Senses—of body and of language—commingle and complicate a peregrinating underlanguage, not so much linguistic as made possible by language's rhyme and rhythm. This underlanguage refuses the permanence of its own constitution via improvisation and continued performance and sets a model for acknowledging aspects of identity that go unheard in standard language use. Morris's sound poetry announces a continued enabling of transformation itself. Her sustained investment in the iterative process keeps tonguing identity into new shapes in order to reveal its public relations and ramifications. The sound of these transfigurations, equally punishing and pleasurable, is the sound of a spell that reinstates flexibility into identity and ethical responsibility into lyric poetry. Morris locates language's core by melting it down and reconstituting it as a tool for ideological adjustment. But as with the girl narrator in "A Little," we must ask, How might language adjust? Or aid justice?

NOTES

1. Go to <www.worldofpoetry.org/usop/land4/htm> or www.writing.upenn.edu/pennsound/x/Morris.html.

2. Alex Ross, "Björk's Saga," *New Yorker* (August 23, 2004): 50.

3. Morris's performance on September 16, 2004, at Eastern Michigan University takes us through a chronological development of her poetics; the performance ends with two sound poems I discuss in this paper, "A Little" and "Chain Gang." To view the performance, go to www.emich.edu/public/english/creative-writing/readingarchive/morris.html. For the most extensive archive of Morris's work, including several poems discussed here, go to PennSound: www.writing.upenn.edu/pennsound/x/Morris .html (2004). These performances offer testimony to the improvisational nature of Morris's work.

4. Harryette Mullen, "Poetry and Identity," in *Telling it Slant: Avant-Garde Poetics of the 1990s*, ed. Mark Wallace and Steven Marks (Tuscaloosa: University of Alabama Press, 2002), 28.

5. Some of Morris's collaborators include Ralph Lemon, Sudha Seetharaman, Trey McIntyre, Arthur Jafa, Xenobia Bailey, Donald Byrd, Graham Haynes, Kevin Bruce Harris, Michael Hill, Jean-Paul Bourelly, Cecilia Smith, DD Jackson, Uri Caine, Ela Troyano, and Badal Roy.

6. J. L. Austin, *How To Do Things With Words*, 2d ed., ed. J. O. Urmson and Marina Sbisà (Cambridge, Mass.: Harvard University Press, 1975).

7. Go to http://www.ubu.com/sound/dutton.html.

8. Gertrude Stein, "Portraits and Repetition," in *Stein: Writings, 1932–1946* (New York: Library of America, 1998 [1935]), 287–312; Henry Louis Gates Jr., *The Signifying Monkey: A Theory of African-American Literary Criticism* (New York: Oxford

University Press, 1998); Amiri Baraka [LeRoi Jones], *The LeRoi Jones/Amiri Baraka Reader*, ed. William J. Harris (New York: Thunder's Mouth Press, 1991), 197.

9. "Gestalt listening" might also be termed "peripheral hearing" after Freud's concept of peripheral consciousness, a level of subconscious awareness such as subliminal perception, where we register information that comes below the threshold of awareness. The degree of involuntary participation and registered cognition is arguable; we both fill in unfinished phrases and register half-heard words when listening to Morris's work. What I am tagging "gestalt listening," Morris calls "the almost heard."

10. Gates, *Signifying Monkey*, 64.

11. Henry Louis Gates Jr., *Figures in Black: Words, Signs, and the "Racial" Self* (New York: Oxford University Press, 1987), 168.

12. This is my transcription; there is no printed source. To hear this piece, go to http://writing.upenn.edu/pennsound/x/Morris.html (2004).

13. For a discussion of crypt words as a tool for modernist writers to engage in racial and gender politics, see Rachel Blau DuPlessis, *Genders, Races and Religious Cultures in Modern American Poetry, 1908–1934* (New York: Cambridge University Press, 2001).

14. Reuven Tsur, *What Makes Sound Patterns Expressive: The Poetic Mode of Speech Perception* (Durham: Duke University Press, 1992), 11.

15. Ibid., 47.

16. The rhetorical tropes subsumed under signifying include naming, marking, testifying, sounding, rapping, playing the dozens, and so forth.

17. Kurt Schwitters, *Ur Sonata*, recording, 1922, <www.ubu.com/sound/schwitters/html>.

18. Yet we can never voice the poem; no one can read the poem aloud because it only exists as a dynamic performance. See Plato and Derrida for diagnostic discussions of oral primacy and perceived authenticity.

19. Sonia Sanchez, *We a BadddDDD People* (Detroit, Mich.: Broadside Press, 1970), 19.

20. Debra Singer, "Tracie Morris." Liner notes to *Soundworks: Whitney Biennial 2002* (New York: Whitney Museum of American Art): 5.

21. Some questions the piece might provoke include: Is she beautiful because she's booty? Or despite being booty? Is she beautiful because she's bound to blackness? Or despite being black? Is she beautiful because she's bound? Is she beautiful because she's she-she or in a tutu? Is she beautiful because she's Bantu? Because she's sheep? Because she's ample? Because of her ample butt? Because she's tooting her horn? Or his horn? Is she beautiful because she ain't shit? Is she bait? Is she bounty?

22. Suzan Lori Parks, Deborah Richards, and Elizabeth Alexander also interrogate the Venus Hottentot construct.

23. Judith Butler, *Excitable Speech: A Politics of the Performative* (New York: Routledge, 1997), 1.

24. Ibid., 36.

25. Gates, *Figures in Black*, 176.

26. Ralph Ellison, *Invisible Man* (New York: Random House, 1980), 9–10.

27. Gertrude Stein, "If I Told Him: A Complete Portrait of Pablo Piccaso," recording, read by the author, <www.factoryschool.org/content/sounds/havanaglen.html>.

28. W.E.B. Du Bois, *The Souls of Black Folk* (New York: Dover, 1994 [1903]), 2.

29. James Joyce, *Ulysses* (New York: Random House, 1990 [1922]), 190.

30. This practice might be patterned on Antonin Artaud's "theater of cruelty," which aims to affront the audience, to engulf them in violence that rattles their moral and emotional tracks. This technique differs for writers like Sonia Sanchez who uses a dual approach of direct, normative grammar and syntactic defamiliarization to emotionally confound the directness of the former.

31. Andrew Welsh, *Roots of Lyric: Primitive Poetry and Modern Poetics* (Princeton: Princeton University Press, 1978): 136–45.

32. I prefer the word "spell" here because its connotations are much more forceful to my ear. "Charm"'s contemporary link with ideas such as "lucky charm" and "charming personality" dilutes its historic punch; Morris's work doles out that other kind of charm in acid droplets.

33. Kathleen Crowne, "'Sonic Revolutionaries': Voice and Experiment in the Spoken Word Poetry of Tracie Morris," in *We Who Love to Be Astonished: Experimental Women's Writing and Performance Poetics*, ed. Laura Hinton and Cynthia Hogue (Tuscaloosa: University of Alabama Press, 2002), 221.

34. Julia Kristeva, *Revolution in Poetic Language*, trans. Margaret Waller, introd. Leon S. Roudiez (New York: Columbia University Press, 1984), 25–30.

35. "What's African About African American Poetry?" *Fence* 1, no. 1 (2001): <www.fencemag.com/v1n1/text/afric_amer.html>.

36. Clarence Major, *Juba to Jive: A Dictionary of African-American Slang* (New York: Penguin, 1994), 56.

37. Fred Moten, *In the Break: The Aesthetics of the Black Radical Tradition* (Minneapolis: University of Minnesota Press, 2003), 42–44. This book provides a rich, extensive meditation on improvisation and black American avant-garde's blurring of music and poetry. Moten stresses among other things the importance of erasure in improvisation and uses Nathaniel Mackey's phrase "that insistent previousness evading each and every natal occasion" as a touchstone.

38. Paul Miller (aka DJ Spooky That Subliminal Kid), *Rhythm Science* (Cambridge, Mass.: Mediawork–MIT Press, 2004), 53–54 and 29.

39. To hear Morris's piece go to <www.writing.upenn.edu/pennsound/x/Morris.html>; Shinehead's song may be heard at <www.mp3.com>.

40. Peter Guralinick, *Sam Cooke: Portrait of a Legend, 1951–1964*, liner notes (New York: ABKCO Records, 2003), 10.

41. Crowne, "Sonic Revolutionaries," 223.

42. Elaine Scarry, *The Body in Pain: The Making and Unmaking of the World* (Oxford: Oxford University Press, 1985).

43. In his essay "The Exhausted," Gilles Deleuze elaborates: "It is not only that words lie; they are so burdened with calculations and significations, with intentions and personal memories, with old habits that cement them together, that one can scarcely bore into the surface before it closes up again." By exhausting words, however, Morris demonstrates what capacities they might discover if freed of these

burdens. Piling up rhythms unfold a multitude of perspectives that bore holes in language's hermetic surfaces. See Deleuze, "The Exhausted," in *Essays Critical and Clinical*, trans. Daniel W. Smith and Michael A. Greco (Minneapolis: University of Minnesota Press, 1997), 173.

BIBLIOGRAPHY

Books by Tracie Morris

Chap-T-her Won: Some Poems by Tracie Morris. New York: TM Ink, 1993.
Intermission. Introduction by Cornelius Eady. New York: Soft Skull Press, 1998.

Selected Poetry and Prose in Anthologies

"Afrofem Aesthetics Manifested." In *Soul: Black Power, Politics and Pleasure*, edited by Richard C. Green and Monique Guillory. New York: New York University Press, 1998.
"Hip Hop Rhyme Formations." In *An Exaltation of Forms: Contemporary Poets Celebrate the Diversity of Their Art*, edited by Annie Finch and Kathrine Varnes. Ann Arbor: University of Michigan Press, 2002.
"The Old Days." In *In Defense of Mumia*, edited by Sam Anderson and Tony Medina. New York: Poets and Writers, 1995.
"on an' on." In *Rock She Wrote*, edited by Ann Powers and Evelyn McDonald. New York: Simon and Schuster, 1995.
"Private Service Announcement," "switchettes (las brujitas)," "Writer's Delight," "Life Saver," and "Step." In *Listen Up! Spoken Word Poetry*, edited by Zoe Anglesey. New York: Ballantine Books, 1998.
"Project Princess." In *The Outlaw Bible of American Poetry*, edited by Alan Kaufman. New York: Random House, 2000.
"Project Princess," "Morenita," and "The Spot." In *Aloud: Voices from the Nuyorican Café*, edited by Migel Algarin, Nicole Blackman, and Bob Holman. New York: Henry Holt, 1993.
"Rasta Not." In *Revival: Spoken Word Artists of Lollapalooza*, edited by Mud Baron, Liz Belie, Juliette Torrez, et al. San Francisco, Calif.: Manic D Press, 1995.
"steeple-peeple." In *110 Stories: New Yorkers Write After September 11*, edited by Ulrich Baer. New York: New York University Press, 2002.
"Why I Won't Wear a Tatoo," "Lovers Total Recall," "Just Say No Blues," and "Prelude to a Kiss." In *Beyond the Frontier: African American Poetry for the 21st Century*, edited by E. Ethelbert Miller. Baltimore, Md.: Black Classic Press, 2002.

Recording Projects (Lyricist/Performer)

Poetry reading and interview with Charles Bernstein. http://writing.upenn.edu/pennsound/x/Morris.html, 2004.
"slave sho' to video a.k.a. Black But Beautiful." *Soundworks: Whitney Biennial 2002*. New York: Whitney Museum of American Art, 2002.

"Project Princess." *Our Souls Have Grown Deep like the Rivers*. Rhino Records, 2000.
"Variation 19." With Uri Caine. *Goldberg Variations*. Uri Caine Ensemble. Winter and Winter Records, 2000.
"All My Life." *All My Life*. Leon Parker. Columbia/Sony Records, 1997.
"Prelude to a Kiss." *State of the Union*. Atavistic Records, 1997.
"Trance-gression/Out of Phase." With Graham Haynes. *Tones for the 21st Century*. Polygram Records, 1997.
"Project Princess." *United States of Poetry*. Mercury Records, 1996.
"Alex." *Alex*. CD audio play. Bavarian Broadcasting Company, Germany, 1995.
"Observations" and "So What?" *Word Up*. Virgin/EMI, Canada, 1993.
"On & On." *Best of the National Poetry Slam*. NuYo/Imago records, 1994.
"Skin." *Folksongs, Folktales*. Kevin Bruce Harris quartet. Tip Toe/Enja Records, 1993.
"Open Letter to a Landlord." *Vivid*. Living Colour, Epic Records, 1989.

Selected Theater Projects, Radio Broadcasts, and Museum Installations

The East New York Project. 651 Arts, New York, New York, 2004.
Afrofuturistic. The Kitchen Performance Space, New York, New York, May 2003.
"slave sho' to video a.k.a. Black but Beautiful," "A Little," "The Mrs. Gets Her Ass Kicked," "untitled a.k.a. Blue Black Blues." Sound poetry installation. 2002 Biennial Exhibition. The Whitney Museum of American Art, 2002.
Sonic Synthesis. The Kitchen Performance Space, New York, New York, 1999.
Grown Over Ivy. The International Festival of Arts and Ideas, Yale University Courtyards, New Haven, Connecticut, 1998.
Geography. Ralph Lemon and Yale Repertory Theater, U.S. tour, 1997.
Black to the Future. P.S. 122, New York, New York, 1996.
Afrofem. P.S. 122, New York, New York, 1995.
Goin' Through Changes. Aaron Davis Hall, New York, New York, May 1995.
Juno the Universal Power Chile. With Jake Ann Jones. National Public Radio Broadcast, 1995.

Selected Criticism

Crowne, Kathleen. "'Choice Voice Noise': Soundsing in Innovative African-American Poetry." In *Assembling Alternatives: Reading Postmodern Poetries Transnationally*, edited by Romana Huk, 219–45. Middletown, Conn.: Wesleyan University Press, 2003.
———. "'Sonic Revolutionaries': Voice and Experiment in the Spoken Word Poetry of Tracie Morris." In *We Who Love to Be Astonished: Experimental Women's Writing and Performance Poetics*, edited by Laura Hinton and Cynthia Hogue, 213–26. Tuscaloosa: University of Alabama Press, 2002.
Damon, Maria. "Was That 'Different,' 'Dissident' or 'Dissonant'? Poetry (n) the Public Spear: Slams, Open Readings, and Dissident Traditions." In *Close Listening: Poetry and the Performed Word*, edited by Charles Bernstein, 324–42. New York: Oxford University Press, 1998.

MYUNG MI KIM

FROM *COMMONS*

FROM "LAMENTA"

229

The transition from the stability and absoluteness of the world's contents to their dissolution into motions and relations.

P: Of what use are the senses to us—tell me that

E: To indicate, to make known, to testify in part

Burning eye seen

Of that

One eye seen

bo-bo-bo   *k-k-k*

Jack in the pulpit   petaling

To a body of infinite size there can be ascribed neither center nor boundary say   .   siphon

Sign scarcity, the greeting—*have you eaten today?*

Signal of peonies   singing given to bullfrogs

Give ear to the quarrels of the marketplace

When the wheel (A) was turned, the gate (B) was raised, thus allowing water to flow from (C) to (D), giving clearance for the ship to pass beneath

lever   .   girt

Host and parasite

Implicated armed band

Where would one live

A custom of wrapping the head in willow branches

315

Why are many buildings necessary with so small a farm area?

The heat of the midday sun is obvious, but the pressure of populations on the inadequate areas of flat land has to be inferred.

For the flock, a brief flash announces possible food

mite   a copper coin of very small value
            a small weight
            a minute particle or portion

detent   stop or catch in a machine which prevents motion and the
            removal of which brings some motor into immediate action
            (as in guns, clocks, watches)

deterge   to wash off or out, to clear away foul or offensive matter from
            the body

s–s–s

how to false bottom log
whom I saw beautiful as a boy

nuph-juk-pahn
nubh-jjuk-paan

shun   .   nestle

ravenous   .   seal

ash   .   gust

318

Their [brilliance and their dependence]

Flowers [gladiolas, zinnia, delphinium]

Offset the houses

What the bluejay exacts [upside down]
[inside] the half-broken sunflower, pecking

Scrip—a small purse carried by a pilgrim, shepherd or beggar

One among fled many
            felt

Any differrent tissue constitutes a heterology

White light after breath (circling the mouth)//

The baby asleep in the house
And two figures down by the barn

It burns. Membrane.

Further carbonization of matter

bellrag   ㅈ
bellslip   *jw*

405

periplus voyage around a coastline or the narrative of such a voyage

muo   the fifty-fifth term in the cycle of sixty used to count years,
months, days, and hours

The fundamental tenet of all military geography is that every feature of
the visible world possesses actual or potential military significance

Little flower,

What day is it

The light stops at glum

O'clock and *f*

A rain saturated tree trunk becomes a feeling

The city of one's birth and the poeple inside it

415

War is there and travel

The same is my sister, brothers, and mother

The father is thrush, white at birth and at dusk

Father is burying ground cool to the touch

This is some color but what color is it

"left their homes after two solid days of attacks"

"they had stayed to take care of their cow"

"the extreme cold froze medicine"

"religion and capitalism intersect in the muddy village twenty miles north of"

424

The central organizing myth of comprehensive knowledge

Bent as light might bend

The openings in the human body

The age that one is

I will be my mother's age also

Color of robin's egg against spring grass

426

jiph-jiph-jiph

Swallow Swallow Bird

This is the gullet

Helmets make cooking pots

Tin cans make roofs

[sparrow, crow]

Not much left
Not much left

705

Spittle, bittle

Lup/   /lapiary

Peregrine's (*f l*)

            sumac

Muri   *dori*

As a head fit without torso

Throat in hand

A farmhouse and outbuildings
An open screen door

So we speak of marauding, flooding

FROM "WORKS"

Sleep took the eye muscle and severed it

In the vernacular   ate   stirred   swept

At the periphery   garbage pigs

: sandscroll :

After a long last

I learn my story

My mother had restaurant

She made noodle soup

It was famous soup

She suffer so much

For so much her life

It burn skin to bone

Scar tissue on top of nerve ending

Ugly power of military

I scream too hot too hot

Naked where clothes were a second before

Cultivation rights

══════════════ ══════

═══════════════════════════

═══════════════════════

too bad

The lower level of the social hierarchy ═════ made up of ═════ who
tilled and ════════ the food

════════ being atomized ═══════════ occurs

══════════════════════ price lists ═══════════════════════

══════════════════════════

As they enter, they cut down grains, tear down the inner and outer walls,
and fill up the ditches and ponds; they exterminate the aged and the weak

In the calendars available, shortages are documented as a result of human
actions: civil wars, piracy, failure to transport food where needed

: has also found safety in the U.S. He's apparently a valued employee at
   Our Way, a compressor plant

: The second and fourth movements will use no speech whatsoever

: Debt burden does kill

Paltry did it

Paltry said so

skilter head .   lifts up and tells simple mother stories

everyday to spout

everyday to alight

everyday to bring one end to the other, close

a pick a pack a frightening fund

that.   wants a biscuit

: I am assured that the global buying frenzy
: I am assured that there is a global buying frenzy

drain in a prophylactic sense

in plain sight cusp of flesh and action

that said: the cost

that said: brittle off the bone and perjure

Constant Reverential Face

Please allow that

Place of feet and water

Please allow that

The oil and seeds

What is the call to call out

laughter visited us early and left

moving around a sequence of debts

there would be the occasion of reaching for a foreign object in the eye

Speaker: She got shot. She did. I saw her.

limbs of pines rope around the waist

neither slaves nor freemen, but who have become part of the soil upon which they work like so many cows and the trees

the schools had been burned down

the teachers had been starved to death

the road had fallen into decay

the bridges were gone

will be eaten
at a ration of quarters
will be eaten
at a ration of fifths

POETICS STATEMENT
Convolutions : the Precision, the Wild

FUGITIVE, UNNAMEABLE, contingent. Nor remnant nor fragment nor refuse. Neither infinite deferral nor rehearsal of uncertainty. Rather, the labor. Of making.

The problem of [the presupposition of] [there already exists] a language for

Regularized language and knowledge. Standing for perceiving and thinking. Serving as arbiter of recognizability, and thus of affiliation. What is occluded in the sociohistorical index.

Fierce unsystematic recombinatory potential of language. The task of aberration   disruption   the provisional. As generative. As relational. Tests of mutually inflected deformations devolutions emendations of nations, languages—of being in time and being in history. Translative. That which is emergent [irreducible] in the cultural order. Forge [to smith]. [Refunction] modes of perception.

Factive . phonotactic . what passes for the actual . aporia
Form's unrest . warfare staged as benevolence . synapse

Heterogeneous conceptions of temporality. Conjunctural.
Historical consciousness as chiasmatic—mobile.   [*cura*]

The practice of the poem is the practice of radical materiality

Poised at the question of the question of the proximal

MAKING COMMON
THE COMMONS

Myung Mi Kim's Ideal Subject

Warren Liu

ONE SALIENT feature of Myung Mi Kim's poetry that general readers and academics alike agree upon is its intense and at times unrelenting opacity. In her first three books, *Under Flag*, *The Bounty*, and *Dura*, the poems concede very little to a reader in search of either narrative, speaker, subject, or even location: instead, they construct meaning through accretion, fragmentation, translation (and mistranslation), and disjunction. It is somewhat surprising, then, to find that the final section of her most recent work, *Commons*, provides what seems to be a commentary on or an explanation of the poems that precede it. Entitled "Pollen Fossil Record," the section reads as an (perhaps intentionally) obscure *ars poetica*, laying out both the rationale and explanation for what might otherwise seem an inaccessibly abstract sequence of poems. Explaining that "*Commons* elides multiple sites: reading and text making, discourses and disciplines, documents and documenting," Kim gestures, exegetically, toward a kind of applied poetic intent, as well as the interpretive practice that such intent might inspire.[1] Curiously, however, the effect of this exegetical musing is double-edged: it serves not only to provide the reader an entry into the work, but warns, in the same breath, the near impossibility of attaining any such position of interpretive clarity.[2] Emphasizing what the text "elides"—what it leaves out, skips over, or literally destroys—the statement actually negates what appears to be, on the surface, an author's explanatory impulse: rather than provide an interpretive framework through which a reader might understand the text, Kim asserts that the text itself is in fact more concerned with all that the text is not. Moreover, this emphasis on what is absent only highlights the question of why what *is* presented is, in fact, present. For the reader looking for a bit of authorial guidance, the answer to the question of what, exactly, lies in the space between "reading and text making, discourses and disciplines, documents and documenting" returns only in the form of a negative: it is that which *Commons* elides.

The verb "elides" perhaps not being explanation enough, Kim reinforces this tone of ambiguous excavation by then raising the apposite question of what might *not* be elided in the work:

> What *is* English now, in the face of mass global migrations, ecological degradations, shifts and upheavals in identifications of gender and labor? How can

the diction(s), register(s), inflection(s) as well as varying affective stances that have and will continue to filter into "English" be taken into account? What are the implications of writing at this moment, in precisely this "America"? (*C* 110)

The quotations around the words "English" and "America" here, much like the missing space between "reading and text making" or "discourses and disciplines," serve as markers of an uncontainable abundance: faced with the overdetermined nature of the terms "English" and "America," what might anyone actually tell us about their constituency? Is such definition possible? Is such interrogation even possible? And yet, this is also to ask: in this particular historical moment, in the face of "mass global migrations" and massive social, economic, and cultural dislocation, what is *not* "English," what is *not* "America"? For Kim, the answer seems to be, everything and everybody, and at the same time, nothing and nobody at all.[3] To suggest that "America" is a definable entity, or that "English" might be a measurable quantity, one must first acknowledge that definition is almost always a matter of negative presence. What is "America"? It's precisely the positive remnant of what "America" is *not*. This duality, this assertion that "what is" is both dependent upon, and distinct from, "what is not," may help explain Kim's initial emphasis on elision. Indeed, to locate *Commons* within the moment of elision, a moment of the "in-between," means also to redefine and resettle the very grounds—the borders and boundaries—of the conspicuous absence that surrounds it.[4] What becomes clear is that *Commons* is thus not simply an exploration of elision, but is also, more important, an interrogation of what even elision might eventually elide. Put another way, one might say that Myung Mi Kim's *Commons* reframes the negative—by negating it.

This is odd explication, indeed, and far from "clear," but perhaps appropriate for a text that flows seamlessly from descriptions of dead robins to philosophical inquiries into the nature of perception.[5] And indeed, the juxtaposition of the general and the specific that structures the two passages cited above is, I believe, far from accidental. For Kim, the exploration of how language functions to mask or suppress the fundamental power relations among *generalized* forms of knowledge production—identified here in terms of "reading," "text making," "discourse," "disciplines," "documents and documenting"—is intimately linked to the recognition that we must also use that same language to define, understand, and uncover *specific* iterations of power (or powerlessness), whether these be in the form of "mass global migrations, ecological degradations," or "upheavals in identifications of gender and labor." In this light, Kim's focus on elision as that which reveals the process of its own functioning becomes rather more pragmatic than poetic, insofar as we agree that language has the potential to both mask *and* reveal the structures of power through which it operates. The function of the elision—the space Kim claims for *Commons*—is thus to both clarify what, through absence, is present, and to disclose how that absence troubles the very notion of *any* positivistic, poetic presence.[6] It is the task of the poetic text, then, to "call into question, to disclose, to make common" these structures of power, to "consider how the polyglot, porous, transcultural presence alerts and alters what is around it" (*C* 110 and 109).

That the very title of the book echoes and amplifies this charge is therefore none too surprising. What is surprising is the apparent contradiction in the assertion itself, in the elided moment between making something "common," and recognizing the rather *uncommon* specificity of "the polyglot, porous, transcultural presence" through which commonality is revealed. Is this not yet another instance of language's ability to mask and incorporate difference? If poetry is to "counter the potential totalizing power of language that serves the prevailing systems and demands of coherence" (*C* 110), how could language possibly serve as a "commons," in which any subject might come to stand for subjectivity in general? What of actual difference, in such a scenario? One is inclined to pity the poor polyglot, whose tongue is thereby made common. I believe, however, that for Kim, difference remains, insofar as one recognizes a distinction between the general sense of language as an idealized "commons," and the specific task of questioning and disclosing, of making "common," the interpretive practices—the ways in which language is received as text, as product, as discourse and discipline— through which the limits of an ideal "commons" is actually contested. This is to say, somewhat simplistically, that the book's title references a noun and the book's practice describes an adjective. What is less obvious is how this seemingly slight difference constitutes two distinct realms of inquiry found throughout all of Myung Mi Kim's work, including *Commons*.[7] Before turning to the specifics of this argument, however, we may find it useful to think more carefully about what it might actually mean for language to operate as a "commons," and how the act of making interpretive practices "common" might in fact contribute to, rather than disrupt, the achievement of such an ideal. And because, in much of Kim's work, the philosophical often freely intermingles with the scientific, it is perhaps not outrageous to turn to a scientist in order to do so.[8]

In his famous essay "The Tragedy of the Commons," Garrett Hardin lays out what is now a well-known scenario, as a rebuttal to "the tendency to assume that decisions reached individually will, in fact, be the best decisions for an entire society."[9] According to Hardin, the "tragedy of the commons" occurs precisely when, confronted with a limited resource (in his scenario, a common pasture open to all herdsman in a community) humans in fact do the exact opposite of the ideal, so that "each man is locked into a system that compels him to increase his herd without limit—in a world that is limited. Ruin is the destination toward which all men rush, each pursuing his own best interest in a society that believes in the freedom of the commons. Freedom in a commons brings ruin to all" ("TC" 254). Although writing specifically about the problem of population control, Hardin's scenario seems applicable (and has been applied) to a variety of topics, ranging from Ultimate Frisbee to the Internet.[10] But can it be applied to language and literature? Judging from the complex constellation of ideas expressed in "Pollen Fossil Record," we might speculatively say that for Myung Mi Kim, at least, it can be applied to *both* language and literature—but not in the same manner. Thus, it's not only possible, but quite plausible, to think of language as the ideal commons, a literally limitless resource from which all of humanity might draw, without fear of scarcity or diminishment.[11] This is to imagine language as a realm similar to Hardin's pretragedy commons, in which "tribal wars, poaching, and disease keep the numbers of both man and beast well below the carrying capacity of the land" ("TC" 254). And indeed, were language only operative in an ideal realm of pure enunciation, there would not necessarily be any impending tragedy. Literature, however, implies resource: not merely in terms of literacy and language acquisition, but also in terms of production, distribution, reception, and specialized discourse in general. Therein lies the tragedy: language might be a limitless resource, but how language becomes literature is a constantly contested territory.[12]

Admittedly, this is a general treatment of highly abstract terminology; it leaves much room for improvement, but serves nicely to illustrate a crucial concern that runs throughout Myung Mi Kim's work: the assertion of the possibility of an ideal language through the exposure of the limits of literature as an embattled terrain of power and subjectivity. Returning, for a moment, to the "Pollen Fossil Record," it becomes clear that for Kim, belief in language as an ideal realm in fact operates in tandem with an ethical responsibility to call out those moments wherein literary practice disrupts or delays the achievement of such ideal. This combination of optimism and skepticism explains how it's possible that the making "common" of such exposure can coexist with the specter of the subject-specific "polyglot" and the historical presence of the "transcultural": on the one hand, Kim expresses a belief in the language as a commons; on the other, she articulates the particular formations of literary practice that inscribe power and subjectivity as a *failure* of that projected ideal. It is for this reason, perhaps, that Kim focuses not on the literary, but on the enunciative, when describing how poetry might serve this ideal, to "contemplate the generative power of the designation 'illegible' coming to speech" (*C* 110), to "change to position of enunciation and the relations within it" (*C* 99). For Kim, the power resides not in the settled, received text, but in that which in fact cannot be read, that which remains "illegible." It is a focused concentration on the transition from illegibility to text that provides for poetry a "generative power," just as it is the revelation of the elided structures of power within the contestation of the legible that traces the degenerative arc of staging literary production as material resource. And indeed, it is the written, the legible, that resettles the elided text as a contested, quantifiable object; notice the emphasis on writing, and not speech, in the question cited above: "What are the implications of writing at this moment, in precisely this 'America'?"

This is, of course, the poetics of elision in action, one best imagined, in fact, as an active, poetic *practice*. Or, in Kim's words, as recitation and repetition: "these rehearsals, not as description, but as activation—actively investigating how legibility is constructed and maintained, how 'English' is made and disseminated" (*C* 110). And here, it's important to note, extratextually, that the difference between language as an ideal "commons," and the making "common" of that which language masks and elides, lies then also in the difference between, for instance, claiming for Kim the title of poet, and proclaiming that Kim is an Asian American poet. A minor, adjectival difference? It would seem not, considering the furious contestation of such amendments within the discourse and discipline of literary criticism. Indeed, this particular transition describes an illuminating instance wherein Kim's poetic practice, her *rehearsals*, allows for a reframing of the discourse of poetics as a literal "field" of disputation—one in which the staking of territory discloses not what language provides as possibility, but rather, what literary production re-scripts as cultural and social power. Indeed, we might notice an echo of this transition in Charles Bernstein's discussion of "packaged" diversity and its consequences. As Bernstein writes,

> I see too great a continuum from "diversity" back to New Critical and liberal-democratic concepts of a common readership that often—certainly not always—have the effect of transforming unresolved ideological divisions and antagonisms into packaged tours of the local color of gender, race, sexuality, ethnicity, region, nation, class, even historical period: where each group or community or period is expected to come up with—or have appointed for them—representative figures we all can know about.[13]

The problem, for Bernstein, is not "diversity" per se, but the ways in which universal ideals of knowable otherness become stand-ins for actual difference and subjective alterity, such that "representative-ness" replicates, rather than interrogates, the fissures and gaps between language as philosophical inquiry and literature as market resource. To become "representative" in the literary marketplace (the hottest product of which is currently "diversity") means, for Bernstein, to forfeit actual difference to the whims of popularity and best-seller lists, to fall prey to "the insidious obsession with mass culture and popularity, here translated into the lingo of a unified culture of diversity" (*AP* 6).

For Bernstein, a more productive way to pose questions of difference is to concentrate on poetic form, rather than to idealize transparent content.

Instead of buying into "the emerging official cultural space of diversity," in which "difference is confined to subject matter and thematic material, a.k.a. local color," poets should focus attention on the operations of language and form, "the political and social meaning of sound, vernacular, non-traditional rhythms—that is, those things that make a text a poem," operations often overlooked by "the conventional forms of dominant culture" (*AP* 6). And while Kim's "Pollen Fossil Record" certainly seems to echo these sentiments—asking, as it does, "What was missing? What was forgotten? What was never learned in the first place? What was and was not written 'correctly'?" (*C* 110)—it also, at the same time, questions the very assumptions that allow Bernstein the space to make such a charge in the first place. And here it should be apparent that while Bernstein, like Kim, envisions language as something of an ideal realm, separate from and untouched by the vagaries of marketplace economics or culturally sanctioned imperatives, he also overlooks the social and political power involved in the reception of that language as such, the structures of academy, publishing house, and lecture hall that articulate (or elide) the struggles behind the transformation of language into literature. Thus, hidden in Bernstein's challenge to "local color" is also an assumption about form that suggests an elision of another sort: that "those things that make a text a poem" are somehow immanent and objective, as opposed to local and subjective.[14] Indeed, what Bernstein neglects to acknowledge here is that he himself, and not a generalized sense of language and form, is one of "those things that make a text a poem." Clearly, Bernstein's complaint raises, without quite answering, the significant question of how, exactly, ethnic subjectivity might then be best represented, *without* replicating the inherent inequalities and disparities of a market economy. If subjectivity cannot be pointed to as difference—if otherness is embedded in form, and not legible content—how then would it even be possible to imagine, much less argue for, Myung Mi Kim as a specifically Asian American poet?[15]

This question returns us not to a discussion of language as a commons, but to a reckoning of how literary production and reception are deeply imbricated with questions of power, discipline, and knowledge production. In this context, to claim Kim as an Asian American poet is not simply to idealize recognizable otherness, but rather, to articulate the continued and continuing inequality of access for Asians to the literary culture of America —to expose both the elision of the Asian from America literature, and the results thereof. Perhaps not unexpectedly, the tension between the desire for language as a commons and an ethically driven exhumation of all that prevents it becomes most fraught in discussions centered around the specificity of ethnic, gendered subjects—as becomes clear during an interview between Myung Mi Kim and James Kyung-Jin Lee. In a response to a question about the age at which she emigrated to America, and its effect on her writing, Kim provides the same type of answer-which-is-no-answer (or, to borrow the title from one of her poems, an "arrival which is not an arrival" [*UF* 32]) that we have already seen above, in her "exegesis" of *Commons*. She states,

> But it strikes me that there's something about being nine or so, where you have enough access to the language that you feel a connection to the culture it's located in, but you have yet to live out the complexities of participating in that culture fully. And, yet again, that culture is embedded in you somehow. In this strange region of knowing and not knowing, I have access to Korea as language and culture, but this access is shaped by rupture (leaving the country, the language). When I engage "Korea"—what resemblance does this have to any "real" place, culture, or language spoken there?[16]

What's most intriguing about this response is the way in which Korea becomes, within the span of a sentence, "Korea." Editorial intrusion or not, I think Kim's meaning here is apparent: much like the "America" of *Commons*, "Korea" signifies both possibility and instability, as that which resides in language (as carrier of culture) and also that which resides, somehow "embedded," in subjectivity (as ruptured essence). The shift from Korea to "Korea" marks not only a semantic turn from this ruptured, internalized essence to externalized, contested knowledge: more significant, it signals a split in subjectivity itself, as a realm of both idealized essence and object of phenomenological inquiry. Whereas there is "access" to "language and culture," it is precisely when the "I" engages Korea as the specific nation-state from which it is ruptured (note the shift from the imagined self-as-other, in the use of the second person, to the first-person declamation), that Korea becomes a spectral fragment of the "real," that Korea becomes "Korea." It should then come as no surprise when, later on in the interview, Kim sees no contradiction in claiming the *necessity* of this essentialized subjectivity even while declaiming the *terms* of that subject's objectification:

> What's of concern to me is the anthology phenomenon, like Korean American this or gay/lesbian that. When categories are perpetuated, when experience is "thematized" (reduced, in other words), what can result is a kind of dismissal. I would hope that what I am doing in my work is raising questions about how the location of Asian American, Korean American, immigrant, female, and so on can resist commodification. (*WM* 97)

It is thus not simply the naming of the Korean, Asian American, immigrant, or female that troubles Kim, but rather, the act of locating that name within the unstable bounds of a specular "Korea" or "America"—as well as the elision of the structures of power inherent in such acts—that her work seeks to rehearse. This, perhaps more than anything, explains Kim's cautionary response to Lee's next question, about whether or not Asian American literature continues to maintain a sense of political insurgency: "Any movement that can name itself has already begun to erase itself" (*WM* 97).

Another echo of the elided, perhaps. Which returns us to the question still unanswered: What are the risks and challenges in reading Myung Mi Kim as an Asian American poet? And, more important, what are the risks and challenges in *not* reading her as such? Is there a way to resolve the breach between language as a commons and the making "common" of literary production's operative restrictions? R. Radhakrishnan poses much the same question, in his essay "Conjectural Identities, Academic Adjacencies," but provides perhaps a more useful context for this particular discussion:

> When I call myself Asian-American am I making a representative identity claim on behalf of a certain group, or am I announcing the legitimacy of a certain institutional formation called Asian-American studies, or am I assuming that the institutional logic of Asian-American studies will be subsumed thoroughly, without remainder or contradiction, by Asian-American macropolitical identity?[17]

Framing the question as one of identity both within and without the frame of disciplinarity, Radhakrishnan makes explicit the implicit divide between calling Kim a poet and naming Kim as an Asian American poet. Just as the former operates on the assumption that language holds no actual territory, so does the latter intrude to remind us that that particular act of elision cannot be resolved simply by making present that which was once absent—all of which is simply to say, the term *Asian American* itself masks as much as it reveals. Radhakrishnan goes on to state this even more clearly:

> There is no representation without "naming" (Asian-America as a name creates a certain interrelationship among the parts that constitute it), and "naming" as a process is symptomatic of the tension between epistemology and politics. If radical epistemology insists on a deconstructive and open-ended process, politics advocates strategic closure.[18]

There is perhaps no better summation of this entire discussion so far than the final sentence of the passage above. And yet, I would suggest that Kim's work further reconfigures Radhakrishnan's thesis, by suggesting that the poetic text is most generative and powerful precisely *because* of its ability to dwell within, and issue from, that very tension between "epistemology and politics."

I would propose, in fact, that this aspect of Kim's work is of particular importance not only for how it rehearses the relation between epistemology and politics, but also for how it challenges critics and readers to actively interrogate their *own* positionality when staking epistemological claims for her work. To rephrase Radhakrishnan's earlier question in terms of Kim's practice: What does one actually gain (or lose) in the process of locating the Asian in American poetry? What does one reveal (or suppress) about one's own position in that act of location and naming? What Kim's work suggests, in fact, is that while it's possible to be both experimentally ideal and politically engaged, to fulfill both Bernstein's plea for formal investigation and Radhakrishnan's charge of political representation, the poetic text must inhabit and enact, rather than *resolve*, the current tensions at hand. That Myung Mi Kim's work does this by exposing the limits and boundaries of disciplinarity and interpretation suggests, perhaps, a perverse willingness to challenge the assumptions of critics and readers of *all* types, including (or especially) those critics and readers that would have Myung Mi Kim be named an Asian American poet (a group in which I include myself). To theoretically recognize this challenge is in itself perhaps a feat none too extraordinary, and in fact is so far all that this discussion has accomplished. A more difficult proposition, clearly is to explore how this recognition might then practically inform readings of Kim's work—an exploration that here must remain somewhat speculative, but perhaps suggestively so.

A fruitful place to begin, I think, is within Kim's first book, *Under Flag*, both because it's the text that has received the most critical attention and because of the manner in which that attention has been directed.[19] While recognizing, to some degree, the experimental qualities of the text, many critics have overlooked the ways in which those qualities might complicate and deepen readings of the text, choosing instead to focus on the possibility of the text's more immediately legible referentiality. Take, for instance, the following lines from Kim's poem "Food Shelter Clothing":

> "In my country" preface to the immigrant's fallow
>
> Field my country ash in water follow
>
> Descent   slur   vowel
>
> Stricken buoys
>
> Span no tongue and mouth
>
> Scripting, hand flat against the mouth
>
> (UF 26)

While I don't think it's unreasonable to suggest that these lines present a moment of relative illegibility—they provide no clear narrative, nor do they seem to suggest any specific, locatable context through which a narrative might flow—I do think that re-scripting the text as legible object is not only possible, but perhaps only natural. What would such a re-scripting look like? One possible answer is provided us by Laura Hyun Yi Kang, who argues that the poem is about "the dynamics of migration and resettlement," particularly in the context of "the armed invasion of Korea by U.S. forces" and the "layering of Korean diasporic movements, especially to the United States."[20] As Kang writes,

> The social marginalization and personal fragmentation of immigrant experience involves a substantial linguistic aspect. . . . It is this hunger that is deprived for the newly arrived immigrant whose experience of linguistic and cultural dislocation is indicated by the three widely dispersed words: "Descent   slur   vowel." In contrast to the American Dream's promise of acceptance and prosperity, immigration is figured as a degrading fall into the incoherence of a "slur" as well as the racist slurs that Koreans are often subject to. . . . What is at the end of this trajectory may be (only) the meaningless isolation of a singular vowel—the individualist American "I."[21]

I think this reading is both absolutely correct and interestingly limited, in part because of the way Kang so clearly posits the stability of the specifically Korean "immigrant" in these lines and throughout her reading of the poem. It's unclear, however, if the lines themselves contain such clarity. Notice, for instance, the contrasting image of potential bounty and possible dearth in the ambiguous function of the word "fallow": as a noun, the word signifies a field plowed but unsown, a field prepared for sowing, but as yet dormant. Similarly, as a verb, "fallow" means both to prepare land for planting and "to become pale or yellow; hence, to fade, wither" (*OED*).[22] This image, of both future abundance and potential diminishment, is further complicated by the enjambment of the word "field" itself, in the next line. While seeming to emphasize the verbal sense of "fallow" as a faded, withered land, the adjectival use of "fallow" in fact need not suggest this at all. Indeed, re-scripting this line as a legible narrative depends heavily on discounting the cyclical *recurrence* of fallowing, sowing, harvesting, and fallowing that the word "fallow" (as either noun, verb, or adjective) implies. Without this sense of repetition, the line might indeed be read as something like, "The phrase 'In my country' is often the preface to the recent (Korean) immigrant's tale of how the *perpetually* fallow fields of her homeland—caused by the (Korean) war's ashy by-product's pollution of the waters—forced her departure. Yet, following her immigration to a new country (the United States), she found not bounty, but racism and further economic decline."

Again, I do not think this is an implausible reading. However, by dwelling momentarily in the illegible, we might begin to notice how the subtext of repetition and recurrence gets echoed not merely in the language (note the repetition of the phrase "my country" and "mouth"), but in the very sounds that an enunciation of that language might create. Notice, for instance, the slow "descent" of the stressed "vowel" as its recurrence ends each of the first three lines: "fallow," "follow," "vowel." Notice too the way the very phrase "slur vowel" describes that process, the slurring of the *a* of "fallow" into the *o* of "follow," and the slide of that *o* into the *aw* sounds of both "vowel" and "mouth." Moreover, the elegant *musicality* of the sounds produced in this sequence of "slur vowel" is itself doubled and redoubled. Doubled, when we recall that the word "slur," aside from describing a "slurred utterance of sound," is also a musical term: a "curved line placed over or under two or more notes of different degrees to show that they are to be played or sung smoothly and connectedly" (*OED*). And it is redoubled, when we pair that secondary sense of "slur" with the definition of "descent" as "a fall, lowering (of the pitch of sound, temperature, etc.)" (*OED*).[23] That this "descent" ends both literally, linguistically, *and* figuratively within the "mouth" is perhaps not insignificant, given Kim's interest in the enunciative moment. What better description of the musicality of language, is there, after all, than this embodied demonstration of Kim's deceptively simple command: "Speak and it is sound in time" (*UF* 13)? Finally, speech as a multiple, musical enunciation becomes coupled to, and is troubled by, the ambiguous function of the word "stricken," which suggests both impending disaster and paralysis even as it provides the possibility of relief; recall that "stricken" is *also* descriptive of music, "of a sound, musical note: produced by striking a blow" (*OED*). The concluding image of these lines serves to reminds us that while speech may be "sound in time," writing is the transcription of that enunciative act, as well as the (possible) cessation of that act's recurrence: "Scripting, hand flat against the mouth." Indeed, we might read the second three lines cited above as expressing something like, "These stricken (struck, musical) buoys are unable to span the tongue and mouth, since in their recurrence, they become script—imagined here as the (writing) hand censoring the (speaking) mouth."

But then, one wonders, is this not also an act of re-inscription, of making the illegible legible? After all, doesn't this reading operate in much the same mode as Kang's, merely substituting the specificity of the Korean immigrant for the more general operations of language—thereby "making common" a different set of figures? These are certainly valid questions, but in the context of Myung Mi Kim's work, questions perhaps not so much indicative of a problematic contradiction as they are emblematic of the productive tension in which her staging of subjectivity resides. Rather than coaxing a settlement of these claims through a legibly positive affirmation of *either* epistemology or politics (setting off, as she suggests, an endless chain of elision), Kim's work instead urges a critical reevaluation of how these two sets of readings are not only related, but necessarily intertwined, as an instance of poetry's interrogative enactment of the irreducible tension between "epistemology and politics" that both qualifies the act of naming and haunts the loss of that name's ideality. Indeed, this duality is embodied not only in the poem's musicality and language, but also in the posited recurrence of such (potential) censure in the word "scripting" itself—a word that evokes writing as product, as "script," even as it invokes the very process of writing as recurrence, as that which is *scripted*. That "script" also signifies performance and practice—as rehearsal—serves to remind us that Kim's work is not simply textual experiment, but also sonic performance, a (momentarily) reproducible instance of enunciation's ability to unmoor language from the stable terra firma of the literary object.[24]

It is a fortunate coincidence for this discussion, perhaps, that the image of a "field" is figured so prominently in the lines examined above; it allows us a deceptively conclusive return back to the commons. I suggest, however, that this return is not only scripted by Kim's work, but also prescriptive, insofar as it suggests that while there may never be an end to the interrogatory rehearsal of making "common" the commons, there is no contradiction in also expressing the possibility that language continues to illuminate moments of its own potential ideality. Thus, rather than interpret Myung Mi Kim's poetry as either a vision of unattainable, idealized essentialism or an elegy of ineluctable (market-based) fragmentation, I would urge a more nuanced view of her poetic practice, one that seeks to reframe the zero-sum binary of "epistemology and politics" as a negatively productive *rehearsal* of the means by which *each position articulates the elision of the other*. In this sense, naming Kim an Asian American poet is not only a statement of political commitment, but is also, equally important, a calling forth of that statement's procedural other: that possible commons in which Asian American poetry is *not* a political necessity. That this ideality may not soon be attained does not suggest, dialectically, that Kim's work is thus under self-erasure, or is threatened by erasure through misreading, misappropriation, or *misidentification*, as I hope this discussion has made clear. In lieu of actual conclusion, then, let us dwell in the speculative, and acknowledge that to truly regard Myung Mi Kim's poetry as she might have us regard it—as a "a projection of the possible state" (*C* 5)—we must both identify in which figurative state such a poetics might ideally reside *and* acknowledge the literal state (and literary territory) from which such poetry issues forth.

NOTES

1. Myung Mi Kim, *Commons* (Berkeley and Los Angeles: University of California Press, 2002), 107. Subsequent quotations from Kim's work will be cited in the text using the following abbreviations: *UF = Under Flag* (Berkeley, Calif.: Kelsey St. Press, 1991); *TB = The Bounty* (Minneapolis: Chax Press, 1996); *D = Dura* (Los Angeles: Sun & Moon Press, 1998); and *C = Commons*.

2. Interestingly, out of all of Kim's texts, only *Commons* provides such intratextual authorial commentary. One is inclined to speculate that, in making the move from

small press publication (earlier publishers of Kim's books include Kelsey St. Press, Chax Press, and Sun & Moon Press) to the "higher-stakes" world of academy-affiliated publication (*Commons* is published by the University of California Press), Kim's work takes on the added burden of having to explicate, in critical terms, its own discursive context—*as content*.

3. A sentiment best illustrated by another line from "Pollen Fossil Record": "————, a word that cannot be translated: it suggests, 'what belongs to the people'" (*C* 109).

4. Elaine Kim, "Poised on the In-between: A Korean American's Reflection on Theresa Hak Kyung Cha's *DICTEE*," in *Writing Self Writing Nation: A Collection of Essays on Dictee by Theresa Hak Kyung Cha*, ed. Elaine Kim and Norma Alarcón (Berkeley, Calif.: Third Woman Press, 1994), 3–30. I take the term *in-between*, with its specific sense of locatable dislocation, from Kim's essay. While her essay focuses on Theresa Hak Kyung Cha's *DICTEE*, there are clear affinities between Cha's text and Myung Mi Kim's poetry, affinities that become clear in the kinds of questions Kim raises through her reading of Cha's work.

5. And, in fact, holds both poles in a single image: "The robin's breast remained inert. Its eyes shone for hours, / but near three o'clock, a fly could be seen rubbing its legs over / the now weeping eye" (*C* 27); note the emphasis here on "eyes" and the subtle shift from immediate perception ("the robin's breast remained inert") to *mediated* perception ("a fly could be seen"), such that by the image's end, it's no longer clear if the robin is, in fact, dead at all.

6. I.e., the process whereby "the inchoate and the concrete coincide" (*C* 107).

7. The significance of slight difference is echoed in the work itself, from the line "alterations through loss or transposition of even a single syllable" to the linguistic enactment of that very process in the command already cited above: "Consider how the polyglot, porous, transcultural presence *alerts* and *alters* what is around it" (*C* 4 and 110; my emphasis).

8. An intermingling well inscribed in the twin images of "Book as specimen / Book as instruction" (*C* 107).

9. Garrett Hardin, "The Tragedy of the Commons," in *Exploring the New Ethics for Survival: The Voyage of the Spaceship Beagle* (Baltimore: Pelican Books, 1973), 254. Originally published in *Science*, December 13, 1968, 1243–48. Subsequent quotes are taken from the former edition and cited in the text using the abbreviation "TC," followed by page number.

10. For an informative list of recent articles that cite Hardin's essay, see http://www.sciencemag.org/cgi/content/full/162/3859/1243 (accessed February 13, 2006).

11. Joseph Jonghyun Jeon, "Speaking in Tongues: Myung Mi Kim's Stylized Mouths," in *Studies in the Literary Imagination* 37, no. 1 (Spring 2004): 1275–48. Jeon's essay provides a useful connection between Kim's work and Walter Benjamin's notion of "pure language," and provides an interesting reading of Kim's work as an instance of how "languages themselves learn to speak each other" (127).

12. Hardin's work is itself not immune to the very tragedy it describes, having been adopted not only by environmentalists and scientists but by the conservative anti-immigration lobby, as well. See, for instance, the website for FAIR (Federation for American Immigration Reform), at http://www.fairus.org (accessed February

13, 2006); FAIR has published Hardin's work as scientific support for its politically charged stance on immigration. See Garrett Hardin, *The Immigration Dilemma: Avoiding the Tragedy of the Commons* (Washington, D.C.: Federation for American Immigration Reform, 1995).

13. Charles Bernstein, *A Poetics* (Cambridge, Mass: Harvard University Press, 1992), 4. Subsequent quotes are cited in the text using the abbreviation *AP*, followed by page number.

14. Whereas for Bernstein form almost organically evokes content—"like the soul and body, completely penetrating and interdependent" (*AP* 8)—for Kim, the question of content is inextricably linked with content's loss, with that which content masks. Indeed, for Kim, form is the rehearsal of ideality's *disruption* by the claims of "illegible" subjectivity. To put it another way: for Kim, form is the *interrogatory rehearsal of the process whereby content resolves into legibility*. As she writes: "Because isolations occur / Uncover the ear / To give form to what is remote, castigated" (*C* 108).

15. This is, unfortunately, an extremely condensed discussion of a complex debate, and I do not mean to single out Bernstein's work here, except to illustrate what seems to be a broad and historic divide, in much criticism of/from experimental and avant-garde poetry, between form as radical political praxis and content as base replication of a market-based demand for recognizable narrative. For an illuminating discussion of this in relation to Asian American poetry, see Dorothy Wang, "Undercover Asian: John Yau and the Politics of Ethnic Self-identification," in *Asian American Literature in the International Context: Readings on Fiction, Poetry, and Performance*, ed. Rocio G. Davis and Sami Ludwig (Hamburg, Germany: LIT Verlag, 2002), 135–55.

16. James Kyung-Jin Lee, interview with author, in *Words Matter: Conversations with Asian American Writers*, ed. King-Kok Cheung (Honolulu: University of Hawaii Press, 2000), 95. Subsequent quotes are cited in the text using the abbreviation *WM*, followed by page number.

17. R. Radhakrishnan, "Conjectural Identities, Academic Adjacencies," in *Orientations: Mapping Studies in the Asian Diaspora*, ed. Kandice Chuh and Karen Shimakawa (Durham: Duke University Press, 2001), 251.

18. Ibid., 251–52.

19. Which is not to say that there has been an overwhelming amount of critical attention paid to Kim's work, as a quick troll of the *MLA International Bibliography* well illustrates. Aside from Jeon's essay already mentioned, and a handful of book reviews, there is a dearth of critical work devoted to Kim's poetry. Three notable exceptions are Charles Altieri's essay on Kim in *Postmodernisms Now: Essays on Contemporaneity in the Arts* (University Park: Penn State Press, 1998), 2–47; Laura Kang's essay, "Compositional Struggles: Re-membering Korean/American Women," in *Compositional Subjects: Enfiguring Asian/American Women* (Durham: Duke University Press, 2002); and Jeannie Chiu's essay "Identities in Process: The Experimental Poetry of Mei-mei Berssenbrugge and Myung Mi Kim," in *Asian North American Identities*, ed. Eleanor Ty and Donald C. Goellnicht (Bloomington: Indiana University Press, 2004).

20. Kang, *Compositional Subjects*, 240–41.

21. Ibid., 241.

22. *Oxford English Dictionary*, 2d ed., s.v. "fallow." Subsequent quotes will be cited in the text using the abbreviation *OED*.

23. Note, also, that "descent" returns us to the "field" in its suggestion of recurrence and "transmission by inheritance" (*OED*).

24. This concern with "scripting" and "script" thus carries over not only into the other poems of *Under Flag*, but into Kim's other texts, as well, shaping a visible trajectory of *intra*textual, subtextual signification that extends throughout her published work. We might locate, in fact, the "preface" to the lines quoted above in "And Sing We," the poem that opens *Under Flag*: "If we live against replication / Our *scripts stricken*" (*UF* 14; my emphasis). It's thus important to emphasize that this particular subtext calls forth and attaches to numerous others that cannot be adequately explored here. One particularly pertinent example relates to a theme already discussed: note the way in which the sequence fallow/follow/vowel *prefigures* the previously cited concern with "alterations through loss or transposition of even a single syllable" in *Commons*. Suggestively, an echo of this subtext also occurs between *Dura* (in the lines "As regards the change of a syllable and consequently / of the whole word" and "Donor: dolor / Placement between *l* and *r*" [*D* 98, 33]) and *The Bounty* (in the paired phrases "distinguish decipher," "parcel partial," and "Call and cull," among others [*B* 15, 18, 23]).

BIBLIOGRAPHY

Books by Myung Mi Kim

The Bounty. Minneapolis: Chax Press, 1996.
Commons. Berkeley and Los Angeles: University of California Press, 2002.
Dura. Los Angeles: Sun & Moon Press, 1998.
Under Flag. Berkeley, Calif.: Kelsey St. Press, 1991.

Interviews

Interview with James Kyung-Jin Lee. In *Words Matter: Conversations with Asian American Writers*, edited by King-Kok Cheung. Honolulu: University of Hawaii Press, 2000.

Selected Criticism

Altieri, Charles. *Postmodernisms Now: Essays on Contemporaneity in the Arts*. University Park: Penn State Press, 1998.
Chiu, Jeannie. "Identities in Process: The Experimental Poetry of Mei-mei Berssenbrugge and Myung Mi Kim." In *Asian North American Identities: Beyond the Hyphen*, edited by Eleanor Ty and Donald C. Goellnicht. Bloomington: Indiana University Press, 2004.
Jeon, Joseph Jonghyun. "Speaking in Tongues: Myung Mi Kim's Stylized Mouths." *Studies in the Literary Imagination* 37, no. 1 (Spring 2004): 1275–48.
Kang, Laura Hyun Yi. *Compositional Subjects: Enfiguring Asian/American Women*. Durham: Duke University Press, 2002.

STACY DORIS

FROM *CONFERENCE*

ᛯ   So my friend sets out for a jungle, which separates me from her. "In the calendar of the long count," says my friend, "the years go in various lengths: 144,000, then 7,200, then 360, then 20, then one days. Nobody knows what determined these years."

ᛰ   BELBEL: Deception would dictate: "I am if I go/If I don't go I'm not," where going is a wave. However, if I go, I am or am not, and if I don't go, the same. That is why ♭'s living makes a life for you, endlessly, elsewhere, nearly always. Why you muſt and will be my sacrifice, despite you.

ᛯ ᛯ   I've ruined everything / To save this practice of a Royalty contemplated through selves, and the high quality of relations and efforts it founds. With the endless end of showing a primacy of ♭ over bird, the drab declares or preaches ♭, but in flight, there's a problem, since air's a bundling bundle of quantities. It blinds and blocks the way to any clarity, as logic is untranslatable to feeling. The role of each is enrichment, which escapes us or you.

ᛰ   BELBEL: You will give your life for what you have or are; you dissolve thus.

ᛯ ᛯ   Because ♭ is flight, not exposition, we (or birds) hollow ♭ in us, then rage at drab inaction. We (or birds) neglecting flight, survive, which is pure drowning or deception, as to admit, even separate from my friend, the sun's setting. Thus flight received a true or false name of sacrifice.

ﭏ   Sacrifice was no amputation or penance, but rather plain movement. Thus an act. Act or proteſt. To sacrifice yourself to breath is belief or embellishment, making of air an unending domain. Is defeat meaning love. Domain is a sum of giving, not of givens. Sacrifice trapped in the hollow of my or birds' hollows. Due to pure expression, thus and from it (cedar's after) did I turn your life away from knowing to juſt affirming, which is sacrifice. You or I vanish thus (after's cedar). Then the sun ... what I said. My miſtake was in replacing the assortment of birds for ♭. Thus something—not nothing—collective inſtalled, meaning perhaps moral or inanimate. And in explaining why birds should be the sacrifice of ♭, but unable to exact ♭'s sacrifice to birds, any definition fails from now on. This, in acts of memory, you forget, which, separating me or us from fear, is our magnitude.

I or birds glide, then, without efficient method, from ♭ to temerity, and in multiplication. A voided vocable, then, applied to each song, thus each cancels other, and nowhere does not accrue in its mere accumulation. Where each is the same, each day. So there are days, meaning hollows. The tale of how speaking begot forgetting. Tale of how ♭ tripped from liberty to license of variable degrees, thus a ſtaircase perhaps.

Thus ♭ may be loſt. Good riddance or farewell.

ﭏ   (Flight 9 9 0)
01:57 Co-Pilot: **Twakaltu ala Allah.**
0:48 Co-Pilot: **Twakaltu ala Allah.**
0:39 Co-Pilot: **Twakaltu ala Allah.**
0:38 Co-Pilot: **Twakaltu ala Allah.**
0:36 Co-Pilot: **Twakaltu ala Allah.**

0:35   Co-Pilot: Twakaltu ala Allah.
0:34   Co-Pilot: Twakaltu ala Allah.
0:32   Co-Pilot: Twakaltu ala Allah.
0:31   Co-Pilot: Twakaltu ala Allah.
0:30   Pilot: Che khabare? Che khabare?

0:29   Co-Pilot: Twakaltu ala Allah.
0:28   Co-Pilot: Twakaltu ala Allah.
0:28   Pilot: Che khabare?

0:21   Pilot: Che khabare, Gamil, Che
        khabare?

0:20   Pilot: Een chiye? Een chiye? Motor
        o khaamoosh kardi?

0:10   Pilot: Boro motor o khaamoosh kon.

0:07   Co-Pilot: Khaamooshe.

0:05   Pilot: Bekesh.

0:05   Pilot: Baa man bekesh.
0:05   Pilot: Baa man bekesh.
0:05   Pilot: Baa man bekesh.
0:05   Pilot: Baa man bekesh.

A MONTH OF VALENTINES

Glycine, my sweet, Without end hung from my skin a bunch of dreams. Pick some. Your Teddybear	My Island Penguin, angel frame: our bodies' reunion drives flamingos insane and mangos again.	Marie-Annie, Love you Me more More my Love's yours. Oscar.

Wolfgang:
 	
A doll for life?
As long as operation
"buns of steel" works.
 	
    Iz.
	To my Love Supreme
	
	from her little
	lotus flower: Bud
	stamen and leaf
	my heart only beats
	with hope of your
	         touch.
	Kevin
		Connie H.
		Since you got up on
		your bike
		my seat is hot
		my chain jumps,
		you know it's great
		to pedal beside you
		and hold your hips
		tight. You're loved
		H-D HARD. I dream
		of a motor
		to chug past your
		molars.
		Pudgy One

My Russian Doily
 	
At the flamboyant
        palace
on its porphyry
        staircase
in your adored
        presence
this sighing lion
huge gusts of wind
howls, abandoned.
Why?
Her Plaything.
	My Daub:
	
	  My lamb, my
	chop, my leg
	my all naked
	my rib, my
	my pork and
	pie. In warm
	my steaming
	you win. Come.
		Eglantine,
		
		Dip my plume
		in your ink again.
		So Long!
		
		Sailor

Ondine,
 	
Amazing muse
you confound my route.
Imagine two lives
internally fused.
 	
Toad.
	Grace,
	        Thank you
	        for last
	marvelous Friday
	I hope next
	privacy and your
	        happiness
	against me.
	
	Love me above all
	I love you above
	        everybody.
	
	Mochi
		Élodie,
		
		As sure as there's
		        Cayenne
		in pepper, life has
		no spice without you,
		dear. My heart spun
		captive in you sugar
		        kisses.
		
		Prickly Pear.

Baby Bat: Big pants little worries many hugs yours hungry. Tom M.	Red Rose: All leather, rare flowers your cavalier lips my pony tail puff to dinosaur shape. Let's fuck. Ph.D.	Zara, The Baronne, Rose on the neck, rage at the spot. Move fade nude arm traces darken words twist things all wrong. Her Vi-count	Duckie All for you only for you long after youth under our roof here: Take these stars for your use. Arthur II.

Soft Squirrel
 	
with the nut-brown
eyes: Twenty years
         later
I still love your fur.
Bury our treasures
all their fall flavors.
 	
Kikki.
	Pulpuce
	
	The shaved mouse
	Pauly the cat
	microwaves deep.
	Be my phoenix.
	
	Prepice
		Xtof:
		
		Hour upon
		hour, year
		after year:
		      More
		a little more
		a little
		more more.
		
		Chico.
			Madame,
			
			Our sunny brooks
			our milky ways
			our chubby bunnies
			
			all stew in plum
			sauce.
			
			Lassie

·Pirouette,
    Papaya.
        Hold me
close to your heart
like the accordionist
under the bridge
of last night.
 	
Pierrot
	Dahlia:
	
	My little mop
	don't rag on love
	it's always great.
	
	        Grrr.
		Bambi,
		
		I love you when
		you love how
		I love you how
		you are. I love
		you when you
		love how you
		love me how
		I do.
		
		The wasp
			Butter,
			
			me better.

Jolly Roger:
 	
      Freaky green
leopard bubble
triply dives
in loving spoonfuls.
 	
Valhalla.
	Carp of the Day:
	
	Scooby scooby doo
	 Bi doo bi doo bi dou
	Scooby doo bi di
	  di dally dally lea
	
	Pompon
		Danish,
		
		Fat bear for hot bunny
		Slippery dish's dream
		        algae
		Gentle fork pierces
		       goodies
		Here comes; get ready.
		
		Scooter.
			Ma Tobias:
			
			Image mirage
			vine your hand
			wrist blue vein
			groin to groin.
			
			Martial

FROM *KNOT*

Time's a free illusion of right's triumph, of reward, which cordons,
Of justice, meaning boundaries; bound. Where law's unruly or limitless,
Respect may be owed perhaps, but at length. Taxing or toxic, continuity's
Sealed in meager endurance. Finite since unbased, having no source.
So that if we's could forget entitlement, I might run as some fluid, brimming
With impunity; wrapped in leaves' rotting to loam, which is, since
Uncertain, a grounds perhaps. Every authority says what is not right and
How it will drown eventually in truths. If a fig moves to even the scent of
Other milk, fruit's a suspension unengulfed by its own cells. Only stability's
The humble goal of thinking and sight, so seeks to mirror. So any self will
Digest their own existence, and end it.

Righteousness's immanence's praying that preys, so surrenders
Discrimination to thirst. Unmuscled, so trusting in force, fairness swallows
People into passage. Avalanches. Heavy, flawed as rock, legality's illogic
Excuses; discharges itself in or as death; masks fleeting thus, and based
On time which it founds, chokes, so stirs emotion. Measure's finite, so of
Limited use, though everywhere applied. So quantity's mistaken in its
Picture of an absolute; equity's most partial, yet fine as an impetus once
Culture implies or legislates ends, so everywhere. Whether or not it exists,
Why would doom need declarations? Laws thus emit sentences unleashed
From clear reason; wraps reason as attraction does. So unrelated, words
Can serve it, mingling. In positing a body, rectitude can't be physically
Envisioned. Trumpets stealth, headless. Pretends to all machinery. Drills.

A ruler who immolates himself is the sole leader to embody integrity,
Which are blind as any judgment or vision, so deems itself impartial.
So a head of state with sight cannot conceive what's commanded.
If retribution had significance it wouldn't need such positing as time;
As life's big lesson. Would not relay myth to inaugurate religion amid
Elements and stuff, storyless. But justice doesn't work. Except that breath
Ignore requital, respiration; even photosynthesis, would cancel its
Charade. The beat of any heart would.

iii, IV

If people could feed on themselves which they can whether in despair or
Pride, time becomes a circulation, reduced and expanded to that, imitating
Digestion. Ingesting decomposes any scrap into functions, whereas eating
Something other than yourself disprove wholeness. What rewards
Rewording might be justice. Then does response outrun responsibility,
Overthrow it, so all government's automatic, total, a model of control based
On nature? If retribution's normal, rule's always enforcing, twisted and
Abstract: flexed. Then days are contaminated by law, and life's a code,
Dead yet leathal. Even putrefaction would be saturated thus: the severed
Hand molder on schedule.

Perhaps in this way all living's starvation, programmed to regurgitate itself,
So cutting off supplies would free, while goods stifle. Thus the excuse
That oneness means bodiless, that what has parts is too bulky for unity.
Indivisible then implies a corpus subtracted, or, origin in amputation. Any
Bomb curls back on its unleashing, so mirrors cause and denies effect.

So repeats; is a refrain. Like all waves, destruction won't break. If so,
Nobody needs to be alive to go on. State equals machine, but runs only
By crashing. Each project attacks what may be in place with the corrosive
Burn of potential. Passivity's the only order: ordains. But breathing counts
Down. Each movement of respiration encodes terror, which flourishes in
Everyone thus, in the midst of hunger and abundance, in the speed of love.
No tourniquet dispels it

iii, VII

POETICS STATEMENT
I Have to Check My e-mail

I WROTE this this summer and thought it might be the start of my poetics statement:

> Poetry is form interrupted and constructed of interruptions. The ability of thought (reflection) to travel, light-like, and anneal to the shapes presented, thereby transforming to their measure. Its processes recognize no singularities, only similarities, imagined, thus enforced, where interruption imposes its continuum.

> Interrupted by all movement: breathing, walking, syncopation, as in originally dance,

. . . and that's as far as I got before interrupting myself. Usually I am interrupting myself from writing in order to check my e-mail. I have to go away to places with no phone lines so as to let myself sit down and write, but no matter what, I interrupt myself, putting on the kettle for tea and such. My process is interruptive. One way of looking at this setup is that I am somehow always writing, and therefore everything I do constitutes an interruption to that, including writing.

Because I have always had many certain problems with form, I consider myself a poet. I have never agreed with form in the sense that it was assigned to me at birth with my body. Why this form and why stay in it for more than an instant? There is no stability of form; all science extols that. Body is an interruption in another interruptive continuum, and vice versa. The reason to create form might be as a way of charting its fleet malleability. Or perhaps form means morph. I wish.

I used to worry that my self-interruptions are some way of hating or punishing myself; of not allowing myself to think. I am still concerned about that. But the evidence is that I'm not interested in form without interruption. Too, I could argue that thinking is a form of interruption. I used to imagine that lyric poetry is about disproving time's actuality by positing potentially indestructible monuments of language. I could say that it is a question of interrupting time.

I am a poet because I don't agree with form as assigned. But once I am a poet, I have problems with poetry and the way it reifies the forms of cultures in which it is written and presented. Sure, poetry flagrantly challenges culture all over the place, but at the same time, and on fundamental levels, it supports its given culture. I might try to explore the idea that poetry might undo the damage it does in part by interrupting its self-proclaimed forms. But I don't think that would be the answer. If the results of my investigation turned out to be positive, thus unified; coherent, they would be at odds with my experience of form as interruption. In experiments, not-so-scientific ones but "scientific" ones as well, the final results are always positive: that's part of Positivism maybe. According to Stephen Hawking, Positivist theory describes and codifies "our" observations by translating them into mathematical models. To me, that sounds like an accurate-enough definition of poetry as well. Poetry is to count, to measure, and such.

There is something ineluctably positivist and celebratory about poetry. That certainly includes protest poetry, which champions a potentially improved reality, and eulogy, which dares hope for eternal life in literary common memory. Greek tragedy, performed at the festivals of Dionysius, vividly embraced the citizens' role as ultimately subordinate in the scheme of things, religious and political. What I'm bombastically pointing out is that while it may simultaneously posit other options and outcomes, poetry revels in things as they are, insofar as there is such a thing as things as they are.

There is no such thing as closeness, if you really think about it, not in reading, not in understanding, not in love. Perhaps that is part of what interferes with being able to know if there are things as they are; perhaps if there were closeness things would be what they are, which is perhaps some kind of (interrupted) continuum. In the impossibility of closeness lies part of the chance of creativity and critique. In a sense that ranges from literal to at least rhetorical, I aim for my poetry to measure and codify observations; not necessarily "my" observations; observations that come to me and that I gather. I love the impossibility of achieving that. For me, the distance between anything and its codification in poetry is by definition a critical, generative distance; a commentary and analysis on the thing and the writing of it, to varying extents. That's a place where I let my hopes play, in the ineluctable distance of closeness. When I was an undergraduate, I studied with John Hawkes whom I greatly admired. He was wonderfully encouraging of my attempts at fiction writing. My most ambitious project entailed a mockery of Justin Harvey Smith's 1899 *The Troubadours At Home; Their Lives And Personalities, Their Songs And Their World*. I am at this point only reasonably certain that this was the title of that book, a somewhat obscure one, though it had been lauded in the writings of Ezra Pound, which is where I picked up the reference. The Hawkes, especially John's beloved wife Sophie, were by coincidence keen on the same book as part of their preparations for a year's upcoming sabbatical in Provence. Smith's style is winning but he is so taken with his subject matter that he devotes long passages to arguing unprovable points of no interest, generally, as I recall, on the topic of ladies' hair and eye color, and as I remember it he preferred green-eyed blondes. Hoping to dramatize the folly of authority, I found imitating this silliness irresistible. Hawkes found my pastiche too close to the original. He also wanted me to return the book to the library, which I did. I did not really question Hawkes's view all at once; instead, I've consistently questioned it over the years.

A way in which I work with closeness in my poetry is through translation. I think some of the fundamental aspects of poetry constitute translation to begin with. Metaphor for me translates any given element into another; rhyme and rhythm translate or equate among sounds and patterns. I feel trapped in translating the same way I feel trapped in language. I write by and through translating and I can make a continuous sense out of my work to date by narrating it as translation: my first book, *Kildare*, translated popular cultural phenomena (video games, comic books, talk shows, b-movies, etc.) into pastoral forms, and the reverse. My second book, *Paramour*, also transposed disparate prosodies on one another, and much of the text was derived by translating writing over and over on itself, in a wild quest to make it end up reading the same back to front and front to back. My third book, *Conference*, is a fake translation of Attar's *Conference of the Birds*, and translates a number of translations of translations along the way: for example, passages from Ibn Arabi's *Treatise on Love*. I have recently completed *Knot*, which sets out to translate everything invisible into written expression via reading, and *Cheerleader's Guide to the World: Council Book*, which is a sandwich-like translation of versions of the *Popul Vuh*, the *Tibetan Book of the Dead*, William Carlos Williams' *Paterson*, and *Secret Autobiographies of Jigme Lingpa* onto today's war-on-terrorism America. I have also published two books in French, which I wrote by translating the style of seventeenth-century French noble memoir authors into the antistyle of an American Girl Scout troop leader residing in Paris just a few years back. *Parlement*, my third French book began with translating *Conference* in order to rewrite it.

Like reading, like a phone call, like thought, like an itch, translation interrupts the originary. Emmanuel Hocquard, whose views have been formative for me, claims independent literary status for a translation, and I have no problem with that. In keeping with this perspective, he eschews the standard facing-page bilingual translation. As a structuring device, I am unceasingly fascinated by the possibilities of this type of *en face* print, and its mirroring conceit. In addition, and perhaps in relation to translation, the other consistent insistence in my work involves the impossibility of self-similarity and accurate reproduction, a concern that gets more and more interesting as electronics and bioengineering bring us ever closer to the unattainable. Poetry offers to belie the fiction of unchanging nature and personality that most writing promotes, and I take up that offer. Characters and other elements surface in my poems in order to morph and elude in keeping with my observations on identity: that it is actually experienced in its moments of change, which are constant and relentless. Just as form is determined for me by interruption, identity is constituted by motion and slippage.

In good keeping with my refusal of what's agreed upon as form, original, and personality, and probably illustrated by my self-interruptive practice, my method is perversity. I obsessively work and rework my manuscripts for years. I know a manuscript is finally finished when I sense that I can't possibly make it any worse. When I can sum up in my mind a roomful of those poets whose opinion I most value and assure myself that each and every one of them will thoroughly detest this new thing I've written, then I know I've taken it as far as I can and it is ready to be sent out and hated by all prospective publishers and readers. Of course I don't really want my work to be hated; I want it to be loved. But for some reason I can only do my job by assiduously courting rejection. There are people who like my work (I am grateful for this). But it is often the case that someone who liked one of my books will be sorely disappointed with the next one I write. Except for the commonalities I've outlined above, my books are disparate. I can't imagine them being otherwise. My work used to be very performable, full of songs and farce. But for a long time I've dreamed of writing things that cannot be read out loud for a variety of reasons. It is interesting to me that some things I never imagined falling out of my approach are now doing so. For example, I set a huge critical store by the power of humor, and my published books to date rely heavily upon it. But toward the end of 2000, I started feeling really too funny for humor anymore. Slotted to appear on September 11, 2001, my book *Conference* was among the many that I feel foresaw and attempted to enter into dialogue with some of the problems that seemed to lead to that day. In the past few years, I have noticed that many poets whom the events affected have begun working in ways that they did not before. That is so moving; if many more people began to go about doing what they do in untried ways, it would make a huge difference. Among other things, September 11, 2001, represents for me an end to culture as I saw it in my imagination. I should mention that I have always been New York–centric; New York = Culture was an assumption I never questioned from the time I was two until recently. In my case, I can't pin certain changes on September 11 as isolated in itself; for me, the moment was a long time coming and the changes are still developing. Part of what that translates to is that I now feel somehow more at home in not knowing where and how I'm heading; I feel that not knowing is a decent approach at this point, one that bears staying with. Actually, poetry tends to think it has the answers; that is one of poetry's eternal claims to fame. Poetry's traditional role is to boast that it knows; that if only others had listened we wouldn't be in whatever mess is at hand. In the past few years it has become increasingly evident to me that there are no answers, that there is no way of proceeding; that finding a provisionally useful question and working with that toward another and another may fit the present circumstances. The present circumstances are a morass, and there is no reason to expect that will end; there is no reason to fantasize that they have ever been otherwise.

THE POETICS OF RADICAL CONSTRAINT AND UNHOOKED BEDAZZLEMENT IN THE WRITING OF STACY DORIS

Caroline Crumpacker

> In terms of geographies and nationalities, the best bet for poetry is delusional space. . . . Any poetry that doesn't somehow begin in a realm of wild fantasy is not worth the writing.
>
> —Stacy Doris

STACY DORIS is interested in love—"love," courtly love, the love lyric, the personals ad, the romance novel—and in the munificence of language, form, and convention generated by love, which she represents as both cultural game and psychological commodity. In Doris's work, the consumption of love is by turns allegorical to, parallel to, foil to, and inseparable from poetic inquiry. Colliding ideals of romantic love with literary traditions—ranging from the English pastoral to mystic Sufi poetry—and the lexicons and communicative gestures inherent in twenty-first-century technocultural life, Doris both celebrates and transgresses literary convention and (historical) ideals of romantic expression. In so doing, she draws her readers into a romantic, violent unveiling and dissection of the borders within which poetry operates, revisiting and enlivening contemporary assumptions governing, among other things, personae, diction, and narrative structure.

Ms. Doris has published four full books of poetry—*Kildare* (Roof Books, 1994), *Paramour* (Krupskaya Press, 2000), *Conference* (Potes & Poets, 2001), and *Knot* (University of Georgia, 2006)—as well as two books in French and copious translations from the French and some from the Spanish. She has also coedited anthologies of French writing in translation including *Twenty One New (to North America) French Writers* (*Raddle Moon* 16, 1997) and *Violence of the White Page* (*Tyuonyi* 9/10, 1991).

Throughout, Doris unearths and enacts the myriad roles of "convention," and manifests a respectful, if audacious, counterpoint. Her use of romantic love as subject matter, as lens, and as parallel makes explicit her vision of literary convention as both playful erotic cosmetic (and hence generative) and old-fashioned restraining device (and hence staid). How and when poetic constraints and tropes can be best engaged and their limitations transgressed, and where these points of engagement and transgression will take poetry in years to come, would seem to be the particulars of Doris's quest—one that brings her to the palindrome, the song, the play-within-a-play, and beyond in search of poetic forms that can contain, explore, and explode the paradoxes of romance and its "delusional space."

Doris is bedazzled and critical, giving us a relentlessly provocative representation of the instability of our poetic models, past and present, and of the intellectual fluidity of terrains that appear opposing but end up enmeshed—or vice versa.

* * *

A savage place! as holy and enchanted
As e'er beneath a waning moon was haunted

By woman wailing for her demon-lover!
—Samuel Taylor Coleridge, *Kubla Khan*

If the Internet is both public square—meeting place for high thinkers, charlatans and wooers of all variety—and a highly controlled and exquisitely marketed resource for state-of-the-art entertainments and enchantments, then its languages necessarily traffic in simultaneity, seduction, expediency, and desire.

Enter *Kildare*, Doris's first full-length book, which pillages the discourse of "electronic entertainments" for rapid-fire drama with characters who feed off the anonymous fantasies of Internet culture, generally inhabiting several interchangeable personae and situations of persona. Moving in and out of comic-book locales including "High-jinx island" and the "Intestine bon-bon factory," these characters speak in the truncated diction of the chat room, inhabiting the social netherworld of the listserv:

Excuse me Miss . . .

Uncle! (TiK) Multiply:
the lotus carpet's hideous.
Down its hatch, goes:

Authority creams/
thighbangling duel over newdom's crown emerald.[1]

Role-playing, shapeshifting and lush imaginative environments speak both to literary and cyberpractice within the pages of *Kildare*, bringing poetry and electronic discourses—otherwise know as "Sir Jewel Box" and "Dame Internet"—into mutual calibration.[2]

Nothing in the book is static; words tremble with double and triple entendres and characters mutate in and out of themselves, often inhabiting multiple personae. A talk-show hostess named Sheila, for example, becomes a nurse-liturgical chorus, Tinkerbell, and a Homecoming Queen, forcing us to mull over the inestimable fallacy of "Sheila" as a fixture of narrative. All this mutability creates something of a cyberpoetic androgene marked by transgendered descriptors such as "Half-man but all caution," "mega-bulbed nymphs," and "not-there guys," while *gamin* is seldom fully parsed out of *gamine*. The transmutation of gender evokes both the liberating properties of the anonymity of cyberspace as well as its more sterile, lifeless qualities. Doris keeps both awarenesses in play in *Kildare*'s erotic action:

> Slices and creams Betty alongside Jill
> soaking their venom (own) marinara UP.
>
> Good girls are fried girls, icing on—Right, uncle?
>
> In a row,
> a rippling muscle valley
> both side to back.[3]

Kildare plays with linguistic and erotic structures much as a modern Internet browser plays with graphic and informational structures. In so doing, the book repositions cyberdiscourse within the imaginative lushness of a romantic-poetic tradition.

Kildare's eponymous second section is a science-fiction explosion enacted by numerous entities ultimately ladled into three composite persons functioning in a videogame mode replete with time capsules, time vises, and gambols through the "butchery pastures" of a wrecked pastoral. Sheila is reincarnated as "Benedictine (pirates' captive)" while language is at a constant pitch of dynamic tour de force:

> Captive-cum-empress in pirate fleet dome
>
> ('else it's back to the slave trade for females
>
> and Latin kids)
>
> She's forced to sip, gussied

up, pinned down.

Come give her a clue, a penny.

Head lube and oil change—then—

speaking only gibberish

martinis her way home.

(She could break you like a pencil,

sweet touch-me heart-o.)

(71)

Kildare is ultimately inconclusive on the larger question of whether the literary potentials—or the romantic potentials—contained within techno-discourse are positive, or even if our pop culture's ever-quickening powers of mutability bode well for poetry. Instead, the book manifests the author's bold insistence on poetry's ability to reflect upon, agitate within, and keep simultaneously a step ahead of (and a watchful step behind) our ever-evolving cultural moment.

Doris ends *Kildare* on a pun (holding the decapitated body of Sheila, Kildare is "stumped") much as she begins the book with a pun ("Probe droids SUCK!"), as if to affirm that, true to the looped time of virtual reality, we have jumped off somewhere near where we jumped on: in "the current technological cultural unconscious' restructuring of space, a conception of the physical world in which locations and identities shift with radical illogic"—an allegorical site for poetic practice.[4]

* * *

> I believe that every gentle lover endures so many toils, so many vigils, exposes himself to so many dangers, sheds so many tears, uses so many ways and means to please his lady love—not chiefly in order to possess her body, but to take the fortress of her mind and to break those hardest diamonds and melt that cold ice, which are often found in the tender breasts of women.
>
> —Baldassare Castiglione, *The Book of the Courtier*

Formulating an assignation between a range of poetic traditions (Ovidian, medieval romantic, pastoral, Shakespearean, etc.) at the masked ball of cyberculture, Doris's second book *Paramour* traces the liaison between "Sir Jewel Box" and "Dame Internet" in their respective, and mutual, languages of love. Proposing that the poetics of love gives shape to both historical and contemporary innovation, Doris ravishes historical poetic territory within the spatial vocabulary of twenty-first-century technology.

Paramour takes courtly love—its ideals and beauty, rules and tyrannies—as locus for investigation. Tracing a through-line from Ovid's *Art of Love* to medieval romance poetry to the Shakespearean sonnet to the romantic poetry of Blake and others, Doris extends the poetics of desire to that paramour, Dame Internet.

Within the libidinal parameters of these forms and venues, lovers cavort and butcher, the lyric sustains and implodes, and sonic pleasures rule. Cue the *Paramour* centerfold, the ethereal core of the booklong palindrome, "A Month of Valentines," an advent calendar for February with twenty-eight poemettes inspired by personals ads in the newspaper and reminiscent of the French *lai*:

> Ondine,
>
> Amazing muse
> you confuse my route.
> Imagine two lives
> internally fused.
>
> Toad.

> Eglantine,
>
> Dip my plume
> in your ink again.
> So Long!
>
> Sailor[5]

And so on, one for each day of the month.

As *Paramour* is a palindrome, all that is written reverses itself. *Boy Book (Songs)* is mirrored back as *Girl Book (Warnings)*, and *How to Love* returns as *LOVE TO, AND HOW*. Within this *Through the Looking Glass* structure, dichotomies such as male/female, lover/beloved, and aggressive/tender are dissolved. In a space that is somewhat transgendered, Doris engages the charms, coquetries, and rituals of courtly love, which manifest most frequently in the erotically entangled characters This and Thus. The sweethearts enter *Paramour* as twins and lovers, Thus female and This male (or so we think, despite warnings abounding such as "They pose as girls sometimes, / But they've got something extra- / spicy in the middle"). They are lovers and parodies of romantic love, and their courtship is at once comic, irreverent, violent, and tender, a fluidity that allows *Paramour*'s performative poetic strategy to become what Doris calls, in the book's introduction, "operatic Ur-text":

Musique n° 1   In the First House
                    House of Lilies
THIS and THUS, twins, tied to two columns of the same colonnade,
arms in the air, facing each other, before the gouty priest and his
engines of torture, sing:

Duet:

CONTINUUM GEMINORUM

Brother, what's   Your heart
gravity   weighs down
without the   my chest:
weight of   a stone
love?   on a frond;
                       a jet
                       on a cloud.

(69)

This and Thus (d)evolve from a parody of idealized romantic love to a prim-
itive and formless coupling. Their story of erotics, violence, absurdity, and
degeneration/regeneration is central to the book's overarching fascina-
tion with the points at which the conventions of love (necessarily) break
down and the points at which the conventions of language break down. In
these points of slippage and fracture, Doris seems to be saying, is the truly
generative environment. Any writing, any loving, "worth the doing" will
end up beyond the parameters set out for it, or those that it sets out for
itself.

Poking in and out of the book's "vivisection" of poetic forms—which
includes not only the palindrome but the rondeau, the aubade, the dramatic
monologue, the ballad, and the prose poem—This and Thus end as the book
ends (to the degree that a merry-go-round can effectively "end"):

the edge open and Thus This rip, root, a-rage, This Thus plunders center of
plunder, ring. This wrench to shreds, convulse, gnaw, Thus grunt.

(138)

Paramour is a celebration of such transgressions/implosions. Demonstrat-
ing that, à la the Internet, nothing—even (or especially) poetic form—is
what it pretends to be. As Brian Kim Stefans writes: "Like Lee Ann Brown's
Polyverse (Sun & Moon), *Paramour* skids through a variety of formal poses,
transmitting its carnal logic through pun and prose, epigraph and song—no
stone left unturned in its quest for momentary satisfaction."[6] Both Brown
and Doris mine poetic potentials by reformulating the questions asked of/by
lyric poetry and placing them in a generative environment of undone syntax
and untied language.

As opposed to Brown or other poets such as Martin Corless-Smith, who are explicitly in conversation with historical poetic moments but are attracted to particular traditions (in Corless-Smith's case, English Romanticism; in Brown's, the Southern American ballad), Doris explores strategies, tropes, parallelisms, and complementarities, across a range of seemingly divergent historical terrains and into contemporary discourses, hunting for their points of connection and breach. Her work takes nothing for granted in its excavation of poetic convention, trying everything on for size. Her points of inquiry are the properties, if not the sinewy contours, of form, boundaries, and trope. She tests the potentials of the work she samples in relation to their points of contact and fracture—where the palindrome meets the merry-go-round. What happens to both structures upon contact and what futurities are proposed at the point of contact?

Doris does not manifest direct answers to these questions. In fact, the questions themselves turn in on themselves as one poetic moment or experiment melts or morphs into the next. Doris never seems to be trying to direct the future of poetic form (the question underlying *Paramour*, as she states in her introduction); rather, she manifests an array of possibilities and, then, their opposites. Inevitably one realizes that there is no answering the questions she poses. The question/answer formulation has imploded.

* * *

To write is to translate.

—Claude Royet-Journoud

Relating the history of poetry in the lexicon of the Internet, laying Ovid at the doorstep of Marie de France, and injecting Sufi mysticism into contemporary poetic analyses are acts of translation in any estimation. Doris notes that she has "always" been a translator: "I remember one time complaining to someone who wanted me to finish the translation I was working on and turn it in, that for me getting out of bed in the morning is a translation." Perhaps because of this, her translations seem to function more as encounters between languages than straightforward renderings into a new tongue. She notes of her two books written in French, "They are not translations but rather I impact English on French . . . like a layer of underpaint or overpaint, sandwiching the two languages, showing French some potential it might not always realize it has."[7]

Doris is one of a handful of younger poets—including Jen Hofer, Monica de la Torre, Eugene Ostashevsky, and others—giving shape to international poetic discourse through her translating, editing, and publishing efforts. She has lived in France, where she published *La Vie de Chester Steven Wiener écrite par sa femme* and *Une Année à New York avec Chester* (both from

P.O.L.) and worked with several French poets, translating their work. She has edited three volumes of English translations of French poetry, as well as a special section of the Parisian magazine *JAVA* that introduced French readers to American poets who had not yet (as of that publication) appeared in French including Kevin Davies, Tim Davis, Lisa Jarnot, Lisa Robertson, Rod Smith, and Catriona Strang. Their work was translated by French poets who might be considered peers, including Christophe Tarkos, Jean-Michel Espitalier, Veronique Pittolo, Nathalie Quintane, and Sabine Macher. Many of the French poets had never translated before, and Doris helped them bring work into French, facilitating a trans-Atlantic conversation that included a section where the French poets asked questions of the Americans.

Doris has also brought some of the most innovative and notable poets writing in France today, including Christophe Tarkos and Dominique Fourcade, into the English language. One of France's most prolific writers and reader/performers, Tarkos (who died in 2005) wrote improvisatory, rhythmic poetry (*le texte expressif*) that meets Doris's "operatic Ur-text" in kaleidoscopic complement. Having published more than twenty-five books of poetry in France, Tarkos's following in the United States is thanks largely to Doris and her husband Chet Wiener. Their selection of his work, *Ma Langue est Poétique* (Roof Books), includes Doris's translations of his work and Wiener's thoughtful introduction.

Literal translation and translation as performance is permutated in Doris's oeuvre by the use of specific texts as palimpest. *Conference* presents Doris's translation-of-sorts of the twelfth-century Persian masterpiece, mystic Sufi poet Farid-Ud-Din-Attar's *The Conference of Birds*. Everything in this book is translated in one way or another; the "Characters Key for Possible Speaking Parts in the Conference" that opens this book, for example, not only situates multiple personhoods as "equal," but also maps a fundamentally trans-object-situation existence in which states of being equal people equal objects via name and symbol:

> Belbel = the Baby-girl commandante Flea = Genocidal Logic = Crow = Angel
> = Luna = Ida Applebroog = Mohammed = US Military Pamphlet #94218 =
> Lolo Ferrari.[8]

In part response, in part distant translation, in part cousin, *Conference* employs the allegorical search/struggle in Attar's epic as theatrical backdrop for a further search for axes of innovative literary potential within the proscriptions of literary history.

Written in rhyming couplets, Attar's poem describes the birds of the world searching for their King/God. At book's end, the birds realize that the source of truth and harmony they have been searching for is, in fact, in themselves. Doris, in *Conference*, gives us a vision of a society similarly blind to its own inherent properties, but one more fractious, more rife with instability, and more brutalized by violent social happenings, slippage of identity and place, and unclear systems of information than Attar's—and, important, one lacking his built-in resolution.

On one level, *Conference* recharges Attar's passionate quest for God vis-à-vis social crisis. Scenes that grab for nostalgia—such as the set piece in which a bunch of birds are doing the twist outside a café while "Me" drinks a Cherry Coke, or a thirteenth-century pastoral where "Friar Dad" and "Friar Me" preach to the birds from a ruined fortress—seem to speak to the desperation of a culture lost in idealized visions of itself. Worse yet, in the incarnation of Genocidal Logic, the quest stalls with the dumb reasoning of war (juxtaposed with imagination):

> GENOCIDAL LOGIC: We each have this choice: die by your own hands or by others'. Their blood-orange eyes.
> THE PYGMY FROM THE JUNGLE: To me the Netherlands is just imagination, but it is real to me.
> GENOCIDAL LOGIC: Everyone whose name begins with H go get everyone whose name begins with M.
> THE PYGMY FROM THE JUNGLE: Take them to the river.
> GENOCIDAL LOGIC: We each have this other choice too: You need to imagine something for it to exist. Can something exist if you can't imagine it?
> THE PYGMY FROM THE JUNGLE: Humanity is part of nature. To survive, you must go against nature completely.
> GENOCIDAL LOGIC: Unnatural acts.
> THE PYGMY FROM THE JUNGLE: The killers kill all day.
> PYGMY FROM THE JUNGLE: The killers kill in shifts.
> *b*: Justice is progressive.
> GENOCIDAL LOGIC: Your problem has found a solution. Die.
> *b*: God no longer wants you. Go now.
>
> (20)

On another level, meanwhile, Doris appears to reject Attar's quest entirely, reaching for something more radical and unresolved than that which has, conveniently, been true all along.

A student of Arabic, Doris is interested in the relationships between European lyric verse and earlier Arab world poetries, both Islamic and pre-Islamic. Concurrent with her study is the relationship between the poetries of spiritual passion such as Attar's (and that of other poets, such as Rumi, who were influenced by him) and their incarnation in the ritualized romantic traditions and poems that later developed in Europe. Doris bridges the two traditions in *Conference*, which stops briefly to nod at Chaucer's *Parliament of Fowls* (wondrously, for Doris's purposes, this is not only another look at the world of birds as allegory, but it is the first recorded Valentine's Day poem) along the way:

> Whan mamockes wer yr mete
> Couchyng yr drousy hedde
> Sometyme in lousy bedde
>
> (58)

Doris asks, as perhaps did Attar, what passionate language can do to reorganize and transgress social structures during times of crisis and searching.

Attar, whose name means *perfumer* and who appears to have been tried for heresy after writing *The Conference of Birds*, is a character in *Conference*. As poetic precursor, and devoted mystic, not to mention as perfumer, Attar is a perfect host for Doris's book, albeit one who seldom appears. Attar is present much as a perfume drifting in from offstage in Doris's most theatrically conceived book.

Conference does not excavate or use poetic form as *Paramour* does; rather, it transcends poetic form and unfolds in prose and dialogue. Its flirtation with literary history, then, arises not from formal but stylistic experiment, long dramatic sequences that make the book as much prose or drama as poetry.

In addition to characters moving with liquid ease in and out of being, *Conference* is populated with symbols that both indicate sets of characters and take on personae of their own (as Cole Swensen notes, these symbols "fly about like errant accents over the pages"), weaving in and out of scenes as a sort of Ur-text of their own.[9] They seem to serve as indicators of a three-dimensional brand of translation in which everything, from characters to place to Attar's poem to moments of lyrical introspection, is in a constant state of transformation. By book's end, each utterance is accompanied by several symbols (each one notating a number of persons and objects and situations) so that, in the obverse of Attar's epic allegorical climax of restored order, the book's characters have spiraled into a textual maelstrom in which nothing "is."

Attar's trial for heresy, which was related to the "incomprehensibility" of *The Conference of Birds*, might be seen as an echo of Ovid's exile, which was due in part to the reception of his ribald *Art of Love*. The real-life implications of poetic enterprise are evident not only in the texts, but in the extra-textual fates of Doris's source materials. Her work speaks to, and from, this seriousness, to the social potentials/inspirations within poetic innovation, and to the libidinal delights to be found in understanding what causes restraint, what use can be made of it and, then, how best to dispense with it. This comes as instruction and warning in *Conference* particularly, where she notes:

Once you embody the rules you are the rules. You are order's center. Thus doubly inanimate.[10]

Doris never simply embodies the rules. She caresses them—Platonically, amorously, always critically—and in so doing gets her writerly hands around their use value in a context of continual literary experiment.

NOTES

1. Stacy Doris, *Kildare* (New York: Roof Books, 1994), 13. Reprints with permission from James Sherry and Roof Books, and the author.

2. Stacy Doris, *Paramour* (San Francisco, Calif.: Krupskaya Press, 2000), 7. Reprints with permission from Krupskaya Press and the author.

3. Stacy Doris, *Kildare* (New York: Roof Books, 1994), 22.

4. Stacy Doris, *Paramour* (Krupskaya Press, 2000), 7.

5. Ibid., 72–3.

6. http://www.arras.net/the_franks/doris_paramour.htm.

7. "How Did I Become a Translator," in *Charting the Here of There: French and American Poetry in Translation in Literary Magazines, 1850–2002*, by Claude Royet-Journoud (New York: New York Public Library and Granary Books, 2002), 140.

8. Stacy Doris, *Conference* (Potes & Poets, 2001), 1. Reprinted with permission from Potes and Poets and the author.

9. www.litmuspress.org/aufgabe/issue2/swensen.htm.

10. Doris, *Conference*, 94.

BIBLIOGRAPHY

Books by Stacy Doris

Une Année à New York avec Chester. Paris: P.O.L., 2000.

Comment Aimer. Translated by Ann Portugal and Caroline Dubois (*Paramour* excerpts). Paris: Creaphis, 1998.

Conference. Bedford, Mass.: Potes & Poets, 2001.

Kildare. New York: Roof Books, 1994. Reprinted PDF download at epc.buffalo.edu/presses/roof/Doris_Kildare.html.

Knot. Athens: University of Georgia Press, 2006.

Paramour. San Francisco, Calif.: Krupskaya, 2000.

La vie de Chester Steven Wiener écrite par sa femme. Paris: P.O.L., 1998.

Translations

Christophe Tarkos: Ma Langue est Poétique. Edited with Chet Wiener. New York: Roof Books, 2001.

Everything Happens. By Dominique Fourcade. Sausalito, Calif.: Post-Apollo Press, 2001.

Family Cinema. Translation from French selections of *Cinéma des familles* by Pierre Alferi. DVD and chapbook. Aubervilliers, France: Les Laboratoires d'Aubervilliers, 2003.

Katalin Molnar. Translation of selections from French of Hungarian poet Katalin Molnar. Rotterdam: Poetry International Festival, 2003.

Tracing. Translation of selections from French of Japanese poet Ryoko Sekiguchi. Providence, R.I.: Duration Press, 2003.

Twenty-One New (to North America) French Writers. Edited with Norma Cole. *Raddle Moon* 16, 1997.

Violence of the White Page. Edited with Emmanuel Hocquard. Tyuonyi 9/10, 1991.

Chapbooks

Implements (for use). With Anne Slacik. Paris: limited edition handmade artbook.

Kildare. Translated by Juliette Valéry. Bordeaux: Format American, 1995.

Marie Antoinette. Bedford, Mass.: a.bacus 89,1999.

Mop Factory Incident. With Melissa Smedley. New York: WSW, 1996.

Le temps est à chacun. Translated by Martin Richet from *Knot.* Marseille: Contrat Maint, 2002.

Selected Prose

"After Language." In *After Language, samtida innovativ anerikansk poesi.* Stockholm, Sweden: OEI, 2001. English version at http://www.ubu.com/papers/oei/doris .html.

"Enquête sur la poésie." *Le Discours Psychanalytique* 12 (October 1994).

"How Did I Become a Translator." In *Charting The Here of There: French and American Poetry in Translation in Literary Magazines, 1850–2002.* New York: New York Public Library and Granary Books, 2002.

Introduction to *Violence of the White Page: Contemporary French Poetry in Translation.* Santa Fe, N.M.: Pederal, 1992. Reprinted PDF download at http://www.durationpress.com/archives/index.html.

"Poetry and this World." In *Writing From the New Coast: Technique.* Stockbridge, Mass.: O-blek, 1993.

"Sampling a Paper." In *A Review of Two Worlds : A Reflexion on French and American Poetry in Translation.* Los Angeles: Otis/University of Southern California, 2003.

"'Those been the cokkes wordes and not myne,' on Comedy and Identity in Poetry." *Boundary 2: 1999, Poetry on the Edge.* Durham: Duke University Press, 1999.

SUSAN WHEELER

THE DEBTOR IN THE CONVEX MIRROR

after Quentin Massys, c. 1514

He counts it out. By now from abroad there are shillings and real—
Bohemian silver fills the new coins—but his haul is gold, écu au soleil,
excelente, mostly: wafers thin and impressed with their marks, milled
new world's gold the Spanish pluck or West African ore Portugal's

slaves sling. The gold wafers gleam in their spill by the scale.
Calm before gale: what bought a sack a century before almost
buys a sack now; the Price Revolution's to come. A third of a mason's—
a master one's—day's wage funds the night's wine, Rhine, for his crew

after a big job wraps up. As for dried herring, his day's wage would buy
fifteen mille for a big do; his workers, just nine—18 stroo. Calm in his
commerce is the businessman, and his wife, their disheveled shelves:
she turns a page; her hands are in God but her gaze is on ange-nobles

and pearls, weights and gold rings—one florin in pan, one in his hand.
What sync they are in: calm their regard, luxe, volupté leur mien.
Fur trimmings on jackets, gemstones on fingers—while the
debtor in the mirror has spent what he has on the red hat he's in.

Prayer book illumined: luxury *that*, and to ignore: only more.
Calmed by the calculation of interest, though the figure's been
clear for a good quarter hour, the moneylender withholds it and waits:
the debtor is better with fuzz in his head. In truth, *he*'s distressed: cares

like the shield impressed in the écu dint the meet of his brow
beneath the red hat. What's he reading? Or faking? Caught in the
curve of an office's alarm, an anti- to crime, a drugstore's big boon
long centuries to come, the debtor—about to receive knell to what

peace he might otherwise recall—worries his page. Ability for
reading silently may not be his; the lender's wife puts him to shame,
though the shame in this is the least of his shames. In the yard
beyond her waits one of his lienors for the gold of another.

Schoolmarms ahoy. Scrap history, the parable, the prayer of the
illustrated hours she trembles to hold. He's got his gold, she's mes-
merized or not by its sheen, the debtor's lost to our reflecting of him—
but it's without, a measurement is made—a figure's gesture on the

gravitate street, the fury of a face *in its face*, behind the door ajar, the
fingers of the lienor demarcating fast the size of a peck or a pecker
not so. *The debt is as large as a giant's back turning, large as*
a vulcanic forge. And

> fragment of the debt imbursed—

> size of its toy—

intense regard.

Fume individually, fume

borrower, clipper, catcher, coiner, getter, grabber, hoarder, loser, lover,
  raiser, spender, teller, thirster—

> scrivener lays out upon collateral, but

what has the red-hat? Zero

> and then sum.

So *here* you are.   Master.

                                              These ideas,
said Friedländer, were "common possession, freebooty, fair game."

A painting by Jan van Eyck eighty years before Massys', glimpsed
and described in Milan but now lost, was its model: banker and wife;

the portrait of Giovanni Arnolfini in a red hat not unlike Massys' debtor
    and,
a year earlier, Arnolfini and his wife at their marriage, we know. In the
    latter,

the self van Eyck daubed in its own convex mirror (one of four figures),
affixed like a crucifix on the backdrop of wall, rides the conjoined hands

as a charm. But nothing foreshadowed the hand of your own.
Your painter's (nineteen, set off for Rome with the jewel of his art)

hand in the gem of its bulge, the hand the pope pronto kissed
with commission—a job, you note, never come through.

Genre derives from the devotional: beauty and *ange* on one side,
deformity by vice on the other, or so said Friedländer. He found the wife's
    gaze

full of dispirit, "lofty sadness." She and her husband are yes tight-lipped.
The palm of the hand, like the open mouth, were Massys' registries

of emotionality, he wrote, but the souls in this painting have neither.
Sentimentally, it *pleases* Massys "to feel sorrow, and grief takes on

mild forms." Worry's otherwise: Massys's St. Anthony, elsewhere,
tempted by courtesans, peaks his brows—wild, broken peaks!—same as

the moneylender's debtor. So much for effects, effects of Massys,
virtuoso, whose pyrotechnics, "new wine poured into old bottles,"

welled "from a kind of nervous energy—in any event, not from the heart."
"*The antithesis of artist*" (Friedländer, still): this, the debtor to Leonardo,

to Van Eyck, may well have known, knowledge well welling his brows
   in the
mirror the moneylender ignores. *My guide in these matters is your self,*

your own soul permeable by beauty, and mine not,
not even by the swirling of facts, leveling—

                 how far, indeed,

can the soul *swim out through the eyes and still return safely to its nest?*
That it be

possible

               I cannot leave. Though around me, and the art,

I fail.

                    Thérèse

was the lookout. She watched the cashier in the convex mirror, and I
watched Jean Shrimpton on the point-of-purchase long before it had
its name.   Thérèse:

               careful, Catholic, pregnant and smoking.

     lips   lipstick

I took the

   cylinder in my fingers and slipped it to Christmas. Thérèse: to the racks,
Seventeen, *Tiger Beat*. A few moments more and we'd be through the door.

                 Maybe it was *in* the painter's hand, *out for a dole*
                     —so close with Clement's promise!—
                           that he sought a soul.

              And these coins, fragments of a web—

Mary sat and did not labor, despite her Martha's sting.

It's still, tonight. The peepers, out, self-
                  restrain.
Sometimes a welling up: I've lost
           thought in images. Night: a blank.
       The stars just stars.
       The sternies prick like whin.
Kid's bicycle on its rim, under the road lamp chill
         as ice.
A soul could be blank as these bald things.
        Are blank. Or so we thought.

So this much we have: banker and wife, waist-up at table, she
with her prayer-book watching the gold coins spill on the surface

before us. What we see in their clothes is the waist-cinch:
her red seamy bodice, his jacket, furred collars and cuffs.

Behind them, just two shelves: account books and objects—
then, out a window or door, two figures obscured but for

faces and heads, one forefinger and thumb in a U.
In the fore of the table, a diverging mirror, gold frame,

askew. And, by his reflected place, we see, we viewers,
sitting right where we are, a red-hatted man who holds

a book to his chin as though he is sunning. Rather,
he's reading—or trying, by the fold in his brow.

Real light, long, late-day, slants through the window
above him where a steeple's filigree's revealed. And that's all.

Most agree the red-hatted reader's the painter; it matches
his portrait from Wiericx's engraving. The clothing's

outdated, the banker's wife's bodice derives from the portrait
Van Eyck did of his wife Margaret in that weird hornèd hat.

And Saint Eligius, patron of goldsmiths, converter of Antwerp,
in Christus' scene, had a curved mirror turned toward outdoors.

Copies of Massys come later. They drop the debtor, insert a
messenger. Imitators of Massys update

                              the coins.

Not
        that the convex tondo, inside of a painting, was not a dozen a dime—
            not just Massys, not just Van Eyck, it was *in the wind* blowing,
        in Brabant, in Ghent, Bruges, Anvers, through the Burgundy hold,
                    fresh off a pub's haul and into the workshop,
            popping up through the guilds   ghastly cliché it was then.

But
        we get   ahead   rewind   to the Lowlands   begin.

Astonishing city. A rube, let's say Charles, onions in sacks slung on his
mule's back, he a standout in his coarse sayette, enters this Antwerp,
inhales as he draws near the docks. Gulls swoop; three Fuggers,
    capitalists,

in wool dickedinnen, speaking abreast in deliberate tread, stop him
cold crossing his path. Street stalls of changers, merchants with money;
crates unloading—fish, sugar—by Spaniards and Danes;

dragomen emitting unrecognizable tongues: such swirl over Charles
in our genre-esque scene. In the movie, we'd hear the THX *clok*,
hooves in their wary trades forth. What little Charles knows of this place

he has heard at the fairs in the mediant towns outlying the western Ypres.
On the way, there'd been Ghent, its self-satisfied sense. Talk there of
trade throttled by this guild or that, trade nip-and-tuck against Bruges':

Antwerp, said an oiler in Deinze, *up-and-comer is it, if you want one
that is. Hub of all nations, market of kings. Nothing there, either,
to stand in the way of a man with ambition or a star in his bush.*

No, if you're smart, you'll go there and quick. Charles had nodded
and drunk from his mug, but the notion then planted by the man
took root. Now, in the pitch of the persons, in the roil of the merchants,

Charles sees there the commerce: purposeful, restive, serene—
a trade's un-self-consciousness, a self-sufficiency in such—
and Charles is impressed. His own small purse, pendant in his

pocket, feels slight but sufficient to one.

                              Anna Bijns, the young lady
says to him not three days later. She's forthright as a slip, and at once
he wants the pocket fuller, a past that's not his. A girl of means, she—

she could show him her whole shelf of books, her writing-room, her
verses that denounce the psalm-sop, Luther. *Like his sins are
worse than ours*, she'll say, to those more worthy of answer.

"Town common to all nations," Guicciardini later wrote of the city.
"First 'capitalist' center . . . in the modern sense," wrote Chlepner.
When Charles and Massys shared Antwerp its reign had just begun;

each week brought scores of foreigners, folded in like butter,
out to let a household kept kempt in local fashion, clean,
its Dinanderie in order and its linens boiled and hung.

Down Gulden street, the house that's held by the Hanseatic corn
market; across the way, the square that will become, in a score of
years, the world's first stock exchange—shops, fragrant with

Portuguese spices, beckon with the latest haul. The merchant
moneylender leans to the obsolescence of his coins—the paper
debts he trades more in leave gold to the unconjoined, sole

debtors like this painter worrying his paper text. *Livre tournois*,
the French would call them, units of money valued at a Roman
pound, and *livre*, *book*: not the first time the two're confused.

Charles, counting his ducats, catches a red hat from the *coin*
of his eye, costume of a century before: it's Massys he sees.
The painter's off to work in the salt crusted air, preparing

—away from the *shadow of a city*, *siphon*, you wrote, of the life
of the studio—

                                       his self to be seen.

New York tonight
                  boils in its heat wave. The sidewalks
burn soles. Haze like a coat warms up the ones out.   Prague

floods.

The market's in side-flip. Each day doubling back

the day before,

lobbing,
the stalk that holds coral bells tracing its arbitrary round. Perhaps
the U on the street

is a score.

Principal export:

ask Bernays, *he'll* know.   Buy low.

The painter in the mirror wants privacy, not this call that invades
the reading of a book. Your own looked out at us, but mine, *Massys*—
disingenuous, masquerading, stressed and damp—doesn't; weightier
things on his mind he's got not. But he only pretends to absorption.
It's we who discern the privacy he wants, we who can see
what he lacks. It's as though we're instructed to trust the lender,
his own fix being more, well, *sequestered.*
The last century mined focus as a notion, and even here in Manhattan,
a delirium of sorts swabbing its streets,
we tread with the intensity of hounds,
plugged into our earpiece conjointments, or collecting loose change
off of cuffs. Massys' grimace underdramatizes our lot.

thassright, that's what makes genres—

pink ribbon, blue bob—
thaler for the watched fob.

No, thalers   come later.

Not much, you prig.

Later enough.

So the grasping soul is unredeemed. *Freak accident—*
yeah, guy goes up a hill in thorns, ends up on a stick.
Not quite, not impaled, more tacked up.   *Yeah.*
And the grasping soul goes clean.

                                        Maybe it's our internalness
we're stuck on.
                              O Captain Me, O Consciousness.
The soul *negotiates* its right of way,

                              O consciousness,

but not without a bargain struck with*out*. Why all
or nothing, is what Charles thinks, watching the painter disappear

O Captain Me
                              in a costume fit to paint. After all,
Charles doesn't know the painter's
destination.

                              In a cloud left by dusty wheels, he

                    O captain me, o

hears a boy call *natura naturata! Red (Flemish) herring!—*
and wells with tears. Impossible   *o consciousness*
that this he heard, silt eyes silt ears

            Copper's up

in an older voice, murmuring, away—strange songs of spring that reach
    the rube in worsted wraps, wheels clattering about his self, while each
    breath, immarginate,

clangs to differentiate its action from the world's.

O captain me.
Sad country sack, negotiant, kneels in the dust to pray.

                                  He crams so much in, Massys. *And then I reached*
that time in life when, all my spices scattered, every story turned
                                                   lapsarian.

Every surface filled with hardware, pots, jetons—a collector's box—
the world impresses back, impresses with a shield or beast or profile of a
    noble sort—
the same impressions, though the edges of each coin be irregular and
    bent—
it being half a century before die standardized.
And even then, this penny black with chewing-gum, that one having seen
the inside of a shoe, this none but a banker's roll—the analogy

goes grim. Or is it metaphor, what we strive for, we

poets. Book-makers with the odds of slugs.

                                    We don't need paintings or / doggerel
                                    and on this too you're true.

                                  The man hand-making his U in the yard
knows Massys's a kite-man, bad risk, a debtor. All glow and show

                    and then off
                                        world, world, world   with him. Each
        time
intent to aliment not only he but they
                                                                world

what comes his way   gives way.

                    Even tonight, here, stampede of slugs
                                                        in all that enters here, in
pages strewn, in air report and digit-pulse: *his way*. The debtor does not
    know his debt to the skittering city. The bank of birds up a skyscraper's
    flank. Patience of his creditors. What does a trust in surfaces ensure but
    faith that the surfaces move?

Blue surroundings. Your nose, welling in the car mirror's arc—
my own in the hubcap hull—

What is this but an arrangement of figures on an open field?
But *they overlap*—and this is the *heart*, despite Friedländer,

the heart of the bind of the debtor: a debt becoming due.
Inveigling the day to take orders from *him*—such a ray from the
cathedral, still in construction, for which Massys' metalwork
is said to encircle a well—the red-hatted man pretends.

The soul encumbers what no other soul knows? Think again.
The mirror lies between two scales—one banker's, one maker's—

and Massys is but writ on its glass. It's the man in the courtyard,
the jig up with fingers, who'll reckon the dark fundamentals

once the weigh-ins are done. And the world impresses him, too.

The *world* overlaps them indentures them both.

                            Car door bangs. Dark Brooklyn, dark
clattering night.

           Though the lineage's strong for the sons of moneylenders,

daughters   don't carry.   They get the short end. *The debtor's excuses*

                                         are many

for the false fealty of her deals.

                  Adept at outline, Friedländer meant. Ready angle of the
couple's arms, echo of the angle in the glass. Her limpid
face lit sole. Debtor's histrionics, a painter's joke
shallow as they go.

Car door creaks its opening, back for a pack
of cigarettes. Side mirror loose, door slam. Wheeled overland

                                  from Venice
the Venetian goods—and cotton, from Levant—
are writ up
                        (in the noon sun and portside)

          and certified lading.
The paper suffices for sugar and salt.

POETICS STATEMENT

Sunday morning, and no chance of a peignoir. Why did it have to be one or the other? I don't think the imagination supplants; it serves. When I work, I try to get out of my own way, to try and treat it as akin to prayer, to align my will with something other than myself. I fail, and I am readily willing to admit that the endeavor is impossible. But I also know from faith that it is the negotiation that matters: the self-reproach, the turning-away, when I've been too lazy or distracted to try to align at all, when the text has adhered to the page like a clump of paste I'm adamant on baking into bread; or the marvel, the turning-toward, that results when I've no idea where a strong passage has come from. When it's wung in, a gift.

To talk about God like you would laundry. To talk about the laundry skirting God. To talk about the laundry where it's God that's meant.

I am aware, too, that this kind of thing veers from Gurdjieff and Yeats to George W and affirmations beside the cash register. Before I "came to believe" (*not* "came to accept Jesus as my personal Saviour," god forbid—why get away from hubris just to grab it back?), I'd scan this and skip ahead. Poets of the past were not made strange by faith, even as late as Auden and Lowell, who were made fallibly human by their negotiations, by their turning from one theological institution to another in fervent crises of faith. Now, we are made self-delusory by it. Or we are taken to be smitten by our own wisdom and certainty—neither of which have I found an iota of, through belief.

Writing is the thing through which I get closest to feeling aligned with something larger. Even though it may happen only five percent of the time, this outstrips anything else I have tried.

What follows from this is an ocean of detailed choices. Like Augustine's self-reconciliation to the paradox of an eternal present, some fairly complicated jerry-rigging goes into keeping up the assumption that once I have waded in—being unable to be anywhere but where I am at any moment, even compass-less, not knowing myself—I can be everywhere and anywhere by way of a will and means other than my own. So, poetics-wise, today I'm in Sargasso, yesterday among the Encantadas, and tomorrow no doubt in the muck of the Hudson near the George Washington Bridge.

SUSAN WHEELER'S
OPEN SOURCE POETICS

Lynn Keller

AN OTHERWISE appreciative reviewer of Susan Wheeler's first collection, *Bag 'o' Diamonds* (1993), quibbled with its "caper-movie title" yet, at least from the perspective available several volumes later, Wheeler's choice reveals a great deal about her sense of poetry's current linguistic resources.[1] To my ear, "bag 'o' diamonds" evokes not so much Hollywood renditions of treasure thieves' escapades as sites like Ye Olde Market in any U.S. shopping mall, where names are manipulated to give contemporary consumerism a comfortingly old-fashioned aura. Situated in Ye Olde Market, Bag 'o' Diamonds might be a shop selling assorted toe rings, beads, and nonprecious jewels. Whether suited to movies or stores, the language Wheeler adopts here is a version of vernacular that is connected with mass culture, popular entertainment, and commodification. Wheeler's poetry reflects an abiding interest in how such debased, clichéd language can acquire renewed force. Her primary strategy is to combine it with many other voices and registers. "The trick is," she says, "to make the multiple Englishes pierce by way of their aggregation, and not in spite of it."[2]

As a piece of linguistic simulacrum, a phrase like "bag 'o' diamonds" is perhaps analogous to the stage gore concocted to simulate deaths in horror films, described within the volume in "Peanut Agglutinin." Easy to scorn, fake blood—like stagy vernacular—turns out to have a place in meaningful experience. As the opening lines put it, "The gore being chili sauce and rice didn't mitigate / the way she died." The poem's title designates peanut as the substance that causes agglutination—presumably, the appearance of the clumping together of red blood cells. But agglutination also denotes a linguistic aggregation: forming words by combining words (more technically, "the formation of words from morphemes that retain their original form and meanings with little change during the combination process" [*Webster's*]). The term, then, designates a process comparable to the dense gluings (*collages* in French, we might note) from which Wheeler constructs her poetry. At the close of "Peanut Agglutinin," the aggregation of several linguistic registers, involvement in mass culture, and spiritual renewal come together in ways that suggest they are intertwined:

> Lissa was tired of peeling grapes for eyeballs,
> And Buck of scooping mayonnaise into insulated gloves.

> Yeah, well here's what she liked: hair, and lots of it,
> peanut brittle—when suddenly, a frost of cicadas,
> rising like Lucifer, hums up the clouds—an
> evening beside you: Do-right, do right again.[3]

It may be precisely because the members of the movie crew are involved in tacky illusion and formulaic plot—blood bags of ketchup in the "ever woods," "this way to the sawmill, inspector!"—that they are out in the world, present to the weird authentic when it suddenly intervenes. And in this revision of the epiphany typical of contemporary lyric, the music of the cicadas and the evening perhaps necessarily takes the form of a refrain also derived from popular culture: specifically, from the 1960s soul music of Aretha Franklin's "Do Right Woman, Do Right Man."

Whether she regards the language and props of mass culture as needed by poets and poetry readers now or just inevitably at hand, Wheeler's tendency is to point toward the grand or lofty or even the precious, approached here in "a frost of cicadas, / rising like Lucifer," and to swerve from the language high culture attaches to them toward some form of popular speech. It's a way, perhaps, of having her cake and eating it too. Thus, Wheeler makes ironic fun of any view of poetry collections as displays of precious jewels, at the same time that she may nonetheless suggest parallels between her hard-edged, multifaceted, syntactically dense constructions and those compressed transformations of coal, diamonds.

If Wheeler seems to be trying to have it both ways, her subsequent prose statements reveal this stance to have been deliberately chosen on a larger scale of poetics, within which her language is merely one element. During the mid- and late 1990s, Wheeler explicitly challenged the prevailing schema of exclusive camps and aesthetics. By September 1996, she was calling attention to how much the divisions between camps—particularly, it seems, those between so-called mainstream and so-called experimentalist writers—were being eroded, and she was urging further opening up of fixed identities. If we insist, she argued, "that power is defined by the borders we assert, we lose the mix. Ann Lauterbach and Alice Notley published by Vintage, Joan Retallack and Leslie Scalapino by Wesleyan: the problem is not what happens with assimilation, a trope that still depends upon opposition, it is rather how do we acknowledge and yet ignore, move through, not so much to accrue the goods . . . but to develop the work."[4]

Acknowledging via Derrida that any attempt at opening up identity and not defining it either with or against another's codified ideas is "necessarily flawed," Wheeler establishes her position as reflecting not naive idealism, but simply a sense of practical necessity if poetry is to remain radical (that is, both antiestablishment and rooted in what is essential).[5] She refuses to regard as depoliticizing assimilation the exploration of resources claimed by avant-garde experimentalists. Advocating *"acting as if"* no one had staked out territories, she claims this "is not assimilationist, but rather selfish in the same sense as is faith. It serves me as does giving coins to those solicitors who are the most obnoxious: I could reason it stupid, but I choose not to, *because it keeps the borders open"* ("WO" 194).

An essay published a few years later brings popular and mass culture into the mix. In "Poetry, Mattering?" Wheeler focuses not on the supposed problem of poets' purported appropriations of other groups' poetic resources, but on assimilations of any resistant expression by the dominant culture and especially mass media, represented by talk-show hosts like Geraldo and Rosie O'Donnell—assimilations whereby what is alternative ends up central and poetry is reduced to marketable personalities: "It may be that . . . the flattening-outs by the steamroller of cultural objectification make impossible any resistance to any aspect of the market-driven culture that isn't, by its own definition as a 'non-coopted' resistance, wholly unknown."[6] Despite the odds, her response remains defiant: "The ambition to find language combinations, structures, methods of composition, that remain *unassimilable* in the broad banality of the cultural market should not be faulted" ("PM" 324). Wheeler goes on to credit the traditional formalist poet and the experimentalist alike with attempting to resist the pervasive banality, albeit with equal inefficacy; she nonetheless urges poets on in resisting "with cobbled solutions" ("PM" 326). In a talk delivered in 2003 Wheeler adopts the term "anodyne eclecticism" to acknowledge the risks she advocates taking—despite potential accusations by politically committed experimentalists of "mere aestheticism"—in seeking a poetics that resists the cultural norms through an assimilationism that aspires to be "ethical in its writing and ethically enlarging in its reading."[7] Recognizing that the results of such assimilative efforts will be unevenly successful, she nonetheless advocates an inclusive approach as "keep[ing] the possibility open for exits we have not foreseen" ("RR" 155). Her own practice suggests that even if market-driven culture threatens poetry's distinction, the language and indeed the forces of that culture have to be taken into account if poetry is to matter.

As the remainder of this essay will demonstrate, the "cobbled solutions" Wheeler has devised in her own attempts to invigorate poetry's radical cultural force involve foregrounding, both formally and in her poems' content, the contemporary "problems" of "steamroller" consumerism/commodification and of artistic assimilation so as ultimately to recast them as opportunities and resources. At a time when many poets were edgy about the politics of borrowing from other camps, Wheeler, in *Smokes* (1998), produced poems that flaunt their borrowings from past writers and traditions and from her near contemporaries (while continuing to draw on popular slang and on images and brand names from popular culture). Though occasionally acknowledging some anxiety about such indebtedness or some dissatisfaction with the resources at hand, more generally the borrowing is grateful, its manner playful and confident. A lesson seems implied: If one can borrow unstintingly from eclectic traditions or diverse precursors, and produce lively writing, why not borrow with equal freedom and openness from a range of contemporary poetic camps? With her third collection, *Source Codes* (2001), as I shall show, Wheeler makes reflection on the relation between artworks and their sources, textual and more broadly cultural, the unifying concern of the volume. Her highlighting of the commonalities between electronic source codes and artistic sources emphasizes that sources are only structures from which one builds, only "scaffolding."[8] They provide, not determinative limits, but supports for exploratory processes. Similarly, the economic dynamics of consumer culture, however problematic for artistic resistance, provide an elaborate set of metaphors and analogues useful for considering options for managing creative and spiritual resources. Wheeler's latest collection, *Ledger*, winner of the 2004 Iowa Poetry Prize, focuses on matters of money in order to continue her explorations of commodification and its effects on both society and individual spirituality. "The Debtor in the Convex Mirror," *Ledger*'s final poem, will provide my concluding demonstration of a poetics analogous to "open source" distribution in the realm of computer programming. Reflecting an ethical stance that resists a narrow concept of ownership as well as a creative principle, open source distribution aims to "develop the work" by making high-level language codes (source codes) visible so that they can be modified by other programmers. In that way, the entire community—not just the individual or company who first developed the program—benefits from improvements made by any interested programmers. Similarly, what I am calling Wheeler's *open source poetics*, which approaches poetic sources and resources as available to all, hopes to foster more effective evasions of the cultural steamroller.

While her prose statements were championing crossover poetries that bridge current aesthetic divides, Wheeler in her own poetic practice was combining with astonishing density the disjunctions and abrupt parataxes Language poets derived from the traditions of collage modernism and the clever formalism of Auden's heirs. Her most audible borrowings in these works, however, were from past poets and earlier works, not from her contemporaries. As Robert Hass noted in his afterword to *Smokes* (his selection for the 1998 Four Way Books Award), her postmodern idiom—"irony, pastiche, non-sequitur, dark wit, wild shifts in diction, a funhouse falling away of narrative continuity from image to image and line to line"—is "by now familiar enough"; what renders the work "exhilarating and unexpected" is her "witty ear." That ear is tuned to the past: "It's as if she took an aspect of postmodernism, of John Ashbery's style, back through Auden to its ancestral roots in Lewis Carroll and Edward Lear and then leapt forward again to make new inventions out of it in the disoriented present."[9]

Hass uses the opening poem to demonstrate, calling attention to its echoing of Robert Frost. In fact, that poem, "He or She That's Got the Limb, That Holds Me Out on It," echoes several other canonical works as well and exemplifies the volume's preoccupation with both the resources and limits of poetic tradition.

> The girls are drifting in their ponytails
> and their pig iron boat. So much for Sunday.
> The dodo birds are making a racket
> to beat the band. You could have come too.
>
> The girls wave and throw their garters
> from their pig iron boat. Why is this charming?
> Where they were nailed on their knees
> the garters all rip. You were expected.
>
> The youngest sees a Fury in a Sentra
> in a cloud. This is her intimation and she balks.
> The boat begins rocking from the scourge
> of the sunset. The youngest starts the song.
>
> (*Smokes* 3)

Initially, the tone is amused, amusing: girls "drifting in their ponytails" lightly mocks female adolescents' preoccupation with their appearance and with egocentric fantasy, rendered particularly absurd by their drifting in a craft that presumably would not float. With the next line, however, these girls become versions of the peignoired woman who dreams by the water in Wallace Stevens's "Sunday Morning," indicating more serious quest. "So much for Sunday" seems to reject the sensual faith of Stevens's protagonist while also announcing a loss of moral and religious moorings. Voices of dead (male) poets are apparently inescapable—rendered playfully in vernacular description of those loud dodo birds—yet their inherited forms and rituals may have lost their charm. Frost's invitation, to which Wheeler pays homage, is also exposed as a failure: you could have come too—but didn't. And where Wordsworth's child in "Intimations of Immortality" trailed clouds of immortal glory, today's child has cloud visions of consumer products: Plymouth Fury and Nissan Sentra. A frightening level of violence pervades the poem, as the drifting girls are forcibly nailed into the position of prayer and prematurely sexualized in a horrific manner, held down as if ready for violation (or are the garters nailed to their bodies, mutilation for beauty?). Yet the youngest refuses to glamorize as epiphany the tacky, latently violent fantasy—a fantasy with roots in lyric tradition, where female figures appear as objects rather than speaking subjects, as well as in contemporary consumer culture. Perhaps aligning her voice with the forces of social disruption that rock the boat, she "starts the song," thereby introducing Wheeler's lyrics that follow.

Wheeler's songs in *Smokes* often deliberately "graft from" model texts by others.[10] The volume contains a poems "after Heine," another "expunging Ponge," a "valentine for Auden,"[11] several distinct echoes of Eliot and of Pound, an allusion to Lowell alluding to Milton in "Casino Night"'s "I might not be right" (*Smokes* 46). The poems often employ regular forms, such as rhymed quatrains or sonnets or even a pantoum, that invoke the patterns of high-cultural tradition. They also imitate biblical cadences or popular forms (for example, the African American folk song about "John Henry" who "laid down his hammer and he died" echoes in "Beavis' Day Off," "and she lay down on fine braids and she cried"). These are all tributes to uses of language Wheeler admires, even as she injects them with extra heterogeneity via bits of vernacular and slang alongside notably esoteric terms. Her sources are prompts for improvisation, not restraining rubrics; this is apparent, for instance, from her play with traditions of literary and vernacular comparison, using cockroaches, in "Sonnet of Alternate Starts for a Poem of Comparison":

> O ya know daguy's a cockroach by dalook but he—
> Like their namesakes, they're drawn to sludge.
> Damn the cockroach life upon the lea.
> What bug shall I compare with you?
> You shittin me, you cockroach mouth.
>
> (*Smokes* 32)

"Ethic" evokes the blackface of John Berryman's Henry to acknowledge some unease about appropriating other voices, particularly from other classes and races: "What business was mine / in the cardboard rune, in the native rap? / I on the tree stump, I missing all" (*Smokes* 11). Yet the poem that opens the second of the volume's two sections, "Ezra's Lament," suggests that it is only self-defeating to worry about the debts incurred in such borrowings. Named for a poet obsessed with financial debt and excessive interest, and who appears twice in the acknowledgments as a source for lines in this volume, "Ezra's Lament" follows the example of Elizabeth Bishop's "Visits to St. Elizabeths" in invoking Pound's obsessiveness through repetitions that recall nursery rhymes. The speaker of Wheeler's quatrains lists his assorted debts on varied scales—"I owed the baker three dollies with heads / I owed the singer a way to recoup," and so forth—and offers a warning:

> Machinate carefully, o if you should go there,
> Clicking the debts like a rotary phone

Where the lifeline is sparked in the vectors.
That frantic believing will break you in two.
(*Smokes* 17)

Apparently, debts pervade every aspect of our existence. But attempting to keep exact track of one's debts, counting through them (as one might click through rosary beads as well as the rotary dial) only proves self-destructive. Listing them may even generate losses in self-respect and creative energy: the broken man's scorn for himself as well as his continued diminution are conveyed in the poem's final stanza, where he labels himself a wank (forties slang for a contemptible person, also meaning to handle one's penis) and where, even as he claims to be giving valuable advice, his commands fade into wistfulness: "O if you should go there in your twenty years / Remember the wank that you cannot repay, / O if you should, there in your twenty years" (*Smokes* 18). What belongs to whom, possession and repayment, seem beside the point, though recognizing the limits of one's self-reliance may be valuable. The one question "Ezra" poses suggests a sense of being ultimately in service of another (an inspiring muse? a life-giving god?) in an economics beyond his ken: "What breath employs me thats salary should be / Paid in tenders I don't understand?" (*Smokes* 17). The question may point toward religious faith; certainly it invites humility. These principles—a humble recognition of the pervasiveness of one's debts, and an acceptance that one can neither avoid nor repay them—extend to artistic indebtedness as well.

Smokes acknowledges that artistic debts are particularly complicated when one's models are living, even if there is a generational separation (as there is, for instance, between Wheeler and Ashbery); both the naturalness and the psychological difficulty of such debts are the subject of the title piece. "Smokes" mixes details describing a young writer's invited visit to an older writer in his apartment in New York's famed Chelsea Hotel, with a series of "suppose[d]" fantasies about what might have happened—or that the young visitor wished would have happened—but didn't. The fantasies highlight the older man's careful attentions to the young man, his valuing of the younger man's opinion (though realism intrudes enough to suggest the attentions are motivated partly by lust or by the forgetful misjudgments of age). Interspersed throughout the narrative are assertions about the order in which plants such as forsythia, daffodils, and johnny-jump-ups bloom in spring, reminders of nature's ordered cycles. The cigarettes in the story—the older writer's Luckys and the younger one's Kools—speak to what has become in our consumer culture a similarly inevitable progression: different generations, different smokes. But acceptance of distinct seasonal/generational achievement is easier with greater historical distance: Imagined as invited by the older poet to read one of his poems in manuscript, the younger responds enviously; it's "a poem to die for" (*Smokes* 13). In contrast, "The older poems—I mean by centuries—have given us enough time to really love them" (14). At the close, however, the young writer accepts his place in the seasons of literary history along with the human limits of those to whom he is indebted. Thus, after imagining what a wonderful adventure it would have been if the older poet had invited the younger into his company, "*Come with us Ethan why don't you?*" the poem returns to reality: "You waited for this, and he didn't. The redbud's a small tree, a scrapper, an adamant. Some are strong, some are weak, some like you with the breath of forgiveness cupping to light a Kool" (*Smokes* 14).

Smokes demonstrates again and again that, once accepted, indebtedness can become a source and a means of celebration. A sense of joy in the language pervades much of the volume, particularly as the poems splash about in their altered allusions and twisted sayings, their variant englishes. Listen, for instance, to the opening stanzas of "The Dogwood and the The," a poem whose serious concern with the difficulty of remembering Christ's sacrifice in the whirling and violent carnival of contemporary culture is only enhanced by the wild glee, the complicit "gaud," of its language:

> The dazzling platters of the many-armed man,
> The hundred plates spinning on the hundred spun fingers,
> A trick whip *Step ON it you* soft in the skim of your skin—
> The eye becomes inured to gaud. The bellicose kids fort up
> The grand screen. *Cool, summa, wahm in the winta*—
> *Hey asshole! Take ya stringy hair out!* The quarter's in,
> (Smokes 8)

The volume's final poem demonstrates Wheeler's relish in having her mind and ear filled with the words of other writers, particularly those now dead. "Chosen" offers a hilarious vision of being haunted and bullied by Bartleby's ghost who assiduously supervises the speaker's writing, holding up Hesiod's map or yelling at her in Norse, as she composes on her computer under flourescent lights. By taking a phrase from Berryman, the final line enacts exactly what it names: "Bone collating—now *that's* a job" (*Smokes* 52). Interpreting the bones as what remains from earlier poets, this is a job Wheeler has chosen, and one she executes with gratitude and spunk.

The "I owed" refrain of "Ezra's Lament" and the private rendezvous of "Smokes" suggest the individualized emphasis in Wheeler's treatment of the dynamics of assimilation and borrowing in *Smokes*. Her next volume, *Source Codes*, reflects a broadened interest in sources and appropriation in cultural contexts that extend well beyond the literary and well beyond the interaction between individual artists and particular texts. The volume's title says as much: in using the phrase "source codes" rather than, say, "sources," Wheeler focuses attention on sets of rules that govern a repeatable process so that the process rather than any particular product or producer is key. As a term designating computer programming languages, "source codes" invokes the electronic transformation of information technologies that has dramatically altered text production, reception, and reproduction; also denoting the boxes with numbers that appear on the backs of mail-order catalogues, the title phrase locates the volume itself as well as its thematic concerns in the context of consumer culture.

The poems in this collection tend to have quite specific sources of diverse kinds: there are found or partially found poems (for instance, one from a viciously misogynist passage in Robert Burton's *Anatomy of Melancholy*), poems "after" portrait studies, poems inspired by specific artistic performances and one by a sign in a restaurant window, a poem that retells a children's story, a commissioned epithalamium, and so on. The only one that imitates a specific poem—a six-stanza imitation of the seven rhymed tercets of Robert Frost's "Provide, Provide"—demonstrates how Wheeler's creations tilt from their sources toward larger social and cultural patterns. Frost's heavily ironic piece presents the cautionary example of the female celebrity who, in aging, falls from having been "the picture pride of Hollywood" to being an impoverished "withered hag"; cynically urging people to protect themselves against "disregard" with wealth, it concludes: "Better to go down dignified / With boughten friendship at your side / Than none at all. Provide, provide!"[12] Where Frost's movie star seems a monitory example of the general fickleness of fortune, Wheeler's imitation-of-sorts details the behavior of a particular social class. It opens with a depiction of widespread famine, perhaps evoking the Irish potato famine: "The thinnest meal on the slightest isle / Sustains but poorly. So: the file / Of men and women, mile and mile." The poem, however, turns out to concern the cravings of the wealthy (the "slightest isle" more Manhattan than Ireland), particularly of art consumers, those ravenous "beauty sluts" for whom buying boas or scavenging antiques might be temporary fashions. Pampered and infantilized by their prosperity, the peripatetic rich live "thumb to mouth." Wheeler concludes with economic analysis that gives center stage to contemporary culture's spiritual poverty; it is the endless craving of the spiritually empty leisured rich that generates the imperative for the rest of society ceaselessly to produce. The profits of that production, of course, may barely enable survival and will not provide spiritual sustenance for either consumers or producers: "The lucky few who do adduce / The food that keeps them from the noose / Will crave on, too. Produce, produce."[13]

Pushing the resources of lyric tradition toward a concern with specific social discourses and with the sources of contemporary social conditions, Wheeler continues to combine torqued versions of regular formalism like Frost's with the fast-cutting, antilyrical disjunctions and fragmented narratives we might associate with, say, the Language writing of Charles Bernstein. Like many of those associated with Language writing, her work foregrounds the ways in which language, especially the languages of mass culture, constructs our world. "Fourteen," for instance, set "just mid-way through a century's detritus," depicts a culture of violence, exploitation, and economic division as it is denied by and created by the mass media and the advertising industry that support capitalist consumption. The scene involves summer rioting and vandalism, taking place in a collage of sounds and images from blaring televisions and radios:

> A child climbs through the glass of the storefront with
> a hold on his mother. Hoppy sights one and dips into
> housewares. The shouts pepper screeches as the wagons
> brake fast. Radios hum Hawkins' revenge at top blast.
>
> (*SC* 19)

In the role of cop, we've got the (white) TV series good guy Hopalong Cassidy, known for battling crime and upholding justice with minimum violence. But here, his "sight[ing] one" sounds ominously as if he's looking though the gun sights, targeting kids—perhaps, if "Hawkins' revenge" refers to the great African American tenor sax player, Coleman Hawkins, black kids. The poem's heavily rhymed and dizzying shifts in linguistic registers or scenes (Hoppy is soon glimpsed in "do-rags" and then, as if with channel switching, Hoppy's a green dog) emphasize the gaps between social classes and races: "the children lay down in the project's sweet gleam, / in a room blinking red from the [police car's] out-bubble turning," while a few lines later "Jack Parr's newest set has fronds behind, waving." While the wealthy, consumers of luxuries like imported teak furniture and Scandinavian pornography, experience no greater discomfort than the indigestion Alka-Seltzer can relieve ("*plop, plop . . . fizz, fizz*"), the boy from the projects—already seen in terms of racist stereotypes of the well-hung black male—is headed for a future of prison, poverty, and legitimate, potentially explosive rage. The poem closes with the boy as another electric appliance, gone haywire:

> The boy's in his lair and the boy is alone, as he sparks,
> as he sparked in the arms of a white man he shone,
> as he will when he sparks in a lockout to come.
> He's a radio. He's a tornado. No dough.
> He's got a big one, size of a A-bomb torpedo.
> The Danes could arrange for the passions to rise
> and the settings not inflame, not quell, not haze
> but in utter placidity backdrop the throes.
> The boy swats the light. He's sparking. He's right.
>
> (*SC* 20)

In this poem, as elsewhere in *Source Codes*, Wheeler's collaging of images and especially slogans associated with American TV shows and consumer product advertising captures the bizarre hybridity and economic disparities of post–World War II American culture: e.g., "in the showroom it gleams *I can't believe* / a perch for McHale, *I ate*, for Have Gun, for Hoss. / A pitcher of teak, a bee in the glass, a deck / wrapping the house with a tree up its neck" [*SC* 20]). Wheeler further cultivates hybridity through the volume's generically mixed construction: *Source Codes* contains nearly as many photo collages as poems, while appendices of poem drafts and html code make up its last third.[14] In place of titles in the table of contents, for each numbered poem or collage Wheeler provides some, usually brief, source information. Often the generality of that information directs readers more toward a cultural context than to tracking down the "originals." For instance, the recurrent attribution, "Figure, *The Economist*," conveys the author's interest in global economics, not the geographical/temporal location of the figure or the article in which the image appeared.

The collages are made from postcards onto which Wheeler glued figures cut from sources designed for mass consumption. Deliberately crude in their technique and often compositionally awkward, the collages are emphatically removed from "mere aestheticism" (a charge sometimes leveled against those who employ techniques associated with Language writing without having evolved from the political contexts that generated Language poetics) and also from the author's personal experience (thwarting the talk-show tendency to read art in terms of personality). While amusingly absurd, many of the images suggest cultural transformations resulting from globalization, secularization, and commodification. A number are interior shots of ornate European cathedrals or dignified historic buildings such as those found in The Hague, now turned tourist attractions; the figures inserted there often seem culturally and racially incongruous (for example, a nearly naked Nigerian soccer fan grins in a cathedral in "Seventeen") or are engaged in activities like kissing or dancing that once would have been entirely inappropriate.

The images could be read as political statements; for instance, "Fifteen," in which an emaciated rifle-bearing African soldier appears to run from Anne Hathaway's bucolic cottage, might locate the sources of contemporary Third World violence in earlier racist colonialism. But such formulaic readings would not do justice to the images' openness to markedly varied readings. This interpretive openness may be one way in which Wheeler counters those who would attach a particular political valence to work they regard as superficially appropriative. Certainly it suggests that in order to understand contemporary society in all its complexity and incongruities and in order to resist the dominant culture's flattening tendencies, we need flexibly to employ multiple source codes, multiple sets of rules. Adopting the terms of her title, we might say Wheeler deliberately thwarts simple modes of reading by scumbling multiple coding languages.

Similarly, the inclusion of drafts in *Source Codes* works against seeing the published version (the poem as consumable product) as the single "real thing," encouraging us to approach artworks as partial records of processes evolving within multifaceted social and cultural circumstances. The reproduced drafts provide evidence not only of the compositional process that yielded cross-outs and verbal substitutions, but also of intellectual contexts (as in a handwritten note, "Kristen Ross on Rimbaud") and technological ones (on the same page, "tech@echostar.com.") (*SC* 74). The contexts of Wheeler's domestic and professional life—free from personal revelations—are evident as well. Thus, one torn-off early draft page reveals LANG above CEN, probably the remains of LANGUAGE CENTERED, alongside some notes about distributing a percentage of the gross; other draft bits appear on a remnant of a concert program (*SC* 103 and 104). Counteracting the possibility that the inclusion of drafts might fetishize the compositional process or—as talk shows do—the creative artist, between the appendixes of "source drafts" for poems in *Source Codes* and in *Bag 'o' Diamonds*, Wheeler inserts a substantial section of html code. This section foregrounds still other kinds of conventions and coding that are sources behind contemporary "creative" writing. With its inclusion, Wheeler also invites readers to think about the sources for an artwork—precedent traditions, specific influences, prompting events, immediate material conditions, and so forth—as acting like source code, which provides a high-level set of instructions from which one can create machine-level instructions, and from there, particular programs and specific documents. Again, *source* is associated with an opening of formal possibility, not with restriction, appropriation, or diminished creativity. Using several source codes—which, metaphorically speaking, could mean drawing on the resources of multiple poetic schools—is, moreover, one way of perhaps jamming the machine, preventing it from following the usual procedures. *Source Codes* keeps suggesting and demonstrating that the deliberate mixing of languages (machine language with "natural" ones, or, more figuratively, visual with verbal media, street language with lofty diction, dissonant cultural contexts, divergent literary traditions) may valuably impede processing-as-usual.

Moving into even more unusual uses of page space and greater formal variety, *Ledger* (2005) richly elaborates Wheeler's long-standing interest in the dynamics of exchange, indebtedness, and profit, whether monetary, aesthetic, and/or spiritual. The volume's closing poem, "The Debtor in the Convex Mirror," provides an apt conclusion to this discussion of Wheeler's embrace of artistic assimilation. Through its title, the poem announces one of its prominent sources, "Self-Portrait in a Convex Mirror," and Wheeler acknowledges her general debts to John Ashbery. Ashbery's celebrated poem is essentially a reflexive monologue in which the poet captures an internal polyphony by tracking the shifts of his attention as he contemplates Francisco Parmigianino's self-portrait. Although his poem acknowledges the particular urban contexts for the painting's creation and its display, Ashbery is primarily concerned with universal processes of consciousness—his own serving as a one-size-fits-all model. Wheeler's poem "after Quentin Massys, c. 1514" is also an ecphrastic work, responding to Massys' painting of the moneylender. In predictable contrast to Ashbery's, hers reflects lively interest in social particularities, especially those involving economic history, as she enters multiple minds and, using several voices, imagines fragments of several people's stories. Thus, with touches of modern vernacular and much musical richness, her opening description of the coins counted out by the moneylender conveys considerable information about early sixteenth-century coinage, wages, and trade:

> He counts it out. By now from abroad there are shillings and real—
> Bohemain silver fills the new coins—but his haul is gold, écu au soleil,
> excelente, mostly: wafers thin and impressed with their marks, milled
> new world's gold the Spanish pluck or West African ore Portugal's
>
> slaves sling. The gold wafers gleam in their spill by the scale.
> Calm before gale: what bought a sack a century before almost
> buys a sack now; the Price Revolution's to come. A third of a mason's—
> a master one's—day's wage funds the night's wine, Rhine, for his crew
>
> after a big job wraps up.[15]

Massys' painting is positioned in the historic trade of artistic ideas as well; by no means original, its ideas and devices were "'common possession, free-booty, fair game,'" as Wheeler has contended poetic ideas and techniques also are (*L* 67). Wheeler notes that the portrait—which later had its own imitators—was modeled on a painting done eighty years earlier by Jan van Eyck, while the "convex tondo" was at the time a "ghastly cliché" (*L* 71).[16] Wheeler's poem, meanwhile, adds another layer to deeply sedimented debates to which Ashbery also contributed in considering, for instance, the possible blankness of the soul. But she enters via a particular moment of economic and ecclesiastic history: in the "[f]irst 'capitalist' center," Antwerp, when "its reign had just begun" and when Luther had begun to preach justification by faith not works (perhaps a consoling perspective for one who portrays herself as a teenage shoplifter hoping to evade the drugstore's convex security mirror) (*L* 73). Her concern is specifically with the redemption of "the grasping soul" (*L* 75), the soul in an era of capitalist acquisitiveness and of problematic focus on the self: "Maybe it's our internalness / we're stuck on. / *O Captain Me, O Consciousness*" (*L* 76).

The mirror, of course, is an ancient figure for representational art, while in all the paintings invoked here, the figure in the mirror is the artist. That "[t]he mirror lies between two scales—one banker's, one maker's—" positions both art and the artist as negotiating between economic or material and spiritual needs (*L* 79). Wheeler remains true to her belief that maintaining rigid boundaries is counterproductive and that we may need the mix if we are to move beyond whatever we're stuck on: "The *world* overlaps them indentures them both" (*L* 79).

NOTES

1. Albert Mobilio, *Voice Literary Supplement* (April 1994): 14.

2. *O·blĕk* 12 (Spring–Fall 1993), special issue, Writing from the New Coast: Technique, ed. Peter Gizzi and Juliana Spahr, 98.

3. Susan Wheeler, *Bag 'o' Diamonds* (Athens: University of Georgia Press, 1993), 8.

4. "What Outside?" *Talisman* 19 (Winter 1998–1999): 192. Subsequent references will appear in the text as "WO."

5. Lack of naïveté is evident also in Wheeler's introduction to a conference roundtable a few months later. Titled "A Tag without a Chit," it was a session on crossovers, or hybrid poetries; among the questions Wheeler posed was whether it is possible to remain unaligned with one camp or another, moving freely in the field and "raiding varied traditions," or whether this position, too, had become a brand, filling a market niche; www.english.rutgers.edu/atag/htm.

6. Susan Wheeler, "Poetry, Mattering?" in *By Herself: Women Reclaim Poetry*, ed. Molly McQuade (St. Paul, Minn.: Graywolf Press, 2000): 321–22. Subsequent references will appear in the text as "PM."

7. Susan Wheeler, "Reading, Raiding, and Anodyne Eclecticism: Word without World," *Antioch Review* (Winter 2004): 148. Subsequent references will appear in the text as "RR."

8. "Interview with Susan Wheeler," conducted by Lynn Keller, *Contemporary Literature* 45 (Winter 2004): 586.

9. Susan Wheeler, *Smokes* (Marshfield, Mass.: Four Way Books, 1998), 55. All subsequent references are to this edition and will appear in the text.

10. Page 9. "Susan Wheeler's Interviews and Profiles" at PreviewPort, www.previewport.com/Home/wheeler-i.html.

11. "Shanked on the Red Bed," according to Wheeler, in *The Best American Poetry, 1998*, ed. John Hollander (New York: Scribner, 1998): 324.

12. Robert Frost, *Complete Poems of Robert Frost* (New York: Holt, Rinehart, and Winston, 1964), 404.

13. Susan Wheeler, *Source Codes* (Cambridge and Applecross, W. Aus.: Salt Publishing, 2001), 7. Further references will appear in the text as *SC*.

14. In the interview with the author, Wheeler states that she had at the time mistakenly understood html, technically a markup language, to be a source code (587).

15. Susan Wheeler, *Ledger* (Iowa City: University of Iowa Press, 2005), 65. Further references will appear in the text as *L*.

16. Lisa Jardine emphasizes the "detailing of commodities" in a van Eyck painting Wheeler mentions as precedent, the portrait of Giovanni Arnofini and his wife at their marriage (with van Eyck as one of four figures in the convex mirror), which Jardine describes as "packed with details of acquisitiveness in fifteenth century Bruges" and as "a celebration of ownership"; *Worldly Goods: A New History of the Renaissance* (New York: Nan A. Talese, an imprint of Doubleday, 1996), 14 and 15.

BIBLIOGRAPHY

Books by Susan Wheeler

Bag 'o' Diamonds. Athens: University of Georgia Press, 1993.
Ledger. Iowa City: University of Iowa Press, 2005.
Record Palace [a novel]. St. Paul, Minn.: Graywolf Press, 2005.
Smokes. Marshfield, Mass.: Four Way Books, 1998.
Source Codes. Cambridge and Applecross, W. Aus.: Salt Publishing, 2001.

Selected Prose

"Apologist for Matter" [on Francis Ponge, *Selected Poems*]. *Denver Quarterly* 30 (Fall 1995): 130–35.
"Gravity No Stretch for the Zip Wit of Rae." In *A Wild Salience: The Writing of Rae Armantrout*, edited by Tom Beckett, 75–79. Cleveland, Ohio: Burning Press, 1999.
"Jokerman." In *Bob Dylan with the Poets and Professors . . . Do You, Mr. Jones?*, 175–91. Chatto and Windus, 2002.
"Joseph Brodsky's Visit." *Denver Quarterly* (Winter 1996–1997): 112–13.
"Poetics," *o·blēk* 12 (Fall 1993). Special issue: Writing from the New Coast: Technique, edited by Peter Gizzi and Juliana Spahr, 96–98.
"Poetry, Mattering?" In *By Herself: Women Reclaim Poetry*, edited by Molly McQuade, 317–27. (St. Paul, Minn.: Graywolf Press, 2000.
"Reading, Writing, and Anodyne Eclecticism: Word without World." *Antioch Review* (Fall 2003): 148–55.
"Round Up 1: Recent Translations from the French." *Denver Quarterly* (Spring 1998): 64–76.
"Round Up 2: Recent Translations from the French." *Denver Quarterly* (Winter 1999–2000): 99–113.
"To Things Their True Names" [Recent translation of Reverdy and Prevert]. *Denver Quarterly* 29 (Spring 1995): 116–23.
"What Outside?" *Talisman* (Fall 1998): 192–95.

Interviews

With Lynn Keller. *Contemporary Literature* 45 (Winter 2004): 573–96.

With Carl Dhiman. *Poetry News* (Spring 2004): 7.
With Micheal Tyrell. *Poetry Project Newsletter* 178 (February–March 2000): 13–14.

Selected Reviews and Criticism

Burt, Stephen. Review of *Smokes. Boston Review* (Summer 1998): http://bostonreview
   net/BR23.3/burt.html.
Keller, Lynn. "Resisting the Cultural Steamroller: Susan Wheeler's *Source Codes.*"
   American Literature 179, no. 1 (March 2007).
Ramke, Bin. "Enhanced and Instrumentalized Looking: Poetry as/and Visual Art."
   American Letters & Commentary (2003): 115–21.
Stefans, Brian Kim. Review of *Smokes. Arras: New Media Poetry and Poetics* [on-line
   journal] http://www.arras.net/the_franks/wheeler_smokes.htm.
———. Review of *Source Codes. Arras: New Media Poetry and Poetics* [on-line journal]
   http://www.arras.net/the_franks/wheeler_source_code.htm.
Yenser, Stephen. "The Poetics of Flash and Speed." In *A Boundless Field: American
   Poetry at Large*, 193–215. Ann Arbor: University of Michigan Press, 2002. (Origi-
   nally published in *Yale Review* [Winter 1999]).

MARK NOWAK

FROM *SHUT UP SHUT DOWN**

From $00 / LINE / STEEL / TRAIN

I.

The basic form is the frame; the photograph of the factory predicts how every one (of the materials) will get used. **and I can remember Mark & I talking about the possibility of Lackawanna becoming a ghost town** Past (participle) past (participant) past (articulating) an incessant scraping (away). **and what would we do. You know—it wasn't just losing a job in the steel industry, but your entire life, the place that you grew up in was going to be gone.** As I scraped (grease, meat, omelettes), the (former) railroad workers and steel workers (still) bullshitting in the restaurant where for eight years I short-order cooked.

*

Who knew

the crisis

from the conditions—

presumably
the Capital [Who]

Note: Complete bibliographies for these poems are available in *Shut Up Shut Down* (Minneapolis, Minn.: Coffee House Press, 2004).

13.

The interruption of the closure, in this instance, by the frame: "LTV [Steel] was able to use its bankruptcy to reduce payments to productive workers." **In the old days when the city bus used to pull up to the factory gate, the driver would call out "butcher shop" or "slaughterhouse."** "In negotiations with the steelworkers union, LTV extracted more takebacks than other, presumably healthier steel companies were able to." **I can remember sitting around the lunch table and everybody at that table, there must have been seven or eight people, had a finger or something missing.** "This gave LTV an advantage over its competitors." **Believe it or not, people felt it was kind of like a badge of honor that they had a finger or something missing, and that would be a topic of conversation.** "Bankruptcy became, through a cultural process that understood bankruptcy as failure, a condition for success."

*

Where are

yards   our

yards where our

no you cannot
    yards [where] away

160.

The men knew that they were risking their jobs in the walkout . . .
but they had got worked up to the point where this didn't seem so
important . . . They were tired of never getting promoted, and they
were tired of being treated

       like dogs

              by . . . White . . .

                          foremen . . .

Get work. Get (worked) over. Get up, get worked up, get working (together)
again.

               *

            Because the photo
       shows [Where]
              stairs [might] mean

       the door the next flight up's
         open*

---

*[except the factory's long since closed]

257.

Because the (brake) past is used because the tearing (past) of the (brick) form is used is used because the fence (in) of the (goddamn) frame is used is used is utterly used against us and by us and upon us and for us is used is used in the present (past) future (form) we are used yet users yet used.

Every day you put your life on the line when you went into that iron house. Every day you sucked up dirt and took a chance on breaking your legs or breaking your back. And anyone who's worked in there knows what I'm talking about.

*

-roads]

Closing

words   :

[Rail

I.

Capitalize the first word
of every sentence, whether or not
it is a complete sentence.
Capitalize the first word of every line
of poetry. **I started work**
on an assembly line
at the huge Westinghouse plant
in East Pittsburgh when I was sixteen.
The work was dull and repetitive.
From 1954 to 1962,
Ronald Reagan served as host
of the television program, "G.E. Theater."
In some modern English poetry forms,
only the first word of the first line
is capitalized, and sometimes
even this is written lower-case.
Six times a year he acted in the dramas
(once starring in a two-part program
as an FBI agent who infiltrates
Communist-front organizations).
We tried to make the time go
by talking to each other.
Capitalize *father* and *mother*
when used in address, but do not
capitalize such nouns
when a possessive pronoun
is used with them.
The remainder of the year
Reagan toured G.E. factories,
speaking to employees and local civic groups on,
as he put it in his autobiography,
"the attempted takeover of the [electrical] industry
by Communists" and "the swiftly rising tide

of collectivism that threatens to inundate
what remains of our free economy."
Sometimes I would fantasize,
making believe I was somewhere other
than at that long bench
with the never-ending noise,
the whining of machines.

9.

"I think [Reagan] forced the strike
so he could show big business that he can and will
beat up on union workers," said Thomas McNut,
president of UFCW Local 400 in Baltimore.
But as the benefits we gained grew,
those of us in the forefront
became targets for red-baiting.
Capitalize the names of organized bodies
and their adherents.
Capitalize Republicans. Shriners
Capitalize Socialists, Elks
They red-baited me.
They red-baited Charlie Newell
and those who represented
the left in our union.
"I get a strange feeling that our democracy
is seriously being challenged when
the administration says. 'Either you work
or we'll destroy you economically,'"
said David Wilson, director-elect
of District 8 of the United Steelworkers.
The only thing they had to throw at us
was that we were "Communists"
or that we were being led around
by the nose by Communists.
Usage differs as to the capitalization
of the word *party.*

the Communist Party
or the Communist party
The "red" label—
people were frightened by it.
From then on,
I don't think there was ever a time
when we weren't vilified by the press.
"Historically, when Americans
have been confronted with laws
that are unfair or unjust,
they have ignored them," Thomas Bradley,
president of the Maryland
and District AFL-CIO said.
"That's how the labor movement began."
It caused a real division in the union.
That's just what the company wanted.
You could not see
the hand of the company openly,
but somehow you knew
it was a hidden force.

17.

Any doubt remaining as to
the Reagan Administration's attitude
toward those who dared to defy it
was erased in March 1982.
A detailed questionnaire
from the Justice Department
arrived at the residence
of each former employee.
One time I was organizing the union.
Next I was selling eggs.
How did that happen?
The cover sheet stated the interrogatories
were for the "convenience" of those appellants
"who do not have counsel."

It also demanded that the interrogatories
"shall be answered under oath."
Therefore the appellant was required
to swear before a notary public
that his answers were complete.
I think it happened
because the left-wing movement
contributed so much
to the strength of the union.
That strength had to be dissipated.
A list of words and expressions
showing their generally accepted capitalization
follows. Note that some words
derived from proper nouns
have developed a special meaning;
these words are no longer capitalized.
American history
bologna sausage
boycott
English literature
poor whites
puritanical ethics
russian dressing
Russian olive
Statement No. 2
un-American
The phrasing of the first question
was particularly significant:
"Are you now, or have you ever been
a member of PATCO?"
Get rid of it. Get it out of here.
If the left could be isolated
out in the country somewhere,
selling eggs,
would there be any reason
to worry?
Would there?

05.25.2000

"The shutdown will mark the first closing of one of the Iron Range's behemoth taconite plants since the 1980s, when a brutal shakeout closed two of eight mines and cut employment in the industry from 16,000 to 6,000."

My stomach dropped to the floor. It was like my stomach was hit by a 10-ton brick. We knew for the last few years that things weren't the best, but we never expected this. It's just unbelievable.

The factory of my father [reduced to rubble] Factory [after factory (shut down)]. Seventeen stories. The blast furnace of my grandfather. The slaughterhouse across from the railroad [terminal] where my father's aunt used to work. Seventeen stories, and every single window shattered [shut up].

*

workers / words / worth / [repeating]

Iron : 21

12.07.2000–01.04.2001

"National Steel's former general manager, his wife and two consultants pleaded guilty in U.S. District Court [in Duluth] Wednesday to a scheme involving more than $240,000 in kickbacks, misappropriations and insurance fraud."

It sucks. It sucks. It sucks. But it's the same old story. You could see it coming for the last 10 years . . . They've already kicked you down to the ground, and now they keep kicking you in the head. I just want it to be over. It's devastating.

Strip mines frame strip malls "gains" as Capital claims its Local. The door [historical], the sometimes [seeming] impenetrable wall. But Luddites broke frames, hundreds of them. And the Range was once Wobbly, too.

*

Wal-Mart / wages / u.s.[w.]a. / away

Aurora : 262

POETICS STATEMENT

Notes toward an Anti-capitalist Poetics II

> "[D]eindustrialization is primarily a feature of successful economic development . . ."

IT IS not poetry that allows Robert Rowthorn (Ph.D., Oxford) and Ramana Ramaswamy (Ph.D., Cambridge) to pen phrases like this in *Economic Issues no. 10* (a 1997 publication of the International Monetary Fund), but it is a poetics. David Harvey has recently termed the scope of just such a poetics "accumulation by dispossession." Harvey makes a lot more sense to those of us who grew up in Detroit, in Youngstown, in Gary, in Buffalo.

The poetics Rowthorn and Ramaswamy project (their "projective verse," so to speak) jettisons the human cost and "the social mark" of factory closures, massive job loss, anomie, et al. Then again, my guess is that Rowthorn and Ramaswamy never lived on my grandfather's block.

The IMF's articulation of a poetics that disregards the vast majority of the people is not new. Ninety years ago in the Junius Pamphlet "The War and the Workers," for example, Rosa Luxemburg dubbed capitalism's dialectic "Dividends are rising, and the proletarians are falling." And as Michael Perelman asserts in *The Invention of Capitalism*, "we hear virtually nothing in classical political economy about the suffering of those who made possible the success of the market society." But the ways this poetics forms (produces) and particularly the ways it transforms (reproduces) are new. It is a poetics of "savage neoliberalism" (Hugo Chávez), market socialization, and the immense privatization of what should be "the commons" of us all (think water, think seeds) that seeks to further secure the stockpiles of Empire for the few (and, as Marx said in *Capital*: "Accumulation of capital is . . . multiplication of the proletariat"). And so when I read in the *New York Times* that Anna McCloy, the wife of the lone surviving miner at Sago, went to Wal-Mart (and the *Times* makes that free nod to advertisement as journalism) to purchase a boom box and a Metallica CD (and that one, too) in hopes of jarring her husband out of his coma, I am pained and furious and tender and embittered at so many (socio-economic, cultural, personal, et al.) levels that I barely know where to begin. And it is *writing*, my poetic praxis, where the disentangling and re-imagining that "Another World is Possible" begins.

In an essay I recently wrote for a symposium on the life and work of Adrienne Rich ("Notes toward an Anti-capitalist Poetics," *Virginia Quarterly Review*), I outlined the vast micro-mobilizations by organized labor and social movements against neoliberal policies and poetics during a single weekend in December 2005, and asked,

> Where are the poems in dialogue with these global people's movements? Where are the poems bridging and building transnational social and aesthetic networks of alternative and agitational modes of grammar and syntax, revolutionary poetic critiques of corporate culture (the contemporary complement to Muriel Rukeyser's *The Book of the Dead*)? Where are the poems (as the Zapatistas described their post-NAFTA *encuentro*) "for humanity and against neoliberalism"? I also want to be able to imagine a future for poetry, as Rich says in "Defying the Space that Separates," "not drawn from the headlines but able to resist the headlines." The questions poets need to be asking today are vital to us all: what is the relationship between a U.S.-controlled agenda for globalization (with Bush-crony Paul Wolfowitz as president of the World Bank) and the future of language and the imagination amidst ubiquitous privatization? Can the free market forces of the U.S. publishing industry (including the massive, almost exclusively non-unionized chain bookstores) and the vastly expanding U.S. model of creative writing production within the MFA industry produce anything other than neoliberal writers and neoliberal tracts? As the U.S. economy transitions from a modernist manufacturing economy to late capitalism's service economy, what would a service economy poetry

and poetics look like, and who among us is prepared to step forward and imagine it?

These are a few of the questions my poetics seeks to address, both through poetry and through on-the-ground organizing work in corporate bookstores and throughout working-class communities and anti-capitalist social movements (see <http://www.urww.org> for more details). And *writing*, something that is to me dialogue and dialectical materialism and documentary and drama all rolled into one, *writing* is my vehicle through which I form and inform (I want an echo of C. L. R. James's famous dictum from *Facing Reality* to ring through here: "Recognize and record." "People all over the world, and particularly ordinary working people in factories, mines, fields, and offices, are rebelling every day in ways of their own invention . . . Their strivings, their struggles, their methods have few chroniclers . . .")

Mine is a *writing* including history, including a bit of creative borrowing from Fred Wah's *Waiting for Saskatchewan* in "$00 / Line / Steel / Train"; a bit of the remix/sample/mash-up techniques from Afrika Bambaataa and Negativland and (ex post facto) DJ Danger Mouse in "Capitalization"; a bit of experimentation with Marxist base-superstructure as poetic form and documentary photography addressing the capitalistic functions of private property in "Hoyt Lakes / Shut Down"; and a bit of Matsuo Basho's *The Narrow Road to the Deep North (Oku no Hosomichi)* and Tillie Olsen's "I Want You Women Up North to Know" and Gwendolyn Brooks's "In the Mecca" and Ernesto Cardenal's *exteriorismo* throughout.

More importantly, post-compositionally (but also pre-composition-ally), these bits and *writings*, these disentanglings and re-imaginings and re-organizings *must* find a way to return to the communities of workers to whom and from whom and of whom they "recognize and record." And so my poetics, my way of making my writing world, my "form and inform," has included staged readings of "Capitalization" at a rally for striking Northwest Airlines mechanics (AMFA Local 33), a reading at the AFL-CIO's annual Labor Day picnic, writing workshops for unions at the Chicago Center for Working Class Studies, public presentations at the North American Labor History Conference in Detroit, a staged reading of another verse play from *Shut Up Shut Down* at the UAW 879 union hall in St. Paul (the women and men who produce the Ford Ranger and who, at the time of this writing, still live in the uncertain "purgatory" (as one local autoworker called it) of Ford's recently released "The Way Forward," a plan that will eliminate 30,000 jobs and close 14 plants by 2012 (on a Luxemburgian note: after the announcement, Ford shares rose 8% on the New York Stock Exchange)).*

*On April 13, 2006—several months after I wrote this poetics statement—Ford announced it would be closing its St. Paul, Minnesota, assembly plant in 2008, ending Ford's 81-year history in the city. 1,900 workers will lose their jobs.

Rowthorn and Ramaswamy's poetics statement concludes that "[d]ein-dustrialization is not a negative phenomenon, but a natural consequence of further growth in advanced economies"—i.e., a further growth in the largely low-wage service sector. They also posit that

> [i]n a service-based economy with fast-changing market conditions, it seems difficult to imagine that a centralized, union-based system will be able to make decisions on appropriate wage differentials. To persist with centralized wage bargaining could, therefore, have adverse consequences for the growth of productivity.

This is not the factual data of political economists, but the dystopian telos of a neoliberal poetics, a "projective verse" of the IMF that Pierre Bourdieu has aptly reframed as a transition from the *economic project of neoliberalization* (deregulation, currency devaluations, privatization of state-owned industries, etcetera) to a more threatening and all-encompassing *political project of neoliberalization* whose goal is nothing less than the methodological elimination and destruction of even the possibility of collective action ("The essence of neoliberalism," 1998). It is the dream (aka nightmare) poetics of "free" capital in a "free" market (see NAFTA, see DR-CAFTA, see FTAA) of "free" workers (temporary, non-unionized, underemployed) in a "free" society (where everything, someday maybe even breathing itself, will become a market transaction). And this is the hegemonic new poetics each of us faces each and every day, whether we acknowledge it or not, when we begin to put words on the page. And, as poets at the very center of Empire, it is our responsibility to respond, to "form and inform," and, borrowing the words from Adrienne Rich, the reason we must write as if our lives depended on it.

MARK NOWAK

Radical Documentary Praxis [Redux]

David Ray Vance

> As capitalism's ever-intensifying imposition of alienation at all levels
> makes it increasingly hard for workers to recognize and name their
> own impoverishment, and eventually puts them in the position
> of having either to reject it in its totality or do nothing at all, the
> revolutionary organization must learn that it can no longer *combat
> alienation by means of alienated forms of struggle*. . . . The proletarian
> revolution is predicated entirely on the requirement that, for the first
> time, theory as the understanding of human practice be recognized
> and directly lived by the masses. This revolution demands that
> workers become dialecticians, and inscribe their thought upon
> practice.   —Guy Debord

MARK NOWAK'S two published volumes of poetry, *Revenants* and *Shut Up
Shut Down*, are brazenly anticapitalist, which in present-day America marks
them as not only radical but potentially heretical.[1] For most Americans the
dissolution of the Soviet Union proved two things unequivocally: (1) that
democracy is superior to communism, and (2) that free market economies
(those subjected to the least possible government restriction) are our only
real hope for assuring economic stability and prosperity at home and across
the globe. Indeed, most Americans have come to view democracy and free
market capitalism as mutually dependent if not synonymous, and, like Mar-
garet Thatcher, most operate from the presumption that "There is no alter-
native."[2]

In her 1997 essay "Why I Refused the National Medal for the Arts," Adri-
enne Rich decried what she saw as the closing down of public discourse
given the broad acceptance of this neoliberal dogma:

> many of us today might wish to hold government accountable, to challenge
> the agendas of private power and wealth that have displaced historical ten-
> dencies toward genuinely representative government in the United States. We
> might still wish to claim our government, to say, *This belongs to us*—we, the
> people, as we are now. . . . We would have to start asking questions that have
> been defined as nonquestions—or as naïve, childish questions. . . . We would
> need to perform an autopsy on capitalism itself.[3]

Two and a half years after Rich penned this critique, an estimated forty thou-
sand people took to the streets of Seattle to protest the policies of the World

Trade Organization, an event that inaugurated subsequent protests against the International Monetary Fund and the World Bank, marking the beginning of what is still a growing antiglobalization/global justice movement.[4] Despite this growing movement, political poetry in America continues to locate itself primarily within the dominant paradigm rather than outside it. That is to say that most political poetry—what there is of it—targets specific governmental administrations and their policies and attitudes rather than the overarching economic ideology and practice that, more and more, explain why these administrations continue to hold power despite their obvious (and fundamentally interchangeable) shortcomings.[5] As Nowak himself points out, "it's embarrassingly difficult to locate poetry (much less a poetics) in U.S.-based literary journals that addresses, engages, and critiques the policies and practices of American empire, neoliberalism, and globalization."[6]

For his own part, Nowak insists on pressing these crucial "nonquestions." For him, there is no distinction between the political and the poetic, a point he makes in "Notes Toward an Anti-Capitalist Poetics II," where he contends that economic theory is but another imaginative act, another way of forming the world via language, therefore constituting a poetic as much as a politic. Moreover, for Nowak poetry is inextricable from the political contexts that limit or otherwise make it possible. Whereas Laura Bush would have us believe it is "inappropriate to turn a literary event into a political forum," Nowak understands that every literary event—every opportunity we take to formulate language, written or otherwise—is politically fraught.[7]

Operating out of this understanding, Nowak joins with others on the fore of the global justice movement to contest two principle neoliberal presumptions. First, that workers' interests—a living wage, education and health care, safe work conditions, clean air and clean water—are "special interests" (read: selfish, self-serving, harmful). Second, that the interests of powerful corporations—profits—are the interests of our nation and the world (read: altruistic, generous, for the greater good). To counter such characterizations and perceptions, Nowak undertakes a documentary praxis that situates these conflicting interests in a more inclusive context, one that acknowledges and accounts for the suffering workers under capitalism endure in the name of safeguarding an economic stability (not to mention prosperity) from which they are themselves excluded. In the process, Nowak forgoes the commonplace tactic of asserting truth claims or otherwise proffering arguments. Instead, by way of his documentary praxis, he constructs a multivalent dialectic that invites readers to inquire critically into the ways capitalism "forms and informs" identity (personal and cultural) and our sense of what is possible in the world.[8]

For students of poetry, Nowak's documentary praxis is certainly not unprecedented. Documentary poetics traces back to early Modernism, most famously in Pound's *Cantos* and Eliot's *The Wasteland*. It is out of this tradition we get Williams's *Patterson*, Olson's *Maximus*, and eventually what comes to be known as the "Poetry of Witness." While poetry has always exhibited a documentary capacity, as numerous scholars have pointed out (William Stott foremost among them), documentary as a genre burst onto the American cultural scene in the 1930s, a seemingly inevitable response to the harsh realities so many people experienced during the Great Depression.[9] In that period, there developed a widespread interest in documenting life, in not only capturing for posterity photographic images and written testimony recounting human experiencing, but also in collecting data of almost every imaginable variety. Documentary's emphasis on evidence and fact spoke to the skepticism that understandably permeated that age.

In his essay "Notes Toward an Anti-Capitalist Poetics," Nowak identifies two poets born of this depression-era tradition that he considers relevant to his own poetic practice: Tillie Olsen and Muriel Rukeyser. Speaking of her poem "I Want You Women Up North To Know" (1934), Nowak credits Olsen with having "employed nearly post-modern techniques of narrative and sampling . . . to produce an early feminist anti-sweatshop poem." In this poem, Olsen borrows liberally from an editorial letter Felipe Ibarro contributed to the *New Masses* in 1934, a letter that lambastes the impoverished living and working conditions of poor workers in the South and accuses northerners who buy the goods these workers produce of profiting on human misery.[10] Like Olsen, Nowak's subject is primarily the plight of workers, and like Olsen he borrows liberally from source materials in constructing his poems. But whereas Olsen uses Ibarro's text only as a springboard for her poem, borrowing less and less of Ibarro's actual phrasing as the poem progresses, Nowak's tendency is to highlight his sources as sources; he doesn't subsume them into his text so much as maintain them as distinct components. He accomplishes this in part by taking pains to structure his poems so that source materials remain identifiable as such and also by habitually providing a thorough bibliography of sources for each poem.[11] Whereas Olsen adapts text from a single documentary source, Nowak always presents his sources in relation to other sources, further emphasizing their textuality.[12]

With its concern for corporate exploitation of workers and its rather more expansive use of documentary sources, Rukeyser's *The Book of the Dead* arguably offers an even more vital, more significant precedent for Nowak's documentary praxis than does Olsen's poem.[13] This text is indicative of the larger trend toward documentary in the 1930s and, as poetry goes, one of the most significant accomplishments to come out of that tradition. Interestingly, Nowak's "Notes Toward an Anti-Capitalist Poetics" was written for a *Virginia Quarterly Review* symposium on Adrienne Rich, herself a staunch advocate of Rukeyser's work; in that essay Nowak not only chastises contemporary poetry for failing to critique corporate culture, but by way of a solution suggests that what is needed is "the contemporary complement to Muriel Rukeyser's *The Book of the Dead*." Nowak's work, it seems clear, is intended to fill that need, to be that contemporary complement.

The commonalities that unite Nowak's and Rukeyser's poetries are readily apparent. Both take as their subject the plight of workers at the hands of capital. Nowak chronicles the suffering that workers (and their families and communities) have endured as a result of the wholesale deindustrialization of what became known as the Rust Belt at the end of the twentieth century, while Rukeyser chronicles what is referred to as the Hawk's Nest Mining Disaster (also called the Gaulley Bridge Tragedy), in which an estimated seven hundred to two thousand workers died (many after years of prolonged suffering) from acute silicosis after mine operators compelled them to work in what were known to be deadly conditions. Both writers accuse corporations of heartlessly exploiting workers and of showing an utter disregard for their lives. Furthermore, both situate these accusations in the larger socioeconomic scheme that is capitalism such that the government is implicated as well. Finally, and most important, both construct their poetry from personal testimonies, newspaper reports, and other forms of historical and personal documentation. In effect, Nowak adapts and updates Rukeyser's documentary approach to serve his purposes and his times. Arguably what most distinguishes Nowak's poetry from Rukeyser's is his rather more skeptical attitude toward language/text as a medium for encapsulating and communicating meaning, an attitude informed by recent cultural theory and very much of our postmodern historical moment.

To clarify what I mean when I refer to Nowak's documentary praxis, I would offer as a fairly typical example the opening section of "Capitalization," a poem sequence from Nowak's second volume, *Shut Up Shut Down*:

> Capitalize the first word
> of every sentence, whether or not
> it is a complete sentence.
> Capitalize the first word of every line
> of poetry. **I started work**
> **on an assembly line**
> **at the huge Westinghouse plant**
> **in East Pittsburgh when I was sixteen.**
> **The work was dull and repetitive.**
> *From 1954 to 1962.*
> *Ronald Reagan served as host*
> *of the television program, "G.E. Theater."*
> In some modern English poetry forms,
> only the first word of the first line
> is capitalized, and sometimes
> even this is written lower-case.

> *Six times a year he acted in the dramas*
> *(once starring in a two-part program*
> *as an agent who infiltrates*
> *Communist-front organizations).*

In these opening lines Nowak establishes the poem's three central frames of reference, or what I term *documentary frames* as each is constructed from a different text or set of texts. The first of these is taken verbatim from Margaret Shertzer's catalogue of the conventions governing capital letter usage in her Reagan-era text *The Elements of Grammar*. Next, in bold print, a first-person account from an unnamed worker; the source of this testimony isn't immediately apparent, but it is in fact taken from Bud and Ruth Schultz's *The Price of Dissent: Testimonies to Political Repression in America*. Last, in italics, an account of Ronald Reagan's early career taken from Christopher Matthew's *New Republic* article "Your Host, Ronald Reagan: From G.E. Theater to the Desk in the Oval Office." Altogether, the poem consists of seventeen separate numbered sections, most all of them spanning at least a page although quite a few are substantially longer. In total, Nowak lists some fifteen separate sources in the bibliography to the poem. These sources range from newspapers and magazine articles from the *Washington Post*, the *New York Times*, *The Economist*, the *New Republic*, to scholarly books published by various university presses, such as Ronald W. Schatz's *The Electrical Workers: A History of Labor at General Electric and Westinghouse, 1923–1960* (University of Illionis Press, 1983).

The poem then "forms and informs" the readers' understanding by alternating and juxtaposing these documentary frames to draw out their interrelatedness—an interrelatedness that the poet has discovered and/or created but which he doesn't assert or state so much as stage. To begin, excerpts from Shertzer's rules of capitalization appear in each and every section of the poem. The process is cumulative, but as we encounter rule after rule in the contexts that Nowak has us encounter them, we become cognizant of their arbitrariness and find ourselves entertaining questions schoolchildren (or second-language learners?) might ask on first being introduced to the concept of capitalizing words: "Who makes these rules? Why these rules and not others? Are we really obliged to go along with this?" We're reminded that inherent in formal convention is a presumption that uniformity is preferable, that we should want everyone to do certain things certain ways.[14] We also come to recognize that the conventions governing capitalization belie a penchant for hierarchy. After all, capitalization in the grammatical sense of the term is essentially a way of privileging certain words and phrases (and by extension hierarchy itself) by affording to them distinction not granted the rabble that is the "uncapitalized."

Obviously, the term "capitalization" does double duty, referring to both the grammatical convention and the introduction of capital (or capitalism) into a system. By virtue of this apposition, the poem opens up the possibility that capitalism (our decision to capitalize) is no less arbitrary and subjective than the rules that govern which letters of which words are placed in uppercase, and that our decision to remain capitalized is similarly conventional and similarly motivated by a penchant for hierarchy—thus the class system. And if capitalism is merely a convention, something people agree to do and maintain as a matter of convenience, then presumably they could collectively choose to do something else, instead. And so the poem invites us to consider the alternatives.

This interrogation of economic capitalism (vis-à-vis grammatical capitalization) then informs our reading of the second documentary frame, which recounts one woman's testimony regarding her experience helping unionize her fellow Westinghouse employees in the 1930s.[15] We learn that after initially succeeding in their efforts, she and her fellow union leaders were accused of being communists, were investigated by the FBI, and were eventually fired from their jobs. This testimony affords us a first-person perspective on the rise and fall of labor unions in twentieth-century America, starting with a period of union expansion immediately after the Great Depression and ending with a period of contraction in the 1950s when McCarthy essentially charged them with being communist fronts and therefore un-American at their core.[16] While this woman's testimony, like all testimony, is necessarily subjective, and while further investigation and scrutiny would be required to gauge its veracity, it behooves us nevertheless to consider the role government may have played in defaming unions and in ultimately weakening their influence in this country. More important, this testimony forms the emotional center of the poem. The suffering this woman endures as a result of her involvement in the union, her sense of being harassed and maligned, gives a human dimension to this economic theorizing and historicizing. In her nameless humanity, she reminds us that the working class is made up of individuals, actual human beings.

This brings us finally to the third documentary frame in the poem, Ronald Reagan. The materials that constitute this frame can be categorized into two parts: (a) reportage about Reagan's work for General Electric before he became president, (b) reportage concerning the part he played in breaking the Professional Air Traffic Controllers' Organization (PATCO) strike in the early 1980s after he became president. While for many Americans this strike was just a blip on the screen, in terms of labor history it marks a critical watershed event. Indeed, it has been argued that the Reagan administration's tough stance against the PATCO strikers ushered in a new era of union busting.[17]

The reportage we get concerning Reagan ultimately invites us to consider how his career before becoming president likely influenced or otherwise predicted the role he would play in breaking the PATCO strike. It further asks us to consider the role big business plays in our democratic system. Reagan was not, after all, a mere employee of G.E.; rather, he was its spokesperson, its representative, the mouthpiece by which its corporate ideology and agenda (including its antiunion propaganda) could be communicated to the country as a whole. Reagan's decision to break the PATCO strike is then potentially indicative of a more pernicious trend, namely, the takeover of government by big business. This trend is especially provocative given neoliberal ideologues that advocate minimal governmental interference in the economic system. Yet, as Reagan exemplifies, government can and does take sides in the conflicts that arise between labor and capital, which certainly constitutes interference so far as labor is one of the market forces that determine capital's course. Finally, this depiction of capitalism as a convention imposed by business interests by way of government influence then calls into question the neoliberal conception of capitalism as the sole survivor of a process of evolutionary social selection and therefore a kind of manifest destiny.

This poem is fairly typical of the way Nowak layers and juxtaposes documentary frames of this sort in his poems. By way of this process, he creates for his readers a multivalent dialectic that doesn't assert claims so much as invite inquiry; the documentary nature of his materials then locates this inquiry in the real world. In this poem, for example, Nowak provides his readers occasion to consider that economic capitalism is finally a historical development, a convention that is the result of human endeavors and interactions, of decisions made by those who have the power to make such decisions, and one that has serious consequences in terms of the quality of life workers experience. But again, this isn't an assertion that Nowak makes, only an inference that his dialectic occasions. Nowak suggests these frames are interrelated or interrelatable by virtue of including them, but it is finally left to the reader to decide how they relate. Remarkably, what Nowak develops by way of this documentary praxis is a didactic poetry that resists being prescriptive, a welcome alternative to the sort of harangue and rant that commonly characterizes political verse.

Interestingly, one of the most significant and most contemporizing influences on Nowak's documentary praxis has been the development of "sampling" in hip-hop and rap music.[18] As Nowak himself puts it, "Afrika Bambattaa and Jam Master Jay taught me to 'sample' long before Ezra Pound did."[19] "Sampling" describes the practice of culling audio tracks from professional recordings—often very recognizable segments, including signature melodies, bass lines, drum tracks, and what have you—and layering them together to create new music. This is the term Nowak uses to describe Olsen's "postmodern technique"; it is also the term he uses to describe his own methods of incorporating textual sources.

Nowak's identification with hip-hop is significant not only for the way it lays claim to a contemporaneous quality for his poetic, suggesting by association that poetry might have a similar potential for social impact and significance, but also for how it reaffirms Nowak's anticapitalist position. Hip-hop began as an antiestablishment, predominantly black, urban, working-class movement, and rappers and hip-hop artists developed sampling primarily as a means to overcome their economic limitations as producers. The practice was, in its origins at least, expressly anticapitalist. In treating all things recorded as being in the public domain, it embodied a willful disregard for copyright. Not surprisingly, sampling as a result became a site of struggle between the rights of corporations and the rights of citizens. Record companies, having a vested interest in (and/or seeing opportunity to profit by) asserting their copyrights, filed lawsuits against artists who sampled their recordings. In turn, the courts have handed down a series of disturbing rulings that essentially eliminated the "fair use" doctrine. This means that artists are legally obliged to secure (that is, purchase) copyright permission even for samples that the court agrees are not immediately identifiable. Were these same rulings applied to written texts, one imagines Nowak's poetry, with its extensive dependence on source materials, might go the way of DJ Danger Mouse's *Grey Album*, which was forced from the market and cannot be purchased (or distributed) legally.

Nowak's use of the term "sampling" also speaks to the way he conceives of documents as sources and obviously informs his perceptions of how they might be made to interact or otherwise speak to one another. While the brief excerpt we looked at from "Capitalization" is suggestive of the way Nowak opens up meaning by juxtaposing and layering sources, it doesn't begin to suggest the variety of forms he engages in his books or the linguistic depth and deftness he displays. Consider, for example, the following lines from section 9 of Nowak's poem "June 19, 1982":

> pushed the frame
> named names
>
> depression repression
> the song the same remains
>
> "Drive your Chevrolet
> through the U.S.A.
>
> America's the greatest
> land of all."
>
> stolen stereo types
> discriminatory democracy

> participatory
> plutocracy
>
> windows replaced
> by the wind
>
> begin
> shattering

We register hip-hop's stylistic influence in these lines, especially in the way the sampled Chevrolet jingle is "mashed-up" or enjambed in order to explode meaning (land stolen / stolen (car?) stereo / stereotype). Similarly, the nod to the Led Zepplin song "The Song Remains the Same" adds yet another layer of reference to the poem, further extending its semantic play. The effect is ironic, so that the jingle becomes itself a subject commented upon by its new context. Additionally, there are the hard rhymes, sprung rhythms and break-beats that characterized so much early rap music, as well as a similar proclivity for recycling the formulaic and familiar to revitalize and make something new of them, a proclivity that can also be conceptualized as a resistance to closure; that is, the presumption that a single artwork can thoroughly encapsulate its subject or otherwise be complete in and of itself.

"June 19, 1982" also offers a ready example of the way Nowak, long-time editor of *XCP: Cross Cultural Poetics* since 1997, uses his documentary praxis to interrogate notions of identity and culture as they have been expounded upon in recent literary and social theory. The poem's title signifies the date that Ronald Ebens and his stepson, Michael Nitz, both white autoworkers (although Nitz had recently been laid off from his job), fatally beat Vincent Chin with a baseball bat.[20] Chin was twenty-seven years old and was attending his bachelor party at a strip club in Detroit when he and Ebens had an altercation. The men came to blows, were ejected from the bar, and then took the fight outside. When Ebens pulled a bat from his car, Chin and his two friends ran. Sometime later (some estimate as much as a half hour had elapsed), Ebens and Nitz caught up with Chin at a nearby McDonalds. Nitz reportedly held Chin down while Ebens used his bat to hit him no fewer than four times in the head and at full force. By all accounts, the anger that led to violence was fueled by Ebens's mistaken belief that Chin was Japanese and that he, therefore, shared in responsibility for the economic hardships autoworkers were experiencing with the downturn in the American auto industry. Witnesses reported Ebens as having said "It's because of you little motherfuckers that we're out of work." As it happens, Chin was Chinese-American, not Japanese. Moreover, he too was an American auto industry worker, a draftsman. Needless to say, Chin's murder highlights the ways identity (and mistaken identity) have real stakes in the world. As feminist critics have long argued, the personal is political.

Altogether, "June 19, 1982" has twelve sections, each comprising four distinct frames. First, in italics, a prose section offering etymological information about the term *employment* or *unemployment*; this text is taken verbatim from Raymond Williams's *Keywords: A Vocabulary of Culture and Society* (Oxford University Press, 1985). Next, in bold text, a first-person self-description that sounds remarkably like what we'd expect to read in a psychological battery test for depression. In fact, this language is taken verbatim from a survey given laid-off steelworkers and reprinted in *Shutdown in Youngstown: Public Policy for Mass Unemployment* (Albany: State University of New York Press, 1983). Following these two parts (both prose paragraphs), the poem ends with right-justified couplets that lyrically delve into the specifics of Vincent Chin's tragic story and to the circumstances that gave rise to that tragedy. Finally, each section includes a photograph on the facing page taken by Nowak. These photographs are all architectural and all give some depiction or another of urban decay. Having already considered the lyric portion of section 9, let's now take up the two prose sections that precede it.

The interaction with idle is particularly interesting. The wide sense, in application to people, can be illustrated from c. 1450: 'To devocionne ever and Contempalcionne / Was sho given and nevre ydel." But in an act of 1530–1 we find the characteristic 'to arrest the side vacaboundes and ydell persones'.

Most of the time I feel blue. I feel like giving up quickly when things go wrong. Things are so bad that I feel as though life is hardly worth living. I am often worried about possible dangers that I cannot control. I am often tempted to give up trying to solve my problems

Both of these prose paragraphs rehearse identity. The first is concerned with the way identity is imposed from outside by social and/or cultural circumstances. The emphasis on etymology reminds us that unemployment is a socially contrived concept, albeit one that has become (at least in our capitalist society) a central defining factor in how we conceptualize ourselves. The second section is then concerned with the interior, emotional being, the psychological state that is symptomatic of a particular self-conception. Of course, we can't help noting the interrelatedness between these two conceptions, such that economic depression causing (or caused by) unemployment gives rise to emotional depression.

Formally speaking, this poem is a loose adaptation of Haibun, a Japanese form in which vivid prose is followed by haiku (often in series) or a short lyric. Nowak takes up this form in three of the five poems in *Shut Up Shut Down*. As Michael Davidson explains, Haibun is particularly suited to Nowak's project: "In Marxist terms, the relationship of prose to poetry replicates the classic division between superstructure and base, between narrative representation of 'real conditions' and the economic realities sustained by (or interpreted through) those representations."[21] Thus, Chin's murder is the result of the economic reality made possible by representation of that reality. Of course, this doesn't in the least justify the actions of the men who killed Chin. It does, however, give their actions context, and forces to the fore the conditions of identity that give rise to hatred, outwardly and inwardly directed, making violence of this sort not just possible, but probable.

Nowak's interrogations of language in this poem—the etymological concerns in the first prose section and the "mash-up" techniques he incorporates in the lyrical section—are indicative of postmodern skepticisms about language as medium for constructing and communicating meaning. It has traditionally been understood that political poetry, poetry that means to motivate public action on the part of its readers, must be transparent. That is, it must present its ideas in a manner directly accessible by the reader, and it must say what it means. But, as Charles Bernstein and others have argued, transparency of this sort is an illusion.[22] Language is itself a formulation inculcated in hegemonic power structures. For a poet intent on writing a poetry that has political influence, practical questions arise as to how this might be accomplished without further reifying the power structures that are already, and necessarily, inscribed in the language. In other words, how is one to construct a poetry that, as Bernstein puts it, "emphasizes its medium as being constructed, rule governed, everywhere circumscribed by grammar & syntax, chosen vocabulary" (41) without undercutting one's own ability to speak out about the world?

Nowak's documentary praxis affords a solution of sorts to this dilemma, or at least a work-around. For starters, as we've already discussed, Nowak doesn't assert claims so much as stage for the reader a dialectic that invites inquiry. As a result, Nowak doesn't claim the sort of authority that presumes language might function transparently. To the contrary, by calling attention to his source materials, Nowak invites us to consider and question his role in constructing these texts. We can't help wondering what he may have excluded and why. His praxis, in other words, doesn't invite us to conceive of a singular, totalizing viewpoint, or what might be called absolute truth. For example, while Nowak's poetry very much insists that we acknowledge the ways in which workers suffer under capitalism, he resists the binaristic thinking that would allow victimization to stand as a singular, defining characteristic. We see this, for example, in "$00 / Line / Steel / Train," where Nowak explains:

Because the (brake) past is used because the tearing (past) of the (brick)
form is used is used is used because the fence (in) of the (goddamn) frame
is used   is used is utterly used against us by us and upon us and for us is

used   is used in the present (past) future (form) we are used yet users yet
used.

This passage insists upon workers' agency. They are acted upon but they also, simultaneously, act. To attend to one or the other is to formulate a frame of reference, but only one. Furthermore, the run-on nature of this passage combined with disruptive parenthetical interjections demands that we acknowledge language as constructed, as other than transparent, and thereby calls upon us to be cognizant of the part we take in constructing meaning from such language.

Nowak incorporates photographic materials into his poems to much the same purpose. Whereas photographs might be expected to stand in for (or represent) the real world as such, by way of Nowak's documentary praxis our attention is constantly drawn to the way knowledge, experience, and understanding are necessarily framed and necessarily limited. Nowak includes photographs to this purpose in both *Revenants* and *Shut Up Shut Down*. In *Revenants*, each section of "Back Me Up" includes a photo on the facing page. These are all architectural photographs depicting neighborhood meeting spots, including a number of taverns, a bowling alley, a liquor store. And yet, none of the photographs is populated with actual persons. *Revenants* is primarily a book about loss: the loss immigrants experience leaving their homes to seek a better life elsewhere, the loss their children experience of a homeland that they've never seen and the mother tongue they don't quite possess, the loss parents and children alike experience as traditional practices are set aside and eventually forgotten, and finally the loss endured when economic upheaval leads to yet another wave of immigration and/or emigration. In depicting what were presumably at one time vibrant social places now hauntingly emptied of people, these photographs emphasize this sense of loss; they point us to what they don't contain as much as what they do. Moreover, Nowak deliberately draws attention to his own part in constructing these photographs, as when he tells us in one case, "We shot this photo / from the parking lot / of a car wash." He further stresses that the photograph as a document is necessarily limited when he tells us, for example, "My father, in his silver / Oldsmobile Acheiva / is just outside this frame."

The images in *Shut Up Shut Down* are also primarily architectural, although some are technically landscapes, and like the photographs in *Revenants*, they are conspicuously devoid of people.[23] In the poem "$oo / Line / Steel / Train," Nowak doesn't actually include images, but each section is titled with a number that refers to a photograph in Bernd and Hilla Becher's 1995 collection *Industrial Façades* (Cambridge, Mass.: MIT Press). The Becher photographs depict various factory buildings, most of them nearly indistinguishable from one another. They are all more or less square and squat, and give little or no indication as to their actual purpose. And all of them are (again like Nowak's photographs) devoid of people. In addition to drawing our attention to the ubiquity of industry and the way it formulates an aesthetic that is seemingly unconcerned with people, by referencing the Becher photographs, Nowak further emphasizes that all documents, including photographs and including his own poems, are always incomplete. There is always something left out, excluded.

The photographs contained in "Hoyt Lakes / Shut Down" function much the same way. This poem takes as its subject the closing down of industry in the Rust Belt and its consequences for the people who live in those communities. The photos contained in this poem are populated with closed fences, gates and doors, closed businesses, and No Trespassing signs. Thematically, then, these images literally depict these communities as being shut up, shut down, and ultimately shut out. But the sense of exclusion extends to the photographs themselves, as well. Simply put, we don't know where the gates and doors are located exactly, or where they lead or used to lead. We don't know finally what it is that is being referenced. We are confronted again and again by the fact that we are shut out of the photographs, that we don't have all the information we should need to determine how, or to what degree, they represent the world.

Ironically, Nowak's use of textual documentation reinforces this sense that we're not getting the whole story, so to speak. Nowak provides extensive bibliographies for each of his poems, yet he doesn't actually indicate for us which materials are derived from which texts. In some cases we can surmise that a given excerpt comes from some specific source listed in the bibliography; in most cases, however, short of doing the legwork of tracking down the original sources, we simply can't know. In this way, the bibliographies acknowledge that these poems are themselves but documents to be skeptically engaged. Furthermore, they remind us that there is more material in the world to consider, that there is indeed a world beyond that which the poems frame. By presenting his readers a dialectical space that doesn't assert meaning but rather occasions it, Nowak simultaneously models and invites the sort of skeptical inquiry he would have us take into that world.

Nowak ends *Shut Up Shut Down* with an all-important call for action in the form of a note from the author which reads:

> If you believe that the bookstore worker who ordered this book from the distributor, placed it on the shelf, rang up your order at the cash register, etc., deserves a living wage, affordable health care, and a voice in the workplace, and you're interested in helping your community's bookstore workers organize for these workplace rights and benefits, please contact the author via the Union of Radical Workers and Writers (URWW) at, http://www.urww.org"[24]

This statement is remarkable not only because it is indicative of Nowak's approach throughout his two published volumes (the two conditionals asking for a conscious evaluation and decision), but also for the way it acknowledges the book itself as materially part of the economic system. Nowak's publisher, Coffee House Press, is a nonprofit entity, but its books enter into the marketplace all the same. And here, as elsewhere, Nowak models for us a form of self-identification that refuses finally to be limited to self-interest. Nowak is not a bookstore worker, yet here takes action to help secure equitable pay for bookstore workers. By way of this act, he defies capitalism's premise that only self-interest can (or should) motivate us to act. Indeed, as a writer, a producer of this product, his self-interests would seem to lie entirely elsewhere. To my way of thinking, Nowak's documentary praxis—in its refusal to concede to such neoliberal ideology, and in its refusal to be either shut up or shut down—performs a much-needed angioplasty on the clotted arteries of American public discourse, clearing way for a more voluminous circulation of ideas and (it is hoped) for a long overdue reconnection with what it means to have a (working) heart.

NOTES

1. Mark Nowak, *Revenants* (Minneapolis, Minn.: Coffee House Press, 2000); and *Shut Up, Shut Down*, with an afterword by Amiri Baraka (Minneapolis, Minn.: Coffee House Press, 2004).

2. See David Harvey, *A Brief History of Neoliberalism* (New York: Oxford University Press, 2005).

3. Adrienne Rich, *Arts of the Possible: Essays and Conversations* (New York: Norton, 2001), 101.

4. See Janet Thomas, *The Battle in Seattle: The Story Behind the WTO Demonstrations* (Golden, Colo.: Fulcrum Press, 2000).

5. The website anthology *Poets Against the War*—however much one may admire its purpose and laud its insistence that poets have a social responsibility to fulfill—more or less exemplifies this tendency. Obviously Language poetry represents something of an exception to this tendency insofar as it utilizes syntactic and semantic disruptions to uncover and critique the ways language itself reifies hegemonic power. Unfortunately, while its originators (and many of their inheritors) are and were very much politically engaged by way of this poetic, faddish imitators have misconstrued Bruce Andrews's call for "writing as politics, not writing about politics" such that much of what passes for Language poetry these days is politically disengaged, especially insofar as linguistic disruptions for their own sake do little to challenge the status quo, the more such disruptions become normalized, expected, fashionable; see Bruce Andrews, "Poetry as Explanation, Poetry as Praxis," in *The Politics of Poetic Form: Poetry and Public Policy*, ed. Charles Bernstein (New York: Roof Books, 1998).

6. Mark Nowak, "Notes toward an Anti-Capitalist Poetics," *Virginia Quarterly Review* 82, no. 2 (Spring 2006): 236–40.

7. Such was the first lady's justification for "indefinitely postponing" (doublespeak for "canceling") a 2003 scheduled White House event to celebrate poetry when she

became aware that a number of invited poets intended to use the forum to protest the Bush administration's war in Iraq; see John Nichols, "Poetic Protests Against War, Censorship," *The Nation* (February 4, 2003).

8. My use of the term *dialectic* is, of course, intended to acknowledge that Nowak's poetic is very much allied with the tradition of dialectical materialism as developed out of the writings of Marx and Engels (vis-à-vis Hegel). See Fredric Jameson, *Marxism and Form: Twentieth-Century Dialectical Theories of Literature* (Princeton: Princeton University Press, 1971). "Forms and informs" is Nowak's phrasing. See Nowak's "Poetics Statement," in this volume.

9. William Stott, *Documentary Expression and Thirties America* (New York: Oxford University Press, 1973). Also see Michael Denning, *The Cultural Front: The Laboring of American Culture in the Twentieth Century* (New York: Verso, 1998).

10. Tillie Olsen, "I Want You Women Up North to Know" (poem), in the *Anthology of Modern American Poetry* (Oxford University Press, 2000). See also Felipe Ibarro, "Where the Sun Spends the Winter: San Antonio, Texas," in *New Masses* (1934); reprinted at http://www.english.uiuc.edu/maps/poets/m_r/olsen/ibarro.htm.

11. Space limitations prevent including the bibliographies in this volume. They are available in the published version of *Shut Up Shut Down* (Minneapolis, Minn.: Coffee House Press, 2003).

12. It is in this sense that I mean to say the dialectic he constructs for his reader is multivalent; always there is more than one source to be accounted for and contextualized by the reader.

13. Muriel Rukeyser, *The Collected Poems* (Pittsburgh: University of Pittsburgh Press, 2005). See also Tom Dayton, *Muriel Rukeyser's Book of the Dead* (Columbia: University of Missouri Press, 2003).

14. As Charles Bernstein points out, the stakes are high when it comes to these conventions. "It's a question of who controls reality. . . . Prescribed rules of grammar & spelling make language seem outside of our control. & a language, even only seemingly, wrested from our control is a world taken from us"; *Content's Dream: Essays 1975–1984*. (Evanston, Ill.: Northwestern University Press, 2001).

15. Nowak's father was a union vice president at the Westinghouse factory in Buffalo, New York, for more than a dozen years, which no doubt helps explain his interest in unions in general and in the history of unions at Westinghouse in particular.

16. See Ellen Schrecker, *Many Are the Crimes: McCarthyism in America* (Princeton: Princeton University Press, 1999).

17. The notion is fairly commonplace although not without its detractors. Using statistical modeling, Traynor and Fichtenbaum concluded that there is "strong evidence that the replacement of striking PATCO members in 1981 was a watershed event in the history of U.S. labor relations." See Thomas L. Traynor and Ruby H. Fichtenbaum, "The Impact of Post-PATCO Labor Relations on U.S. Union Wages," *Eastern Economic Journal* 23, no. 1 (Winter 1997): 61–72.

18. See Jeff Chang, *Can't Stop Won't Stop: A History of the Hip-Hop Generation* (New York: Picador, 2006).

19. Nowak names a host of other artists who have influenced his approach (not all of them associated with hip-hop or early rap), including DJ Danger Mouse, the

Clash, Kraftwerk and Negativland. The quotation is from Piers Hugill's "Class War in the Rust Belt," *Jacket Magazine* 28 (2005): online.

20. I've culled details of the case from Reynolds Farley and Judy Mullin, "Detroit: The History and Future of the Motor City" at http://detroit1701.org/Detroit_Homepage.html (accessed April 20, 2006). Nowak also cites Christine Choy and Renee Tajima, *Who Killed Vincent Chin?* (New York: Filmmakers Library, 1998).

21. Michael Davidson, "On the Outskirts of Form: Cosmopoetics in the Shadow of NAFTA" (unpublished book chapter, September 7, 2005).

22. Bernstein, *Content's Dream*, 70.

23. None of the photographs Nowak includes in either of his books actually depicts people. One reviewer asserts that the cover photograph for *Shut Up Shut Down* depicts three workers flying an upside-down American flag—an international sign for distress—above the blast furnace at the Bethlehem Steel plant in 1983, but this is a misreading of the image. The workers are not present in the photograph.

24. The URWW successfully helped organize one of the two Borders bookstores in the United States that are at present unionized (the one in Minneapolis).

BIBLIOGRAPHY

Books By Mark Nowak

Shut Up, Shut Down [afterword by Amiri Baraka]. Minneapolis, Minn.: Coffee House Press, 2004.
Revenants. Minneapolis, Minn.: Coffee House Press, 2000.
Visit Teepee Town. Coedited with Diane Glancy. Minneapolis, Minn.: Coffee House Press, 1999.
Then, and Now: Selected Poems, 1943–1993 [ed.]. By Theodore Enslin. Orono, Me.: National Poetry Foundation, 1999.
XCP: Cross Cultural Poetics [ed.]. Nos. 1–17 (1997–present).

Selected Prose

"Notes Toward an Anti-Capitalist Poetics." *Virginia Quarterly Review* 82, no 2 (Spring 2006): 236–40.
"'To Commit Suicide in Buffalo is Redundant': Music and Death in Zero City, 1982–1984." In *Goth: Undead Subculture*, edited by Lauren Goodlad and Michael Bibby. Durham: Duke University Press, 2006.
¡Workers of the Word, Unite and Fight! Long Beach, Calif.: Palm Press, 2005.

Interviews

Chicago Postmodern Poetry, http://www.chicagopostmodernpoetry.com/nowak.htm.

Selected Criticism

Boykoff, Jules. "Shut Up Shut Down" (review). *Labor History* 46, no. 3 (August 2005).

Davidson, Michael. "On the Outskirts of Form: Cosmopoetics in the Shadow of NAFTA" (unpublished).

Derksen, Jeff. "Poetry and the Landscape of Neoliberalism." *West Coast Line* 46 (Spring 2005).

Gilbert, Alan. *Another Future: Poetry and Art in a Postmodern Twilight.* (Middletown, Conn.: Wesleyan University Press, 2006).

Hugill, Piers. "Class War in the Rust Belt." *Jacket Magazine* 28 (2005); online.

Meadows, Deborah. "Poetics of De-Industrialization." *Jacket Magazine* 18 (2002). Reprinted, in Spanish translation, in *Encuentro: antología de poesía americana* (Havana, Cuba: Casa de Letras).

Michalski, David. "Cities Memory Voices Collage." In *Art and The Performance of Memory: Sounds and Gestures of Recollection*, edited by Richard Cándida-Smith. New York: Routledge, 2002. This collection is reprinted as *Text and Image: Art and the Performance of Memory* (Philadelphia: Transaction Publishers, 2006).

Roediger, David. "'More Than Two Things': The State of the Art of Labor History." *New Working-Class Studies*, edited by John Russo and Sherry Lee Linkon. Ithaca: Cornell University Press, 2005.

Schultz, Susan. "Borrowed Lines." *Boston Review* (January–February 2006).

KENNETH GOLDSMITH

"PAGE ONE" FROM *THE DAY*

"All the News
That's Fit to Print"
The New York Times
Late Edition
New York: Today, mainly sunny and noticeably less humid, high 79.
Tonight, clear, low 62. Tomorrow, sunny and cool, high 76. Yesterday,
high 86, low 73. Weather map is on Page D8.
VOL. CL . . . No. 51,873
Copyright © 2001 The New York Times
NEW YORK, TUESDAY, SEPTEMBER 11, 2001
$1 beyond the greater New York metropolitan area.
75 CENTS
Photographs, clockwise from top left, by Librado Romero, Ruby
Washington, Ruth Fremson and James Estrin / The New York Times
THE HOME STRETCH On the last day of campaigning, the
mayoral candidates scoured the city for votes. Clockwise from top Peter F.
Vallone, Alan G. Hevesi and Mark Green talked with voters in Brooklyn
and Manhattan. The polls are open from 6 a.m. to 9 p.m. Page B1
Nuclear Booty:
More Smugglers
Use Asia Route
By DOUGLAS FRANTZ
ISTANBUL, Sept. 10 — The police in Batumi, a Black Sea port in
Georgia, heard a rumor in July that someone wanted to sell several pounds
of high-grade uranium for $100,000. The most tantalizing aspect of the
tip was that one of the sellers was reportedly a Georgia Army officer.

All sorts of scoundrels have tried nuclear smuggling in recent years. Many are amateurs; most of what they try to peddle proves useless for making bombs.

But the possible involvement of an army officer gave the Batumi case a measure of deadly seriousness, beyond its status as another example of how the smuggling of nuclear material has shifted to Central Asia.

On the morning of July 20, the local antiterrorist squad burst into a small hotel room near the port, just outside the Turkish border. They arrested four men, including an army captain named Shota Geladze.

On the floor of the room, in a glass jar wrapped in plastic, sat nearly four pounds of enriched uranium 235, according to Revaz Chantladze, one of the police officers. The quantity was less than is usually required for a small atomic bomb.

Subsequent analysis yielded differing opinions. A Western diplomat
Continued on Page A10
City Voters Have Heard It All
As Campaign Din Nears End
By JIM DWYER
The first time the phone rang, Victoria Ehigiator was elbow deep in a sink of soapy dishes. She dried her hands and picked up the phone. It was Al Sharpton on the line, calling about the primary election. He said his piece, and she went back to the dishes. A few minutes later, the phone rang again, and she lifted herself from the bubbles once more.

That time it was Fernando Ferrer. And then it was Gloria Davis. Followed by Adolfo Carrión.

As one digitized caller after another dropped into her home, thanks to new technology that can swamp the telephones in a ZIP code or an entire city with the actual voice of, say, Ed Koch, urging a vote for Peter Vallone, Ms. Ehigiator started to suspect that very few people in New York were not running for something — whether it was mayor, comptroller, public advocate, borough president or City Council.

And as for those few who weren't candidates, they all seemed to be calling her about those who were.

Had Bill Bradley actually phoned her about Herb Berman? And who was Herb Berman, anyway? (Psst: he's a council member running for comptroller.)

"There was another guy — his name starts with S," said Ms. Ehiglator, of Morrisania in the Bronx, offering no other clues. "I'm trying to do the Sunday dishes but I never got off the phone with all these animated voice messages. It was a real fiesta of phone calls."

Today is the end of the busiest primary campaign around here that anyone can remember, and the candidates are ganging up on the small fraction of the electorate that customarily decides such races. From the high cliffs of northern Manhattan to the ocean foam at Rockaway Beach, New Yorkers report they are coping by slamming down the phone faster, throwing out the mail sooner,

Continued on Page B5

a Nation of Early Risers,

Morning TV Is a Hot Market

By BILL CARTER

How much morning television can one nation watch?

Ever since the owlish Dave Garroway ambled through the "Today" program on NBC starting in 1952, sometimes accompanied by a chimpanzee, television screens have greeted awakening Americans with the combination of hard news, feature reports and soft celebrity interviews that has come to be known as the morning news program.

But the competition for bleary eyes has grown more intense as media conglomerates have awakened to

the idea that changing lives, heightened interest from advertisers and other factors have made the morning one of the few areas of growth in the television business.

That trend was underscored last week when CNN raided its rival all-news cable network, Fox News, and took the anchor Paula Zahn for a new morning program it will begin next spring from inside the Time & Life Building at 50th Street on the Avenue of the Americas in Midtown Manhattan.

According to Fox executives, reading from the offer sheet they said CNN gave to Ms. Zahn, CNN agreed to triple her salary, bringing it over the $2 million mark.

The figure would be by far the most money CNN has ever paid for an anchor, far more than double what CNN agreed to pay to Aaron Brown, the anchor it has brought in from ABC to lead a prime-time newscast.

The raid and Fox's response — a lawsuit — represent the latest nasty interchange between Fox News and CNN, and serve as a proxy for a larger corporate battle between

Continued on Page C16
Updated news: www.nytimes.com

School Dress Codes vs. a Sea of Bare Flesh

By KATE ZERNIKE

MILLBURN, N.J., Sept. 7 — In the tumult of bare skin that is the hallway of Millburn High School, Michele Pitts is the Enforcer.

"Hon, put the sweater on," she barks at a pair of bare shoulders.

"Lose those flip-flops," to a pair of bare legs.

One student waves her off as Mrs. Pitts crosses her arms in a "Cover that cleavage" sign. "You talked to me already," the girl insists, then promises, "Tomorrow!" as she disappears around a corner.

Baseball caps, a taboo of yesteryear, pass by unchallenged, having slipped in severity on a list of offenses that now include exposed bellies, backs and thighs. For Mrs. Pitts, the assistant principal, there is simply too much skin to cover.

With Britney Spears and CosmoGirl setting the fashion trends, shirts and skirts are inching up, pants are slipping down, and schools across the country are finding themselves forced to tighten their dress codes and police their hallways.

This fall, New York State is requiring all public school districts to adopt dress codes as part of a larger code of conduct. In North Carolina, the bill that allowed schools to post the Ten Commandments also required them to institute dress codes.

The days when torn jeans tested the limits are now a fond memory. Today, schools feel the need to remind students that see-through clothing is not appropriate. (The Liverpool Central School District, near Syracuse, learned this when two high school girls showed up on Halloween dressed in Saran Wrap. Only one appeared to be wearing underwear.)

In the new dress codes, spaghetti straps are forbidden (straps must be no less than an inch and a half

Don Standing

for The New York Times

The dress code

at Millburn High

School aims to

raise standards and self-respect.

It frowns on low

necklines, bared

shoulders, flip-

flops and spa-

ghetti straps.

wide), as is clothing that "bares the private parts"; fishnet stockings and shirts; T-shirts with lewd messages; flip-flops or other clothing more suited to the beach; and skirts or shorts above mid-thigh. Boys cannot wear tank tops or

Continued on Page B7

INSIDE

Mrs. Dole to Run for Senate

Elizabeth Dole plans to announce that she will run in 2002 for the Senate seat being vacated by Jesse Helms of North Carolina. PAGE A16

Afghan Rebel's Fate Unclear

A day after a bombing aimed at the leader of the opposition to the Taliban, there were conflicting reports as to whether he survived. PAGE A15

Morgan Stanley Bias Suit

The Equal Employment Opportunity Commission filed a sex-discrimination suit against Morgan Stanley Dean Witter. BUSINESS DAY, PAGE C1

FOR HOME DELIVERY CALL 1–800-NYTIMES

0 354613937201

Giants Fail in Opener

The Giants allowed touchdowns in every quarter as the host Denver Broncos rolled to a 31–20 victory.

SPORTSTUESDAY, PAGE D1

Debate Over Shark Attacks

Commercial fishermen are at odds with scientists over the reason for a spate of highly publicized shark attacks. SCIENCE TIMES, PAGE F1

Scientists Urge
Bigger Supply
Of Stem Cells
Report Backs Cloning
to Create New Lines

By SHERYL GAY STOLBERG

WASHINGTON, Sept. 10 — A panel of scientific experts has concluded that new colonies, or lines, of human embryonic stem cells will be necessary if the science is to fulfill its potential, a finding that is likely to inflame the political debate over President Bush's decision to restrict federally financed research to the 64 stem cell lines that are already known to exist.

In a 59-page report that examines the state of human stem cell science, the panel also endorsed cloning technology to create new stem cells that could be used to treat patients. Mr. Bush strongly opposes human cloning for any reason, and the House of Representatives voted in July to outlaw any type of cloning, whether for reproduction or research.

The report by the National Academy of Sciences, perhaps the nation's most eminent organization of scientists, is scheduled to be made public on Tuesday morning at a news conference in Washington. It does not address Mr. Bush's policy directly, though it strongly supports federal financing for stem cell research.

"High quality, publicly funded research is the wellspring of medical breakthroughs," said the report, a copy of which was provided to The

New York Times by Congressional supporters of stem cell research. It added that federal financing, and the government oversight that comes with it, "offers the most efficient and responsible means of fulfilling the promise of stem cells to meet the need for regenerative medical therapies."

Though the academy often issues its reports in response to requests from the government, it embarked on this study on its own earlier this year. The study was not an exhaustive review of the scientific literature in stem cells, but was rather intended to examine the prospects for the on this study on its own earlier this year. The study was not an exhaustive review of the scientific literature in stem cells, but was rather intended to examine the prospects for the research and to make policy recommendations. The report was written

Continued on Page A18

Strict Arsenic Limit Sought

Strict standards for arsenic in drinking water, suspended by the Bush administration, were justified, experts have concluded. Page A20.

KEY LEADERS TALK
OF POSSIBLE DEALS
TO REVIVE ECONOMY
BUSH IS UNDER PRESSURE
Lott Open to More Tax Cuts —
Democrat Sees Temporary
Dip Into Social Security
By ALISON MITCHELL
and RICHARD W. STEVENSON

WASHINGTON, Sept. 10 — Key figures in both parties responded to the darkening economic outlook today by exploring possible compromises on additional tax cuts, and the Democratic chairman of the Senate Budget Committee suggested that such a deal could involve the politically perilous step of tapping temporarily into the Social Security surplus.

Pressure mounted on President Bush to drop his cautious approach to dealing with the weakening economy, much of it from within his own party. Republicans are voicing growing concern that the White House has underestimated public unease about the economy and the threat it poses to members of Congress up for re-election next year.

Confronted with polls showing that support for Republicans was eroding even before the government reported on Friday that the unemployment rate had surged, nervous Republicans moved on a variety of fronts.

In the House, Republican leaders agreed tonight to take up legislation in committee on Tuesday that would require automatic spending cuts if any Social Security money was spent on other government programs in the current fiscal year.

After accounting for the slowing economy and the tax cut signed into law by Mr. Bush in June, the Congressional Budget Office projected last month that the government would spend $9 billion of Social Security receipts in the fiscal year that ends Sept. 30. Both parties now expect that figure to be higher.

The White House sent a memorandum to all cabinet agencies today asking them to look for possible budget cuts as the administration develops tax and spending proposals for its next budget.

In the Senate, Trent Lott of Mississippi, the minority leader, said he was open to an idea floated by Democrats for a tax cut for workers who had not qualified for the current rebate. Workers who do not make enough money to pay federal income taxes but who still pay the payroll taxes that finance Social Security and Medicare will not receive rebate checks this year.

Mr. Lott said he would like to see

Continued on Page A20

Traced on Internet,

Teacher Is Charged

In '71 Jet Hijacking

By C.J. CHIVERS

Thirty years after a black-power revolutionary hijacked a jetliner from Ontario to Cuba and disappeared, Canadian and federal authorities matched the fingerprints he left on a can of ginger ale in the airplane with those of a teacher in Westchester County and charged the teacher with the crime yesterday.

The teacher, Patrick Dolan Critton, 54, of Mount Vernon, N.Y., was charged with kidnapping, armed robbery and extortion in United States District Court in Manhattan. He is facing extradition to Canada, where a detective had tracked him down through a simple Internet search.

The authorities said that Mr. Critton, a fugitive for 30 years, had been hiding in plain sight for the last seven years, working as a schoolteacher, using his real name, raising two sons and mentoring other children. Even one of the police officers who arrested him said he had the appearance and demeanor of a gentleman.

But as a young man, the authorities said, Patrick Dolan Critton was a revolutionary with a taste for the most daring of crimes.

By 1971, when he was 24, he was wanted by the New York City police on charges that he participated in a bank robbery that led to a frantic gun battle with the police, and that he had worked in a covert explosives factory on the Lower East Side, where the police said he made pipe bombs with other members of a black liberation group, the Republic

Continued on Page B6

POETICS STATEMENT
Being Boring

I AM the most boring writer that has ever lived. If there were an Olympic sport for extreme boredom, I would get a gold medal. My books are impossible to read straight through. In fact, every time I have to proofread them before sending them off to the publisher, I fall asleep repeatedly. You really don't need to read my books to get the idea of what they're like; you just need to know the general concept.

Over the past ten years, my practice today has boiled down to simply retyping existing texts. I've thought about my practice in relation to Borges's Pierre Menard, but even Menard was more original than I am: he, independent of any knowledge of *Don Quixote*, reinvented Cervantes' masterpiece word for word. By contrast, I don't invent anything. I just keep rewriting the same book. I sympathize with the protagonist of a cartoon claiming to have transferred x amount of megabytes, physically exhausted after a day of downloading. The simple act of moving information from one place to another today constitutes a significant cultural act in and of itself. I think it's fair to say that most of us spend hours each day shifting content into different containers. Some of us call this writing.

Kenneth Goldsmith | 361

In 1969, the conceptual artist Douglas Huebler wrote, "The world is full of objects, more or less interesting; I do not wish to add any more." I've come to embrace Huebler's ideas, though it might be retooled as, "The world is full of texts, more or less interesting; I do not wish to add any more." It seems an appropriate response to a new condition in writing today: faced with an unprecedented amount of available text, the problem is not needing to write more of it; instead, we must learn to negotiate the vast quantity that exists. I've transformed from a writer into an information manager, adept at the skills of replicating, organizing, mirroring, archiving, hoarding, storing, reprinting, bootlegging, plundering, and transferring. I've needed to acquire a whole new skill set: I've become a master typist, an exacting cut-and-paster, and an OCR demon. There's nothing I love more than transcription; I find few things more satisfying than collation.

John Cage said, "If something is boring after two minutes, try it for four. If still boring, then eight. Then sixteen. Then thirty-two. Eventually one discovers that it is not boring at all." He's right: there's a certain kind of unboring boredom that's fascinating, engrossing, transcendent, and downright sexy. And then there's the other kind of boring: let's call it boring boring. *Boring boring* is a client meeting; *boring boring* is having to endure someone's self-indulgent poetry reading; *boring boring* is watching a toddler for an afternoon; *boring boring* is the seder at Aunt Fanny's. *Boring boring* is being somewhere we don't want to be; *boring boring* is doing something we don't want to do.

Unboring boring is a voluntary state; boring boring is a forced one. Unboring boring is the sort of boredom that we surrender ourselves to when, say, we go to see a piece of minimalist music. I recall once having seen a restaging of an early Robert Wilson piece from the 1970s. It took four hours for two people to cross the stage; when they met in the middle, one of them raised their arm and stabbed the other. The actual stabbing itself took a good hour to complete. Because I volunteered to be bored, it was the most exciting thing I've ever seen.

The twentieth-century avant-garde liked to embrace boredom as a way of getting around what it considered to be the vapid "excitement" of popular culture. I'll never forget being at a sound poetry festival with Jackson Mac Low in Miami Beach more than a decade ago. Jackson was railing against popular culture, dance music, anything with a beat, anything that reeked of entertainment. I really couldn't understand what he was talking about. For a younger generation, popular culture is very sophisticated. Everyone in advertising today has a degree in semiotics, setting up a condition whereby artists, seeing the complex ads, go into the studio and make work about the advertising, which feeds subsequent ads, and so on. But later that night, back in the hotel room, I was channel surfing and came across a 1950s Lawrence Welk rerun. It was unbearably stupid, wrapping its boredom in the guise of "entertainment" and suddenly it occurred to me that in his day, Jackson was right. A powerful way to combat such crap was to do the opposite of it, to be purposely boring.

By the 1960s and '70s in art circles this type of boredom—boring boring—was often the norm. I'm glad I wasn't around to have to sit through all of that stuff. Boredom, it seems, became a forced condition, be it in theater, music, art, or literature. It's no wonder people bailed out of boredom in the late 1970s and early '80s to go into punk rock or expressionistic painting. After a while, boredom got boring.

And then, a few decades later, things changed again: excitement became dull and boring started to look good again. So here we are, ready to be bored once more. But this time, boredom has changed. We've embraced unboring boring, modified boredom, boredom with all the boring parts cut out of it. Reality TV, for example, is a new kind of boredom. "An American Family," broadcast in the early 1970s—strutting its ennui—was the old boredom; "The Osbournes"—action-packed boredom—is the new. There's no one more tedious than Ozzy Osbourne, but his television presence is the most engagingly constructed tedium that has ever existed. We can't take our eyes off the guy, stumbling through the dullness of his own life.

Our taste for the unboring boring won't last forever. I assume that someday soon it'll go back to boring boring once again, though for reasons and conditions I can't predict at this time. But until then, even though I construct boring works, I wouldn't dream of forcing you to sit through an extended reading of my work: at least not without a fair warning, giving you an out, a chance for you to edit the dull parts by fast forwarding, leaving the room, or switching me off.

I do a weekly radio show that, most weeks, is extremely challenging listening, often veering into boring boring territory (I've played shows of two men snoring for three hours, to name one example), but I don't mind doing this because no one's forcing you to listen straight through. If you don't like it, you simply get up, turn it off, and put something else on.

In the same vein, as I said before, I don't expect you to even read my books cover to cover. It's for that reason I like the idea that you can know each of my books in one sentence. For instance, there's the book of every word I spoke for a week unedited. Or the book of every move my body made over the course of a day, a process so dry and tedious that I had to get drunk halfway though the day in order to make it to the end. Or my most recent book, *Day*, in which I retyped a day's copy of the *New York Times* and published it as a 900-page book. Now you know what I do without ever having to have read a word of it.

Let me go into more detail about *Day*. I would take a page of the newspaper, start at the upper-lefthand corner and work my way through, following the articles as they were laid out on the page. If an article, for example, continued on another page, I wouldn't go there. Instead, I would finish retyping the page I was on in full before proceeding to the next one. I allowed myself no creative liberties with the text. The object of the project was to be as uncreative in the process as possible. It was one of the hardest constraints a writer can muster, particularly on a project of this scale; with every keystroke came the temptation to "fudge," "cut-and-paste," and "skew" the mundane language. But to do so would be to foil my exercise.

Everywhere there was a bit of text in the paper, I grabbed it. I made no distinction between editorial and advertising, stock quotes or classified ads. If it could be considered text, I had to have it. Even if there was, say, an ad for a car, I took a magnifying glass and grabbed the text off the license plate. Between retyping and OCR'ing, I finished the book in a year.

Far from being boring, it was the most fascinating writing process I've ever experienced. It was surprisingly sensual. I was trained as a sculptor and moving the text from one place to another became as physical, and as sexy as, say, carving stone. It became this wild sort of obsession to peel the text off the page of the newspaper and force it into the fluid medium of the digital. I felt as if I were taking the newspaper, giving it a good shake, and watching as the letters tumbled off the page into a big pile, transforming the static language that was glued to the page into movable type.

As good as the process was, that's how good I felt the end result to be. The day I chose to retype, the Friday before Labor Day weekend of 2000, was a slow news day. Just the regular stuff happened, nothing special. But in spite of that, after it was finished, it became clear that the daily newspaper —or in this case *Day*—is really a great novel, filled with stories of love, jealousy, murder, competition, sex, passion, and so forth. It's a fantastic thing: the daily newspaper, when translated, amounts to a 900-page book. Every day. And it's a book that's written in every city and in every country, only to be instantly discarded in order to write a brand-new one, full of fresh stories the next day. After reading the newspaper over breakfast for twenty minutes in the morning, we say we've read the paper. Believe me, you've never really *read* the paper.

There was something so satisfying about this exercise that I wanted to see what would happen when I applied it to other types of print media. So I went ahead and retyped an issue of *Vogue*, which yielded fantastically minimal results. Imagine a fashion magazine denuded of its images. What are you left with? In the beginning of a fashion magazine there are dozens of two-page advertising spreads that are all images, containing almost no text. What emerged were exquisite little lines—almost fashion haikus—about products, locations, prices, and so forth. And in the back where there is more text, it was completely different than the *New York Times*; *Vogue* is full of juicy gossip and over-the-top language, making for a totally new book. I called that book *Month*.

My next idea was to do a weekly—obviously called *Week*—so I chose to retype an issue of *Newsweek*, which was, well, as dull as *Newsweek* itself is. That project definitely fell on the boring side of boring.

I got to wondering if I'm simply masochistic, doing these sorts of projects so I decided to do a reality check and try a boring exercise with my generally bored students: I gave them the simple instructions to retype five pages of their choice. I came in the next week, dreading their response to the most dry, dull, assignment I could give them. But much to my surprise, they were charged—as charged as I was during my retyping of the *Times*. Their responses were varied and full of revelations: some found it enlightening to become a machine (without ever having known Warhol's famous dictum "I want to be a machine"). Others said that it was the most intense *reading* experience they ever had, with many actually embodying the characters they were retyping. Several students became aware that the act of typing or writing is actually an act of performance, involving their whole body in a physically durational act (even down to noticing the cramps in their hands). Some of the students became intensely aware of the text's formal properties and for the first time in their lives began to think of texts not only as transparent, but opaque objects to be moved around a white space. Others found the task Zen-like and amnesia-inducing (without ever having known Satie's "Memoirs of an Amnesiac" or Duchamp's desire to live without memory), having the text alternately lose then regain meaning. Out of the class of eighteen, there was only one girl who didn't have some sort of a transcendental experience with the mundane act of typing. She was a waitress who took it upon herself to retype her restaurant's menu in order to learn it better for work. She ended up hating the task and hating her job even more. It was an object lesson in the difference between voluntary and involuntary boredom. It's hard to turn the dreary world of work into unboring boredom.

The class learned that it's hard to be bored when creating a work of art. But what about an audience's reception to such work? I think that there were a handful of artists in the twentieth century who intentionally made boring work, but didn't expect their audiences to fully engage with it in a durational sense. It's these artists, I feel, who predicted the sort of unboring boredom that we're so fond of today.

Andy Warhol, for instance, said of his films that the real action wasn't on the screen. He's right. Nothing happened in the early Warhol films: a static image of the Empire State Building for eight hours, a man sleeping for six. It is nearly impossible to watch them straight through. Warhol often claimed that his films were better thought about than seen. He also said that the films were catalysts for other types of actions: conversation that took place in the theater during the screening, the audience walking in and out, and thoughts that happened in the heads of the moviegoers. Warhol conceived of his films as a staging for a performance, in which the audience were the superstars, not the actors or objects on the screen.

Gertrude Stein, too, often set up a situation of skimming, knowing that few were going to be reading her epic works straight through. (How many people have linearly read every word of *The Making of Americans*? Not too many, I suppose.) The scholar Ulla Dydo, in her magnificent compilation of the writings of Gertrude Stein, remarked that much of Stein's work was never meant to be read closely at all; rather, she was deploying visual means of reading. What appeared to be densely unreadable and repetitive was, in fact, designed to be skimmed, and to delight the eye (in a visual sense) while holding the book. Stein, as usual, was prescient in predicting our reading habits. John Cage, too, proved to be the avant-garde's Evelyn Wood, boiling down dense modernist works into deconstructed, remixed Cliff Notes; in his "Writing Through *Finnegans Wake*" he reduced a 628-page tome to a slim 39 pages, and Ezra Pound's 824-page *Cantos* to a mere handful of words.

* * *

I'm getting out of the boredom business, friends. I recently embarked upon my latest project, a piece that would completely turn my entire practice on its ear. I wanted to work with *extraordinary* language, *dramatic* language; language drenched with *emotion*. Excitement is what I'm after now. After thinking about what I could do for some months, I hit upon the perfect project. I would redo my *New York Times* piece, only instead of retyping a "normal" news day, I would retype the issue of the *New York Times* published on the morning of September 11, using the exact same method I did for *Day*.

I've now just finished the first section of the paper and I can tell you that it's doing everything that I want it to. I've embarked on an epic unboring boring work. It's been a highly emotional experience retyping this paper, full of events that never happened: sales that were canceled, listings for events that were indefinitely postponed, stories deemed to be big news one day were swept off the pages of the paper of record forever, stock prices that took a huge dive the next day, and so forth. I think you get the idea. I love the idea of doing something so exciting in the most boring way possible or vice versa.

At a reading I gave recently—and I *do* do short readings occasionally—the other reader came up to me after my reading and said incredulously, "You didn't write a word of what you read." I thought for a moment and, sure, in one sense—the traditional sense—he was right; but in the expanded field of appropriation, uncreativity, sampling, and language management in which we all habit today, he couldn't have been more wrong. Each and every word was "written" by me: sometimes mediated by a machine, sometimes transcribed, and sometimes copied; but without my intervention, slight as it may be, these works would never have found their way into the world. When retyping a book, I often stop and ask myself if what I am doing is really writing. As I sit there, in front of the computer screen, punching keys, the answer is invariably yes.

AFFECT AND AUTISM

Kenneth Goldsmith's Reconstitution of Signal and Noise

Raymond McDaniel

I

THERE EXISTS an old Situationist dream: the concept of a book bound in sandpaper, that when placed or removed from a bookcase contributes to the destruction of the books between which it is shelved.[1] Hardly the model of poetic community, but an experimental impulse is also often a corrective one; an almost moral sense that what has been done ought to be undone, or at least done *less*. So nested in this fanciful suggestion rests a radical ambition: that within literature's conventions lies the means by which writing itself may be utterly reconfigured, at the expense of the previous configurations whose terms both delimit and invite the possibilities of dramatic restructuring. Both despite and because of his origins as a fine artist, Kenneth Goldsmith's commitment to "uncreativity" realizes the Situationist project and invigorates *art* by striking directly at *artifice*. What distinguishes Goldsmith from his forerunners—Dadaists, Situationists, concrete poets, Fluxus adventurers and Oulipo antipractitioners—is his commitment to literalize, to make fully manifest, the idea of literal-mindedness, and thereby "purge" his art of the creative impulse each of the above movements identified as the specter by which art is haunted.

Literal-mindedness suggests the most useful entrance to Goldsmith's work. Literal-mindedness, of course, is easily confused with simplicity—a state itself subject to grievous misapprehension. Otherwise astute observers of Goldsmith's writing rely upon the apparent simplicity of his methods: in her review of *Day*, Lucy Raven notes: "This discrepancy between the simple idea and its dictionary-size manifestation marks the fulcrum of *Day*'s complexity."[2] And Brian Kim Stefans writes: "Kenneth Goldsmith has made a career out of creating, through masochistically tortuous writing practices, impossibly long, but very simply conceived books that follow through to the bitter end on some writing tick."[3] While reviews correctly identify the conceptual elegance of Goldsmith's formal parameters, we shall initially examine the relationship between simplicity or literal-mindedness and the hint of pathology implied by "masochistically tortuous writing" that bespeaks "some . . . tick." In short, we shall address the frequency and ease with which Goldsmith's practice evokes the language and aura of psychological disorder, especially the wavelength of the spectrum of autism syndromes now identified as Asperger's Disorder.

The most recent edition of the *Diagnostic and Statistical Manual of Mental Disorders* characterizes the diagnostic criteria for 299.80, Asperger's Disorder, as follows:

A. Qualitative impairment in social interaction, as manifested by at least two of the following:
  1. marked impairments in the use of multiple nonverbal behaviors such as eye-to-eye gaze, facial expression, body postures, and gestures to regulate social interaction
  2. failure to develop peer relationships appropriate to developmental level
  3. a lack of spontaneous seeking to share enjoyment, interests, or achievements with other people (e.g. by a lack of showing, bringing, or pointing out objects of interest to other people)
  4. lack of social or emotional reciprocity

B. Restricted repetitive and stereotyped patterns of behavior, interests, and activities, as manifested by at least one of the following:
  1. encompassing preoccupation with one or more stereotyped and restricted patterns of interest that is abnormal either in intensity or focus
  2. apparently inflexible adherence to specific, nonfunctional routines or rituals
  3. stereotyped and repetitive motor mannerisms (e.g., hand or finger flapping or twisting, or complex whole-body movements)
  4. persistent preoccupation with parts of objects[4]

We must of course be cautious when we apply diagnostic criteria originally designed for one sphere to a completely unrelated area; caution necessarily compounded when the criteria at hand are originally meant to address medical and psychological conditions widely perceived as liabilities in important areas of social functioning. Yet reliance upon psychological descriptors is not accidental; indeed, it can be quite useful if we maintain strict efforts to avoid pathologizing the objects to which we turn these medical and psychological terms. And it is also worth noting that psychological diagnoses are themselves not static; they are equally subject to potential abuse and potential evolution. It is particularly useful to consider the evolution of the spectrum of conditions now known collectively as autism, the general category into which Asperger's falls. Once we regarded autism syndrome behaviors as the likely result of insufficient and/or inappropriate maternal attention; we institutionalized individuals who demonstrated those behaviors. We now perceive these behaviors, however, with a far greater degree of subtlety as regards both their origins and their consequences, and it is this more sophisticated imagination that lends itself to an examination of Kenneth Goldsmith's "uncreative practice" and noninterventionist writing. The most telling shift in our collective imagination is exemplified by the following specification of Asperger's: "There is no clinically significant general delay in cognitive development or in . . . adaptive behavior . . . and curiosity about the environment."

This (relatively recent) acknowledgment by the American Psychological Association is critical: that Asperger's children and other persons who display certain autism behaviors possess the full measure of cognitive capability. What this acknowledgment reveals is that we now appreciate that our prior measurements for determining the base criteria for intelligence overvalued what we mistook for *intuition*: for instance, the ability to discern the meaning of a smile or a grimace or any of a countless number of context-dependent cues we once cavalierly assumed were natural and inevitable expressions of meaning. This shift is important for the instruction of those with Asperger's, because it suggests that they can learn social cues they same way they learn multiplication tables or musical scales. Indeed, many of these children not only find it easier to learn the likes of mathematics or musical notation, they sometimes retreat to these methodologies because they offer a *more* genuinely intuitive system of meaning than the base social cues we normally assume to be foundational. And what this suggests in turn is that we distinguish between categories of sense-making that encompass self-replicating and self-limiting laws (such as mathematics) and those that do not (such as language as expressive of shared, social, community "nodes" of meaning). The utility of this distinction for purposes of locating Goldsmith's work in the experimental "tradition" is that deliberate pursuit of derangement of the senses—both the literal senses and the conventions and norms to which they correspond—has been the foundation stone of experimental poetry since Rimbaud, at least.[5]

The irony of this pursuit, and the discrepancy upon which Goldsmith has so precisely played, is that the very methods upon which the quest depends have served only to reinforce the conditions derangement is meant to unsettle. If creativity is the focusing of language to the object of the poet's will, but that poet is necessarily immersed in the same meaning-lattice as the language itself, then exits to derangement cannot be achieved via any "creative" act. What we need is not more creativity, but less; and as the consciousness from which creativity springs also contains the language to which the artist might apply that creativity, what we finally need is less *artist*.

This construct is hardly sophisticated, but the peculiar genius of Kenneth Goldsmith is his dogged insistence on eliminating from his methodology any fold or complication of the construct in which an indulgent artistry might hide. When he speaks of *purging* his work, he transmits his understanding of the invidious means by which auctorial will asserts itself at the expense of true derangement. Goldsmith is becoming relentlessly literal-minded in the conception and execution of his writing—and what, finally, is Asperger's Disorder but a neurologically hardwired literalism, an ability (as opposed to a curse) to apprehend data without the filters in which auctorial will becomes inevitably trapped? Goldsmith has declared his devotion to "the practice of non-interventionalist writing: transcription, retyping, copying; moving information from one place to another as a valid writing practice," but the nature of information itself is utterly at question in this practice.[6]

Each of Goldsmith's projects for the last several years participates, with greater and lesser degrees of success, in this project of literalization; each of these projects echolocates intriguingly against psychological descriptors.

The second and fourth of the *DSM*'s criteria for qualitative impairment enjoy analogues to Goldsmithian projects. "Failure to develop peer relationships to appropriate levels" and "lack of social and emotional reciprocity" are telling descriptors of Goldsmith's *Soliloquy*, which consists of every word Goldsmith spoke in one week. Because *Soliloquy* faithfully records Goldsmith's utterances in multiple social contexts, but to the exclusion of the language of the other parties with whom Goldsmith conducts his social exchanges, the text defines lack of reciprocity, and thereby reveals the exhaustive vacuity of quotidian discourse. More important, this withdrawal of the dialogic element renders the standard markers of conversational discourse strange. Because the text is wholly unedited, this vacuity and estrangement also documents the fragility of so-called peer relationships. Consider this excerpt, pertaining to Goldsmith's meeting with Marjorie Perloff (who has, ironically enough, been one of Goldsmith's most lucid and elaborate defenders):

> Um, well, I actually have a great meeting, um, I'm having lunch with, uh, one of the most powerful literary critics you know in the in academia in the country. It's her, Marjorie Perloff and, uh, I'm meeting her actually at the MOMA Members Dining Room for lunch today. And she's deeply powerful and I'm going to get her, I hope, to write a blurb for the back of my book and promote it.[7]

As mortifying as this is, those fragments of necessarily one-sided conversations that do not expressly offer opportunities for social treachery are no less banal, and in bulk become transformingly alien:

> "Yeah, if you were if you were taping you'd have 5 times as many tapes as me. I have very few tapes from this week. No, it's much better than it was. It's way better. Yeah. I don't mind, you know, it's just an industrial noise right now it's just it used to sort of scream and whine and, you know, no, it's a lot better."

Of *Soliloquy*, he writes that "If every word spoken daily in New York City were somehow to materialize as a snowflake, each day there would be a blizzard"—which indicates that Goldsmith is less interested in the immediate social and emotional effect of the language as it becomes fragmented than he is in the texture and volume of the fragments themselves, as they literally fill the vacuum constructed as neutral or otherwise valueless.[8] Or, as Gordon Tapper puts it, "Like the practitioners of concrete poetry, Goldsmith wants us to look at language so as to confront it as abstract visual images that represent utterance. He also wants us to see that language occupies space, and lots of it."[9]

Offhanded descriptions of Goldsmith's work that draw upon psychological diagnoses similar to what we've done here are not uncommon: John Strausbaugh describes Goldsmith's *No. 111.2.7.93–10.20.96/6* as "a 606-page tour de force of . . . *something*. Linguistic OCD maybe?"[10] Given that the text to which Strausbaugh refers is a book-length poem that itemizes Goldsmith's reading over the course of three years, from February 7, 1993, to October 20, 1996, this description, while glib, is hardly inexact. The precision of the recording frame satisfies most criteria for *compulsive*, in that it allows no apparent room for manipulation but does not account for or justify its own precision. But the *obsessive* elements appear in Goldsmith's arrangement of the texts, according to alphabetical order, all phrases rhyming with the letter R, sorting these entries by number of syllables, starting with entries of one syllable for chapter 1, progressing through entries of two syllables, three syllables, and further, concluding with a complete transcript of D. H. Lawrence's "The Rocking-Horse Winner," the 7,228 syllables of which end on the word "winner."[11]

Goldsmith's *No. 111* approximates the *DSM*'s criteria for restricted repetitive behaviors, especially the "restricted patterns of interest . . . abnormal in intensity or focus" and "apparently inflexible adherence to specific, nonfunctional routines or rituals." In his pursuit of the *schwa* phoneme, Goldsmith could not have elected a more seemingly random quest, but it is exactly this variousness that allows him to introduce a version of the "space occupation" that fulfills social dimensions even more fully than does *Soliloquy*. Goldsmith's interest in conventionally neglected texts has a sometimes polar quality: there's the *New York Times* transcribed in *Day* on one end, and then there's the individual's every utterance of *Soliloquy* on the other. We can think of these cultural poles as *hard ephemera* and *soft ephemera*, respectively, and Goldsmith routinely applies digital technology to reconstitute the ephemeral properties of each—via the transfer of data to a digital "larval stage" from which he manages the text to its new form. But as an advocate for the potential of the reconstitutive medium itself, Goldsmith insists (quite logically) that digital media can be at least as hospitable to poetics as print, whose material properties allow him perpetual opportunities for manipulations that draw attention to the whole disorienting range of words as space-complicating objects.[12] But Goldsmith seems progressively less interested in exploiting those digital media he has done so much otherwise to celebrate. Correspondent to this, *No. 111.2.7.93–10.20.96/6*, Goldsmith's most successful fusion of hard and soft ephemera to date, is ironically also the text whose methodology most powerfully resists the facility of digital manipulation. Goldsmith counted and allocated his syllable-ziggurats by hand and eye, and the reward for this labor is the unpredictable fecundity of the following:

> Amber Valetta, be a wallflower, digging the fucker's, Welcome Back Kotter, lick chops and basta . . .

> Einstein once asked with sadness and wonder, either of the higher or the lower, Emily Dickinson worse than ever, emphasize how glad you are to see her, endure no light being themselves obscure . . .

> nothing's gonna change my clothes every anymore, now get your meaty paws away from that buzzer, now there's a question that ought to get us somewhere, Objects In Mirror Are Closer Than They Appear, objects of desire that once defined their eras, of course {NAK} (sense 2) i.e. "I'm not here", oh my sagging gonads, aching pulsating sore, "Oh!" she exclaimed "It's like a dick but much smaller!", On the next Phil: Real Incest and Real Survivors . . .

> Eeeaaarrrghh! I pictured smashing his face in . . . kicking his scrotum back into his torso . . . digging the fucker's eyes out . . . going for a field goal with his head over and over . . . , even if it is not good for us we become addicted. And we become enslaved. And when we become enslaved we are constantly thinking of that thing wherever we are, from the mountains to the prairies . . . FUCK MISS AMERIKA . . . to the oceans . . . NO NO HO CHI MINH . . . white with foam . . . 1 2 3 4 WE DON'T WANT YOUR FUCKING WAR . . . God bless Amerika, grab me Chewie. I'm slipping—hold on. Grab it almost . . . you almost got it. Gently now all right easy easy hold me Chewie. Chewie! With a little higher just a little higher . . .

It is difficult to imagine a more catholic collection, equally evidential of the complex and unpredictable interweaving of ephemera from which language is constructed. While this work persuasively documents that unalloyed language contains greater potential for creative affect than more traditionally tooled "creative" writing, the drawback to *No. 111.2.7.93–10.20.96/6*, as Goldsmith himself admits, is that the text, for all its superficial randomness, is nevertheless heavily edited.[13]

In a move away from this reliance on editorial intervention that simultaneously inverts the *DSM*'s criteria for "persistent preoccupation with parts of objects," we must consider Goldsmith's *Day*, a full transcription of the complete contents of the Friday, September 1, 2000, edition of the *New York Times* in 9-point Bookman Old Style font that dissolves the very "parts" that make a newspaper intelligible:

Elsewhere today, a bomb exploded
near a public market in the southern
town of Kabacan, wounding at least 13
people, officials said.
The police said they suspected that another Muslim
rebel group, the Moro Islamic
Liberation Front, was responsible.
the original razor scooter
hot@bloomingdales

Or,

A great gift idea!
British Begin Human Testing of H.I.V. Vaccine

Or,

Despite an unusual two-year suspen-
Continued on Page D5.

In the following description of *Day*, Brad Ford communicates the diffi-
culty of registering the full measure of *Day*'s cumulative effect:

> Yet the reader has to look deeper than the articles. More is happening than
> words coming together to tell a story. I suppose if I were of a certain ilk and
> had read straight through, the first jump would have warned me. But also, the
> ads are obvious admonitions. *Day*'s format takes most typography and visual
> clues away from the reader. The ads are clearly not ads—they are copy and
> have no pictures, which is a different experience. The eye-catching tricks of
> Madison Avenue are stripped of all but caps and exclamations, and it deflates
> them or makes them comedy. Maps become columns of place names and a line
> for scale (0 miles 300). This is not quite the *New York Times*."[14]

But in fact, *Day* is *precisely* the *New York Times*. The deletion of "visual
clues" forces the reader to apprehend the girth and perversity of the *Times*
as assemblage, as a monolith that—via the refusal of the literal that context-
dependency secures—manages to hide its miraculous properties in the shal-
low labyrinth of its everyday use.

2

Aside from the mysteries of their neurological details, autism syndromes
such as Asperger's usefully reveal some of the previously occluded dangers
of how we have become too unconscious in our use of *context* to determine
sense. As established, individuals who displays Asperger's tendencies may find
the code of tics and facial arrangements that conventionally allow deter-
minations of emotional register elusive. These persons lack some measure

of the innate capacity to deduce emotion via expression, and thereby raise serious questions about what "innate" actually means. While those with Asperger's syndrome can be educated to recognize these patterns and associate them with their likely emotional and social analogues, the process by which they are educated must address, and somehow incorporate, the student's conviction that even the most basic and seemingly fundamental layers of human social interaction do not make sense. When we use the term *sense*, of course, we must distinguish between those patterns that make sense relative to their internal features (a smile indicates pleasure; a smile's absence indicates pleasure's lack, at least; an inverted smile—a frown—indicates displeasure) and those patterns that seem to participate in universal order, such as musical scales and certain mathematical processes. In the case of the former, logic alone cannot help one predict all the rules one might need to navigate the cataracts of the system successfully. But those with autism profiles often find the latter kind of sense easier to master, perhaps because it is proportionately easier to derive a constellation of meaning from a single star, a single segment from which greater and more elaborate iterations of the base logic can be deduced.

Those who work closely with Asperger's individuals thus note the way in which their own perceptions of their behavior and assumptions undergo a rigorous and often surprising reformulation. To step outside a methodology so deeply socialized as to appear "natural" is to experience shock, confusion, delight—a host of reactions that characterize the essence of estrangement, the pursuit of which over the last one hundred years describes a catalogue of means by which poets have struggled to alchemize "plain" language into a language through which this estrangement could occur. Yet the insistence on plain language—on a context from which evocative poetry must, by definition, then deviate—has crippled poets' ability to estrange. To believe that plain language, quotidian language, must be internally modified to become poetry and thereby achieve strangeness: this is the mistake of trying to fly by jumping *really hard*.

It's easy to mock Goldsmith's books before you've read them; even at the level of the hook, they readily appall, as Goldsmith will admit. Of his transcription for *Day*, he confesses, "never have I faced a writing process this dry, this extreme, this boring."[15] He then proceeds to quote John Cage: "If something is boring after two minutes, try it for four. If still boring, then eight. Then sixteen. Then thirty-two. Eventually one discovers that it is not boring at all."[16] Corollary to this boredom-as-defense-against-disorientation, there are peppered liberally throughout reviews of Kenneth Goldsmith's writing admissions of how *funny* it can often be; how the juxtapositions that accumulate through the processes of his literalized projects become both odd and ha-ha. But juxtaposition as a means to achieve disorientation reaches a point of diminishing returns very quickly: note the original effect of Duchamp's

Fountain, and the speed with which it has become a kind of visual shorthand for the cheap obviousness of modern and postmodern "tricks." The disorientation *Fountain* once achieved depends upon an enjambment of contexts. What is this, but the language of metaphor writ large, and what is metaphor but the exhausted handmaiden of creativity itself, the self-defeating impulse Goldsmith strives to quash? Metaphor functions by unmediated conflation of objects derived from uncommonly situated contexts. But the limited utility of metaphor regarding the inducement of disorientation rests in metaphor's reification of the contexts it otherwise seeks to manipulate. Here is X and here is Y: while we may not be familiar with the juxtaposition of the two, and while that juxtaposition may open the door to an observation or apprehension of both objects that deviates from the observations more commonly associated with their original contexts, it cannot but reassert the legitimacy of the contexts it manipulates. The effect of disorientation—its blast radius, as it were—is delimited by the perceiver's ability to determine what does or does not belong. And that ability, rather than being undermined by that apparent and initially radicalizing effect of juxtaposition, is rather *reinforced* by it. This is why the appropriate appreciation of Goldsmith's achievement lies not in its incidental and accidental metaphors, but in the much more discomfiting effects of its cumulative estrangements. And this is why comparisons between Goldsmith's methodology and the literal-mindedness of Asperger's prove persuasive; both suggest the cognitive flaw in reliance upon juxtaposition as the most accurate and inevitable means of orientation, of meaning.

Those who encountered *Fountain* for the first time, enjoyed (or at least felt) the jolt provided by the superimposition of the hidden quotidian—the subsocial space reserved for bodily functions—on the tableau of high art, of refined cerebration. But that jolt was bought at the expense of cementing the disjunction between the two contexts. In order for Duchamp's effort to disarm his audience's suppositions to work at all, it had to confirm that audience's belief in their collective ability to discern high and low, public and private. Disorientation by juxtaposition pulls the rug out from under the victim of art only to remind them of the solidity of the ground on which the rug rests. The victim stumbles, but does not really fall.

By now, of course, juxtaposition's tricks are more than exhausted; they've become a trope, more obvious in their effect than the supposedly obvious assumptions they are meant to illustrate. If the visual arts are, as Goldsmith frequently quotes Brion Gysin as saying, always fifty years ahead of their literary counterparts, then poetry has more than compensated for the gap by way of its long dependence on metaphor as both technique and, in large measure, defining property.[17]

I do not mean, however, that the original function of metaphor and juxtaposition—to restore the strangeness of the specific—has or can be abandoned. What I do mean is that more extreme strategies are required for the achievement of the condition juxtaposition once aspired to induce; Kenneth Goldsmith and his "extreme writing" successfully secure the strangeness his forebears sought but failed to fully to reach. In place of juxtaposition, Goldsmith practices a form of *textual amplification*. By virtue of pathological loyalty to the textual consequences of his originating designs, Goldsmith's work regularly injects text not into a field by which it can be compared to other texts, but into a vacuum, in which the dimensions and properties of the text simultaneously swell and shrink. *Day*, for instance, may initially be read against the more common newsprint format from which it is derived, but the *whole* of *Day* soundly defeats any such comparison.

In its transparent dependence upon concept, Goldsmith's work resembles the project- and process-based conception of Oulipo, but differs in one obvious yet radical fashion: Goldsmith executes what Oulipo merely posits.[18] This execution represents more than mere perseverance on Goldsmith's part; it establishes the necessary importance of literal-mindedness, of engineered autism, as practice. Oulipian experiments deny practice not as matter of intransigence, but as a matter of principle: theoretically speaking, once articulated, the idea of a writing project has achieved everything that the project itself ever could. From the Oulipian perspective, to *apply* an Oulipian conceit defeats the very purpose of contriving the conceit itself. The artist who pursues the conceit's execution therefore adopts either a deep misunderstanding of the conceit itself or a willful naïveté. Goldsmith clearly falls into this latter category, and his deliberate "naïveté" has proved consistently resourceful, putting the lie to the Oulipian dis-emphasis on actual product. Indeed, his efforts in this area are reminiscent of John Cage's famous response to the criticism that anyone could do what he did. "Of course they could," he replied, "but they don't."[19] Goldsmith shares with Cage a conviction that for all the elegance of the conception, the pluralities engendered by the concept's application are worthwhile in their own right, indeed, redemptive of the concept's promise.

Several of Goldsmith's more recent works demonstrate the dual means by which the product redeems the act of production. With projects such as *1.11* or *Fidget* or *Soliloquy*, Goldsmith describes and executes methodologies that, as he himself notes, result in texts that in no fundamental way resemble alternative executions of the inspiring methodology. This bespeaks one kind of product-based utility, which is the virtue of specificity as unpredictable by methodology. Any effort to reproduce the particular effect of works like *Fidget* or *Soliloquy* would fail, regardless of fidelity to the general rule from which each is derived. It is important to note, however, that this "failure" is limited only to the Oulipian standard of concept-over-product, thereby suggesting the flaw in the Oulipian imagination. Indeed, works like *Fidget* demonstrate that the specificity of the product can elicit far greater degrees of provocation than their conceptual inspirations. Of course, the extreme nature of these projects (record and transcribe your every word for a week; transcribe your every gesture for a day) also dovetails neatly with the amplification effect introduced above. The very excess of the conceptions results in text that, injected into a context-vacuum, approaches a quality that disorients simply by scale, or confusion thereof. This is the disorientation that redeems the promise of juxtaposition, but without the circuitous dependencies that hobble metaphor.

While his inheritance of Cage's concerns is obvious, and his adoptions of some Oulipian precepts equally clear, Goldsmith is geometrically more than poetry's analogue to Cage or Oulipo's idiot-savant son. In fact, Goldsmith is on record as having a "peevish" response to the gap between the promises of Cage's rhetoric and Cage's willingness to adhere in practice to the demands he made at the level of theory: he claimed that Cage, "whose mission it was to accept all sound as music, failed; his filter was on too high. He permitted only the sounds that fell into his worldview. Commercial sounds, pop music, lowbrow culture, sounds of violence and aggression, etc. held no place in the Cagean pantheon."[20] Goldsmith tacitly presents himself as the cure to the affliction even Cage was unwilling to remedy completely. Goldsmith's particular criticism of Cage's unwillingness to follow to the full extent of its logical consequence the claim that all sound, including its absence, should be thought of as constitutive of music, manifests in Goldsmith's own marriages of hard and soft ephemera. Fully applied loyalty to Cagean standards leaves little room for the kind of performative specificity for which Cage was well known. Goldsmith strikes directly at this disjunction and identifies the privileged position of compositional or auctorial control—of "creation"—as that which interferes with a full realization of Cage's claim. It is this interference that the arc of Goldsmith's art seeks to eliminate, and within that arc Goldsmith himself is not immune to the suasions of interventionalist writing. *Soliloquy*, for example, creates a perpetual opportunity for interventionist manipulations; while Goldsmith remains committed to the transcription of his every spoken word, the occasion of the project proves as fluid a provocation as any of the other social contexts for which Goldsmith appears willing to tweak his language.

The position at which we finally arrive is one at which Goldsmith seems forced to choose between methodological demons. On this axis, there is the threat of principled inconsistency, à la Cage, and at the other, a dis-emphasis of product, à la Oulipo. Works such as *Fidget* and *Soliloquy* ably demonstrate the flaws of Oulipian hyperconceptuality by tendering infinitely diverse degrees of specificity; they also, however, invite the kind of manipulation of material that Goldsmith finds so irritating in Cage.

Goldsmith resolves this dilemma by placing greater faith in Cage's principles than Cage did himself. The result is the full advent of his "uncreativity," and the ascension of his amplification strategy. Unlike his previous works, the newer projects of *Day* and *The Weather* truly *do* produce texts that would maintain uniform properties regardless of the multiplicity of their executions. So this virtue of product-and-process is lost, but the effects of amplification undiluted by auctorial temptations more than regain what is thereby compromised. These products more closely resemble those of Warhol (especially the Warhol of *Empire*, his eight-hour film of a static shot of the Empire State Building) than they do those of Cage; *The Weather* in particular synthesizes the sometimes contradictory impulses of Goldsmith's work.[21]

3

> A couple of breaks of sunshine over the next couple of hours, what little sunshine there is left. Remember, this is the shortest day of the year. Looks like the clear skies hold off till later on tonight. It will be brisk and cold, low temperatures will range from twenty-nine in some suburbs to thirty-eight in midtown. Not a bad shopping day tomorrow, sunshine to start, then increasing clouds, still breezy, with a high near fifty. Couple of showers around tomorrow night, er, tomorrow evening, into early tomorrow night, otherwise partly cloudy later on, low thirty. For Monday, windy and colder with sunshine, a few clouds, high forty-two. And then for, er, Christmas Eve, mostly sunny, but with a chilly wind, high near forty degrees. For Christmas itself, cloudy with a chance for rain or snow, high thirty-six. Forty-three degrees right now and cloudy, relative humidity is fifty-five percent in midtown. Repeating the current temperature forty-three going down to thirty-eight in midtown.

Goldsmith himself: "I'm intrigued with the simplest and often overlooked aspect of situations. With the web, people tend to be dazzled (blinded) by the more complicated aspects of the web—from data-driven artworks to Flash—whilst tending to minimize the social, political, and artistic implications of that upon which the whole system is built."[22]

To return to situations, simple, overlooked: the Situationists, who derived their name from this superficially modest yet hyperbolically ambitious goal, believed that art as understood to that point interfered with, rather than facilitated, this dream. The text from *Year* is none other than the weather itself; approximations of that perpetually ineffable phenomenon are among the oldest of poetic, "creative" enterprises. *Year* is less and more. It is our accumulated narrative, our speech *about* and not *of*; as such it places the failure of description, the impossibility of ever containing that in which you are immersed, at the focus of our attention. In its scale and humble specificity, its admixture of alertness and unconsciousness, the text promises the most elemental properties of the world will be sufficient to the demands the poetic impulse makes upon that world. And in his enormous and detailed erasures, his deliberately engineered autistic lucidity, Kenneth Goldsmith whisks away clouds in favor of their sky, which he proves to be anything but empty.

NOTES

1. As with much of the Situationist agenda, Guy Debord has his fingers all over this: for more of the same, see his "The Situationists and the New Action Forms in Politics and Art," in *Internationale situationiste*, Destruktion AF RSG 6 (Odense, Denmark: Galerie EXI, 1963). And of course, *La Société du Spectacle* (Paris: Champ Libre, 1971).

2. Lucy Raven, "Review of *Day*," http://epc.buffalo.edu/authors/goldsmith/ (2003).

3. Brian Kim Stefans, "Little Review of *Day*," wings.buffalo.edu/epc/authors/goldsmith/bks_day.html (2003).

4. American Psychiatric Association, *Diagnostic and Statistical Manual of Mental Disorders DSM-IV-TR*. American Psychiatric Association (June 2003). If you want to appreciate the degree to which diagnosis both follows and predicts presupposition and prejudice, you cannot go wrong with a chronological scan of the *DSM* and its "revisions."

5. It's worth noting that for all the collective overreliance of that quote in the justification of "experimental" writing, there are relatively few who consider why Rimbaud focuses in this pursuit on grammar and matter, one formal and one sensual, and bypasses the realm of ideas altogether.

6. Personal correspondence with the author, although Goldsmith has said very much the same in his deliberate references and justifications of his work.

7. Goldsmith and Perloff actually have the occasion to discuss this encounter. Marjorie Perloff, "A Conversation with Kenneth Goldsmith," *Jacket* (February 21, 2003).

8. The most recent reference of this claim appears in Goldmsith's never-ending and mutable "statement of poetics," for lack of a more accurate phrase; http://epc.buffalo.edu/authors/goldsmith/theory.html.

9. Gordon Tapper, "Kenneth Goldsmith: Bravin Post Lee," *zingmagazine* (1997).

10. John Strausbaugh, "Kenneth Goldsmith's No. 111." *New York Press* (1997).

11. Amusing yet telling anecdote: Goldsmith claims to have never read "The Rocking-Horse Winner," even as he was folding it into his text. He merely counted it, a task apparently prohibitive of reading as conventionally understood—which proves Goldsmith's point well, if accidentally.

12. Personal correspondence with the author.

13. Personal correspondence with the author. Note that "editing" here, while defined so that it still interferes with the full application of noninterventionist writing, is still not quite "editing" in the normal literary sense.

14. Brad Ford, "A Provincial Review of Kenneth Goldsmith's *Day*"; http://epc.buffalo.edu/authors/goldsmith/ (2003).

15. Ibid.

16. Goldsmith is quoting Cage in an essay about how boring Goldsmith finds

himself and his own work. Goldsmith, Kenneth. "Being Boring," http://www.writing
.upenn.edu/~wh/boring.html.

17. Goldsmith's detailing of this quote, and his use of it, appears in the Perloff interview cited above.

18. Adherents of Oulipo would not, of course, think that the lack of "product" proved any kind of failure or lapse; nor would they necessarily judge those products (such as Perec's "A Void" a failure for being a potential literature made "real."

19. Goldsmith references here John Cage from his *Silence*; for a transcript of the relevant passages, see http://www.zakros.com/mica/soundart/s04/cage_text.html.

20. Kenneth Goldsmith, "Uncreativity as a Creative Process." http://drunken boat.com/db5/goldsmith/uncreativity.html (2000).

21. A happy irony: one of the most astute short descriptions of this film can be found on MoMA's website, where the description accompanies an opportunity to buy a print of a still from the film. Of course, the whole film is more or less a still, but . . .

22. Personal correspondence with author.

BIBLIOGRAPHY

Books and Compact Discs by Kenneth Goldsmith

I'll Be Your Mirror: The Selected Andy Warhol Interviews, 1962–1987. New York: Carroll & Graf, 2004.
Nothing Special. Seattle, Wash.: Staalplaat, 2004. Collaboration with People Like Us (CD).
Day. Great Barrington, Mass.: The Figures, 2003.
Soliloquy. New York: Granary Books, 2001.
Fidget. Toronto: Coach House Books, 2000.
6799. New York: *zingmagazine*, 2000.
Gertrude Stein on Punctuation. Newton, N.J.: Abaton Books, 1999.
No. 111 2.7.96–19.20.96. Great Barrington, Mass.: The Figures, 1997.
73 Poems. With essays by Robert Mahoney, John Schaefer, and Geoffrey Young. Brooklyn, N.Y.: Permanent Press, 1994. Accompanying collaborative CD with composer/vocalist Joan LaBarbara. New York: Lovely Music, Ltd., 1994.
No. 110 10.4.93–10.7.93. New York: Beans Dear? Press, 1993.

Selected Criticism

Arning, Bill. "Kenneth Goldsmith." *Poliester* (Fall 1998).
Belgum, Erik. "Interview with Kenneth Goldsmith." *Read Me* 4 (Winter 2000).
Bessa, A. S. "Exchanging email with Kenneth Goldsmith." *zingmagazine* 3 (Winter 2000).
Bök, Christian. "How Poems Work: Kenneth Goldsmith's *No. 111*." *Toronto Globe and Mail* (May 11, 2000).
Boon, Marcus. "Ether Talk: Kenneth Goldsmith." *The Wire* (June 2002).

Dorward, Nate. "You Know Him, Reader." *The Gig* 7 (November 2000).

Ford, Brad. "A Provincial Review of Kenneth Goldsmith's *Day*." (http://epc.buffalo .edu/authors/goldsmith/ (2003).

Goode, Chris. 2004. "What's it for?" *The Gig* 16 (February 2004).

Hoffberg, Judith. Review of *Fidget. Umbrella* 23, no. 2 (September 2000).

Jaeger, Peter, and Scott Pound. "Introduction to Pulp Theory." *Open Letter* 10, no. 5 (Spring 1999).

Levin, Kim. "Voice Choice." *Village Voice* (April 12, 1994).

Levine, Stacey. "Snickering for Joy: No. 111 2.7.93–10.20.96." *American Book Review* (January–February 1998).

Lin, Tan. "Information Archives, the De-Materialization of Language, and Kenneth Goldsmith's Fidget and No. 111 2.7.93–10.20.96." http://epc.buffalo.edu/authors/ goldsmith/lin.html (1998).

Ludwig, Jenny. Review of *Fidget. Boston Review* (October–November 2001).

Ngai, Sian. "Stuplimity: Shock and Boredom in Twentieth-Century Aesthetics." *Postmodern Culture* 10, http://muse.jhu.edu/journals/postmodern_culture/.2000 (2000).

Nufer, Doug. "The Creativity Racket." *Muse Apprentice Guild* (2003).

Perloff, Marjorie. "'Concrete Prose': Haroldo de Campos's Galáxias and After." http://epc.buffalo.edu/authors/perloff/perloff_decampos.html (1998).

———. "A Conversation with Kenneth Goldsmith." *Jacket* (February 21, 2003).

———. "Noticings." *Sulfur* (Fall 1994).

———. "Vocable Scriptsigns: Differential Poetics in Kenneth Goldsmith's *Fidget*." Toronto: Coach House Press, 2000.

———. 1998. "Yang Introduction: Younger American Poets." *Yang*, no. 2. Antwerp, Belgium, 1998.

Princenthal, Nancy. "Fidget: Artist's Book Beat." *On Paper* (November–December 1998).

Raven, Lucy. Review of *Day*. http://epc.buffalo.edu/authors/goldsmith/ (2003).

Rubinstein, Raphael. "Appropriative Writing." *American Poetry Review* (March–April 1998).

Ryan, Kyra. "Avant-Garde and Opera Free: Kenneth Goldsmith's *Fidget*." *Utne Reader* (August 2000).

Silverton, Mike. "LaBarbara/Goldsmith: Seventy-Three Poems." *Fanfare* (September–October 1994).

Smith, Roberta. "Kenneth Goldsmith 'Soliloquy' at Bravin Post Lee." *New York Times* (February 18, 1997).

Strausbaugh, John. "Afterwords." *New York Press* (July 2002).

Tapper, Gordon. "Kenneth Goldsmith: Bravin Post Lee." *zingmagazine* (1997).

Workman, Michael. Review of *Soliloquy. New Art Examiner* (May–June 2002).

CONTRIBUTORS

CHARLES ALTIERI is professor of English at the University of California, Berkeley, where he teaches twentieth-century American and British literature. He is the author of eight books on modern American poetry and theories of the arts, most recently *The Particulars of Rapture: An Aesthetics of the Affects* (Cornell University Press, 2004), and *The Art of Twentieth Century American Poetry* (Blackwell, 2005).

RICK BENJAMIN teaches poetry and community practice courses at both Brown University and the Rhode Island School of Design. He is also the state director of River of Words, a K–12 ecological education project experienced through the lens of poetry and the visual arts, and the co–executive director of the Rhode Island Service Alliance, a nonprofit organization that administers AmeriCorps and other national service programs in the state. His poems have appeared in several journals, most recently *Watershed*.

STEPHEN BURT is associate professor of English at Macalester College in Saint Paul, Minnesota. He is the author of *Randall Jarrell and His Age* (Columbia University Press, 2002) and the editor of *Randall Jarrell on W. H. Auden* (Columbia University Press, 2005); he also has authored two books of poems, *Popular Music* (which won the Colorado Prize for 1999) and *Parallel Play* (Graywolf, 2006), and a chapbook, *Shot Clocks: Poems and an Essay for the WNBA* (Harry Tankoos Books, 2006). His essays and articles on modern and contemporary poetry have appeared in *ALH* (American Literary History), *The Believer, Boston Review, College Literature, Jacket, London Review of Books, Modern Philology, PN Review, Times Literary Supplement*, and *Yale Review*.

JOSHUA CLOVER has published two books of poems: *Madonna anno domini* (Louisiana State University Press, 1997) and *The Totality for Kids* (University of California Press, 2006). His contribution to the Modern Classics series for the British Film Institute, *The Matrix*, was published in 2005. He is an associate professor of English literature at the University of California, Davis, a contributor to the *New York Times*, and the poetry editor for the *Village Voice Literary Supplement*.

CAROLINE CRUMPACKER lives with her partner Tom O'Malley and their daughter Colette in upstate New York. She is an editor for *Fence Magazine*, a contributing editor for *Circumference Magazine* and curator for the Bilingual Poetry Reading Series at the Bowery Poetry Club in Manhattan. She received a fellowship from the Fine Arts Work Center in Provincetown, Massachusetts, in 2001–2002. Her translations, essays, and poems have appeared in the books *Talisman Anthology of Contemporary French Poetry* (Talisman, 2004); and *Love Poems by Younger American Poets* (Verse Press, 2004) and in magazines including *American Letters and Commentary, Boston Review, Can I Have My Ball Back? Chicago Review, Denver Quarterly, DoubleChange, Fence, Germ, Hors Bord* (in French), *Jubilat, L'Oeil de Bouef* (in French), *Lungfull! No, Ploughshares, Poetry Project Newsletter, Seneca Review,* and *Volt.*

Stacy Doris is the author of *Cheerleader's Guide to the World: Council Book* (Roof, 2006), *Knot* (University of Georgia Press, 2006), *Parlement* (P.O.L, 2005), *Conference* (Potes & Poets, 2001), *Paramour* (Krupskaya, 2000), and *Kildare* (Roof, 1995). Written semi-anonymously in French are *La vie de Chester Steven Wiener écrite par sa femme* (P.O.L, 1998), and *Une année à New York avec Chester* (P.O.L, 2000). In addition she has edited a dossier of new American writing in French for *Java*, and coedited the following collections of French poetry translated by American poets: with Chet Wiener and Christophe Tarkos: *Ma Langue est Poétique—Selected Work* (Roof, 2001); with Norma Cole: *Twenty-two New (to North America) French Poets* (Raddle Moon, 1997); with Emmanuel Hocquard: *Violence of the White Page: Contemporary French Poetry in Translation* (Pederal, 1992). She is an assistant professor of creative writing at San Francisco State University.

Peter Gizzi grew up in Pittsfield, Massachusetts. He is the author of *The Outernationale* (Wesleyan University Press, 2007), *Some Values of Landscape and Weather* (Wesleyan University Press, 2003), *Artificial Heart* (Burning Deck, 1998), and *Periplum and Other Poems 1987–1992* (Salt Publishing, 2004). He has also published several limited-edition chapbooks, folios, and artist books. His work has been anthologized both here and abroad and has been translated into numerous languages. Gizzi's honors include the Lavan Younger Poet Award from the Academy of American Poets (1994) and fellowships from the Howard Foundation (1998), The Foundation for Contemporary Performance Arts (1999), and The John Simon Guggenheim Memorial Foundation (2005). His editing projects have included *o·blēk: a journal of language arts* (1987–1993), *The Exact Change Yearbook* (Carcanet, 1995), and *The House That Jack Built: The Collected Lectures of Jack Spicer* (Wesleyan University Press, 1998). He teaches at the University of Massachusetts at Amherst. More can be found at http://epc.buffalo.edu/authors/gizzi.

Kenneth Goldsmith has been called the author of some of the most "exhaustive and beautiful collage work yet produced in poetry" by *Publishers Weekly*. The author of seven books of poetry, founding editor of the online archive UbuWeb (http://ubu.com), and the editor of "I'll Be Your Mirror: The

Selected Andy Warhol Interviews," Goldsmith is also the host of a weekly radio show on New York City's WFMU. He teaches writing at the University of Pennsylvania, where he is a senior editor of *PennSound*, an online poetry archive. More about Goldsmith can be found on his author's page at the University of Buffalo's Electronic Poetry Center: http://epc.buffalo.edu/authors/goldsmith.

CHRISTINE HUME is the author of *Musca Domestica* (Beacon, 2000), winner of the Barnard New Women Poets Prize, and *Alaskaphrenia* (New Issues, 2004), winner of the Green Rose Award, and Small Press Traffic's 2005 Best Book of the Year. She is an associate professor of English at Eastern Michigan University.

LYNN KELLER is professor of English at the University of Wisconsin–Madison. She is the author of *Re-making It New: Contemporary American Poetry and the Modernist Tradition* (Cambridge University Press, 1987) and *Forms of Expansion: Recent Long Poems by Women* (University of Chicago Press, 1997) and coeditor with Cristanne Miller of *Feminist Measures: Sounding in Poetry and Theory* (University of Michigan Press, 1994). She is coeditor, with Alan Golding and Adalaide Morris, of the Contemporary North American Poetry series from the University of Iowa Press. Her current project is a book on recent experimental poetry by American women.

MYUNG MI KIM is the author of *Commons* (University of California Press, 2002). Kim's other books include *Dura* (Sun & Moon, 1998), *The Bounty* (Chax Press, 1996), and *Under Flag* (Kelsey St. Press, 1991). She is professor of English at the State University of New York at Buffalo.

KIMBERLY LAMM is completing her Ph.D. in English at the University of Washington. Recent work has appeared in *Callaloo, Michigan Feminist Studies*, and the collection *Transnational, National, and Personal Voices: New Perspectives on Asian American Asian Diasporic Women Writers*.

MARK LEVINE's books are *Debt* (William Morrow, 1993), *Enola Gay* (University of California Press, 2000), and *The Wilds* (University of California Press, 2006). He has also written journalistic nonfiction for the *New York Times Magazine*, the *New Yorker, Outside*, and many other magazines. He has received a Whiting Writers' Award and a fellowship from the NEA, and has taught at the University of Montana and, since 1999, at the Iowa Writers Workshop, where he is an associate professor.

WARREN LIU holds a Ph.D. in English from the University of California, Berkeley, and is an assistant professor of English at Oberlin College. He is currently completing work on a manuscript entitled "The Object of Experiment: Figurations of Subjectivity in Asian American Literature."

SABRINA ORAH MARK was raised in Brooklyn, and received a B.A. from Barnard College, and an M.F.A. from the Iowa Writers' Workshop. Her poems have appeared or are forthcoming in *American Letters and Commentary, American Poet, The Canary, Conduit, Denver Quarterly, Gulf Coast*, the *Indiana Review, Jubilat, Volt*, and other journals. Her poems also appear in *Legitimate Dangers: American Poets of the New Century* (Sarabande Books, 2006). Her first book of poems, *The Babies*, a collection of prose poems, won the 2004 Saturnalia Books Poetry Prize (judged by Jane Miller), and was recently published by Saturnalia Books. She is currently completing a Ph.D. in English (creative writing) at the University of Georgia in Athens.

RAYMOND MCDANIEL is the author of *Murder* (2004) and the forthcoming *Saltwater Empire*, both published by Coffee House Press. He writes monthly essays about contemporary poetry for the *Constant Critic* and teaches at the University of Michigan, Ann Arbor.

TRACIE MORRIS has worked in multiple media: printed text, theater, dance, music, and film. She has toured extensively throughout the United States, Canada, Europe, Africa, and Asia. Her work has also been featured in commissioned pieces for several organizations including Aaron Davis Hall, the International Festival for the Arts, the Kitchen Performance Space, Franklin Furnace, Yale Repertory Theater (for choreographer Ralph Lemon), the Whitney Biennial, and the Jamaica Center for Arts and Learning. Awards include: NYFA Fellowship, Creative Capital Fellowship, the National Haiku Slam Championship, and an Asian Cultural Council Fellowship. She is the author of two poetry collections, *Intermission* and *Chap-T-her Won*. Tracie Morris holds multiple degrees from Hunter College, CUNY, and New York University.

MARK NOWAK is author of *Revenants* and *Shut Up Shut Down* (afterword by Amiri Baraka) as well as coeditor (with Diane Glancy) of *Visit Teepee Town: Native Writings after the Detours* (all from Coffee House Press). He is the editor of *XCP: Cross Cultural Poetics* and the director of the Union of Radical Workers and Writers <http://www.urww.org>. His essay on gothic-industrial music and deindustrialization in the Rust Belt was recently published in *Goth: Undead Subculture* (Duke University Press). Nowak is currently editing a collection of essays written by workers who organized their bookstores in the United States and Canada and facilitating a "poetry dialogue" (through the UAW and NUMSA) with autoworkers at Ford plants in the United States and South Africa.

PAUL OTREMBA is a Ph.D. candidate at the University of Houston. His poetry and reviews have appeared in such magazines as the *Virginia Quarterly Review, New England Review, American Literary Review*, and *Tikkun*, where he served as assistant poetry editor.

D. A. POWELL is assistant professor of English at University of San Francisco. His most recent book, *Cocktails* (Graywolf, 2004) was a finalist for the National Book Critics' Circle and the Lambda Book Awards.

CLAUDIA RANKINE is the author of four collections of poetry, most recently *Don't Let Me Be Lonely* (Graywolf Press). She is coeditor with Juliana Spahr of *American Women Poets in the 21st Century* (Wesleyan University Press). A recipient of the Academy of American Poetry fellowship, she teaches at Pomona College.

LISA SEWELL is the author of two books of poems, *The Way Out* (Alice James Books, 1998) and *Name Withheld* (Four Way Books, 2006). Recipient of grants and awards from the National Endowment for the Arts, the Leeway Foundation, the Pennsylvania Council on the Arts, and the Fine Arts Work Center in Provincetown, she lives in Philadelphia and teaches at Villanova University.

JULIANA SPAHR was born in Chillicothe, Ohio, in 1966. Her books include *The Transformation* (Atelos, 2007), *This Connection of Everyone with Lungs* (University of California Press, 2005), *Fuck You-Aloha-I Love You* (Wesleyan University Press, 2001), *Everybody's Autonomy: Connective Reading and Collective Identity* (University of Alabama Press, 2001), and *Response* (Sun & Moon Press, 1996). She is coeditor with Claudia Rankine of *American Women Poets in the 21st Century* (Wesleyan University Press), and she coedits the journal *Chain* with Jena Osman (archive at http://www.temple.edu/chain). She frequently self-publishes her work (archive at http://people.mills.edu/jspahr).

COLE SWENSEN is the author of nine volumes of poetry; her latest book, *Goest* (Alice James Books, 2004), was a finalist for the National Book Award. Other volumes have won the National Poetry Series, the Iowa Poetry Prize, the San Francisco State Poetry Center Book Award, and Sun & Moon's New American Writing Award. Her work has appeared in various journals including *Conjunctions*, *American Poetry Review*, and the *Boston Review*, and has been translated into French, Swedish, and Norwegian. She also translates contemporary French poetry, prose, and art criticism; recent work appears in the *Yale Anthology of 20th Century French Poetry*; her translation of Jean Frémon's *Island of the Dead* won the PEN USA 2004 Award for literary translation. She divides her time between Washington, D.C., Paris, and Iowa, where she teaches at the Iowa Writers' Workshop.

DAVID RAY VANCE is a doctoral candidate in the Creative Writing Program at the University of Houston and is coeditor of *American Letters and Commentary*. His poetry collection *Vitreous* was winner of the 2005 Del Sol Press Poetry Prize. He is presently visiting assistant professor at the University of Texas at San Antonio.

KAREN VOLKMAN is the author of *Crash's Law* (Norton, 1996) and *Spar* (University of Iowa Press, 2002), which received the Iowa Poetry Prize and the James Laughlin Award. Recipient of awards and fellowships from the NEA, the Poetry Society of America, and the Akademie Schloss Solitude, she teaches in the MFA program at the University of Montana.

SUSAN WHEELER is the author of four collections of poetry, *Bag 'o' Diamonds* (University of Georgia Press, 1993), *Smokes* (Four Way Books, 1998), *Source Codes* (Salt Publishing, 2001), and *Ledger* (University of Iowa Press, 2005); and of *Record Palace*, a novel (Graywolf Press, 2005). Her awards include the Witter Bynner Prize for Poetry from the American Academy of Arts and Letters, the Norma Farber First Book Award from the Poetry Society of America, two Pushcart Prizes, and fellowships from the John Simon Guggenheim Foundation and the New York Foundation for the Arts. Her work has appeared in eight editions of the Scribner anthology *Best American Poetry*, as well as in the *Paris Review*, *London Review of Books*, *Verse*, *Talisman*, the *New Yorker*, and many other journals. On the creative writing faculty of Princeton University, she has also taught at Columbia University, the University of Iowa, Rutgers, and New York University.

KEVIN YOUNG is the author of five poetry collections, most recently *For the Confederate Dead* (Knopf, 2007), *Black Maria* (Knopf, 2005), a film noir in verse, and *Jelly Roll: A Blues* (Knopf, 2003), winner of the Paterson Poetry Prize and a finalist for the National Book Award and the *Los Angeles Times* Book Prize. His first book, *Most Way Home* (Zoland Books, 1998), was a National Poetry Series selection and winner of the John C. Zacharis First Book Award from *Ploughshares*. Young is also the editor of *Giant Steps: The New Generation of African American Writers*, the Library of America's *John Berryman: Selected Poems*, and the Everyman's Pocket Poets series volumes *Blues Poems* and *Jazz Poems*. The recent recipient of fellowships from the Guggenheim Foundation and the National Endowment for the Arts, Young is currently Atticus Haygood Professor of English and Creative Writing and curator of the Raymond Danowski Poetry Library at Emory University in Atlanta, Georgia.

INDEX

Descartes, Rene, 114
Dickinson, Emily, 57, 163, 203, 207
Documentary poetry: and Mark Nowak, 12, 334, 337–49; and Juliana Spahr, 7
Dollimore, Jonathan, 87, 91, 92, 93
Doris, Stacy, 1, 3, 10–11, 384; *Une Annee a New York avec Chester*, 284; "Boy Book (Songs)," 282; *Conference*, 267–69, 276, 278, 285–88; and corporeality, 274; and cyber culture, 11, 279–284; and form, 10, 274–75, 276–78; and gender issues, 280; "Girl Book (Warnings)," 282; "How to Love," 282; "I Have to Check my E-mail," 274–78; and identity politics, 277; *Kildare*, 276, 279, 280–81; *Knot*, 272–73, 276, 278; and language (breakdown of), 283; and language (electronic discourse), 279–84; and language (materiality of), 10; and language (performative), 285–86; and language (translation), 276–78; and love, 278–79, 282–84; "LOVE TO, AND HOW)," 282; and mass media, 279–84; *A Month of Valentines*, 270–71, 282; *Paramour*, 270–71, 276, 279, 282–84, 287; "The Poetics of Radical Constraint and Unhooked Bedazzlement in the Writing of Stacy Doris" (Crumpacker), 278–89; and popular culture, 281; and reception, 277–78; and translation, 285–87; *Twenty One New (to North America) French Writers*, 279; *La Vie de Chester Steven Wiener ecrite par sa femme*, 284; *Violence of the White Page*, 279
Doty, Mark, 6
Douglas, Mary, *Purity and Danger*, 90
DuBois, W. E. B., 197
Duchamp, Marcel, 365; *Fountain*, 374–75
Dugan, Alan, 191
Dumas, Alexander, *The Count of Monte Christo*, 117
Duncan, Robert, 84, 86
Dutton, Paul, 210; "Reverberations," 217
Dydo, Ulla, 366

Eliot, T. S., 86, 309; *The Wasteland*, 174, 338
Ellison, Ralph, 190; *Invisible Man*, 225

Enlightenment, The, 30, 165; Rene Descartes, 114
Epistemology, and politics in Myung Mi Kim, 259–63
Espitalier, Jean-Michel, 285

Farmer, Steve, 107
Feminist theory: 55; Judith Butler, 224; Julia Kristeva, 91, 228. *See also* gender issues
Finley, Ruth, 142–43
Fluxus, 12, 367
Ford, Brad, 373
Form: and content, in Joshua Clover, 165, 170; in Karen Volkman, 60–67; and elision in Myung Mi Kim, 254–57; and ideal readers in Joshua Clover, 168; as long lines in D. A. Powell, 84, 87; in Mark Nowak, 345; the political and social meanings of, 257; in Stacy Doris, 274–75, 282–284; as play, in Joshua Clover, 166, in Susan Wheeler, 309; problems with, in Stacy Doris, 10, 275–78; traditional and contemporary in Karen Volkman, 54–55; in Kevin Young, 193–94, 202. *See also* Collage; Language; Sampling
Fourcade, Dominique, 285
Fragmentation, in Peter Gizzi, 109–11; in Kenneth Goldsmith, 371; in Myung Mi Kim, 252, 263; in Tracie Morris, 217–20; in D. A. Powell, 88, 93; in Susan Wheeler, 312–13. *See also* Language; Postmodernism
Frost, Robert, 308; "Directive," 88; "Provide, Provide," 312

Gates, Jr., Henry Louis, 217–18
Gender issues: in Juliana Spahr, 137, 143, 144–45; in Tracie Morris, 219, 223–24, 229; in Stacy Doris, 280; in Susan Wheeler, 308
Genet, Jean, 91–92
Ginsberg, Allen, 82
Gizzi, Peter, 1, 3, 6, 7, 11, 384; "An Allegory of Doubt," 117; "Beginning with a Phrase from Simone Weil," 97–98; "Chateau If," 105, 117; "Etudes, Evidence, or a Working Definition of the

Mallarme, Stephane, 169

Mann, Ron, 210

Mark, Sabrina Orah, 5, 386; "Mark Levine: The Poetics of Evidence," 29–42

Martin, Robert K., 85

Marx, Karl, 164–65; *Capital*, 333

Marxism, 55; in Joshua Clover, 164–65, 173; in Mark Nowak, 334, 345–46

Mass culture: as information technology in Susan Wheeler, 304–307, 311–12; and loss, in Peter Gizzi, 6, 111, in Kevin Young, 8, 193–98. *See also* Consumer culture, Mass media, Popular culture

Mass media: Internet, in Stacy Doris, 279–84, in Kenneth Goldsmith, 361–81, in Juliana Spahr, 142–43, in Kevin Young, 9, 193–207. *See also* Mass culture and Popular culture

Massys, Quentin, 316

Matthew, Christopher, 340

McDaniel, Raymond, 12–13, 386; "Affect and Autism: Kenneth Goldsmith's Reconstitution of Signal and Noise," 367–81

McGrath, Connell, 115

Milton, John, 309

Modernism, 2, 4, 107–109, 115, 164, 168, 307; and documentary poetics, 337–38; and the New York School, 6, 109

Modernity, 30

Monette, Paul, 6; *Borrowed Time*, 84

Morris, Tracie, 1, 9, 386; and African American culture, 211–12; and Black Arts movement, 9, 223; and Black Power movement, 223–26; and the blues, 212; "Chain Gang," 212, 214, 230–31; and consumer culture, 215; and the corporeality of voice, 215, 217, 221, 224; and fragmentation, 217–20; and gender issues, 219, 223–24, 229; and historicity, 224; and identity politics (language of), 226–28; and identity politics (ritual), 218–21; "Improvisational Insurrection: The Sound Poetry of Tracie Morris" (Hume), 215–35; and language (and hegemony), 224; and language (and improvisation), 225–28;

and language (performative), 216–18; "A Little," 211, 214, 218–22, 231; and minimalism, 217–20; "The Mrs.Gets Her Ass Kicked," 212, 214, 217; and music influences, 210, 212, 227, 229–30; and popular culture, 210, 212, 218, 227, 229–30; "Procrastination/Self-Flagellation," 211; "Project Princess," 210–216; and psychoanalysis, 228; and race issues, 211–12, 223–26; "slave sho' to video a.k.a. Black But Beautiful," 222–29; "Sound Making Notes," 210–15; and subjectivity (and corporeality), 220–21

Morrison, Toni, *Beloved*, 191

Moxley, Jennifer, 61

Mullen, Harryette, 216

Multicultural poetry, 3

Music influences: blues, in Kevin Young, 9, 193, 199–207, in Tracie Morris, 212, 227; disco in D. A. Powell, 85, 93; hip-hop, in Tracie Morris, 210, 227, in Mark Nowak, 12, 342–44, in D. A. Powell, 86, in Kevin Young, 9, 193; jazz, in Tracie Morris, 210, 218, 227, in Kevin Young, 198; pop, in Tracie Morris, 212, in D. A. Powell, 85, in Susan Wheeler, 11, 305, in Kevin Young, 9, 193; sampling, in Tracie Morris, 229–30, in Mark Nowak, 12, 334, 342–43

Negri, Antonio, and Michael Hardt, *Empire*, 138

Neoliberalism, 332–35, 336–37

New Criticism, 55

New York School, 6; influence on Peter Gizzi, 109

Nietzsche, Friedrich, *Beyond Good and Evil*, 116

Notley, Alice, 305

Nowak, Mark, 1, 3, 11–12, 386–87; "$00/Line/Steel/Train," 320–23, 334, 346–48; and anti-establishment, 343; "Back Me Up," 347; and capitalism, 11–12, 332–35, 336–49; "Capitalization," 324–27, 334, 339–40, 343; and deindustrialization, 332–35, 336–49; and documentary poetry, 12, 334, 337–49; "Hoyt Lakes/Shut Down," 329–331,

Volkman, Karen, 1, 3, 5, 6, 8, 9, 54–55, 388; "Bitter seed—scarred semblance—psyche," 49; "Brown is the flat gestation of a maze," 46–47; "Casanova in Love," 58; "Chronicle," 59; *Crash's Law*, 54, 55–59; "The first greeting on a bright sift," 46; and form, 54–55, 60–67; "Grey airs, grey stirs," 48; "I never wish to sing again as I used to," 44; "I won't go in today," 43; and identity, 60; "Infernal," 57–58; "Infidel," 57–58; "It could be a bird that says summer," 45–46; "Kiss Me Deadly," 63; and language (materiality of), 56–64; and language (performative), 58; and language (representational), 56; "Lifting whither, cycle of the sift," 50; and lyric "I," 55–67; "No noise subracts it," 45; *Nomina*, 55, 56, 64–67; "O verb, o void," 44–45; "One might start here," 51–53; "Persephone at Home," 59; and post-Romantic, 5; "The Red Shoes," 58; "Reticulation of a premise," 5, 48–49; "Shrewd star," 62; *Spar*, 54, 56, 59–63; "A Space for Desire and the Mutable Self: Karen Volkman's Experimentations with the Lyric" (Otremba), 55–70; and subjectivity (destablized), 55; and subjectivity (and form), 60–67; and subjectivity (interrogation of), 56; "There comes a time to rusticate the numbers," 43–44; "The thing you do you keep or claim," 49–50; "What is this witness, the watching ages," 47; "What we know," 61–62

Wah, Fred, *Waiting for Saskatchewan*, 334
Waldrop, Keith, 115
Waldrop, Rosmarie, 54, 115; "Form and Discontent," 60; *Reluctant Gravities*, 60
Wallace, Mark, 3
Warhol, Andy, 194–95, 365–66; *Empire*, 378
Warner, Michael, *Publics and Counterpublics*, 140
Washington, Booker T., 197
Welsh, Andrew, 226–27
Wheeler, Susan, 1, 3, 11, 303, 388; "after Quentin Massys, c.1514," 316; and anti-establishment, 305; *Bag 'o' Diamonds*, 304, 315; "Beavis' Day Off," 309; "Casino Night," 309; "Chosen," 311; and collage, 304–306, 314; and consumer culture, 11, 304–17; "The Debtor in the Convex Mirror," 290–302, 307, 315; "The Dogwood and the The," 311; "Ethic," 309; "Ezra's Lament," 309–310; "Fifteen," 314; "Fourteen," 313; and fragmentation, 312–13; and gender issues, 308; "He or She That's Got the Limb, That Holds Me Out on It," 308; and identity (fixed), 305–6; and language (and computer programming), 307–12; and language (and improvisation), 309; and language (of mass culture), 304–5, 313, 315; and language (musicality of), 316; and language (vernacular), 304, 309, 316; *Ledger*, 307, 315–17; and mass culture, 306; and music influences, 11, 305; "Peanut Agglutinin," 304–5; "Poetry, Mattering?," 306; and popular culture, 305–6; and reception, 304; "Seventeen," 314; "Smokes," 310–11; *Smokes*, 306–11; "Sonnet of Alternate Starts for a Poem of Comparison," 309; *Source Codes*, 307, 311–15; "Susan Wheeler's Open Source Poetics" (Keller), 304–19; and writing, 303, 315
Whitman, Walt, 82, 85, 93, 108, 207
Wiener, Chet, 285
Williams, Raymond, *Keywords: A Vocabulary of Culture and Society*, 345
Williams, William Carlos, 109, 112; *The Descent of Winter*, 191; *Patterson*, 338; *Spring and All*, 191
Wilson, Robert, 362
Winkfield, Trevor, 113
Wolfowitz, Paul, 333
Wood, Evelyn, 366
Wordsworth, William, "Intimations of Immortality," 308
Writing: and the body in D. A. Powell, 82; creative, in Kenneth Goldsmith, 369, in Susan Wheeler, 315; as preservation in Kevin Young, 190–92; and spirituality in Susan Wheeler, 303. *See also* Form, Language, Subjectivity